C000229167

Complete Nepali

Teach® Yourself

Complete Nepali

Michael Hutt, Krishna Pradhan and
Abhi Subedi

First published in UK 1999 as *Teach Yourself Nepali* by Hodder Education. An Hachette company.

First published in US 1999 by The McGraw-Hill Companies, Inc.

This edition published in 2016 by John Murray Learning

British Library Cataloguing in Publication Data: a catalogue record for this title is available from the British Library.

Library of Congress Catalog Card Number: on file.

9781444101973

10

Typeset by Cenveo® Publisher Services.

Printed and bound in Great Britain by CPI Group (UK) Ltd., Croydon, CR0 4YY.

John Murray Learning policy is to use papers that are natural, renewable and recyclable products and made from wood grown in sustainable forests. The logging and manufacturing processes are expected to conform to the environmental regulations of the country of origin.

Carmelite House
50 Victoria Embankment
London EC4Y 0DZ
www.hodder.co.uk

Contents

Meet the authors **xi**

Only got a minute? **xiii**

Only got 5 minutes? **xv**

Only got 10 minutes? **xvii**

How to use the book **xxiii**

The Nepali script and sound system **xxvii**

1 **Are you Bindu?** **2**

1 ***Meeting the bus*** **2**
is and *are* in Nepali; first person pronouns (*I*, *we*); second person pronoun (*you*); *I am*, *you are*, *we are* with **ho**; nouns; asking and answering questions

2 ***Arriving at the college*** **8**
third person pronouns (*he*, *she*, *they*); *he is*, *she is*, *it is*, *they are* with **ho**; *this*, *that*, *these* and *those*; adjectives

2 **How far is it to Kathmandu, brother?** **16**

3 ***A view of Kathmandu*** **16**
pronouns with **cha**; **ali** *quite* and **dherai** *very*, *many*; questioning words (interrogatives); the simple sentence

4 ***Near and far*** **22**
postpositions: **-mā**, **-bāṭa**, **-dekhi**; using relationship terms to address people

3 **How many?** **30**

5 ***Students at the language school*** **30**
the Nepali numerals; numbers of people

6 ***Setting up the exam room*** **32**
numbers of things; how many?

7 ***Kamal and Amrit*** **35**
possession of portable items; using numbers without classifiers

4 **Whose is it?** 42

8 ***Jyoti's houses*** 42
ownership: **-ko**, **-kī**, **-kā** with nouns and names;
words for *and*: **ra**, **ani**; *I know, you know*, etc. using **thāhā**

9 ***Ratan's motorcar*** 46
ownership using **-ko**, **-kī**, **-kā** with unchanged ('direct case')
pronouns; *my, your, our; one's own*: emphasizing ownership
using **āphno**; asking questions: the use of **ki**

10 ***Whose book is this?*** 50
ownership using **-ko**, **-kī**, **-kā** with changed ('oblique case') pronouns;
interrogatives: **kasko** *whose*, **keko** *of what*, **kahā̃ko** *of/from where?*

5 **What do you do?** 56

11 ***The cook and the pilot*** 56
the dictionary form of verbs; the habitual present tense; using
the habitual present tense; **dheraijaso** *usually;* **mātrai** *only,*
pani *also, too, even;* **kahile?** *when?,* **kahilekāhī̃** *sometimes,*
kahilyai pani *never;* modes of transport; new postpositions:
-pachi *after,* **-samma** *up to, until,* **-ko lāgi** *for*

12 ***Women in the villages*** 65
the habitual present tense: feminine forms; times of day;
days of the week; frequency: **paṭak**

6 **Give me 500 rupees** 72

13 ***Hiring a rickshaw*** 72
the imperatives; the postposition **-lāī** as object marker; the habitual
present tense: alternative negative forms; the postposition **-tira**
towards; the negative particle **na;** **tara** *but,* **ta** *though;* **hawas** and
huncha: *OK, all right*

7 **The best** 84

14 ***Towns and villages*** 84
comparatives and superlatives; likes and dislikes using
man parnu; kina *why,* **kinabhane** *because*

8 **I came yesterday** 90

15 ***Sandhya drops by*** 90
the simple past tense; the simple past forms of **hunu** *to be:* **thiyo** and
bhayo; location and movement; *someone* and *something:* the uses
of **kehī** and **kohī**

16 ***A visit from Shankarprasad*** 99
transitive and intransitive verbs; transitive verbs and the suffix **-le**; further uses of **-le**; parts of the body

9 I'll go when I've eaten **106**

17 ***A day off work*** **106**
two verbs with the same subject: the **-era** participle; the reported speech-marker **re**

18 ***A chance encounter in Darjeeling*** **113**
the continuous tenses in **-dai cha**; *which one? this one!* the uses of **cāhī̃**; other forms of the conjunctive participle; expressions of age; further relationship terms

10 In the market **124**

19 ***Out shopping*** **124**
needed and *available:* **cāhinu** and **pāinu**; food vocabulary; using **-lāī** instead of **-ko lāgi**

11 It seems fine to me **132**

20 ***A place to stay in Kathmandu*** **132**
feelings: the use of nouns with **lāgnu**; *how do you like Nepal?* using adjectives with **lāgnu**; more passive verbs; *similar to* **jasto**; making adjectives into adverbs

12 Where has he gone? **142**

21 ***A late start*** **142**
the completed present tense; stating the time of day using **bajyo**

22 ***Which countries have you visited?*** **148**
the completed past tense; reporting speech using **bhanera**; *because it is, because it was: the* **-eko** participle with **-le**; using the **-eko** participle as an adjective; ordinal numbers

13 Dear Raju ... **158**

23 ***An exchange of letters*** **158**
using the **-eko** participle as a verb; *how long is it since ...?*; seeing or hearing another person's actions; the **-eko** participle with **ho** or **hoina**; thoughts and intentions using **bhanera** and **bhaneko**; *what does this word mean?*; the Nepali year

14 If it rains ... **168**

24 ***Out trekking*** **168**
real conditional sentences; using **holā** to mean *perhaps, might be;* the **-ne** participle as an adjective; using the **-ne** participle to talk about future actions; the verb **pugnu** *to arrive, suffice*

15 I'll go next year **178**

25 ***Going home for Dasain*** **178**
the probable future tense; the infinitive + **lāgnu**: *what does it cost to …? how long does it take to…?;* words for approximately

16 What should I do? **188**

26 ***Arriving at Tribhuvan International Airport*** **188**
must, should, don't have to; must, had to; the verbs **milnu** and **milāunu**

17 You're not allowed in **198**

27 ***Americans at Pashupati temple*** **198**
is it all right to …? using the infinitive with **huncha/hũdaina**; *they don't allow you to …;* **bhaera** *being* and **bhaera pani** *despite being;* religion in Nepal

18 I can learn Nepali **206**

28 ***How many languages can you speak?*** **206**
to be able to …; to get to, manage to; describing a verb; *to learn to, teach to; to want to …;* verbs meaning *to believe*

19 At the doctor's **216**

29 ***Kalyani visits the doctor*** **216**
expressing purpose; beginning to do something; after doing something; remembering and forgetting; before doing something: postpositions beginning with **-bhandā**

20 The map of Nepal **228**

30 ***The map of Nepal*** **228**
using **parnu** with locations; *above, below, beyond:* more postpositions beginning with **-bhandā**; the use of **bhanne** to mean *named;* the use of **bhanne** to mean *that*

21 I used to smoke 236

31 ***Bad habits*** 236
the habitual past tense; finishing, stopping, quitting; *while doing, immediately after doing; will have to, used to have to;* wishing, hoping and deciding

22 Shall I make tea? 248

32 ***Cancelling the tea party*** 248
may I? verbs in the subjunctive; doing something for another person: compound verbs with **dinu**; trying and seeking

23 If he'd taken the medicine 256

33 ***A death in the neighbourhood*** 256
already done: compound verbs with **saknu**; unreal conditional sentences; the short completed present tense; realization: using **rahecha** at the end of sentences; the verb **cinnu** *to know, to recognize*

24 If that's how it is ... 264

34 ***Two porters and a folksong*** 264
compound verbs with **hālnu**; continuous tenses using **rahanu**; short real conditional sentences

Appendices 273

Cardinal numbers 273

Kinship terms 275

Key to exercises 276

Nepali–English glossary 293

English–Nepali glossary 315

Meet the authors

Michael Hutt is the Professor of Nepali and Himalayan Studies at SOAS (the School of Oriental and African Studies) in London. He completed a PhD on the history of the Nepali language and its literature at SOAS in 1984 and has been engaged in teaching and research relating to Nepal there since 1987.

Krishna Pradhan is the Senior Lector in Nepali at SOAS, where he teaches undergraduate, postgraduate and non-degree courses in Nepali language. Krishna took his BA in Economics and History and an MA in Sociology from Tribhuvan University, Kathmandu. He began his professional career by teaching American and British volunteers in Kathmandu in 1982. Later he worked at the American mission (US Embassy and USAID), where he taught Nepali to American diplomats and development officers as well as Fulbright professors, scholars and many PhD candidates from American universities. Krishna taught for Cornell University's 'Cornell Nepal study programme' in Kathmandu, and he was a visiting lecturer at Cornell in 1997 and 2000. Since he joined SOAS in 2004 he has developed a range of new audio and video materials for students of the Nepali language and completed a new online Nepali dictionary.

Abhi Subedi was born in eastern Nepal and educated in Nepal and Britain. He is a professor of English at Tribhuvan University in Kathmandu and an established writer who has published works in both Nepali and English, including plays, essays, poems and literary criticism and history. He has also translated works from English into Nepali and from Nepali into English. He writes regular columns in Nepal's Nepali and English-language media and is very closely associated with language pedagogy, especially the teaching and syllabus writing of English in Nepal. Besides English, Subedi has taught Nepali to expatriates in Nepal at different times: these have included tourists, ambassadors, freaks, priests and lovers.

Only got a minute?

Nepali is spoken by 25–30 million people, mostly in Nepal, Sikkim, Darjeeling and Bhutan. Although there are some regional variations, the vast majority understand the modern standard form of the language that we teach you in this course.

The book requires you to learn the Devanagari script, which is ordered very logically and is surprisingly easy to master. Once you can read the script, you will find it a very trusty guide to the correct pronunciation of Nepali: much better than the Roman alphabet for English!

Although Nepali is an Indo-Aryan language, and is therefore related to English, there are some important differences between the two languages: Nepali puts the verb at the end of a sentence rather than in the middle; the levels of politeness used to address another person in Nepali are more wide ranging than they are in English; Nepali does not really have equivalents for the English words 'yes', 'no' and 'please'; most Nepali nouns are masculine unless they are both human and female; and the system of Nepali verbs is more complex (although also more regular) than the English equivalent.'

There are many good reasons for studying Nepali. Perhaps you are planning to trek in the Himalaya, to live and work in a Nepali community or simply to eat in a Nepali restaurant in the west. In all of these situations, a knowledge of Nepali will gain you new friends and open your eyes to a new way of seeing the world.

Only got 5 minutes?

Nepali is a member of the Indo-Aryan family of languages. It is the lingua franca of the central and eastern Himalaya and the national language of Nepal. Roughly half of Nepal's 28 million people speak Nepali as their mother tongue, while the remainder have as their first language either another Indo-Aryan language or a Tibeto-Burman language. However, the proportion of the population that speaks and understands Nepali probably exceeds 80%. There may also be as many as 6 million speakers of Nepali living outside Nepal, mainly in India (especially Sikkim and Darjeeling) and southern Bhutan.

Historically, Nepali spread gradually eastward across the region, as kings speaking an early version of the language conquered and unified the many small kingdoms that had existed there since the early medieval period. The language was taken to India and Bhutan during the 19th and 20th centuries by migrants from eastern Nepal, and further abroad as the common language of 'Gurkha' soldiers.

Today, the modern standard form of Nepali is well established and almost universally understood by Nepali speakers and written Nepali varies very little across the Nepali-speaking world.

Learning Nepali

This book requires you to learn the Devanagari script in which Nepali and several other major Indian languages are written. Although there are more signs and symbols to memorize than in the Roman alphabet, the alphabet is ordered very logically and is the best aid to correct pronunciation.

You will find that some Nepali words are less alien than you expected and you will encounter words with which you may be familiar from reading English books about India or Nepal or by South Asian authors. Of course, this does not mean that you will not have to memorize a large number of new words, but you will find them interesting and sometimes even musical and this chore will often become a pleasure.

Admittedly, Nepali pronunciation can be a challenge for learners whose first language is English. For instance, you have to learn to think more carefully about your breathing and the position of your tongue when you are pronouncing certain consonants. With practice, you will probably become very good at this. If you don't, however, this will not be a major problem because Nepali speakers will still understand most of what you say.

One of the major differences between Nepali and English grammar lies in the area of word order within sentences. Whereas English sentences conform to the pattern subject–verb–object, e.g. 'I speak Nepali', Nepali conforms to subject–object–verb, *ma nepālī bolchu*, 'I Nepali speak'. The system of Nepali personal pronouns is also more elaborate than that of

English. For instance, there are four levels of politeness available when addressing another person as 'you'.

Nepali does not really have equivalents for the English words 'yes', 'no' and 'please'. A question will invariably end with a verb and the answer will simply repeat that verb, using either its affirmative form to mean 'yes' or its negative form to mean 'no'. The politeness of a request is implicit in the form of the verb that is used and is not conveyed through an equivalent of 'please'.

Grammatical gender is not an important consideration for students of Nepali, because Nepali treats almost all nouns as masculine unless they are both human and female.

Whatever your motives for learning Nepali may be, this book is designed to enable those with no previous knowledge of the language to progress to a point where they can communicate effectively in Nepali on a range of everyday topics and can also read and write.

Only got 10 minutes?

Nepali is a member of the Indo-Aryan group of languages, which includes most of the languages of the northern half of the Indian subcontinent. These languages are derived from Sanskrit in much the same way that the European Romance languages (French, Spanish, Italian, etc.) are derived from Latin and each has developed its own distinctive character over the course of many centuries.

Nepali functions as a lingua franca across much of the central and eastern Himalaya and it is the national language of Nepal. Nepal is one of the world's most linguistically diverse countries: a total of 61 indigenous nationalities are officially recognized and many of these have their own language. The population of Nepal is growing rapidly and in 2009 it was estimated to be about 28 million. Roughly a half – primarily the higher caste and politically dominant Brahmins (Bahuns) and Chetris – speak Nepali as their mother tongue, while the remainder have as their first language either an Indo-Aryan language such as Maithili, Bhojpuri, Awadhi or Hindi or a Tibeto-Burman language such as Tamang, Newar, Gurung, Magar, Limbu, Tibetan or one of the many Rai languages. However, the level of bilingualism with Nepali is now very high in most parts of the country and the proportion of the population that speaks and understands Nepali probably exceeds 80%.

There may be as many as 6 million speakers of Nepali living outside Nepal. Nepali is recognized by the Indian Constitution as a major language of India because of its dominance in Sikkim and the Darjeeling district of West Bengal and although Bhutan has its own national language, Dzongkha, Nepali is also widely spoken and understood there, especially in the south.

Nepali acquired the role of a 'link language' during the medieval and early modern period because the need arose for communication to take place between people speaking many different languages as new states and kingdoms came into existence. It spread gradually eastwards from the west of what is now Nepal as a part of a process of conquest and unification led by kings who spoke an early version of Nepali first known as Khas Kura and later as Gorkhali. The language was taken to Darjeeling, Sikkim, Bhutan and the hill states of northeast India during the 19th and 20th centuries by migrants from eastern Nepal who came to work on tea plantations or to cultivate lands that were newly opened for agriculture. In addition to this, Nepali travelled further abroad as the common language of 'Gurkha' soldiers serving in the Indian and British armies.

Dialectal variation in Nepali occurs as one travels from west to east, but it is mainly a feature of colloquial village speech in the far west. As the language of education, government, and broadcast and print media, the modern standard form of Nepali is well established and almost universally understood by Nepali speakers. The version of standard Nepali spoken in north east India and Bhutan has some special features, but these are mostly restricted to vocabulary and are quite easily learnt. Written Nepali varies very little across the Nepali-speaking world.

Learning Nepali

THE DEVANAGARI SCRIPT

If you are a beginner in Nepali and you have never studied an Asian language before, you may be expecting it to be very difficult to learn. This will be partly because it is written in a script that you cannot read. Some learners decide that they will not attempt to learn to read or write the language because they imagine that it will be too much of a challenge and that in any case all they want to do is converse, not engage in literary study. This is a serious mistake, for several reasons. First, it is much easier to master the Devanagari script than its appearance might suggest. Ask any one of the hundreds of millions of people who are literate in Hindi, Gujarati, Marathi, Sanskrit or Bengali: these languages all use a form of Devanagari. Although there are more signs and symbols to memorize (33 consonants and 11 vowels) than in the Roman alphabet, the alphabet is ordered in a beautifully scientific way and (except in a tiny number of cases) every letter is always pronounced exactly the same – and there are no capital letters. Second, if you do *not* learn the script, you will have to learn Nepali by using an adapted form of the Roman alphabet, all set about with an array of dots and dashes. This is a much less satisfactory way of representing the correct pronunciation of a Nepali word and the quality of your spoken Nepali will suffer as a consequence. Third, anyone who has travelled in a country where non-Roman scripts predominate will know that an inability to read the world around you can feel deeply alienating. Yes, you will often see English on signposts and advertisements in Nepal, but you will see much more Nepali and if you can read it you will find that it tells you a great deal more.

VOCABULARY

Nepali's use of a non-Roman script obscures the fact that it, like all of the other Indo-Aryan languages, is actually a fellow member of the broad Indo-European family, which includes English. Latin and Sanskrit share a common ancestor, so you will find that some words are less alien than you expected: for example, 'I' is *ma,* 'name' is *nām,* 'person' is *mānche,* 'new' is *nayā̃.* Also, you will encounter words with which you may be familiar from reading English books about India or Nepal or by South Asian authors: 'village' is *gāun,* 'tea' is *ciyā* (pronounced 'chyaa'), 'letter' is *cithī.* Of course, much of the vocabulary will be wholly new to you and the task of memorizing a large number of new words that is a part of learning any language should not be underestimated. The point here, however, is that Nepali is not wholly alien for a speaker of a western European language: there are points of connection and commonality.

PRONUNCIATION

It has to be admitted that the correct pronunciation of Nepali does sometimes present the foreign learner with challenges. For example, the alphabet makes a clear distinction between consonants that are dental (pronounced with the tongue against the front teeth) and retroflex (pronounced with the tongue against the roof of the mouth) and between consonants that are aspirated (pronounced breathily) and consonants that are not. So you will from time to time be required to pronounce a 'd' while simultaneously breathing out quite strongly and pressing your tongue against the roof your mouth. With practice, you will succeed in doing this to some degree and you may even perfect it. If you don't quite manage it, however, the consequences will not be disastrous and it is difficult to conceive of a situation in which it will lead to your being misunderstood. The worst that will happen is that the Nepali to whom you are speaking will notice that you are pronouncing that particular word like a typical foreign speaker; they will probably be too polite to point this out.

GRAMMAR

One of the major differences between Nepali and English grammar lies in the area of word order within sentences. Whereas English sentences conform to the pattern subject–verb–object, e.g. 'I speak Nepali', Nepali conforms to subject–object–verb, *ma nepālī bolchu*, 'I Nepali speak'. Once this has been internalized, however, it does not present the learner with any major difficulty.

The system of Nepali personal pronouns is more elaborate than that of English, and teaches the foreign learner a lot about relationships within families and about social hierarchy. For instance, there are four levels of politeness available when addressing another person as 'you'. You will address someone as *yahā̃* when you need to be exceptionally polite or deferential, as *tapāī* when you are being ordinarily polite, as *timī* because you consider them your friend and equal or as *ta* because you are intimate with them in some way, because they rank far below you in the social hierarchy or simply because you wish to insult them.

Nepali does not really have equivalents for the English words 'yes', 'no' and 'please'. A question will invariably end with a verb and the answer will simply repeat that verb, using either its affirmative form to mean 'yes' or its negative form to mean 'no'. Most foreigners who have spent time in Nepal know that *cha* means 'yes, there is some' and *chaina* means 'no, there isn't any'. The politeness of a request is implicit in the form of the verb that is used and is not conveyed through an equivalent of 'please'. So, a command is blunt: *kām gara!* 'work!' and the politest form of request takes longer: *kām garnuholā*, 'please work'.

Grammatical gender is not an important consideration for students of Nepali, because Nepali treats almost all nouns as masculine unless they are both human and female. This removes one of the difficulties faced by learners of Nepali's close relative, Hindi, not to mention its distant cousin, French. To speak Nepali well, you do need to be able to use feminine endings for verbs and adjectives when they refer to a sister, a mother, a daughter or a wife. If you want to be poetic when the need arises, you may like to know that feminine gender can also be used when referring to the planet earth and to the cow, which is a sacred symbol of Hinduism.

The standard dictionary form of the majority of Nepali adjectives ends in *-o*, which is actually the ending that should be used when the adjective is being used to describe a singular masculine noun. Formal Nepali grammar requires this to change to *-ī* when the adjective is being used to describe a feminine noun and *-ā* when it is being used to describe a plural noun. However, because so many Nepali speakers do not have the language as a mother tongue and also because educational standards in Nepal remain regrettably low, you will find that quite a few grammatical rules, including this one, are honoured mainly in the breach. As a foreign speaker of the language, you may sometimes have to choose between different levels of grammatical correctness, according to the company you are in at the time.

If you look up the Nepali for verbs such as *to eat, to go* or *to forget* in a dictionary, you will find that they all consist of one or two syllables followed by the ending *-nu*: *khānu, jānu, birsanu*. Like English, Nepali uses changes in the verb to denote different times, as in *I forget* (present), *I forgot* (past), *I will forget* (future). These changes are referred to as tense. In Nepali, the verb endings for each tense are dependent on three factors: *time* (past, present, future, etc.), *category* of the verb, and *person*. The rules surrounding the use of Nepali verbs are probably the most complex area of Nepali grammar and the versatility of the verb system provides the language with much of its character. The unique one- or two-syllable root of each verb provides the stem for a range of different endings, each devoted to a particular tense. There are some conceptual difficulties for the foreign learner here, because Nepali observes distinctions that may be new – between transitive and intransitive verbs, for instance, or between existential and descriptive functions. These shed fascinating light on Nepali attitudes to such matters as time and agency and remind you that you are learning a language that functions in a cultural context that is very different from your own.

Using your Nepali

People study Nepali for a variety of reasons. Perhaps you intend to travel to Nepal, or to Sikkim or Darjeeling, for a holiday or a trekking expedition. If so, you will be looked after and guided by Nepalis who speak English – but along the way you will also encounter many who do not or whose English is very limited. Even the ability to make simple enquiries and engage in light conversation in Nepali will distinguish you from the crowd of ordinary tourists and trekkers. It will make you new friends and will enable you to engage with the society and culture through which you are passing at a much deeper level.

Or perhaps you are preparing to work or conduct research during an extended period in a Nepali-speaking environment, in which case you will have to ask yourself how much you will understand of what is going on around you without an understanding of the language. How much will you really learn for yourself if you have to rely on translators and interpreters or simply communicate only with the small minority of Nepalis who can speak to you in English on the topics you need to understand?

Increasingly, Nepali speakers may be found in the cities of Europe, the Gulf states and the USA and nowadays Nepali restaurants may be found in the most surprising locations, from Washington DC to Truro. So it may be that you wish to learn Nepali because you are in regular contact with members of a Nepali community in your home town or neighbourhood.

Like every language, Nepali has a range of different styles and levels of sophistication. A hillfarmer who has a Tibeto-Burman language as his mother tongue may use the same verb ending for all genders, numbers and levels of politeness, because for him Nepali is a workaday link language that enables him to communicate with people who have other languages as their mother tongue. In contrast, an educated urbanite will use various verb endings that depend not only on the number and gender of the subjects performing the actions of the verbs, but also on how polite s/he chooses to be about them. By and large, the Nepali in this book is that which Nepali speakers use unself-consciously in the various situations that are introduced. Where choices arise, however, we err towards the more grammatically correct. While accepting that some Nepali speakers would not make quite the same choices in everyday conversation, we take the view that it is better to learn rules before learning the exceptions to those rules. Similarly, the language of this book admits only a handful of English words, although many Nepali speakers (particularly in the capital) do make free use of English vocabulary in their conversation.

This book is designed to enable those with no previous knowledge of the language to progress to a point where they can communicate effectively in Nepali on a range of everyday topics, and can also read and write. For some we hope it will provide a basis for further study of Nepali literature, society and culture, and the gateway to a lifelong relationship with this beautiful language and the people who speak it.

How to use the book

The book is divided into 24 units. Each unit contains from one to three Nepali dialogues (in **Unit 13,** instead of a dialogue, there is an exchange of letters, in **Unit 20** a prose passage). In the first four units all of the Nepali appears in both Devanagari (the script in which Nepali is written) and Roman transliteration. Each dialogue is followed by a box setting out the new vocabulary it *contains,* and a literal English translation. Each dialogue or passage is followed by a section of more detailed grammatical explanation including further examples and exercises. The key to each exercise is given at the end of the book, followed by a complete end vocabulary.

You should begin by learning the characters of the Devanagari script and their pronunciation. Although the book can be used on its own, the descriptions of the sound of each character can only be approximate and the CD that is available to accompany the book will be of great help to you in developing accurate pronunciation at an early stage.

You may choose how to approach each unit: you might wish to learn the dialogue and its meaning first by hearing and repeating it, and then work through the translation and the grammar section to understand why it means what it does; alternatively, you might prefer to work through the grammar section first and then turn back to the dialogue to see the grammar in action, as it were. Whichever way you approach each unit, it is important not to move on until you have:

- mastered the dialogue;
- fully digested the grammar section and the examples it contains;
- learned all new vocabulary;
- completed the exercises and checked them against the key;
- repeated the exercises if they were not correct the first time.

The grammatical explanations are intended to be as clear and jargon-free as possible, although it is not possible to explain the structures of a language without using some grammatical terminology. The book cannot claim to cover every feature of Nepali, but it does contain all of the most common verb constructions and a basic vocabulary of some 1600 words. It will equip you with what you need to speak and read, and if you continue with Nepali after you have mastered this book your vocabulary and your familiarity with more complex constructions will grow very quickly. As well as helping you to master the Nepali language, the dialogues are also intended to provide you with an insight into Nepali culture and daily life.

Further reading

Other beginners' courses in Nepali include Tika B. Karki and Chij K. Shrestha's *Basic Course in Spoken Nepali* (Kathmandu, various editions), Ganga Prasad Uprety's *Basic Nepali for Foreigners*

(Kathmandu, Makalu Publication House, 2008), and David Matthews's *A Course in Nepali* (London, School of Oriental and African Studies, 1984). The first of these has been used for many years to teach Nepali to Peace Corps volunteers without introducing the Devanagari script. The third adopts a more academic approach and also introduces more complex grammatical structures.

Once you have completed *Complete Nepali*, you will find the following textbooks useful: M.K. Verma and T.N. Sharma's *Intermediate Nepali Structure* and *Intermediate Nepali Reader*, both published by Manohar Publishers in New Delhi in 1979; and Michael Hutt's *Modern Literary Nepali: an Introductory Reader*, published by Oxford University Press in New Delhi in 1997.

The best Nepali-English dictionaries currently on the market are *A Practical Dictionary of Modern Nepali*, produced by an editorial board headed by Ruth Laila-Schmidt and published by Ratna Sagar Publishers in New Delhi in 1993 and Gautam's Up-To-Date Nepali-English Dictionary, compiled by Choodamani Gautam and published by Gautam Prakashan, Biratnagar, in 2001. Ralph Turner's celebrated Nepali dictionary, first published in 1930, was reprinted in India in 1981; this is a work of immense interest, but is perhaps a little forbidding for a beginner in the language.

For a general introduction to Nepal, we recommend *State of Nepal*, edited by Kanak Mani Dixit and Shastri Ramachandaran and published by Himal Books in Kathmandu in 2002, and John Whelpton's *A History of Nepal* (Cambridge University Press, 2005). Although it is a work of fiction, Manjushree Thapa's novel *The Tutor of History* (Penguin India, 2001) is also an excellent way of acquainting yourself with Nepali society.

For English translations from modern Nepali literature, see Michael Hutt's *Himalayan Voices: an Introduction to Modern Nepali Literature* (University of California Press, 1991); and Lil Bahadur Chettri's *Mountains Painted with Turmeric* (Columbia University Press, 2008).

Acknowledgements

The authors wish to thank Govinda Giri Prerana, Bindu Subedi and John Whelpton for their invaluable comments and suggestions on various sections and drafts of the book, and the Research and Publications Committee of the School of Oriental and African Studies for facilitating this collaboration. We are also grateful to Subhas Rai for providing us with the drawings that illustrate a number of the dialogues.

Abbreviations & symbols

M	middle (case)	Dr	doctor
L	low (case)	Er.	elder
H	high (case)	Yr.	younger
Q	question	Mat.	maternal
A	answer	Pat.	paternal

S	statement	bro	brother
m.	masculine	sis	sister
f.	feminine	D	daughter
cj.ptc.	conjunctive participle	S	son

Flags those passages that you can listen to on the recording that accompanies this book.

Vocabulary boxes follow each dialogue. Use these to make sure you've understood the dialogue.

The **exercises,** throughout the book, give you plenty of opportunity to practise the Nepali language points as you learn.

The **grammar** section gives a clear explanation of the grammatical issues explored in that chapter.

The Nepali script and sound system

00.01

When you have read through this section, listen to the recording, so that you can hear the vowels and consonants of the Devanagari script.

Nepali is written in the **Devanāgarī** (or 'Nagari') script, which is also used for Hindi, Sanskrit and Marathi, with only minor modifications being made to accommodate the special features of the Nepali sound system. Devanagari is a phonetic script, which means that almost every word is pronounced exactly as it is written: learning a character means also learning a sound. The system comprises three kinds of characters: vowels, consonants, and conjunct characters. There are no capital letters.

Vowels

The Devanagari script has 11 vowels. Every vowel except अ a has two symbols. The first symbol is the full form of the vowel, called the *vowel character*. This is used when the vowel is the first letter of a word or syllable, and when it follows another vowel. The second symbol is the *vowel sign*, which is used after a consonant, i.e. when the vowel is the second letter of a syllable. The alphabet begins with the vowels, and the vowel characters are shown on the following page.

अ	**a**	like the 'a' in *ago*, but like the 'o' in *pot* when it follows a labial consonant (a consonant pronounced on the lips)
आ	**ā**	like the 'a' in *f**a**ther*
इ	**i**	like the 'ee' in ***fee**t*; rarely like the 'i' in *h**i**t*
ई	**ī**	like the 'ee' in *f**ee**t*
उ	**u**	like the 'oo' in *f**oo**d*; rarely like the 'u' in *p**u**t*
ऊ	**ū**	like the 'oo' in *f**oo**d*
ऋ	**ṛ**	like the 'ri' in *t**ri**p*, ***ri**pple* (only occurs in words borrowed from Sanskrit)
ए	**e**	like the first part of the vowel sound in *m**a**de*
ऐ	**ai**	like the 'oy' sound in *b**oy*** or the 'i' sound in *qu**i**te*
ओ	**o**	like the first part of the vowel sound in *h**o**le*
औ	**au**	like the 'ow' sound in *c**ow***

Consonants

00.02

The Devanagari script has 33 consonants. The traditional Indian system very helpfully orders consonants according to the way they are pronounced, and they are listed here in alphabetical order. Each of the first five groups of consonants has as its final member a nasal consonant (a consonant pronounced through the nose).

Each Devanagari character is followed by a Roman transliteration which consists of the consonant followed by the letter **a**. This is because, in the absence of any other vowel sign, each consonant is held to contain the inherent अ **a** vowel. Because each Devanagari consonant therefore comes to represent a syllable, some scholars call the Devanagari system **a** 'syllabary' rather than an 'alphabet'. In words that end in a consonant, the inherent **a** of the final letter is sometimes pronounced, but is more often silent. This final **a** will appear in transliteration only when it is to be pronounced.

Two important contrasts that exist in Nepali, but not in English, should be pointed out. The first is between *aspirated* and *non-aspirated* consonants, the second between *dental* and *retroflex* consonants.

- Aspirated consonants are pronounced with a strong expulsion of breath, while non-aspirated consonants are pronounced with only minimal breath being expelled. The amount of breath expelled during the pronunciation of an English consonant is usually somewhere between these two extremes, so discipline is required to learn the Nepali way: less breath than normal while uttering a non-aspirated consonant, much more breath than normal while uttering an aspirated one. Hold a mirror in front of your face as you practise, and compare the extent to which it clouds up in each instance! Or put a hand in front of your mouth to feel the difference. Take care also to utter each aspirate consonant as a single sound: although the second letter of the Roman transliteration of Devanagari aspirates is 'h', this is there to indicate the expulsion of breath, not to suggest that there are two separate sounds.
- To pronounce Nepali words correctly, it is also important to differentiate between dental consonants and retroflex consonants, and most particularly between dental **ta** and **da** and retroflex **ṭa** and **ḍa**. For dental consonants the tongue should touch the back of the upper front teeth, for retroflex consonants it should be curled back up against the roof of the mouth. For the English 't' and 'd' the tongue is held somewhere between these two positions, which sounds like a retroflex to a Nepali speaker's ear. Learners therefore need to work harder to pronounce dental consonants than they do to pronounce retroflex ones, though they often imagine the opposite.

Velar or guttural consonants (pronounced in the throat)

क	**ka**	as the 'k' in *s**k**it*
ख	**kha**	as **ka** but with a strong release of breath

ग	**ga**	as the 'g' in *go*
घ	**gha**	as ga but with a strong release of breath
ङ्	**ṅ**	as the 'n' in *si**n**g*

Palatal consonants (pronounced at the palate or the upper gum-line)

च	**ca**	like the 'ch' in ***ch**eese*, but with less release of breath and pronounced with the tip of the tongue touching the lower front teeth
छ	**cha**	somewhere between the 'ch' in ***ch**eese* and the 'ts' in ***t**sar*, pronounced with a strong release of breath
ज	**ja**	as the 'j' in ***j**ug*
झ	**jha**	as **ja** but with a strong release of breath
ञ	**ña**	as the 'n' in *i**n**jury*

Retroflex consonants (pronounced with the tongue curled back to touch the palate)

ट	**ṭa**	like the 't' in *s**t**op*, but with the tongue curled up to touch the roof of the mouth
ठ	**ṭha**	as **ṭa** but with a strong release of breath
ड	**ḍa**	*when the first letter of a syllable:* as the 'd' in ***d**ug*, but with the tongue curled up to touch the roof of the mouth *in the middle or at the end of a word:* as the 'r' in ***r**ug*, but with the tongue curled up to touch the roof of the mouth
ढ	**ḍha**	as **ḍa** but with a strong release of breath
ण	**ṇa**	like the 'n' in *a**n**d*, but with the tongue curled up to touch the roof of the mouth

Dental consonants (pronounced with the tongue touching or close to the upper front teeth)

त	**ta**	like the 't' in ***t**ip*, with the tip of the tongue against the back of the upper front teeth
थ	**tha**	as **ta** but with a strong release of breath
द	**da**	as the 'd' in ***d**ip*
ध	**dha**	as **da** but with a strong release of breath
न	**na**	as the 'n' in ***n**ip*

Labial consonants (pronounced on the lips)

प	**pa**	as the 'p' in ***p**ot*
फ	**pha**	as **pa** but with a strong release of breath; often like the 'f' in ***f**ather*

ब	**ba**	as the 'b' in ***b**ud*
भ	**bha**	as **ba** but with a strong release of breath; sometimes like a breathy 'v' as in ***d**river*
म	**ma**	as the 'm' in ***m**ud*

Semi-vowels

य	**ya**	as the 'y' in ***y**es*
र	**ra**	like the 'r' in ***r**un*, but pronounced with a trill of the tongue, not on the lips
ल	**la**	like the 'l' in ***l**ot*, but pronounced with the tongue further forward
व	**va**	pronounced either as the 'b' in ***b**ud* or as the 'w' in ***w**orse*

Sibilant ('hissing') consonants

श	**śa**	as the 'sh' in *s**h**un*, but also frequently pronounced 's'
ष	**ṣa**	as the 'sh' in *s**h**un*, but also frequently pronounced 's'
स	**sa**	as the 's' in ***s**un*

Aspirate consonant

ह	**ha**	as the 'h' in ***h**ug*

Script exercise 1 Make a flash card for each character, with the Devanagari letter on the front and the Roman transliteration on the back. Use these to help you memorize each character.

Script exercise 2 Write out the following Nepali words in Devanagari:

jhan	saral	thap	bhavan	kamal	had
chad	bakhat	jarah	yas	ṭhag	ḍar
tara	gaṇa	śahar	daśak	nabh	vaś
calan	ṭaṭh	ma	ghar	phaṭ	rath
dhaval	ḍhab	lay	paḍha	ṣaṭh	khatam

Constructing syllables

Every vowel except अ **a** has a vowel sign which is added to a consonant to form a syllable. The अ **a** vowel is inherent in the consonant itself. When a vowel other than अ **a** is added to a consonant, it automatically replaces the अ **a** vowel. Vowel signs are attached to the consonant क् k in the following ways:

क् **k**	+	अ **a**	=	क	**ka**
क **ka**	+	आ **ā**	=	का	**kā**
क **ka**	+	इ **i**	=	कि	**ki**
क **ka**	+	ई **ī**	=	की	**kī**
क **ka**	+	उ **u**	=	कु	**ku**
क **ka**	+	ऊ **ū**	=	कू	**kū**
क **ka**	+	ऋ **ṛ**	=	कृ	**kṛ**
क **ka**	+	ए **e**	=	के	**ke**
क **ka**	+	ऐ **ai**	=	कै	**kai**
क **ka**	+	ओ **o**	=	को	**ko**
क **ka**	+	औ **au**	=	कौ	**kau**

A vowel sign is generally attached to the stem or downstroke of a consonant – to the foot of the downstroke in the case of उ **u**, ऊ **ū**, and ऋ **ṛ**, to the head of the downstroke in the case of ए **e** and ऐ **ai**, as an additional downstroke attached by a loop to the head of the stem in the cases of इ **i** and ई **ī**, and as an additional downstroke with or without extra elements in the cases of आ **ā**, ओ **o**, and औ **au**. क **ka** is a single-stemmed consonant, but some consonants have two downstrokes, and in such cases the vowel sign must be attached to the right-hand member of the pair. The consonant ग **ga** is an example:

ग	गा	गि	गी	गु	गू	गृ	गे	गै	गो	गौ
ga	**gā**	**gi**	**gī**	**gu**	**gū**	**gṛ**	**ge**	**gai**	**go**	**gau**

The consonant र **ra** is an exception to these general rules when it takes the vowel signs ु **-u** and ू **-ū**. Instead of attaching these to the foot of the downstroke, you should allow them to nestle higher up in the crook of the character:

र	+	उ	=	रु **ru**
र	+	ऊ	=	रू **rū**

A consonant can only support one vowel at a time. In words in which one vowel follows directly after another, the second vowel must always appear as a full vowel character. Thus, to write the word **duī** *(two)* you must write दु **du** followed by ई **ī** in its full form: दुई. Similarly, note the spellings खाउ **khāu**, गाई **gāī**, and लिए **lie**.

Script exercise 3 Write out the following Nepali words in Devanagari:

luṭapīṭ	bemausam	aghāunu	ghṃā	anauṭho
auṣadhi	bhautik	risāunu	ainā	deū
khicaḍī	dobāṭo	gūḍh	hariyo	ukusamukus

itarinu	janatā	yahī	nakhāū	choṭakarī
oḍār	bṛhat	phūladānī	guruko	śarīr
sāikal	jhilimili	taipani	bhailo	vīṇā
śiśī	yātāyāt	āmā	thego	īśān
ḍaul	eghāra	ūṣār		

Nasalization

Every vowel can be nasalized. To pronounce a nasalized vowel, direct as much as you can of the breath that is involved in its pronunciation towards the nasal cavity. In Nepali, nasalization is indicated by a sign called चन्द्रबिन्दु **candrabindu** (literally, *moon dot*), whose name describes its appearance well: ँ. In Roman transliteration, nasalization is represented by a *tilde* over the vowel (e.g. **ã**).

The चन्द्रबिन्दु **candrabindu** is written either over the nasalized vowel itself, e.g. कहाँ **kahā̃**, or above the consonant to which the vowel is attached, e.g. गरूँ **garū̃**, हुँ **hũ**. If any part of the vowel is written above the headstroke, the चन्द्रबिन्दु **candrabindu** is reduced to its बिन्दु **bindu** or 'dot', e.g. छिंडी **chĩḍī**, गरें **garẽ**.

In some Nepali words it is customary to represent nasalization not with the चन्द्रबिन्दु **candrabindu** but with a conjunct of which the first member is one of the nasal consonants. The two most common combinations are:

ङ्	**ṅ**	+	क	**ka**	=	ङ्क	**ṅka**
ङ्	**ṅ**	+	ग	**ga**	=	ङ्ग	**ṅga**

Thus, certain words can be spelled in two different ways: हाँगो **hā̃go** or हाङ्गो **hāṅgo**; गुरुंग **gurũg** or गुरुङ्ग **guruṅg**. The conjuncts tend to be used in words that are felt to be unique to the language, while चन्द्रबिन्दु **candrabindu** is used in words that Nepali shares with Hindi, Sanskrit, etc.

Script exercise 4 Write out the following Nepali words in Devanagari:

hā̃	chāyā̃	nayā̃	gāũ	sā̃ga
gāũchu	āinā̃	diinā̃	tapāī̃	jā̃daina
pā̃c	aũlo	garẽ	sā̃sār	ā̃khā
guruṅg	chā̃gā	mnā̃n	aṅg	

Conjunct characters

The spellings of many Nepali words involve the combination or clustering of two or more consonants; these combinations are known as *conjuncts*. By joining two consonants in this way, you cancel out the inherent अ **a** between them.

Certain combinations produce what are in effect new characters rather than recognizable combinations of their constituent consonants. These *special* conjuncts are listed below:

Special conjunct characters

क **ka**	+	ष **ṣa**	=	क्ष **kṣa** (often pronounced 'che')
ज **ja**	+	ञ **ña**	=	ज्ञ **jña** (pronounced 'gya')
श **śa**	+	र **ra**	=	श्र **śra**
त **ta**	+	त **ta**	=	त्त **tta**
त **ta**	+	र **ra**	=	त्र **tra**
द **da**	+	य **ya**	=	द्य **dya**

HALF CHARACTERS

More than half of all the conjuncts are formed simply by dropping a downstroke from the first member and then joining what remains to the full form of the second member. For instance, to produce the conjunct **gya**, consisting of the consonants ग **ga** and य **ya**, remove the second downstroke of ग **ga** to produce ग् and add this to the full form of य **ya** to produce the conjunct ग्य.

The following table shows all the half characters, followed by examples of ways in which they are combined with full characters to form conjuncts.

Full character		***Half character***	***Examples***
क्	**k**	क्	क्क **kka,** क्ख **kkha,** क्ट **kṭa**
क्ष	**kṣa**	क्ष्	क्ष्म **kṣma,** क्ष्य **kṣya**
ख	**kha**	ख्	ख्य **khya,** ख्न **khna,** ख्छ **khcha**
ग	**ga**	ग्	ग्य **gya,** ग्ल **gla,** ग्व **gva**
घ	**gha**	घ्	घ्छ **ghcha,** घ्न **ghna,** घ्य **ghya**
च	**ca**	च्	च्च **cca,** च्छ **ccha,** च्य **cya**
ज	**ja**	ज्	ज्ज **jja,** ज्य **jya,** ज्व **jva**
झ	**jha**	झ्	झ्य **jhya,** झ्द **jhda,** झ्न **jhna**
ञ	**ñ**	ञ्	ञ्च **ñca,** ञ्ज **ñja**
ण	**ṇ**	ण्	ण्ट **ṇṭa,** ण्ठ **ṇṭha,** ण्य **ṇya**
त	**ta**	त्	त्म **tma,** त्य **tya,** त्स **tsa**
त्त	**tta**	त्त्	त्त्व **ttva**
थ	**tha**	थ्	थ्य **thya**
ध	**dha**	ध्	ध्छ **dhcha,** ध्य **dhya,** ध्व **dhva**
न	**na**	न्	न्त **nta,** न्द्र **ndra,** न्ह **nha**

प	**pa**	ट	**प्ठ pṭha, प्प ppa, प्स psa**
फ	**pha**	फ्	**फ्न phna**
ब	**ba**	ब्	**ब्ज bja, ब्द bda, ब्ब bba**
भ	**bha**	भ्	**भ्य bhya**
म	**ma**	म्	**म्न mna, म्प mpa, म्ह mha**
य	**ya**	य्	**य्य yya**
ल	**la**	ल्	**ल्क lka, ल्द lda, ल्ल lla**
व	**va**	व्	**व्य vya**
श	**śa**	श्	**श्य śya, श्ल śla, श्व śva**
ष	**ṣa**	ष्	**ष्ठ ṣṭha, ष्ण ṣṇa, ष्य ṣya**
स	**sa**	स्	**स्क ska, स्ट sṭa, स्त sta**

THE HALANT

If the diagonal stroke called हलन्त **halant** is placed at the foot of a consonant, it removes its inherent अ **a.** हलन्त **halant** is used regularly in verbs, but very rarely in other words. It is also used to show that a conjunct exists between two consonants whose joining cannot be represented in any other way. The round or oval characters ट, ठ, ड, ढ, द cannot drop a downstroke and remain recognizable. For this reason, if they are the first member of a conjunct they will keep their full form and the junction will be effected by the हलन्त **halant**, e.g.

ड	**ḍa**	+	ड	**ḍa**	=	ड्ड	**ḍḍa**
ट	**ṭa**	+	द	**da**	=	ट्द	**ṭda**
ठ	**ṭha**	+	म	**ma**	=	ठ्म	**ṭhma**
ट	**ṭa**	+	न	**na**	=	ट्न	**ṭna**

CONJUNCTS CONTAINING THE CONSONANT र RA

When र **ra** is the first member of a conjunct combination, it takes a form known as रेफ **reph**, which is a hook (ॅ) written above the headstroke of the second member of the conjunct combination, e.g. गर्छ **garcha**, गर्न **garna**. If a vowel sign follows the consonant to which र **ra** is being joined, the रेफ **reph** sign must move to the right, i.e. to the end of the syllable it precedes: गर्दा **gardā**, भर्ती **bhartī**, गर्ने **garne**.

When र **ra** is the first member of a conjunct of which the second member is य **ya**, it is written instead as a curved dash: गर्‍यो **garyo**, पर्‍यो **paryo**.

When र **ra** is the second member of a conjunct it is written as a diagonal slash down from the left of the lower part of the downstroke of the first member of the conjunct: राम्रो **rāmro**, उग्र **ugra**. If the first member of the conjunct has two stems, the diagonal slash will be added to the right-hand stem. If the first member of the conjunct is an oval or round consonant, a slightly different form is used: ड्र **ḍra**, ट्र **ṭra**. Note also the forms स्र **sra,** ह्र **hra**, श्र **śra**.

OTHER SPECIAL CASES

If the second member of a conjunct is य **ya** and the first member is a retroflex consonant, the य **ya** takes a special form (ट्य):

ट	**ṭa**	+	य	**ya**	=	ट्य	**ṭya**
ड	**ḍ**	+	य	**ya**	=	ड्य	**ḍya**

Conjuncts that consist of two identical retroflex consonants may be represented with the characters arranged vertically, e.g.

ट	**ṭa**	+	ट	**ṭa**	=	ट्ट	**ṭṭa**

The consonants द **da** and ह **ha** form the following special conjuncts:

द **da**	+	ग **ga**	=	द्ग **dga**	ह **ha**	+	र **ra**	= ह्र **hra**
द **da**	+	द **da**	=	द्द **dda**	ह **ha**	+	व **va**	= ह्व **hva**
द **da**	+	ध **dha**	=	द्ध **ddha**	ह **ha**	+	ल **la**	= ह्ल **hla**
द **da**	+	भ **bha**	=	द्भ **dbha**	ह **ha**	+	म **ma**	= ह्म **hma**
द **da**	+	व **va**	=	द्व **dva**	ह **ha**	+	न **na**	= ह्न **hna**

00.03

Script exercise 5 Write out the following Nepali words in Devanagari:

kakṣā	jñān	natra	śrīmān	hlāsā	vidyā
divya	mahattā	lakṣya	hāttī	garchin	śānti
subbā	sakdaina	śabda	bhāgya	haptā	ṭhaṭṭā
pakkā	aḍḍā	jhyāl	āphno	phyā̃knu	rāmro
kṛṣṇa	dṛśya	pradhān	paddhati	bharyāṅ	viśva
bhañjyāṅg	pañcāyat	garthyo	khelcha	kāṭyo	garyo
kāṭhmāḍaũ	paḍhyo	vīrendra	bujhnu	mvāī	kyā
dhvani	āgrejī	kvāppa	prakhyāt	icchā	acyūt
ujjval	ṭrak	aṇḍā	utkṛṣṭa	tattva	ātmā
drava	dvārā	ārambh	rāṣṭra	svāsthya	hissī

Visarga

Visarga is a sign like a colon (but with its dots further apart) that occurs at the end or in the middle of certain words. It is pronounced as **ha** and is transliterated as **ḥ**. The only word in this book that requires **visarga** is दुःख **duḥkha**.

Numerals

The Nepali numerals are as follows:

१	२	३	४	५	६	७	८	९	०
1	2	3	4	5	6	7	8	9	0

Dictionary order

अ	**a**	क	**ka**	ठ	**ṭha**	ब	**ba**
आ	**ā**	ख	**kha**	ड	**ḍa**	भ	**bha**
इ	**i**	ग	**ga**	ढ	**ḍha**	म	**ma**
ई	**ī**	घ	**gha**	ण	**ṇa**	य	**ya**
उ	**u**	ङ्	**ṅa**	त	**ta**	र	**ra**
ऊ	**ū**	च	**ca**	थ	**tha**	ल	**la**
ऋ	**ṛ**	छ	**cha**	द	**da**	व	**va**
ए	**e**	ज	**ja**	ध	**dha**	श	**śa**
ऐ	**ai**	झ	**jha**	न	**na**	ष	**ṣa**
ओ	**o**	ञ	**ña**	प	**pa**	स	**sa**
औ	**au**	ट	**ṭa**	फ	**pha**	ह	**ha**

The nasalized form of a vowel always precedes its unnasalized form in the dictionary order: thus, words beginning with अँ will come before words beginning with अ, words beginning with कुँ before words beginning with कु, etc.

Stress and accent

In Sanskrit, the language from which Nepali originally developed, consonants are always pronounced with their inherent अ **a** unless हलन्त **halant** is there to cancel it out. In Nepali, however, this is no longer the rule. The हलन्त **halant** is used only to mark the absence of a final अ **a** at the end of certain verb endings where without it some ambiguity of meaning could arise, or to mark the absence of the inherent अ **a** between two consonants that cannot be conjoined to form a conjunct in any other way. Otherwise, some words that end in a consonant but no vowel sign are pronounced with a final अ **-a**, whereas others are not. Although the best way to learn pronunciation is by hearing Nepali words spoken, certain rules can be discerned here.

The following categories of words should usually be pronounced as they are written (i.e. with the inherent अ **a** unless this is cancelled out with the हलन्त **halant**):

1 verb forms, where the हलन्त **halant** is used whenever necessary to cancel the inherent अ **a: दिएर diera, गर gara, गर्छन् garchan, पढ्छन् paḍhchan**;

2 most adverbs and postpositions: **तर tara, बाहिर bāhira, आज āja, तिर -tira**;

3 repetitive onomatopoeic words: सललल **salalala**;

4 words of one syllable: म **ma,** त **ta**;

5 words whose final syllable is a conjunct: कर्म **karma,** भक्त **bhakta**;

6 most words ending in a semi-vowel: मह **maha,** शिव **śiva**.

An inherent **-a** is usually not pronounced:*

1 at the end of postpositions of two or more syllables that are written as separate words (i.e. that are not joined to the noun or pronoun they follow): समेत **samet,** बाहेक **bāhek**;

2 in words (other than verbs) consisting of Cv-Ca: दिन **din,** or V-Ca: औल **aul**;

3 in words (other than verbs) consisting of Cv-Cv-Ca: नेपाल **nepāl,** विकास **bikās,** किताब **kitāb**;

4 in words consisting of Cv-Ca-Cv-Ca, where both medial and final अ **a** are dropped: किनमेल **kinmel,** खलबल **khalbal,** तरवार **tarvār,** लतपत **latpat**.

*Cv = syllable consisting of consonant + any vowel (including **v a**). Ca = syllable consisting of consonant + **v a**.

Punctuation

Devanagari now employs all of the punctuation symbols used in English, with the exception of the full stop. This consists instead of a single downstroke: ।

Samples of Nepali handwriting

मेरो नाम अभि सुवेदी हो।

मेरो नाम माइकल हट हो।

मेरो नाम कृष्ण प्रधान हो।

KEY TO SCRIPT EXERCISES

Script exercise 2

झन	सरल	थप	भवन	कमल	हद
छद	बखत	जरह	यस	ठग	डर
तर	गण	शहर	दशक	नभ	वश
चलन	टठ	म	घर	फट	रथ
धवल	ढब	लय	पढ	षठ	खतम

Script exercise 3

लुटपीट	बेमौसम	अघाउनु	घृणा	अनौठो
औषधि	भौतिक	रिसाउनु	ऐना	देऊ
खिचडी	दोबाटो	गूढ	हरियो	उकुसमुकुस
इतरिनु	जनता	यही	नखाऊ	छोटकरी
ओडार	बृहत	फूलदानी	गुरुको	शरीर
साइकल	झिलिमिलि	तैपनि	भैलो	वीणा
शिशी	यातायात	आमा	थेगो	ईशान
डौल	एघार	ऊषार		

Script exercise 4

हाँ	छायाँ	नयाँ	गाउँ	सँग
गाउँछु	आइनँ	दिइनँ	तपाईं	जाँदैन
पाँच	औंलो	गरें	सँसार	आँखा
गुरुङ्ग	छाङ्गा	मनाङ्	अङ्ग	

Script exercise 5

कक्षा	ज्ञान	नत्र	श्रीमान	ल्हासा	विद्या
दिव्य	महत्ता	लक्ष्य	हात्ती	गर्छिन्	शान्ति
सुब्बा	सक्दैन	शब्द	भाग्य	हप्ता	ठट्टा
पक्का	अड्डा	झ्याल	आफ्नो	फ्याँक्नु	राम्रो
कृष्ण	दृश्य	प्रधान	पद्धति	भ्याङ्	विश्व
भञ्ज्याङ्ग	पञ्चायत	गर्थ्यो	खेल्छ	काट्यो	गऱ्यो
काठ्माडौं	पढ्यो	विरेन्द्र	बुझ्नु	म्वाई	क्या
ध्वनि	अँग्रेजी	क्वाप्प	प्रख्यात	इच्छा	अच्यूत
उज्ज्वल	ट्रक	अण्डा	उत्कृष्ट	तत्त्व	आत्मा
द्रव	द्वारा	आरम्भ	राष्ट्र	स्वास्थ्य	हिस्सी

Credits

Front cover: Lynx/Iconotec.com/Photolibrary.com

Back cover and pack: © Jakub Semeniuk/iStockphoto.com, © Royalty-Free/Corbis, © agencyby/iStockphoto.com, © Andy Cook/iStockphoto.com, © Christopher Ewing/iStockphoto.com, © zebicho – Fotolia.com, © Geoffrey Holman/iStockphoto.com, © Photodisc/Getty Images, © James C. Pruitt/iStockphoto.com, © Mohamed Saber – Fotolia.com

Pack: © Stockbyte/Getty Images

1 तिमी बिन्दु हौ ?
Are you Bindu?

In this unit you will learn:

- ▶ ***how to identify yourself and others***
- ▶ ***how to ask and answer simple questions***
- ▶ ***how to exchange greetings***
- ▶ ***how to address people politely***
- ▶ ***how to apply adjectives to nouns***

1 Meeting the bus

01.01

Gita and Bindu, two young women from Hetauda, have just arrived in Kathmandu to take up their college courses. Bimal Kumar, a senior male student, has been sent to meet them.

बिमल कुमार **Bimal Kumār**	नमस्ते ! **namaste!** Hello!
गीता **Gītā**	हजुर ? **hajur?** Pardon?
बिमल कुमार **Bimal Kumār**	नमस्ते ! तिमी गीता हौ ? **namaste! timī Gītā hau?** Hello! Are you Gita?
गीता **Gītā**	हो, म गीता हुँ । नमस्ते । **ho, ma Gītā hũ. namaste.** Yes, I am Gita. Hello.
बिमल कुमार **Bimal Kumār**	अनि तिमी बिन्दु हौ ? **ani timī Bindu hau?** And are you Bindu?
बिन्दु **Bindu**	हजुर, म बिन्दु हुँ । **hajur, ma Bindu hũ.** Yes, I am Bindu.
बिमल कुमार **Bimal Kumār**	ल, राम्रो । म बिमल कुमार हुँ । **la, rāmro. ma Bimal Kumār hũ.** Right, good. I am Bimal Kumar.

बिन्दु	नमस्ते बिमल कुमारजी ! तपाई सन्चै हुनुहुन्छ ?
Bindu	**namaste Bimal Kumārjī! tapāī̃ sancai hunuhuncha?**
	Hello Bimal Kumarji! Are you well?
बिमल कुमार	सन्चै । तिमीहरू नि ?
Bimal Kumār	**sancai. timīharū ni?**
	I am well. How about you?
गीता	सन्चै ! तपाई शिक्षक हुनुहुन्छ ?
Gītā	**sancai! tapāī̃ śikṣak hunuhuncha?**
	We are well. Are you a teacher?
बिमल कुमार	होइन, म विद्यार्थी हुँ । तिमीहरू पनि विद्यार्थी हौ, होइन ?
Bimal Kumār	**hoina, ma vidyīrthī hũ. timīharū pani vidyārthī hau, hoina?**
	No, I am a student. You are students too, aren't you?
बिन्दु	हजुर, हामीहरू पनि विद्यार्थी हौं ।
Bindu	**hajur, hāmīharū pani vidyārthī haũ.**
	Yes, we are students too.

Quick vocab

नमस्ते ! **namaste!**	hello! (Hindu greeting; also used for *goodbye*)
हजुर ? **hajur?**	yes? pardon?
तिमी… हौ **hau?**	you are ... or are you ...?
हो **ho**	yes (literally, is)
म… हुँ **ma ... hũ**	I am ...
अनि **ani**	and
हजुर **hajur**	yes

ल **la**	there! or that's it!
राम्रो **rāmro**	good
बिमल कुमारजी **Bimal Kumārjī**	-jī is added to his name for politeness *
सन्चै **sancai**	well, in good health
तपाईं... हुनुहुन्छ ? **tapāī̃ hunuhuncha**	you are ... or are you ...?
नी ? **ni ?**	what about ...?
तिमीहरू **timīharū**	you (plural)
शिक्षक **śikṣak**	teacher
होइन **hoina**	no (literally, is not)
पनि **pani**	too, also
विद्यार्थी **vidyārthī**	student, students
होइन ? **hoina?**	is that not so?
हामीहरू ... हौं **hāmīharū ... haũ**	we ... are

*Some Nepali speakers add the suffix- **ज्यू-jyū** to names instead. The suffix -**जी -jī** is common to both Hindi and Nepali.

Grammar

1 *IS* AND *ARE* IN NEPALI

In English, you say that something or someone *is* large, or *is* a policeman, or *is* in Kathmandu. But in Nepali, a distinction is made between two different kinds of *is*, and in the plural between two kinds of *are*. These two forms are:

a The **हो ho** form which normally defines the thing or person you are talking about with a noun:

ऊ प्रहरी हो ।	**ū praharī ho.**	He is a policeman.
यो काठ्माडौं हो ।	**yo kāṭhmāḍaũ ho.**	This is Kathmandu.

b The **छ cha** form which describes with an adjective, or locates a thing or person:

त्यो ठूलो छ ।	**tyo ṭhūlo cha.**	That is big (describing).
ऊ काठ्माडौंमा छ ।	**ū kāṭhmāḍaũmā cha.**	He is in (-mā) Kathmandu (locating).

If you wish to say that something is large you must use **छ cha** for *is,* because you are describing it; if you wish to say that someone is in Kathmandu, you must again use **छ cha** for *is,* because you are locating them; but if you wish to state that someone is a policeman you must use **हो ho** for *is*, because you are defining him. **छ cha** and **हो ho** have different forms, depending on which of the Nepali pronouns (the words for *I, we, you, he, she, it* and *they*) is their subject. These forms are introduced in the pages that follow.

2 FIRST PERSON PRONOUNS (*I, WE*)

The first person pronouns are म **ma** *I* and हामी **hāmī** *we*. हामी **hāmī** *we* is sometimes used to mean *I* in place of म **ma**, though not with the pomposity of the English 'royal we'. When it is necessary to make it absolutely clear that हामी **hāmī** is intended to mean *we* in the plural, the pronoun is pluralized to become हामीहरू **hāmīharū**.

3 SECOND PERSON PRONOUN (*YOU*)

When speaking to a person, you must address that person using a pronoun (a word for *you*) that reflects whether you are senior to him/her, or vice versa, and to what degree. This kind of seniority can depend, among other things, on age difference, family relationships, gender or social class.

● INSIGHT

Although there are three levels of 'you' in Nepali, depending on the age or social status of a person addressed, it is suggested that non-Nepali speakers of Nepali use the polite form as much as possible, unless they are dealing with small children.

The three levels of politeness, working upward, are:

LOW	(intimate or contemptuous)
MIDDLE	(familiar)
HIGH	(polite and super-polite)

LOW: the intimate or contemptuous तँ **tã** (*you* or *thou*) is used to address a social inferior (a junior servant, one's own small child, an animal, etc.), to express contempt or anger (one driver to another after a collision between their cars, perhaps!), or to address someone with whom one's relationship is intimate. Foreign speakers of Nepali will never use this pronoun. It can only be used to address an individual, and therefore has no plural form.

MIDDLE: the familiar तिमी **timī** (roughly equivalent to the French *tu*) is used to address persons significantly younger or of lower social standing than oneself (servants, children, etc.) or to address friends with whom an established informal relationship exists. To form the plural, you add the pluralizing suffix -हरू **-harū**.

HIGH: the polite तपाईं **tapāĩ** (roughly equivalent to the French *vous*) is used to address most equals and all superiors except those to whom especial deference is due. (Foreign speakers of Nepali inevitably find themselves using this word for *you* more commonly than any other. In fact, they will probably feel more comfortable using it to address people, such as servants or porters, whom Nepalis would tend to address as तिमी **timī**.) To form the plural, you add the pluralizing suffix -हरू **-harū**.

The super-polite हजुर **hajur** is sometimes used to express especial deference when addressing someone. It takes the same verb-forms as the other High pronouns. It might be used by a lower grade employee to address his employer, for example, or by a new bride to address her husband. It is also used as a polite word of assent (हजुर ! **hajur!** *Yes!*) or to indicate that one has not heard or understood (हजुर ? **hajur?** *Pardon me?*).

4 I AM, YOU ARE, WE ARE *WITH* हो HO

Singular		
म हुँ	**ma hũ**	I am
तँ होस्	**tã hos**	you (Low) are
तिमी हौ	**timī hau**	you (Middle) are
तपाईं हुनुहुन्छ	**tapāĩ hunuhuncha**	you (High) are
Plural		
हामी हौं	**hāmī haũ**	we are (occasionally I am)
हामीहरू हौं	**hāmīharū haũ**	we are
तिमीहरू हौ	**timīharū hau**	you (Middle) are
तपाईंहरू हुनुहुन्छ	**tapāĩharū hunuhuncha**	you (High) are

Negatives					
Each affirmative form of हो **ho** has a negative form:					
Affirmative			***Negative***		
हुँ	**hũ**	I am	होइन	**hoina**	I am not
हौं	**haũ**	we are	होइनौं	**hoinaũ**	we are not
होस्	**hos**	you (Low) are	होइनस्	**hoinas**	you (Low) are not
हौ	**hau**	you (Middle) are	होइनौ	**hoinau**	you (Middle) are not
हुनुहुन्छ	**hunuhuncha**	you (High) are	हुनुहुन्न	**hunuhunna**	you (High) are not

INSIGHT

The use of the demonstrative pronouns यो **yo** and त्यो **tyo** can be the key to enhancing your vocabulary. Point to things and ask questions using the demonstrative pronouns, e.g. 'what is this?' or 'what is that?'

5 NOUNS

Nearly all Nepali nouns have masculine gender. The only feminine nouns are those that are female and human. Many feminine nouns end in **-ī**. Here are some examples of feminine nouns:

केटी	**keṭī**	girl	आइमाई	**āimāī**	woman
आमा	**āmā**	mother	छोरी	**chorī**	daughter
दिदी	**didī**	elder sister	बहिनी	**bahinī**	younger sister
श्रीमती	**śrīmatī**	wife	साली	**sālī**	wife's younger sister

There is no definite article *the* in Nepali, nor is there an indefinite article *a*. Therefore a sentence such as ऊ विद्यार्थी हो **ū vidyārthī ho** can be translated as *s/he is a student* or as *s/he is the student*, depending on the context.

All nouns, and most pronouns, are pluralized simply by adding the suffix -हरू **-harū**:

Singular			Plural		
मान्छे	**mānche**	person	मान्छेहरू	**mānceharū**	people
नेपाली	**nepālī**	Nepali	नेपालीहरू	**nepālīharū**	Nepalis
तपाईं	**tapāī̃**	you (High)	तपाईंहरू	**tapāī̃harū**	you people (High)
तिमी	**timī**	you (Middle)	तिमीहरू	**timīharū**	you people (Middle)

However, it is not necessary to attach -हरू **-harū** to a noun when some other word in the sentence makes it clear that the noun is plural. In the following sentences, the word that takes the plural suffix is the one that the speaker wishes to emphasize:

हामीहरू शिक्षक हौं । **hāmīharū śikṣak haũ.** We are teachers.

There is no need to add -हरू **-harū** to शिक्षक **śikṣak** as well as to हामी **hāmī**. हामी **hīmī** is emphasized.

तिमीहरू विद्यार्थी हौ । **timīharū vidyārthī hau.** You are students.

There is no need to add -हरू **-harū** to विद्यार्थी **vidyārthī** as well as to तिमी **timī**. तिमी **timī** is emphasized.

हामी शिक्षकहरू हौं । **hāmī śikṣakharū haũ.** We are teachers.

शिक्षक **śikṣak** is emphasized.

तिमी विद्यार्थीहरू हौ । **timī vidyārthīharū hau.** You are students.

विद्यार्थी **vidyārthī** is emphasized.

● INSIGHT

Nepali syntax places the subject at the beginning of a sentence and the verb at the end. All the other words are arranged between the subject and the verb, their exact location depending on the relationship between them and the verb and the subject.

6 ASKING AND ANSWERING QUESTIONS

In everyday spoken Nepali, the only difference between a statement and a question is the intonation. To put it simply: the tone of your voice goes up at the end of a question, while at the end of a statement it goes down:

यो काठ्माडौं हो ।	**yo kāṭhmāḍaũ ho.**	This is Kathmandu.
	(हो **ho** pronounced in a low tone)	
यो काठ्माडौं हो ?	**yo kāṭhmāḍaũ ho?**	Is this Kathmandu?
	(हो **ho** pronounced in a rising tone)	

Nepali does possess words for *yes* and *no:* these are अँ **ã** and अहँ **ahã** respectively.

Q यो काठ्माडौं हो ?	**yo kāṭhmāḍaũ ho?**	Is this Kathmandu?
A अँ, काठ्माडौं हो ।	**ã, kāṭhmāḍaũ ho.**	Yes, this is Kathmandu.
or		
A अहँ, पोखरा हो ।	**ahã, pokharā ho.**	No, this is Pokhara.

However, when answering a question it is more common to respond with the affirmative or negative form of the verb with which the question ended:

Q यो काठ्माडौं हो ?	**yo kāṭhmāḍaũ ho?**	Is this Kathmandu?
A हो, काठ्माडौं हो ।	**ho, kāṭhmāḍaũ ho.**	Yes, this is Kathmandu.
or		
A होइन, यो पोखरा हो ।	**hoina, yo pokharā ho.**	No, this is Pokhara.

हजुर **hajur** is often used for *yes:*

Q त्यो रमेश हो ?	**tyo Rameś ho?**	Is that Ramesh?
A हजुर, रमेश हो ।	**hajur, Rameś ho.**	Yes, that's Ramesh.

Often, हो **ho** *is* and होइन **hoina** *is not* are also used to mean *yes* and *no* regardless of the verb in the question:

Q तपाईं रमेशजी हुनुहुन्छ ?	**tapāī̃ Rameśjī hunuhuncha?**	Are you Rameshji?
A हो, म रमेश हुँ ।	**ho, ma Rameś hũ.**	Yes, I am Ramesh.
or		
A होइन, म ओम हुँ ।	**hoina, ma Om hũ.**	No, I am Om.

2 Arriving at the college

01.02

Gita and Bindu reach the college with Bimal Kumar.

गीता **Gītā**	यो महेन्द्र महाविद्यालय हो ? **yo Mahendra mahāvidyālay ho?** Is this Mahendra College?
बिमल कुमार	हो । यो महेन्द्र महाविद्यालय हो ।

Bimal Kumār	**ho. yo Mahendra mahāvidyālay ho.**	
	Yes. This is Mahendra College.	
बिन्दु	ती मान्छेहरू को हुन् ?	
Bindu	**tī mānceharū ko hun?**	
	Who are those people?	
बिमल कुमार	तिनीहरू विद्यार्थी हुन् । यो सलील हो, त्यो गणेश हो, र तिनीहरू माया र अम्बिका हुन् ।	
Bimal Kumār	**tinīharū vidyārthī hun. yo Salīl ho, tyo Gaṇeś ho, ra tinīharū Māyā ra Ambikā hun.**	
	They are students. This is Salil, that is Ganesh, and those are Maya and Ambika.	
गीता	अनि त्यो मान्छे शिक्षक हो ?	
Gītā	**ani tyo mānche śikṣak ho?**	
	And is that person a teacher?	
बिमल कुमार	हजुर । वहाँ डाक्टर रमेश थापा हुनुहुन्छ । नमस्कार डाक्टर थापा !	
Bimal Kumār	**hajur. vahā̃ ḍākṭar Rameś Thāpā hunuhuncha. namaskār ḍākṭar Thāpā !**	
	Yes. He is Dr Ramesh Thapa. Hello, Dr Thapa!	
रमेश थापा	नमस्कार बिमल कुमारजी । वहाँहरू को हुनुहुन्छ ?	
Ramesh Thāpā	**namaskār Bimal Kumārjī. vahā̃harū ko hunuhuncha?**	
	Hello, Bimal Kumarji. Who are they?	
बिमल कुमार	वहाँहरू गीता खड्का र बिन्दु शर्मा हुनुहुन्छ । नयाँ विद्यार्थीहरू ।	
Bimal Kumār	**vahā̃harū Gītā Khaḍkā ra Bindu Śarmā hunuhuncha. nayā̃ vidyārthīharū.**	
	They are Gita Khadka and Bindu Sharma. New students.	
रमेश थापा	नमस्ते, नमस्ते ।	
Ramesh Thāpā	**namaste, namaste.**	
	Hello, hello.	
गीता र बिन्दु	नमस्ते हजुर ।	
Gītā ra Bindu	**namaste hajur.**	
	Hello, sir.	

V Quick vocab

महेन्द्र महाविद्यालय **Mahendra mahāvidyālay**	*Mahendra College*
ती **tī**	those
मान्छेहरू **mānceharū**	people
को **ko**	who?
हुन् **hun**	are

र **ra**	and
डाक्टर **ḍākṭar**	doctor
नमस्कार **namaskār**	hello or goodbye (more formal than नमस्ते **namaste**)
नयाँ **nayā̃**	new

Exercise 1

Answer the following questions about yourself:

१ तपाई बिमल कुमार हुनुहुन्छ ? **tapāī̃ Bimal Kumār hunuhuncha?**

२ तपाई विद्यार्थी हुनुहुन्छ ? **tapāī̃ vidyārthī hunuhuncha?**

३ तपाई नेपाली हुनुहुन्छ ? **tapāī̃ nepālī hunuhuncha?**

• INSIGHT

Listen carefully and imitate accordingly to make your pronunciation as close as possible to that of the native speaker. Continue to speak anyway even if you mispronounce words, because the more you speak the more you learn.

Grammar

7 THIRD PERSON PRONOUNS (HE, SHE, THEY)

If you are speaking about a person, the pronoun you choose must reflect whether that person is senior or junior to you in age, social class, etc., and must also indicate whether s/he is in the proximity or not when you speak. The same three levels of politeness exist here that apply to the second person pronouns, although they are not exact equivalents in terms of their usage:

LOW	(simple reference)
MIDDLE	(polite reference)
HIGH	(honorific reference)

LOW third person pronouns are:

ऊ **ū** he/she

यो **yo** it, this

त्यो **tyo** it, that

ऊ **ū** *he/she* is used to refer to a person in his/her absence when there is no need to talk about that person with deference or politeness. ऊ **ū** cannot be used as a pronoun to refer to things or objects, and is used only to refer to human beings.

While यो **yo** and त्यो **tyo** both mean *it*, the difference between them is that यो **yo** refers to something near to the speaker ('this') while त्यो **tyo** refers to something away from the speaker ('that'). यो **yo** and त्यो **tyo** have the plural forms यी **yī** and ती **tī** respectively: the first of these is often pronounced without its initial *y*, i.e. **ī**.

यो **yo** and त्यो **tyo** can also sometimes be used to mean *he* or *she,* but this can sound impolite and it is better to use only ऊ **ū** to refer to people at this level of politeness.

Middle pronouns उनी **unī**, यिनी **yinī** and तिनी **tinī** are in their singular forms generally a feature of cultured or literary Nepali rather than of colloquial speech. When they are used in speech, they refer most commonly to women. They are used to refer to persons who are felt to deserve a modicum of honorific reference, but not the full-blown honorific grade (one example might be a man speaking about his wife).

उनी **unī** and तिनी **tinī** have distant reference, while यिनी **yinī** refers to a person who is physically close to the speaker. The plural forms उनीहरू **unīharū**, यिनीहरू **yinīharū** and तिनीहरू **tinīharū** are used much more commonly in speech than the singular forms, and here they are simply pronouns that refer, politely but not exceptionally politely, to persons in the plural. उनीहरू **unīharū** is in most contexts the word you should use to refer to people as *they.*

HIGH pronouns यहाँ **yahā̃** and वहाँ **vahā̃** and their plural forms यहाँहरू **yahā̃harū** and वहाँहरू **vahā̃harū** are used to refer to persons very politely in their presence and absence respectively. Inevitably, you will be more polite about a person who can hear what you are saying, so वहाँ **vahā̃** is generally used only for persons deserving especial deference and respect: one's parents, teacher, etc. वहाँ **vahā̃** is often pronounced and sometimes written as उहाँ **uhā̃**. (*Note* यहाँ **yahā̃** may also be used as a very polite form of the second person pronoun 'you'.)

8 HE IS, SHE IS, IT IS, THEY ARE WITH हो HO

Singular		
LOW		
ऊ हो	**ū ho**	s/he (distant, Low) is
यो हो	**yo ho**	it/ this (nearby, Low) is
त्यो हो	**tyo ho**	it/that (distant, Low) is
MIDDLE		
उनी हुन्	**unī hun**	s/he (distant, Middle) is
यिनी हुन्	**yinī hun**	s/he (nearby, Middle) is
तिनी हुन्	**tinī hun**	s/he (distant, Middle) is
HIGH		
यहाँ हुनुहुन्छ	**yahā̃ hunuhuncha**	s/he (nearby, High) is
वहाँ हुनुहुन्छ	**vahā̃ hunuhuncha**	s/he (distant, High) is
Plural		
LOW		
यी हुन्	**yī hun**	they (nearby, Low) are
ती हुन्	**tī hun**	they (distant, Low) are
MIDDLE		
उनीहरू हुन्	**unīharū hun**	they (distant, Middle) are

यिनीहरू हुन्	**yinīharū hun**	they (nearby, Middle) are
तिनीहरू हुन्	**tinīharū hun**	they (distant, Middle) are
HIGH		
यहाँहरू हुनुहुन्छ	**yahā̃ harū hunuhuncha**	they (nearby, High) are
वहाँहरू हुनुहुन्छ	**vahā̃ harū hunuhuncha**	they (distant, High) are

Negatives					
Each affirmative form of हो **ho** has a negative form:					
affirmative			***negative***		
LOW SINGULAR					
हो	**ho**	is	होइन	**hoina**	is not
LOW PLURAL & MIDDLE SINGULAR					
हुन्	**hun**	are/is	होइनन्	**hoinan**	are not/is not
HIGH SINGULAR & PLURAL					
हुनुहुन्छ	**hunuhuncha**	is/are	हुनुहुन्न	**hunuhunna**	are not/is not

To be (using हो **ho** to define people's nationalities). Here are some examples:

Affirmative

म अँग्रेज हुँ ।	**ma ā̃grej hū̃.**	I am English.
हामी जर्मन हौं ।	**hāmī jarman haū̃.**	We are German.
तिमी भारतीय हौ ।	**timī bhāratīya hau.**	You (M) are Indian.
तपाई नेपाली हुनुहुन्छ ।	**tapāī̃ nepālī hunuhuncha.**	You (H) are Nepali.
ऊ अमेरिकाली हो ।	**ū amerikālī ho.**	S/he (L) is American.
उनी पाकिस्तानी हुन् ।	**unī pākistānī hun.**	S/he (M) is Pakistani.
वहाँ चिनियाँ हुनुहुन्छ ।	**vahā̃ ciniyā̃ hunuhuncha.**	S/he (H) is Chinese.

Negative

म जर्मन होइन ।	**ma jarman hoina.**	I am not German.
हामी अँग्रेज होइनौं ।	**hāmī ā̃grej hoinaū̃.**	We are not English.*
तिमी अमेरिकाली होइनौ ।	**timī ameriikālī hoinau.**	You (M) are not American.
तपाईं चिनियाँ हुनुहुन्न ।	**tapāī̃ ciniyā̃ hunuhunna.**	You (H) are not Chinese.
ऊ हिन्दुस्तानी होइन ।	**ū hindustānī hoina.**	S/he (L) is not Indian.
उनी नेपाली होइनन् ।	**unī nepālī hoinan.**	S/he (M) is not Nepali.
वहाँ पाकिस्तानी हुनुहुन्न ।	**vahā̃ pākistānī hunuhunna.**	S/he (H) is not Pakistani.

Note:* The terms अमेरिकन **amerikan *American* and अँग्रेज **ā̃grej** *English* are often used to refer generally to foreigners or white people.

तँ **tã**, the Low word for *you*, would not be used in sentences such as the above. An example of its use would be:

तँ मूर्ख होस् ।	**tã mūrkh hos.**	You (L) are an idiot.

9 THIS, THAT, THESE AND THOSE

यो **yo** and त्यो **tyo** and their plural forms यी **yī** and ती **tī** are most commonly used as adjectives to mean *this, that, these* and *those:*

त्यो मान्छे नेपाली हो ।	**tyo mānche nepālī ho.**	That person is Nepali.
यो केटा विद्यार्थी हो ।	**yo keṭā vidyārthī ho.**	This boy is a student.
ती मान्छेहरू अँग्रेज होइनन् ।	**tī mānchehartū āgrej hoinan.**	Those people are not English.
यी बहिनीहरू गीता र बिन्दु हुन् ।	**yī bahinīharū Gītā ra Bindu hun.**	These young girls are Gita and Bindu.

10 ADJECTIVES

Adjectives are of two types:

a inflecting adjectives which end in the vowel **-ओ -o**,

b invariable adjectives ending in some other vowel, or in a consonant.

The endings of adjectives of type (a) must change ('inflect') according to the number and gender of the noun they describe. The endings are:

-ओ **-o** in the masculine singular,

-ई **-ī** in the feminine singular,

-आ **-ā** in the masculine and feminine plural.

a Inflecting adjectives

ठूलो राजा	**ṭhūlo rājā**	great king
ठूला राजाहरू	**ṭhūlā rājāharū**	great kings
राम्रो केटा	**rāmro keṭā**	good boy
राम्रा केटाहरू	**rāmrā keṭāharū**	good boys
सेतो किताब	**seto kitāb**	white book
सेता किताबहरू	**setā kitābharū**	white books
सानी केटी	**sānī keṭī**	small girl
साना केटीहरू	**sānā keṭīharū**	small girls

b Invariable adjectives

गरीब किसान	**garīb kisān**	poor farmer
गरीब किसानहरू	**garīb kisānharū**	poor farmers
सफा कोठा	**saphā koṭhā**	clean room

सफा कोठाहरू	**saphā koāhāharū**	clean rooms
धनी मान्छे	**dhanī mānche**	rich man / person
धनी मान्छेहरू	**dhanī mānchеharū**	rich men / people
नयाँ कलम	**nayā̃ kalam**	new pen
नयाँ कलमहरू	**nayā̃ kalamharū**	new pens

● INSIGHT

Following the rules of grammar may be difficult when you are learning a new language but in the long run you will feel happy, because you will be speaking standard Nepali correctly.

Exercise 2

Complete the following sentences with the appropriate form of हो **ho** to form an affirmative statement. Work in transliteration first, then write the sentences out in Devanagari:

१	म अँग्रेज...	**ma ãgrej...**
२	हामी विद्यार्थी...	**hāmī vidyārthī...**
३	तिमी हिन्दुस्तानी...	**timī hindustānī...**
४	तिमीहरू किसान...	**timīharū kisān...**
५	तपाईं शिक्षक...	**tapāī̃ śikṣak...**
६	ऊ शिक्षक...	**ū śikṣak...**
७	उनी धनी मान्छे...	**unī dhanī mānche...**
८	ती मान्छेहरू प्रहरी...	**tī mānchеharū praharī...**
९	वहाँ नेपाली...	**vahā̃ nepālī...**
१०	यहाँहरू भारतीय...	**yahā̃harū bhāratīya...**

Exercise 3

Convert the affirmative statements into negative statements by changing the forms of the verbs.

Exercise 4

Translate into Nepali, giving both the script and the transliteration forms, taking care to give the adjectives the correct endings:

1 good farmer

2 big book

3 rich girl

4 new boy

5 good king

6 rich farmers
7 good books
8 small girls
9 poor boys
10 rich kings

The most important things for the reader to remember

1 हो ho or **होइन hoina** is also used as an expression 'yes/no' but, more importantly, it is a 'to be' verb which is used to identify object, person or place.

2 There are different ways of exchanging greetings, which depend on the relative age or social status of the speakers. They include **नमस्ते namaste, नमस्कार namask'r, दर्शन darshan** etc.

3 Nepali uses the appropriate conjugated forms of **हो ho** according to subject, so that people can be referred to properly, according to their age and social status.

4 The use of **यो yo** and **त्यो tyo** as demonstrative pronouns and their plural forms **यी yī** and **ती tī,** as well as their oblique forms.

5 **जी jī** is added at the end of Nepali names to express respect while addressing and referring to people. The polite response to this address is **हजुर hajur**.

6 **हरू harū** is a plural marker which is attached to nouns or pronouns. But **हरू harū** is usually left out if an adjective denoting quantity has already been used.

7 Nepali has its own terms for different nationalities: **नेपाली nepālī, भारतीय bhāratīya अमेरिकी amerikī, अंग्रेज** *angrej*, etc.

8 Nepali adjectives are changed to reflect whether the nouns they describe are singular, plural or feminine, e.g. **ठूलो ṭhūlo, ठूला ṭhūla, ठूली ṭhūlī**.

2 काठ्माडौं कति टाढा छ दाइ ?

How far is it to Kathmandu, brother?

In this unit you will learn:

- ***how to describe and ask about things and people***
- ***how to discuss distances and locations***
- ***how to use relationship terms to address people***

3 A view of Kathmandu

02.01

Two villagers have reached a hilltop overlooking the Kathmandu Valley. From there they can see Kathmandu and the villages that surround it. They discuss the view.

रामे **Rāme**	त्यो शहर काठ्माडौं हो, होइन ? **tyo śahar kāṭhmāḍaũ ho, hoina?** That city is Kathmandu, isn't it?
धने **Dhane**	हो, त्यो शहर काठ्माडौं हो । **ho, tyo śahar kāṭhmāḍaũ ho.** Yes, that city is Kathmandu.
रामे **Rāme**	काठ्माडौं ठूलो छ, होइन ? **kāṭhmāḍaũ ṭhūlo cha, hoina?** Kathmandu is big, isn't it?
धने **Dhane**	हो, धेरै ठूलो छ । **ho, dherai ṭhūlo cha.** Yes, it's very big.
रामे **Rāme**	काठ्माडौं कस्तो छ ? राम्रो छ ? **kāṭhmāḍaũ kasto cha? rāmro cha?** What is Kathmandu like? Is it nice?
धने **Dhane**	राम्रै छ । **rāmrai cha.** It's quite nice.
रामे **Rāme**	अनि त्यो कुन गाउँ हो ? **ani tyo kun gāũ ho?** And which village is that?
धने **Dhane**	त्यो गाउँ होइन, भक्तपुर शहर हो । **tyo gāũ hoina, bhaktapur śahar ho.** That is not a village, that is Bhaktapur city.

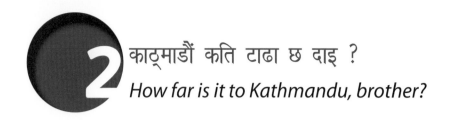

रामे	ए । त्यो शहर सानो छ, होइन ?
Rāme	**e. tyo śahar sāno cha, hoina?**
	Oh, I see. That city is small, isn't it?
धने	हो, अलि सानो छ । धेरै ठूलो छैन । तर भक्तपुर धेरै पुरानो शहर हो ।
Dhane	**ho, ali sāno cha. dherai ṭhūlo chaina. tara bhaktapur dherai purāno śahar ho.**
	Yes, it is quite small. It is not very big. But Bhaktapur is a very old city.

V QUICK VOCAB

शहर **śahar**	city
धेरै **dherai**	very
छ **cha**	is
कस्तो **kasto**	like what? how?
राम्रै **rāmrai**	quite nice
कुन **kun**	which?
गाउँ **gāũ**	village
भक्तपुर **bhaktapur**	Bhaktapur
ए **e**	Oh, I see
अलि **ali**	quite
तर **tara**	but
पुरानो **purāno**	old

Exercise 5

02.02

Answer the following questions in Nepali about **Dialogue 3**. If your answer to 1 is in the affirmative, write the Nepali for *Yes, Kathmandu is big*; if your answer is negative, write the Nepali for *No, Kathmandu is not big, it is small*, and so on.

१. काठ्माडौं ठूलो छ ?	**kāṭhmāḍaũ ṭhūlo cha?**
२. भक्तपुर गाउँ हो ?	**bhaktapur gāũ ho?**
३. काठ्माडौं राम्रो छ ?	**kāṭhmāḍaũ rāmro cha?**
४. काठ्माडौं ठूलो शहर हो ?	**kāṭhmāḍaũ ṭhūlo śahar ho?**
५. भक्तपुर पुरानो छ ?	**bhaktapur purāno cha?**
६. भक्तपुर नयाँ शहर हो ?	**bhaktapur nayā̃ śahar ho?**

Grammar

11 PRONOUNS WITH छ CHA

You must use the हो **ho** form of the verb *to be* if you are defining something or someone with a noun, but if you are locating the thing or person you are talking about or describing it with an adjective you must use the छ **cha** form. The High forms हुनुहुन्छ **hunuhuncha** (affirmative) and हुनुहुन्न **hunuhunna** (negative), which were introduced in **Unit 1**, are the same regardless of whether they are defining, describing or locating. The other forms are as follows:

Verb form		Pronoun(s)
छु	chu	म **ma**
छौं	chaũ	हामी **hāmī** and हामीहरू **hāmīharū**
छस्	chas	तँ **tã**
छौ	chau	तिमी **timī** and तिमीहरू **timīharū**
छ	cha	ऊ **ū** यो **yo** त्यो **tyo**
छन्	chan	उनी **unī** यिनी **yinī** and तिनी **tinī** यी **yī** and ती **tī**
		उनीहरू **unīharū,** यिनीहरू **yinīharū** and तिनीहरू **tinīharū**

Negatives					
Each affirmative form of छ has a negative form:					
Affirmative			***Negative***		
छु	**chu**	(I) am	छैन	**chaina**	am not
छौं	**chaũ**	(we) are	छैनौं	**chainaũ**	are not
छस्	**chas**	(you) are (L)	छैनस्	**chainas**	are not
छौ	**chau**	(you) are (M)	छैनौ	**chainau**	are not
छ	**cha**	is (L)	छैन	**chaina**	is not
छन्	**chan**	is (M) / are (L)	छैनन्	**chainan**	is/are not

Feminine forms of छ cha

If you are talking *to* a particular woman or girl and addressing her as तँ **tã** or तिमी **timī** you can choose to use the following feminine forms of छ **cha**:

तँ छेस्	**tã ches**	you (Low) are
तिमी छ्यौ	**timī chyau**	you (Middle) are

If you are talking *about* a particular woman or girl and intend to use the Low pronoun for *she* (ऊ **ū**), you can choose to use the feminine form of छ **cha**, which is छे **che**:

ऊ छे	**ū che**	she (Low) is

If you are talking *about* a particular woman or girl and are using one of the Middle words for *he* or *she* (उनी **unī**, यिनी **yinī**, or तिनी **tinī**), you can choose to use the feminine form of छन् **chan**, which is छिन् **chin**:

उनी छिन्	**unī chin**	she (distant, Middle) is
यिनी छिन्	**yinī chin**	she (nearby, Middle) is
तिनी छिन्	**tinī chin**	she (distant, Middle) is

These feminine forms are not used very consistently in everyday spoken Nepali, but they are often used by men to refer politely to their wives and other female relatives, and they should always be used in the written language. There are no feminine negative forms of छ **cha**.

● INSIGHT

Knowledge of छ *cha* and its conjugated forms should help you memorize all other verb conjugations in the present tense, because they appear at the end of each verb tense, e.g. म जान्छु *ma jānchu*, म जाँदै छु *ma jā̃dai chu*, म गएको छु *ma gaeko chu*.

12 अलि ALI QUITE AND धेरै DHERAI VERY, MANY

Nepali adjectives can be qualified or emphasized by putting the words अलि **ali** *quite* or धेरै **dherai** *very* in front of them.

ऊ अलि दुब्लो छ ।	**ū ali dublo cha.**	He is quite thin.
राम धेरै मोटो छैन ।	**Rām dherai moṭo chaina.**	Ram is not very fat.
उनी अलि होची छिन् ।	**unī ali hocī chin.**	She is rather short.
म धेरै अग्लो छु ।	**ma dherai aglo chu.**	I am very tall.

A second way to qualify or emphasize an adjective is to change its ending to -ऐ **-ai** if it ends in a vowel or to add -ऐ **-ai** to the end of the word if it ends in a consonant:

दुब्लो	**dublo**	thin	दुब्लै	**dublai**	quite thin
मोटो	**moṭo**	fat	मोटै	**moṭai**	quite fat
होचो	**hoco**	short in stature	होचै	**hocai**	rather short in stature

अग्लो	**aglo**	tall	अग्लै	**aglai**	fairly tall
राम्रो	**rāmro**	good, nice	राम्रै	**rāmrai**	nice enough
सानो	**sāno**	small	सानै	**sānai**	rather small
सफा	**saphā**	clean	सफै	**saphai**	clean enough

धेरै **dherai** *very* has a second meaning, which is *many.* It means *very* when it comes before an adjective, but if it comes before a noun, or on its own, it means *many:*

Q नेपालमा धेरै शहरहरू छन् ?	**nepālmā dherai śaharharū chan?**	Are there many cities in Nepal?
A अहँ, धेरै छैनन् ।	**ahã, dherai chainan.**	No, there are not many.

But if you want to ask *are there many big towns in Nepal?* you have the problem that धेरै ठूला षहरहरू **dherai ṭhūlā śaharharū** could be taken to mean *very big cities* instead of *many big cities.* You get over this problem by moving the position of धेरै **dherai** in the sentence:

Q नेपालमा ठूला शहरहरू धेरै छन् ?	**nepālmā ṭhūlā śaharharū dherai chan?**	Are there many big cities in Nepal? ('are big cities many in Nepal?')
A अहँ, धेरै छैनन् ।	**ahã, dherai chainan.**	No, there are not many.

One other commonly used word is अलिकति **alikati** *a small quantity of*, which should only be used to qualify nouns:

अलिकति दूध	**alikati dūdh**	a little milk
अलिकति चिनी	**alikati cinī**	a little sugar
अलिकति पानी	**alikati pānī**	a little water

13 QUESTIONING WORDS (INTERROGATIVES)

In Nepali, many questioning words (called *interrogatives*) begin with a क **k-** and belong to a group of words that follows a set pattern. Those beginning with य **y-** are 'this-words', those beginning with त्य **ty-** or उ **u-** are 'that-words', and those beginning with क **k-** are words that ask a question.

'this-word'		*'that-word'*		*interrogatives*	
	ऊ	**ū** he/she		को	**ko** who?
यो	**yo** it/this	त्यो	tyo it/that	के	**ke** what?
यो	**yo** it/this	त्यो	**tyo** it/that	कुन	**kun** which?
यति	**yati** this much	त्यति	**tyati** that much	कति	**kati** how much?
यस्तो	**yasto** like this	त्यस्तो	**tyasto** like that	कस्तो	**kasto** like what?
यहाँ	**yahā̃** here	त्यहाँ	**tyahā̃** there	कहाँ	**kahā̃** where?

उति **uti** and उस्तो **usto** are alternative forms for *that much* and *like that* respectively.

Because कुन **kun** means *which?*, an enquiry that involves the use of कुन **kun** may use either the verb हो **ho** or the verb छ **cha**:

यो कुन देश हो ?	**yo kun deś ho?**	Which country is this?
यो देश नेपाल हो ।	**yo deś nepāl ho.**	This country is Nepal.
पसलमा कुन साबुन सस्तो छ ?	**pasalmā kun sābun sasto cha?**	In the shop which soap is cheap?
काठ्माडौंमा कुन होटेल राम्रो छ ?	**kāṭhmāḍaũmā kun hoṭel rāmro cha?**	In Kathmandu, which hotel is good?

Because कस्तो **kasto** means *like what?*, a question in which it is used usually asks for a 'describing' reply. So, an enquiry that involves the use of कस्तो **kasto** usually uses the verb छ **cha**:

यो देश कस्तो छ ?	**yo deś kasto cha?**	What is this country like?
यो देश राम्रो छ ।	**yo deś rāmro cha.**	This country is good.
यो पानी कस्तो छ ?	**yo pānī kasto cha?**	What is this water like?
यो पानी सफा छ ।	**yo pānī saphā cha.**	This water is clean.

However, it is also possible to ask *what kind of country is this?*, in which case you are asking for a 'defining' statement and calling for the use of हो **ho**:

यो कस्तो देश हो ?	**yo kasto deś ho?**	What kind of country is this?
यो धेरै धनी देश हो ।	**yo dherai dhanī deś ho.**	This is a very rich country.
यो कस्तो पानी हो ?	**yo kasto pānī ho?**	What kind of water is this?
यो मैलो पानी हो ।	**yo mailo pānī ho.**	This is dirty water.

INSIGHT

It is important to know the question words and their usages, not only so that you can get a range of information but also so that you can learn how to respond properly to each kind of question in Nepali. This opens up a new horizon for learning Nepali.

14 THE SIMPLE SENTENCE

You have no doubt realized by now that Nepali has a different word order from English. In Nepali, the natural place for the verb is at the end of a sentence. Simply, an English speaker says *I am English,* while a Nepali speaker says:

म नेपाली हुँ।	**ma nepālī hũ.**	'I Nepali am.'
तपाईं विद्यार्थी हुनुहुन्छ ।	**tapāī̃ vidyārthī hunuhuncha.**	'You student are.'

Unless there is some good reason for it not to, a Nepali sentence will always begin with a subject and end with a verb: everything else will come in between. If a change is made to this word order it has an effect on the meaning of a sentence: it may emphasize something, or express hesitation or doubt:

नेपाली हुँ म ।	**nepālī hũ ma.**	I'm a Nepali, I am!
विद्यार्थी हुनुहुन्छ तपाई ?	**vidyārthī hunuhuncha tapāĩ?**	Are you a student, then?

4 Near and far

02.03

Salil has just arrived in town and he needs to visit the bank and the post office. He asks Rane, a passer-by, for directions.

सलील **Salīl**	ए भाई, नमस्ते ! यहाँ हुलाक घर छ ? **e bhāi, namaste! yahā̃ hulāk ghar cha?** Oh (younger) brother, hello! Is there a post office here?
रने **Rane**	छ दाइ । **cha dāi.** Yes, (elder) brother.
सलील **Salīl**	यहाँबाट हुलाक घर कति टाढा छ ? **yahā̃bāṭa hulāk ghar kati ṭāḍhā cha?** How far is the post office from here?
रने **Rane**	धेरै टाढा छैन, नजिकै छ दाइ । **dherai ṭāḍhā chaina, najikai cha dāi.** It's not very far, it's quite near, (elder) brother.
सलील **Salīl**	त्यहाँ बैंक पनि छ ? **tyahā̃ baĩk pani cha?** Is there a bank there too?
रने **Rane**	छ, बैंक पनि छ । ठूलै छ । **cha, baĩk pani cha. ṭhūlai cha.** Yes, there's a bank too. It's quite big.
सलील **Salīl**	हुलाक घरदेखि बैंक धेरै टाढा छ ? **hulāk ghardekhi baĩk dherai ṭāḍhā cha?** Is the bank very far from the post office?
रने **Rane**	अहँ, त्यो पनि नजिकै छ । बैंक र हुलाक घर यहाँबाट टाढा छैन । **ahã, tyo pani najikai cha. baĩk ra hulāk ghar yahā̃bāṭa ṭāḍhā chaina.** No, that's quite near too. The bank and the post office are not far from here.

सलील	आज बैंक र हुलाक घरमा भीड छ ?	
Salīl	**āja baĩk ra hulāk gharmā bhīḍ cha?**	Are the bank and the post office crowded today?
रने	छैन दाइ । आज बैंक र हुलाक घर बन्द छन् । आज सरकारी बिदा छ ।	
Rane	**chaina dāi. āja baĩk ra hulāk ghar banda chan. āja sarkārī bidā cha.**	No, (elder) brother. Today the bank and the post office are closed. There's a government holiday today.

Quick vocab

भाइ **bhāi**	(younger) brother
यहाँ **yahā̃**	here
हुलाक घर **hulāk ghar**	post office
दाइ **dāi**	(elder) brother
यहाँबाट **yahā̃bāṭa**	from here
कति **kati**	how much?
टाढा **ṭāḍhā**	far, distant
नजिकै **najikai**	quite near
त्यहाँ **tyahā̃**	there
बैंक **baĩk**	bank
हुलाक घरदेखि **hulāk ghardekhi**	from the post office
आज **āja**	today
भीड **bhīḍ**	crowd
घर **ghar**	house, home, building
बन्द **banda**	shut, closed
सरकारी **sarkārī**	governmental
बिदा **bidā**	holiday

INSIGHT

Body language also conveys messages all the time. Nodding your head for 'yes' or 'no', flapping your hands for 'no, there is not', and the gestures for 'come here' and 'go there' are all everyday acts in Nepali daily life and also essential parts of communication.

Grammar

15 POSTPOSITIONS: –मा -MĀ, –बाट -BĀṬA, –देखि -DEKHI

In English there is a category of words called prepositions: *to, at, in, from, for,* etc. These are called prepositions because they come *in front of* the noun or pronoun they are acting upon:

to *the man,* ***at*** *the house,* ***from*** *London,* etc. The Nepali equivalents of these words are called postpositions because they come *after* the noun they are acting upon: *the man* ***to****, the house* ***at****, London* ***from***. In writing they must always be joined to the end of the noun or pronoun.

The postposition **-मा mā** means *in, at* or *on:*

नेपालमा	**nepālmā**	in Nepal
टेबुलमा	**ṭebulmā**	on the table
बैंकमा	**baĩkmā**	at the bank

Two other postpositions that are used in **Dialogue 4** are -बाट **-bāṭa** *from* and -देखि **-dekhi** *from, since.* Both of these mean *from,* but only -देखि **-dekhi** can also be used with expressions of time:

काठ्माडौंबाट	**kāṭhmāḍaũbāṭa**	from Kathmandu
लण्डनदेखि	**lanḍandekhi**	from London
आजदेखि	**ājadekhi**	from today
हिजोदेखि	**hijodekhi**	since yesterday

If you need to ask how far away something is, you will use the adjective **टाढा ṭāḍhā** *distant* with one or other of these two postpositions. When stating or discussing distances, the word **टाढा ṭāḍhā** must usually be retained, even when you also mention some units or measures of distance.

भक्तपुरबाट काठ्माडौं कति टाढा छ ?	**bhaktapurbāṭa kāṭhmāḍaũ kati ṭāḍhā cha?**	How distant is Kathmandu from Bhaktapur?
भक्तपुरबाट काठ्माडौं आठ माइल टाढा छ ।	**bhaktapurbāṭa kāṭhmāḍaũ āṭh māil ṭāḍhā cha.**	Kathmandu is eight miles distant from Bhaktapur.

If you wish to say that something has been the case for a certain period of time, and still is the case, you should use -देखि **-dekhi** with the present tense of the verb:

म हिजोदेखि नेपालमा छु ।	**ma hijodekhi nepālmā chu.**	I am in Nepal since yesterday.
अबदेखि म नेपालमा छु ।	**abadekhi ma nepālmā chu.**	From now on I am in Nepal.

Units of distance

Nepalis think in terms of both miles and kilometres, though the metric system is gradually becoming prevalent:

आठ माइल	**āṭh māil**	eight miles
नौ किलोमिटर	**nau kilomiṭar**	nine kilometres

In the hills of Nepal, a traditional measure of distance is the **कोस kos,** which is usually interpreted to mean *two miles*, or sometimes *half an hour's walk*. Foreigners walking in Nepal often find the **कोस kos** an elusive concept, perhaps because it measures distance partly in terms of the time taken to travel it, and because Nepalis are naturally much more adept at negotiating the steep ups and downs of their landscape than foreign visitors.

16 USING RELATIONSHIP TERMS TO ADDRESS PEOPLE

It is common practice in Nepali for people to address others, whether they are strangers, friends, or acquaintances, by using a relationship term. Obviously, you need to judge which term is appropriate for the person you are addressing, but it is perfectly acceptable to address a male younger than yourself as भाइ **bhāi** *younger brother*, or a female who is older than you as दिदी **didī** *elder sister*. Elderly people may be addressed as बा **bā** *father* or आमा **āmā** *mother*; no stigma is attached to age in Nepal. These terms are often also added to people's personal names in conversation: अमिता दिदी **Amitā didī,** सलील भाइ **Salīl bhāi.** A chart of kinship terminology is given in the Appendices.

नेपाली परिवार **nepālī parivār** A Nepali family

1 To be addressed and referred to with High pronouns

बुवा, बा	**buvā** or **bā**	father
आमा, मा	**āmā** or **mā**	mother
बुवा-आमा, बा-आमा	**buvā-āmā** or **bā-āmā**	mother and father
हजुरबा, बाजे	**hajurbā** or **bāje**	grandfather
हजुरआमा, बज्यै	**hajurāmā** or **bajyai**	grandmother

2 To be addressed with High pronouns and usually referred to with High (male) or Middle (female) pronouns

स्वास्नी, श्रीमती	**svāsnī** or **śrīmatī***	wife
लोग्ने, श्रीमान्	**logne** or **śrīmān***	husband
दिदी	**didī**	elder sister
दाइ, दाज्यू, दाजु	**dāi** or **dājyū** or **dāju**	elder brother

3 To be addressed with Middle pronouns and usually referred to with Low (male) and Middle (female) pronouns

भाइ	**bhāi**	younger brother
बहिनी	**bahinī**	younger sister
छोरा	**chorā**	son
छोरी	**chorī**	daughter
छोराछोरी	**chorāchorī**	sons and daughters
नाति	**nāti**	grandson
नातिनी	**nātinī**	granddaughter
नाति-नातिनी	**nāti-nātinī**	grandchildren

*When referring to a known individual, the foreign speaker should use the honorific terms श्रीमान् **śrīmān** and श्रीमती **śrīmatī.** लोग्ने **logne** and स्वास्नी **svāsnī** are used to refer to husbands and wives more generally. In rural areas, some people use the words जोई **joī** or बूढी **būḍhī** ('old woman') for *wife* and पोई **poī** or बूढा **būḍhā** ('old man') for *husband*.

● INSIGHT

Nepali uses relationship terms to address or attract the attention of strangers. The terms used depend on the age and gender of the person. The idea behind this usage is to create a friendly situation in order to facilitate communication.

Exercise 6

Translate the following sentences into Nepali, referring to the box above for the correct levels of politeness when choosing which form of the verb to use.

1 Younger brother is at school.

2 Elder brother is in Darjeeling.

3 Elder sister is at Mahendra Mahāvidyālay.

4 Tomorrow mother and father are at home.

5 There are many brothers and sisters in the family.

Exercise 7

Convert the affirmative Nepali sentences you have completed for Exercise 6 into negative statements, by changing the forms of the verbs.

Exercise 8

Look at the simple map of the part of Nepal in which you are staying, showing:

1	सरस्वती मन्दिर	**sarasvatī mandir**	Saraswati temple
2	बजार	**bajār**	marketplace
3	पसलहरू	**pasalharū**	shops
4	बैंक	**baĩk**	bank
5	हुलाक घर	**hulāk ghar**	post office
6	प्रहरी थाना	**praharī thānā**	police station
7	होटेल	**hoṭel**	hotel
8	डाँफे लज	**ḍā̃phe laj**	Danphe Lodge
9	सेती खोला	**setī kholā**	Seti Khola (a river)
10	सडक	**saḍak**	road

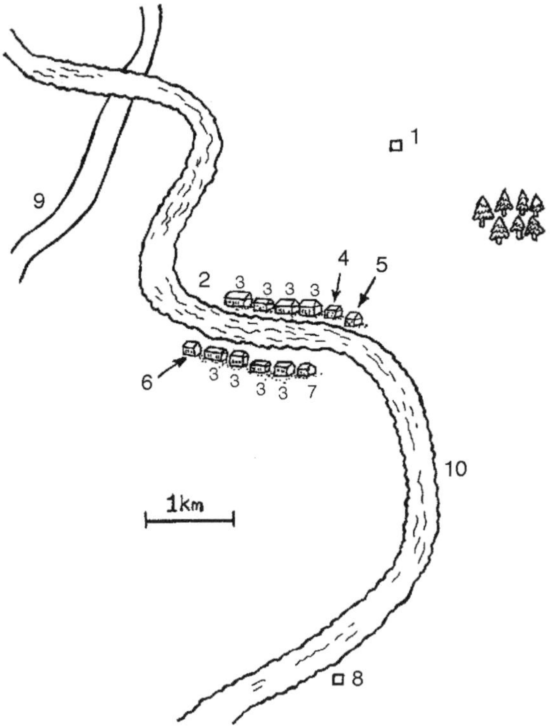

Referring to the map, and assuming that you are staying in the lodge, answer the following questions in Nepali:

१ प्रहरी थाना नजिक छ ?	**praharī thānā najik cha?**
२ हुलाक घर टाढा छ ?	**hulāk ghar ṭāḍhā cha?**
३ लजबाट बजार कति टाढा छ ?	**lajbāṭa bajār kati ṭāḍhā cha?**
४ बजारमा के के छ ?	**bajārmā ke ke cha?**
५ प्रहरी थाना कहाँ छ ?	**praharī thānā kahā̃ cha?**
६ सरस्वती मन्दिर बजारबाट कति टाढा छ ?	**sarasvatī mandir bajārbāṭa kati ṭāḍhā cha?**

The most important things for the reader to remember

1 छ *cha* is used with adjectives to describe and also to locate a thing, person or place, e.g. घर राम्रो छ **ghar rāmro cha,** 'the house is nice', कलम टेबुलमा छ **kalam ṭebulmā cha,** 'a pen is on the table'.

2 Remember the conjugation of छ **cha** with all pronouns in Nepali.

3 Knowledge of question words and their uses will help you to collect all kinds of information. Also be aware of the difference between कसको **kasko** – कस्तो **kasto** and कस्तो **kasto** – कसरी **kasarī**.

4 नै is an emphasis marker and its vowel sound ऐ **ai** can be added to the end of any part of speech. E.g.: ठूलो **ṭhūlo** 'big', ठूलै **ṭhūlai** 'quite big'. घरमा **gharmā** घरमै **gharmai** 'at home'.

5 There is an important difference between अलिअलि **aliali**, which is used with adjectives, e.g. अलिअलि पिरो **aliali piro** 'a little bit spicy' and अलिकति **alikati**, which is used with quantitative uncountable nouns, e.g. अलिकति भात **alikati bhāt** 'a little rice'.

6 The postposition बाट **bāṭa** 'from' is used in relation to place, देखि **dekhi** 'from, since' usually in context of time but less commonly for place and मा **mā** 'in, on, at' to indicate location. They are attached to the nouns in their written form.

3 कति ?
How many?

In this unit you will learn:

▶ ***how to count and enumerate people, things and units***

▶ ***how to talk about portable possessions***

5 Students at the language school

03.01

The Minister for Education is visiting a school and is asking the teacher how many students are studying each language.

मन्त्री	नेपाली कक्षामा कतिजना विद्यार्थीहरू छन् ?
mantrī	**nepālī kakṣāmā katijanā vidyārthīharū chan?**
	How many students are there in the Nepali class?
शिक्षक	दसजना विद्यार्थी छन् । पाँचजना केटा र पाँचजना केटी ।
śikṣak	**dasjanā vidyārthī chan. pā̃cjanā keṭā ra pā̃cjanā keṭī.**
	There are ten students. Five boys and five girls.
मन्त्री	ए । अनि अँग्रेजी कक्षामा कतिजना विद्यार्थीहरू छन् ?
mantrī	**e. ani ā̃grejī kakṣāmā katijanā vidyārthīharū chan?**
	Oh, I see. And how many students are there in the English class?
शिक्षक	त्यो कक्षा अलि ठूलो छ । नौजना केटा र दसजना केटी छन् । जम्मा उन्नाइसजना विद्यार्थीहरू छन् ।
śikṣak	**tyo kakṣā ali ṭhūlo cha. naujanā keṭā ra dasjanā keṭī chan. jammā unnāisjanā vidyārthīharū chan.**
	That class is quite big. There are nine boys and ten girls. All together there are 19 students.
मन्त्री	नेपाली कक्षामा विदेशीहरू मात्रै छन् ?
mantrī	**nepālī kakṣāmā videśīharū matrai chan?**
	Are there only foreigners in the Nepali class?
शिक्षक	विदेशीहरू मात्रै छन् मन्त्रीज्यू । तीनजना चिनियाँ, पाँचजना अँग्रेज, र दुईजना जर्मन छन् ।
śikṣak	**videśīharū mātrai chan mantrījyū. tīnjanā ciniyā̃, pā̃cjanā ā̃grej, ra duījanā jarman chan.**
	There are only foreigners, Minister. Three Chinese, five English and two Germans.

Quick vocab

मन्त्री **mantrī**	minister
कक्षा **kakṣā**	class
मा **mā**	in
कतिजना **katijanā**	how many?
दसजना **dasjanā**	ten
पाँचजना केटा **pā̃cjanā keṭā**	five boys
पाँचजना केटी **pā̃cjanā keṭī**	five girls
नौजना केटा **naujanā keṭā**	nine boys
दसजना केटी **dasjanā keṭī**	ten girls
जम्मा **jammā**	all together, in total
उन्नाइसजना **unnāisjanā**	19
विदेशीहरू **videśīharū**	foreigners
मात्रै **mātrai**	only
मन्त्रीज्यू **mantrījyū**	form of address for a minister

Grammar

17 THE NEPALI NUMERALS

The Nepali numerals are very similar to the Hindi numerals, with only a few exceptions. The system is complex, and it is necessary to learn each number from one to 100 as a separate item of vocabulary, though each group of ten has its own internal logic and it is occasionally possible to guess! The first ten numbers are given here, both on their own and with the classifier suffixes they often need to take (as explained below). You are advised to learn the numbers in sets of ten (see the appendices).

Numbers and numeral classifiers: summary

	number		*+ human classifier*	*+ non-human classifier*
1	१	एक **ek**	एकजना **ekjanā**	एउटा (एकवटा) **euṭā (ekvaṭā)**
2	२	दुई **duī**	दुईजना **duījanā**	दुइटा (दुईवटा) **duiṭā (duīvaṭā)**
3	३	तीन **tīn**	तीनजना **tīnjanā**	तीनवटा **tīnvaṭā**
4	४	चार **cār**	चारजना **cārjanā**	चारवटा **cārvaṭā**
5	५	पाँच **pā̃c**	पाँचजना **pā̃cjanā**	पाँचवटा **pā̃cvaṭā**
6	६	छ **cha**	छजना **chajanā**	छवटा **chavaṭā**
7	७	सात **sāt**	सातजना **sātjanā**	सातवटा **sātvaṭā**
8	८	आठ **āṭh**	आठजना **āṭhjanā**	आठवटा **āṭhvaṭā**
9	९	नौ **nau**	नौजना **naujanā**	नौवटा **nauvaṭā**
10	१०	दस **das**	दसजना **dasjanā**	दसवटा **dasvaṭā**

18 NUMBERS OF PEOPLE

When you are using numbers to enumerate human nouns – i.e. words that represent people – you should add the classifier -जना **janā** to the end of the number. It is incorrect to say एक मान्छे **ek mānche** *one person:* the correct form is एकजना मान्छे **ekjanā mānche.** If the number is plural, there is no need to add the plural suffix -हरू **-harū** to the noun, because the number already tells you that there is more than one person and therefore -हरू **-harū** is superfluous:

एकजना मान्छे	**ekjanā mānche**	one person
दुईजना लोग्ने-मान्छे	**duījanā logne-mānche**	two men (literally, husband-person)
तीनजना स्वास्नी-मान्छे	**tīnjanā svāsnī-mānche**	three women (literally, wife-person)

The words मान्छे **mānche** and मानिस **mānis** are interchangeable, though the first is used more commonly. Both mean *person,* but unless qualified by the addition of स्वास्नी **svāsnī** (*woman/wife*) they can usually be taken to represent a male.

Exercise 9

03.02

Answer the following questions in Nepali on **Dialogue 5**:

नेपाली कक्षामाः	**nepālī kakṣāmā:**
१. कतिजना विद्यार्थीहरू छन् ?	**katijanā vidyārthīharū chan?**
२. कतिजना अँग्रेजहरू छन् ?	**katijanā ãgrejharū chan?**
३. कतिजना जर्मनहरू छन् ?	**katijanā jarmanharū chan?**
अँग्रेजी कक्षामाः	**ãgrejī kakṣāmā:**
४. कतिजना विद्यार्थीहरू छन् ?	**katijanā vidyārthīharū chan?**
५. कतिजना केटाहरू छन् ?	**katijanā keṭāharū chan?**
६. कतिजना केटीहरू छन् ?	**katijanā keṭīharū chan?**

6 Setting up the exam room

03.03

Poshan, a junior teacher, is setting up a room for an examination. Ramesh, the principal, comes to check that all is well.

रमेश **Ramesh**	यो कोठामा कतिवटा टेबुल छन् ? **yo koṭhāmā kativaṭā ṭebul chan?** How many tables are there in this room?
पोषण **Poshan**	दसवटा छन् हजुर । **dasvaṭā chan hajur.** There are ten, sir.
रमेश	अनि कतिवटा मेच छन् ?

Ramesh	**ani kativaṭā mec chan?**
	And how many chairs are there?
पोषण	आठवटा मात्रै छन् ।
Poshan	**āṭhvaṭā mātrai chan.**
	There are only eight.
रमेश	ए । कक्षामा दसजना विद्यार्थी छन्, होइन ?
Ramesh	**e. kakṣāmā dasjanā vidyārthī chan, hoina?**
	Oh, I see. There are ten students in the class, aren't there?
पोषण	हजुर, दसजना छन् । अर्को कोठामा दुई-चारवटा मेच छन् ।
Poshan	**hajur, dasjanā chan. arko koṭhāmā duī-cārvaṭā mec chan.**
	Yes, there are ten. There are a few chairs in the next room.
रमेश	ठीक छ । कलम र कागजहरू पनि ठीक छन् ?
Ramesh	**ṭhīk cha. kalam ra kāgajharī pani ṭhīk chan?**
	OK. Are the pens and papers OK too?
पोषण	हरेक टेबुलमा एउटा कलम र कागज छ हजुर ।
Poshan	**harek ṭebulmā euṭā kalam ra kāgaj cha hajur.**
	On each table there is a pen and paper, sir.

V Quick vocab

कोठा **koṭhā**	room
कतिवटा **kativaṭā**	how many?
टेबुल **ṭebul**	table
दसवटा **dasvaṭā**	ten
मेच **mec**	chair
आठवटा **āṭhvaṭā**	eight
मात्रै **mātrai**	only
अर्को **arko**	other, next
दुई-चारवटा **duī-cārvaṭā**	two or four (= 'a few')
ठीक **ṭhīk**	fine, correct
कलम **kalam**	pen
कागज **kāgaj**	paper
हरेक **harek**	each, every
एउटा **euṭā**	one or a

Grammar

19 NUMBERS OF THINGS

When you are using numbers to enumerate non-human nouns – i.e. animals and inanimate objects – you must always add the classifier -वटा **vaṭā** to the end of the number. It is incorrect to say चार किताब **cār kitāb** *four books*: the correct form is चारवटा **cārvaṭā kitāb.** Again, -हरू **-harū** is superfluous when the number is plural.

The classifier -वटा **vaṭā** is not pronounced as it is spelled: the correct pronunciation is 'auṭā'. It is added to the numbers in a rather less regular way than the classifier -जना **janā.** When it is added to एक **ek** one, the combination produces एउटा **euṭā**, pronounced and often spelled यौटा **yauṭā**, and when it is added to दुई **duī** *two* the combination produces दुइटा **duiṭā**, pronounced 'dwīṭā'. For obvious practical reasons, these two are used very commonly in everyday spoken Nepali.

एउटा किताब	**euṭā** ('yauṭā') **kitāb**	one book
दुइटा मेच	**duiṭā** ('dwīṭā') **mec**	two chairs

Perhaps because Nepali does not have an indefinite article *a,* एउटा **euṭā** is often used with human nouns, e.g. एउटा मान्छे **euṭā mānche** *one man* or *a man* to refer to a person about whom the speaker feels no need to be especially polite.

● INSIGHT

वटा *vatā* is sometimes used to count the number of children as well, e.g. एउटा छोरा *eutā chorā* 'one son' as well as with a person to indicate generalization, e.g. एउटा मान्छे *eutā mānche* 'a human'.

20 HOW MANY?

When you are asking the question *how many?* you must add one of the classifiers to the interrogative कति **kati**, the choice of classifier depending upon whether you are asking about people or other things. Because -जना **janā** can only be used to enumerate people and -वटा **vaṭā** can only be used to enumerate things and animals, the combination of a number plus a classifier can also be used on its own:

घरमा कतिजना मान्छे छन् ?	**gharmā katijanā mānche chan?**	How many people are in the house?
दसजना छन् ।	**dasjanā chan.**	There are ten.
घरमा कतिवटा कोठा छन् ?	**gharmā kativaṭā koṭhā chan?**	How many rooms are there in the house?
तीनवटा छन् ।	**tīnvaṭā chan.**	There are three.

However, when the question concerns units of measurement, कति **kati** can be used without a classifier suffix (see **Grammar 22**).

● INSIGHT

The Nepali classifiers वटा *vatā* and जना *janā* are used only with numbers but you can say धेरैजना meaning 'many people' where मान्छे 'people' is understood, because जना is only used for people anyway. However, you can't say धेरैवटा *dheraivatā* because वटा can be used with any object or animal.

7 Kamal and Amrit

03.04

Kamal bumps into Amrit on the street. Kamal, an office worker, always has money to spare, while Amrit, a young student, is always penniless.

कमल **Kamal**	अहो अमृत भाइ ! **aho Amṛt bhāi!** Oh, Amrit!
अमृत **Amrit**	नमस्कार कमल दाइ ! **namaskār Kamal dāi!** Hello, Kamal!
कमल **Kamal**	नमस्कार ! अहिले कतातिर ? **namaskār! ahile katātira?** Hello! Where are you off to now?
अमृत **Amrit**	घरतिर । **ghartira.** Home.
कमल **Kamal**	अनि हालखबर कस्तो छ ? **ani hālkhabar kasto cha?** And how are things?
अमृत **Amrit**	राम्रै छ । **rāmrai cha.** Fine.
कमल **Kamal**	आज तिमीसँग पैसा छ ? **āja timīsãga paisā cha?** Do you have any money on you today?
अमृत **Amrit**	मसँग ? अलिकति छ । दुई रुपियाँ मात्रै छ । **masãga? alikati cha. duī rupiyã mātrai cha.** On me? I have a little. I have just two rupees.
कमल **Kamal**	केही छैन । आज मसित पचास रुपियाँ छ । **kehī chaina. āja masita pacās rupiyã cha.** It doesn't matter. I've got fifty rupees today.
अमृत **Amrit**	मसँग न पैसा छ न चुरोट छ । तपाईंसँग चुरोट छ ? **masãga na paisā cha na curoṭ cha. tapāĩsãga curoṭ cha?** I have neither money nor cigarettes. Do you have a cigarette?
कमल **Kamal**	छ, मसँग एक बट्टा याक चुरोट छ । **cha, masãga ek baṭṭā yāk curoṭ cha.** Yes, I have a packet of Yak cigarettes.

अमृत **Amrit**	आहा, याक चुरोट राम्रो छ ! **āhā, yāk curoṭ rāmro cha!** Oh, Yak cigarettes are good!	
कमल **Kamal**	होइन, तिमी सानो केटा हौ । धुम्रपान खराब छ । **hoina, timī sāno keṭā hau. dhūmrapān kharāb cha.** No, you are a small boy. Smoking is bad.	

Quick vocab

अहो **aho**	(an exclamation of pleasure or surprise)
अहिले **ahile**	now
कता **katā**	where, in which
तिर **tira**	towards
घरतिर **ghartira**	towards home
हालखबर **hālkhabar**	news
तिमीसँग **timīsãga**	with you
पैसा **paisā**	money
मसँग? **masãga?**	with me?
केही छैन **kehī chaina**	it doesn't matter
आज **āja**	today
मसित **masita**	with me
दस रुपियाँ **das rupiyã**	ten rupees
चुरोट **curoṭ**	cigarette
न ... न ... **na ... na**	neither ... nor ...
एक बट्टा **ek baṭṭā**	one packet
आहा **āhā**	(another exclamation of pleasure or surprise)
धूम्रपान **dhūmrapān**	smoking (a rather highflown Sanskrit term)
खराब **kharāb**	bad

Grammar

21 POSSESSION OF PORTABLE ITEMS

Nepali does not have a verb that is the equivalent of the English *to have* or *to own*, but establishes ownership and possession in different ways. The first way is used in relation to things that someone can carry around on his/her person. Often, these are things that are disposable or acquired temporarily: money, for instance, comes and goes, and items such as pens generally run out of ink and have to be discarded.

Possession is indicated by using either one of two postpositions that both have exactly the same meaning: *with*. The two words are -सँग **sãga** (sometimes spelt सङ्ग **saṅga**) and -सित **sita**. These are added directly on to nouns, names and pronouns:

केटासँग	**keṭāsãga**	or	केटासित	**keṭāsita** with the boy
कुमारसँग	**Kumārsãga**	or	कुमारसित	**Kumārsita** with Kumar
मसँग	**masãga**	or	मसित	**masita** with me

Having added one or other of these words to the possesser, all that is left to create a simple statement of possession is to state the thing possessed and end with the verb, which is always छ **cha** (because you are *locating* the possession on the person of the possessor):

त्यो मान्छेसँग दुई रुपियाँ छ ।	**tyo mānchesãga duī rupiyā̃ cha.**	That man has two rupees (on his person).
ऊसँग एउटा कलम छ ।	**ūsãga euṭā kalam cha.**	He has a pen (on his person).

If the statement or question is about someone *not* possessing something, use the negative form of छ **cha**.

मसित पैसा छैन ।	**masita paisā chaina.**	I don't have any money (on my person).
गीतासँग साबुन छैन ।	**Gītāsãga sābun chaina.**	Gita does not have any soap (with her).

22 USING NUMBERS WITHOUT CLASSIFIERS

When you are talking about sums of money, weights and measures, units of time, distances, or any other kind of measure or unit, there is no need to add a classifier to the numerals involved, or to use the plural suffix -हरू **-harū**. Nor is it correct to use the plural form of a verb when its subject is a plural numerical quantity.

Currency

The Nepali रुपियाँ **rupiyā̃** *rupee* consists of 100 पैसा **paisā**. There are also special words for a quarter-rupee (सुका **sukā**) and a half-rupee (मोहर **mohar** or मोहोर **mohor**), though these terms have fallen into disuse as a result of inflation. The abbreviation for *rupee* is Rs. in Roman script, and रु॰ **ru.** in Devanāgarī. The Nepali rupee is sometimes referred to as the ने॰ रु॰ **ne. ru.** (short for नेपाली रुपियाँ **nepālī rupiyā̃**), to distinguish it from the भा॰ रु॰ **bhā. ru.** (भारतीय रुपियाँ **bhāratīya rupiyā̃**) or Indian rupee.

Weights and capacities

There are two systems of measuring weights and quantities current in Nepal. One is the metric European system of kilogrammes (किलो **kilo**), the other is a more complicated traditional system based on capacity, which is particularly suited to measuring quantities of grain:

चौथाई	**cauthāī**	one quarter of a **mānā**
आधा माना	**ādhā mānā**	half a **mānā**
एक माना	**ek mānā**	one **mānā** (= 0.7 litres or 20 ounces)
एक कुरुवा	**ek kuruvā**	(= two **mānā**s)
एक पाथी	**ek pāthī**	(= eight **mānā**s)
एक मुरी	**ek murī**	(= 20 **pāthī**s)

Neither kind of unit requires the use of classifiers or plural suffixes:

एक किलो आलु	**ek kilo ālu**	one kilo of potatoes
पाँच किलो स्याउ	**pā̃c kilo syāu**	five kilos of apples
दुई माना चामल	**duī mānā cāmal**	two **mānās** of rice
एक पाथी दाल	**ek pāthī dāl**	one **pāthī** of lentils

Note that words such as *cup* and *pot* are also treated as measures of quantity in phrases such as the following, and therefore the numbers do not take a classifier:

दुई कप चिया	**duī kap ciyā**	two cups of tea
एक पाट चिया	**ek pāṭ ciyā**	one pot of tea

Units of time

एक सेकण्ड	**ek sekaṇḍ**	one second
एक छिन	**ek chin**	one moment
दुई मिनेट	**duī mineṭ**	two minutes
तीन घण्टा	**tīn ghaṇṭā**	three hours
चार दिन	**cār din**	four days
पाँच हप्ता	**pā̃c haptā**	five weeks
छ महिना	**cha mahinā**	six months
सात वर्श	**sāt varṣa**	seven years

Exercise 10

Translate the following sentences into Nepali:

1 I have ten rupees and a packet of cigarettes.

2 We have been in Nepal for three weeks.

3 There are ten men, three women and five boys in the post office.

4 How much money do you have with you?

5 That Indian man has no money, but the Nepali boy has ten rupees.

6 The rich farmer has ten **pāthī**s of rice and ten kilogrammes of potatoes.

7 There are two cups of tea on each table.

8 The teacher has no books and the students have no pens.

> **INSIGHT**
>
> When you say 'I have a pen' in Nepali, you say मसित कलम छ *masita kalam cha*, which can be translated into English as 'I have a pen with me'. It implies that the pen is with me at the moment.

Exercise 11

Write six Nepali sentences that define each of the people in the left-hand column as teachers, using an appropriate form of the verb *to be* from the right-hand column. Then do the same thing for each once again, but this time locating them at home.

भाइ	**bhāi**	हुनुहुन्छ	**hunuhuncha**
दिदी	**didī**	हो	**ho**
भाइहरू	**bhāiharū**	छन्	**chan**
दाज्यू	**dājyū**	हुन्	**hun**
आमा	**āmā**	छ	**cha**
म	**ma**	छिन्	**chin**
शिक्षक	**śikṣak**	हुँ	**hũ**
घरमा	**gharmā**	छु	**chu**

Exercise 12

03.05

Translate into Nepali:

1 one week
2 two men
3 three books
4 four boys
5 five rupees
6 six chairs
7 seven women
8 eight classes
9 nine kilos
10 ten foreigners
11 two kilos
12 seven and a half kilos
13 three **pāthīs**
14 two and a half **mānās**
15 three rupees and seventy-five **paisā**
16 nine and a half rupees.

The most important things for the reader to remember

1 The Nepali classifier वटा **vaṭā** is used to express the number of inanimate objects or animals, e.g. एकवटा किताब **ekvaṭā kitāb**, 'one book'. There is a very commonly used short form of वटा **vaṭā**, एउटा **euṭā**, दुइटा **duiṭā**, etc.

2 जना **janā** is used to count the number of people such as दुईजना शिक्षक **duījanā śikṣak** 'two teachers', दसजना विद्यार्थी **dasjanā vidyārthī** 'ten students'.

3 सँग **sãga** or सित **sita** is used with छ **cha** to indicate the possession of portable things that people normally carry with them, such as money, bag, umbrella, matches or cigarettes, etc. e.g. मसँग पैसा छ । **masãga paisā cha**, 'I have money'.

4 The classifiers वटा **vaṭā** and जना **janā** are not used with money, measurement and weights or unit of time, e.g. दस रुपियाँ **das rupiyā̃** 'ten rupees', एक किलो आलु **ek kilo ālu** 'one kilogramme of potatoes', एक घण्टा **ek ghaṇṭā** 'one hour'.

5 Nepali uses the English words 'second' and 'minute', but other units of time are very useful to memorize: दुई घण्टा **duī ghaṇṭā** 'two hours', तीन दिन **tīn din** 'three days', एक हप्ता **ek haptā** 'one week', दुई महिना **duī mahinā** 'two months', चार बर्ष **cār varṣa** 'four years'.

4 कसको हो ?

Whose is it?

In this unit you will learn:

- *how to talk about ownership*
- *how to express and ask about knowledge*
- *how to ask further questions*

8 Jyoti's houses

04.01

Anil and Bijay are comparing notes on Jyoti, a new acquaintance.

अनिल **Anil**	ज्योतिका कतिवटा घरहरू छन् ? तपाईंलाई थाहा छ ? **Jyotīkā kativaṭā gharharū chan? tapāī̃lāī thāhā cha?** How many houses does Jyoti have? Do you know?
बिजय **Bijay**	थाहा छ । ज्योतिका दुइटा घर छन् : एउटा सानो र एउटा ठूलो । **thāhā cha. Jyotikā duiṭā ghar chan: euṭā sāno ra euṭā ṭhūlo.** I know. Jyoti has two houses: one big and one small.
अनिल **Anil**	ए । ज्योतिको सानो घर कहाँ छ ? **e. Jyotiko sāno ghar kahā̃ cha?** Oh, I see. Where is Jyoti's small house?
बिजय **Bijay**	ज्योतिको सानो घर बजारमा छ । त्यहाँ ज्योतिको बुवाको एउटा पसल पनि छ । **Jyotiko sāno ghar bajārmā cha. tyahā̃ Jyotiko buvāko euṭā pasal pani cha.** Jyoti's small house is in the marketplace. Jyoti's father has a shop there too.
अनिल **Anil**	अनि ज्योतिको ठूलो घर नि ? **ani Jyotiko ṭhūlo ghar ni?** And what about Jyoti's big house?
बिजय **Bijay**	ज्योतिको ठूलो घर पोखराबाट दुई कोस टाढा छ । **Jyotiko ṭhūlo ghar Pokharābāṭa duī kos ṭāḍhā cha.** Jyoti's big house is two kos away from Pokhara.
अनिल **Anil**	त्यो घर निक्कै ठूलो छ ? **tyo ghar nikkai ṭhūlo cha?** Is that house very large?

बिजय **Bijay**	हो, निक्कै ठूलो छ । त्यो घरमा दसवटा कोठा छन् । **ho, nikkai ṭhūlo cha. tyo gharmā dasvaṭā koṭhā chan.** Yes, it's very large. There are ten rooms in that house.
अनिल **Anil**	ज्योतिको परिवार पनि ठूलो छ ? **Jyotiko parivār pani ṭhūlo cha?** Is Jyoti's family large too?
बिजय **Bijay**	ठूलो छैन, तर उनीहरू धनी छन् । हरेक शहरमा ज्योतिको बुवाका दुई-चारवटा पसल छन् । **ṭhūlo chaina, tara unīharū dhanī chan. harek śaharmā Jyotiko buvākā duī-cārvaṭā pasal chan.** It's not large, but they are rich. Jyoti's father has several shops in every town.
अनिल **Anil**	अनि ज्योतिका दाजु-भाइ छैनन् ? **ani Jyotikā dāju-bhāi chainan?** And does Jyoti not have any brothers?
बिजय **Bijay**	छैनन् । ज्योतिकी एउटी बहिनी छ, कान्ती । हिजोआज उनी दार्जीलिङ्गको एउटा स्कूलमा छिन् । **chainan. Jyotikī euṭī bahinī cha, Kāntī. hijoāja unī Darjeelingko euṭā skūlmā chin.** No. He has one sister, Kanti. Nowadays she is at a school in Darjeeling.

Quick vocab

ज्योतिक **Jyotīkā**	Jyoti's, belonging to Jyoti (plural possessions)
थाहा **thāhā**	knowledge, information
ज्योतिको **Jyotīko**	Jyoti's, belonging to Jyoti (single possession)
कोस **kos**	a measure of distance, roughly two miles
निकै **nikai**	very (used only with adjectives)
दाजु-भाइ **dāju-bhāi**	brothers
ज्योतिकी **Jyotiki**	Jyoti's, belonging to Jyoti (female possession)
एउटी **euṭī**	one (feminine ending)
हिजोआज **hijoāja**	nowadays
दार्जीलिङ्ग **Dārjīliṅg**	Darjeeling
स्कूल **skūl**	school

Grammar

23 OWNERSHIP: -को -KO, - की -*KĪ*,- का -*KĀ*, WITH NOUNS AND NAMES

Unless you are using -सँग **-sãga** or -सित **-sita** to talk about possessions that are 'with' an owner at the time, the particle -को **-ko** must be used to link an owner to a thing that is owned. The particle performs the same function, and occurs in the same place in a sentence or phrase, as the 'apostrophe s' ('s) in English, and can be attached to nouns and names in the same way:

रामको किताब	**Rāmko kitāb**	Ram's book
सेतीको बुवा	**Setīko buvā**	Seti's father

However, -को **-ko** behaves like an inflected adjective in that the vowel must change according to the number and gender of whatever is owned – to **-ī** when a female human noun is owned, and to **-ā** when the owned nouns are plural:

रमेशकी आमा	**Rameśkī āmā**	Ramesh's mother
नेपालका गाउँहरू	**Nepālkā gāũharū**	Nepal's villages

As in statements of possession using -सँग **-sãga** or -सित **-sita**, statements of ownership involve the use of the verb छ **cha**:

रमेशका दुईजना दाजु छन् ।	**Rameśkā duījanā dāju chan.**	Ramesh has two elder brothers.
बिन्दूको दाजु छैन ।	**Bindūko dāju chaina.**	Bindu does not have an elder brother.

However, if something is being identified as a belonging then it becomes necessary to use हो **ho** instead of छ **cha**:

यो सानो घर ज्योतिको हो ।	**yo sāno ghar Jyotiko ho.**	This small house is Jyoti's.
ऊ बिन्दूको दाजु होइन ।	**ū Bindūko dāju hoina.**	He is not Bindu's elder brother.

It is possible to use -को **-ko** in a string of ownerships:

ज्योतिको साथी	**Jyotiko sāthī**	Jyoti's friend
ज्योतिको साथीको बुवा	**Jyotiko sāthīko buvā**	Jyoti's friend's father
ज्योतिको साथीको बुवाको घर	**Jyotiko sāthīko buvāko ghar**	Jyoti's friend's father's house
ज्योतिको साथीको बुवाको घरका झ्यालहरू	**Jyotiko sāthīko buvāko gharkā jhyālharū**.	Jyoti's friend's father's house's windows

24 WORDS FOR AND: र RA, अनि ANI

So far you have met two different Nepali words that are both translated as *and*. र **ra** is used to link pairs or the members of a group of nouns, pronouns, or names:

ज्योति, अम्बिका र राम	**Jyoti, Ambikā ra Rām**	Jyoti, Ambika and Ram
बैंक र हुलाक घर	**baĩk ra hulāk ghar**	the bank and the post office

अनि **ani**, on the other hand, is used to mean *and* when we wish to introduce another topic or to ask an additional question: it can often mean *and then*. In spoken Nepali, a sentence can never begin with र **ra**, but it is possible to begin a sentence with अनि **ani**.

अनि बैंक कहाँ छ ?	**ani baĩk kahā̃ cha?**	And where is the bank?
अनि ?	**ani?**	And then? anything else?
अनि तिमी को हौ ?	**ani timī ko hau?**	And who are you?

A third word for *and* that is used only in scholarly, formal or official contexts as a substitute for र **ra** is the Sanskrit loan तथा **tathā.**

25 I KNOW, YOU KNOW, ETC. USING थाहा THĀHĀ

थाहा **thāhā**, often pronounced **thā**, means *knowledge* or *information*. The most common way to state that you know something is to say that the knowledge exists *for you* or *to you*, using the postposition -लाई **-lāī**, which means *to* or *for*:

मलाई थाहा छ ।	**malāī thāhā cha.**	I know ('to me there is knowledge').
तपाईंलाई थाहा छैन ।	**tapāĩlāī thāhā chaina.**	You do not know ('to you there is not knowledge').
बिन्दूलाई पक्का थाहा छ ?	**Bindūlāī pakkā thāhā cha?**	Does Bindu know for sure? ('to Bindu is there certain knowledge?').

These questions and statements are frequently abbreviated:

थाहा छ ।	**thāhā cha.**	I know.
थाहा छ ?	**thāhā cha?**	Do you know?
थाहा छैन ।	**thāhā chaina.**	I don't know.

● INSIGHT

'To know' in Nepali is expressed in two ways: थाहा हुनु *thāhā hunu* and चिन्नु *cinnu*. The subject of the first one is the knowledge of something or someone and the verb is not conjugated. The subject of the second one is the person who is knowing or recognizing and the object is another person. It is conjugated.

9 Ratan's motorcar

04.02

Subir and Anand have just spotted their friend Ratan driving past in a red car.

सुबीर	रातो मोटरमा त्यो को हो ?
Subīr	**rāto moṭarmā tyo ko ho?**
	Who is that in the red car?
आनन्द	रतन, होइन ?
Ānand	**Ratan, hoina?**
	It's Ratan, isn't it?
सुबीर	हो, त्यो रतन हो ।
Subīr	**ho, tyo Ratan ho.**
	Yes, that's Ratan.
आनन्द	त्यो रातो मोटर रतनजीको आफ्नो मोटर हो ?
Ānand	**tyo rāto moṭar Ratanjīko āphno moṭar ho?**
	Is that red car Ratanji's own car?
सुबीर	होइन, रतनको साथीको मोटर हो ।
Subīr	**hoina, Ratanko sāthīko moṭar ho.**
	No, it's Ratan's friend's car.
आनन्द	तपाईंको पनि मोटर छ ?
Ānand	**tapā̃īko pani moṭar cha?**
	Do you too have a car ?
सुबीर	अहँ, मेरो मोटर छैन । तर मेरो दाज्यूको एउटा मोटर छ ।
Subīr	**ahã, mero moṭar chaina. tara mero dājyūko euṭā moṭar cha.**
	No, I don't have a car. But my elder brother has a car.
आनन्द	तपाईंको दाज्यूको मोटर कस्तो छ ?
Ānand	**tapā̃īko dājyūko moṭar kasto cha?**
	What's your elder brother's car like?
सुबीर	दाज्यूको मोटर अलि पुरानो छ, तर राम्रो छ, एकदम राम्रो । तपाईंको मोटर छ कि छैन नि ?
Subīr	**dājyūko moṭar ali purāno cha, tara rāmro cha, ekdam rāmro. tapā̃īko moṭar cha ki chaina ni?**
	Elder brother's car is rather old, but it's nice, really nice. So do you have a car or not?
आनन्द	छैन! मेरो एउटा साइकल मात्रै छ ।
Ānand	**chaina! mero euṭā sāikal mātrai cha.**
	No! I have only a bicycle.

Quick vocab

रातो **rāto**	red
मोटर **moṭar**	car
आफ्नो **āphno**	own
साथी **sāthī**	friend
एकदम **ekdam**	really, very
साइकल **sāikal**	bicycle

Exercise 13

Answer the following questions about **Dialogue 9**:

१ रतनजीको आफ्नो मोटर छ ?	**Ratanjīko āphno moṭar cha?**
२ रातो मोटर रतनको हो ?	**rāto moṭar ratanko ho?**
३ सुबीरको आफ्नो मोटर छ ?	**Subīrko āphno moṭar cha?**
५ सुबीरको दाज्यूको मोटर छ कि छैन ?	**Subīrko dājyūko moṭar cha ki chaina?**

Grammar

26 OWNERSHIP USING -को -KO, -की -KĪ, -का -KĀ WITH UNCHANGED ('DIRECT CASE') PRONOUNS

The postposition -**को** -**ko** can be added to two kinds of pronouns in exactly the same way that it is added to nouns and names, i.e. without requiring any change to be made to these pronouns. The two categories are:

i The most polite pronouns (**तपाईं tapāī̃**, **यहाँ yahā̃**, **वहाँ vahā̃**, **हजुर hajur**),

ii Plural pronouns that end in -**हरू**.

यहाँको शुभनाम के हो ?	**yahā̃ko śubhanām ke ho?**	What is this person's name?*
वहाँको काम के हो ?	**vahā̃ko kām ke ho?**	What is his job?
उनीहरूको लुगा अनौठो छ !	**unīharūko lugā anauṭho cha!**	Their clothing is strange!

*Using **शुभनाम śubhanām** *auspicious name* to ask a personal name is more polite than using **नाम nām**.

> **INSIGHT**
>
> Although there are formally three forms of possessive markers in the written form of Nepali (को *ko*, का *kā*, and की *kī*) for singular, plural and feminine form respectively, in spoken Nepali, you will often hear people using को *ko* for all of them.

27 MY, YOUR, OUR

-को **-ko** cannot be added to the pronouns म **ma I**, तँ **tã** *you*, तिमी **timī** *you* and हामी **hāmī** *we*. Instead, these four pronouns have special ownership ('genitive') forms:

म	**ma**	I	becomes	मेरो	**mero**	my, mine
तँ	**tã**	you	becomes	तेरो	**tero**	your, yours
तिमी	**timī**	you	becomes	तिम्रो	**timro**	your, yours
हामी	**hāmī**	we	becomes	हाम्रो	**hāmro**	our, ours

मेरो नाम जेनी हो ।	**mero nām Jenī ho.**	My name is Jenny.
तिम्रो नाम सोनाम होइन, छिरिङ्ग हो ।	**timro nām Sonām hoina, Chiring ho.**	Your name is not Sonam, it is Tsering.*
हाम्रो थर अधिकारी हो ।	**hāmro thar Adhikārī ho.**	Our family name is Adhikari.

* These are both Tibetan names, current among people who live along Nepal's northern border, and also among Tibetan refugees in Nepal. Nepali does not have a letter to represent the Tibetan sound **ts**, so it uses छ **ch** instead.

Exercise 14

Create sentences that state ownership, using the elements provided:

Owner	**Quantity**	**Possession**
E.g. I	2	houses
= मेरा दुइटा घर छन्	**merā duiṭā ghar chan**	I have two houses
1 Dhan Bahādur's wife	2	elder sisters
2 I	0	mother and father
3 My mother	4	grandchildren
4 They	0	sons and daughters
5 He (High)	9	cows (गाई **gāī**)
6 We	5	fat buffaloes (भैंसी **bhaĩsī**)

28 ONE'S OWN: EMPHASIZING OWNERSHIP USING आफ्नो ĀPHNO

The word आफ्नो **āphno** means *own* and can be used with any of the possessive pronouns. It does not matter whether it is being used to mean *my own* or *your own* or anyone else's *own*; the word remains the same. It is an adjective, however, so its ending must change according to the number and gender of the thing or things owned:

मेरो आफ्नो साथी	**mero āphno sāthī**	my own friend
तपाईंका आफ्ना छोराछोरी	**tapāīkā āphnā chorāchorī**	your own children
अमिताकी आफ्नी बहिनी	**Amitākī āphnī bahinī**	Amita's own younger sister

To emphasize that the thing that is owned is the owner's very own possession and does not belong to anyone else, the ending of **आफ्नो āphno** is changed to **-ai**:

रमेशको आफ्नै साइकल ।	**Rameśko āphnai sāikal.**	Ramesh's very own bicycle.
अमिताकी आफ्नै बहिनी ।	**Amitākī āphnai bahinī.**	Amita's very own younger sister.
यिनीहरू मेरा आफ्नै छोराछोरी हुन् ।	**yinīharū merā āphnai chorāchorī hun.**	These are my own children.

29 ASKING QUESTIONS: THE USE OF कि KI

The word order of a question in Nepali is exactly the same as the word order of a statement: when spoken, the difference lies in the intonation; when written, the only difference between a statement and a question is the absence or presence of a question mark. However, Nepali speakers frequently end a question with the questioning word **कि ? ki?** which literally means *or…?* **हो कि ? ho ki?** and **छ कि ? cha ki?** mean *is it or…?* and *is there or…?*

यो तपाईंको आफ्नो साइकल हो कि ?	**yo tapāīko āphno sāikal ho ki?**	*Is this your own* bicycle, or …?
तपाईंको घरमा साइकल छ कि ?	**tapāīko gharmā sāikal cha ki?**	Is there a bicycle in your house, or …?

The question might also include the negative form of the verb, to mean *is it or isn't it?* or *is there or isn't there?*

चिया हो ?	**ciyā ho?**	is it tea?
चिया हो कि ?	**ciyā ho ki?**	is it tea or…?
चिया हो कि होइन ?	**ciyā ho ki hoina?**	is it tea or not?
चिया छ ?	**ciyā cha?**	is there any tea?
चिया छ कि ?	**ciyā cha ki?**	is there any tea or…?
चिया छ कि छैन ?	**ciyā cha ki chaina?**	is there any tea or not?

These last three questions carry the implication that if there is any tea the speaker would like to drink it. Similarly, a sentence such as:

तपाईंको घरमा नुन छ कि ?	**tapāīko gharmā nun cha ki?**	Is there salt in your house?

suggests that the person asking the question is in need of salt.

• INSIGHT

When कि *ki* is used between two entities, it means 'or' in Nepali. When it is used at the end of a question it also indicates some degree of politeness for the person who is being addressed because it allows him to say 'no'.

Exercise 15

Translate into Nepali:

1 You (Middle) are my son's friend, aren't you? Is your name Gautam (**gautam**)?

2 Is your (Middle) friend's father's name Ganesh Man (**gaṇeś mān**)? Do you know or don't you?

3 His (High) name is Laksmi Nath (**lakṣmī nāth**). I know that.

4 My home is not far from here. Where is your (Middle) home?

5 Your (High) father is at the bank. Does your mother know?

6 Their (Middle) cows are in our field. Don't they know?

7 Our family name is Pokharel (**pokharel**). We are Brahmins.

8 This is not your (Middle) watch. It is my mother's.

Exercise 16

Write a simple account of the members of your family, along the following lines:

My name is ... My home is in ...

In my family we are ... people: (list the members of your family, using relationship terms).

Next, give the following information about each member of your family:

My elder sister's name is ...

She is in ... (give the name of the town where she lives).

Repeat this information for each member of your family.

If any of your siblings is married, state the name of their husband or wife.

10 Whose book is this?

04.03

रश्मि **Raśmi**	यो कसको किताब हो ? **yo kasko kitāb ho?** Whose book is this?
प्रीति **Prīti**	मेरो विचारमा त्यो सूर्यकी छोरीको किताब हो । **mero vicārmā tyo Sūryakī chorīko kitāb ho.** I think that is Surya's daughter's book.

रश्मि **Raśmi**	सूर्यकी छोरी छ र ? मलाई थाहा छैन । **Sūryakī chorī cha ra? malāī thāhā chaina.** Does Surya have a daughter then? I don't know.
प्रीति **Prīti**	मेरो विचारमा उनका एकजना छोरा र एकजना छोरी छन् । **mero vicārmā unkā ekjanā chorā ra ekjanā chorī chan.** I think he has one son and one daughter.
रश्मि **Raśmi**	छोरीको नाम के हो त ? **chorīko nām ke ho ta?** What's the daughter's name then?
प्रीति **Prīti**	थाहा छैन । **thāhā chaina.** I don't know.
रश्मि **Raśmi**	छोराको नाम के हो ? **chorāko nām ke ho?** What's the son's name?
प्रीति **Prīti**	उसको नाम गिरीश हो । **usko nām Girīś ho.** His name is Girish.
रश्मि **Raśmi**	अनि उसको उमेर कति हो ? थाहा छ ? **ani usko umer kati ho? thāhā cha?** And how old is he? Do you know?
प्रीति **Prīti**	उसको उमेर कति हो थाहा छैन । **usko umer kati ho thāhā chaina.** I don't know how old he is.
रश्मि **Raśmi**	ए ठीकै छ नि ! किताबमा गिरीशको नाम छ । यो किताब उसैको हो । **e ṭhīkai cha ni! kitābmā Girīśko nām cha. yo kitāb usaiko ho.** Oh, it's OK. Girish's name is on the book. This book is his.

V Quick vocab

कसको **kasko** — whose?
विचार **vicār** — thought, opinion
र ? **ra?** — indeed? then?
उमेर **umer** — age
उसैको **usaiko** — his (and no-one else's)

Exercise 17

Answer the following questions about **Dialogue 10**:

१ सूर्यका कतिजना छोराछोरी छन् ?	**Sūryakā katijanā chorāchorī chan?**
२ प्रीतिको विचारमा सूर्यकी छोरी छ कि छैन ?	**Prītiko vicārmā Sūryakī chorī cha ki chaina?**
३ सूर्यको छोराको नाम के हो ?	**Sūryako chorāko nām ke ho?**
४ अनि किताबमा कसको नाम छ ?	**ani kitābmā kasko nām cha?**

Grammar

30 OWNERSHIP USING -को -KO, -की -KĪ, -का -KĀ WITH CHANGED ('OBLIQUE CASE') PRONOUNS

Nepali grammar has only two cases. A noun or pronoun is always in either the 'direct' case, which means that it remains as it appears in a dictionary, or the 'oblique' case, which means that its ending might need to change.

A word will always take the 'oblique case' when a postposition has been added to it; whether this means that its ending actually has to change depends on what the word is. Generally, nouns do not change in the oblique case, but certain pronouns do. When -को **-ko** is added to pronouns (except (i) the most polite forms, (ii) plurals ending in -हरू **-harū** and (iii) म **ma,** तँ **tã,** तिमी **timī,** and हामी **hāmī** – see **Grammar 26 and 27**), the pronouns have to be modified slightly, and are said then to have changed into the oblique case, from their original, unchanged direct case:

direct case		*oblique case*		**+ को -ko**		
ऊ	**ū**	उस	**us**	उसको	**usko**	his/her
यो	**yo**	यस	**yas**	यसको	**yasko**	his/her/its
त्यो	**tyo**	त्यस	**tyas**	त्यसको	**tyasko**	his/her/its
उनी	**unī**	उन	**un**	उनको	**unko**	his/her (polite)
यिनी	**yinī**	यिन	**yin**	यिनको	**yinko**	his/her (polite)
तिनी	**tinī**	तिन	**tin**	तिनको	**tinko**	his/her (polite)

The oblique forms of the pronouns यो **yo** *this* and त्यो **tyo** *that* are not pronounced exactly as they are spelled:

direct form		*oblique form*		*pronunciation*
यो	**yo**	यस	**yas**	**'es'**
त्यो	**tyo**	त्यस	**tyas**	**'tes'**

When the postposition -लाई **-lāī** is added to the oblique forms of यो **yo**, त्यो **tyo**, and ऊ **ū** the word is often pronounced as if the '**s**' has been lost and the '**l**' has been doubled:

	spelling	*pronunciation*
यसलाई	**yaslāī**	**'ellāī'**
त्यसलाई	**tyaslāī**	**'tellāī'**
उसलाई	**uslāī**	**'ullāī'**

All of the pronouns in the box above must change to their oblique forms whenever a postposition is added to them. The examples given in the box show what happens when the postposition is -को **-ko**, but exactly the same changes are necessary when other postpositions are involved:

उनलाई थाहा छैन ।	**unlāī thāhā chaina.**	S/he does not know.
यसमा चिनी छ ?	**yasmā cinī cha?**	Is there (any) sugar in this?

An exception to this rule is the postposition -सँग **-sãga** *with,* which is always added to the unchanged ('direct case') form of a pronoun:

ऊसँग पैसा छैन ।	**ūsãga paisā chaina.**	He has no money (on his person).

When यो **yo** and त्यो **tyo** are being used before a noun to mean *this* and *that*, they should take their oblique form if a postposition is added to the noun.

यो शहर	**yo śahar**	this town
becomes		
यस शहरमा	**yas śaharmā**	in this town
त्यो दिन	**tyo din**	that day
becomes		
त्यस दिनदेखि	**tyas dindekhi**	since that day

However, this is a rule that is often ignored in everyday spoken Nepali. It is particularly likely to be ignored if यो **yo** and त्यो **tyo** are separated from the noun they describe by another adjective or adjectives. The longer the following phrase becomes, the more permissible it is to use the direct form यो **yo** *this* instead of its oblique form यस **yas:**

In this town:	यस शहरमा	**yas śaharmā**
or	यो शहरमा	**yo śaharmā**
In this big town:	यस ठूलो शहरमा	**yas ṭhūlo śaharmā**
or	यो ठूलो शहरमा	**yo ṭhūlo śaharmā**
In this big old town:	यस ठूलो पुरानो शहरमा	**yas ṭhūlo purāno śaharmā**
or	यो ठूलो पुरानो शहरमा	**yo ṭhūlo purāno śaharmā**

यी **yī** *these* and ती **tī** *those* do not take oblique forms:

यी शहरहरू	**yī śaharharū**	these towns
यी शहरहरूमा	**yī śaharharūmā**	in these towns
ती घरहरू	**tī gharharū**	those houses
ती घरहरूबाट	**tī gharharūbāṭa**	from those houses

31 INTERROGATIVES: कसको KASKO *WHOSE*, केका KEKO *OF WHAT*, कहाँका KAHĀKO *OF/FROM WHERE*?

The Nepali word for *who?* is को ? **ko?** When the -को **-ko** that links owner to owned is added to the को **ko** that means *who?*, the latter must change to its oblique form, which is कस **kas**:

को **ko** who?	+	-को **-ko** *'s*	=	कसको **kasko** whose?

कसको किताब	**kasko kitāb**	whose book?
कसका छोराहरू	**kaskā chorāharū**	whose sons?
कसकी बहिनी	**kaskī bahinī**	whose sister?

Most other interrogatives (e.g. के **ke** *what?*, कहाँ **kahā̃** *where?*) do not have an oblique form, so they do not change when -को **-ko** is added to them:

यो केको मासु हो ?	**yo keko māsu ho?**	What kind of meat is this?
त्यो कुखुराको मासु हो ।	**tyo kukhurāko māsu ho.**	That is chicken' meat.

In English it is said that a person is 'from' a particular place, if that is where that person resides or has his/her origin. In Nepali, the same expression uses the genitive -को **-ko**, instead of any word meaning *from:*

ऊ कहाँको मान्छे हो ?	**ū kahā̃ko mānche ho?**	Where is he from? (literally, 'he is a person of where?')
ऊ गोरखाको मान्छे हो ।	**ū Gorkhāko mānche ho.**	He is from Gorkha. (literally, 'he is a person of Gorkha')
यो कहाँको चामल हो ?	**yo kahā̃ko cāmal ho?**	Where is this rice from?
त्यो पोखराको चामल हो ।	**tyo Pokharāko cāmal ho.**	It is rice from Pokhara.

Exercise 18

Create sentences that state ownership, observing grammatical rules to the letter and using the elements provided:

Owner	**Quantity**	**Possession**
E.g. he	2	house
= उसका दुइटा घर छन्	**uskā duiṭā ghar chan**	he has two houses

1 That boy	2	houses
2 This big village	only 1	teashop
3 He (Low)	8	daughters
4 She (Middle)	4	sons
5 This man	many	friends
6 Who	0	friend?

The most important things for the reader to remember

1 The possessive forms तपाईंको **tapāĩko**, तपाईंका **tapāĩkā**, तपाईंकी **tapāĩkā** translate as 'your' for singular, plural and feminine possessions, respectively.

2 Nepali expresses ownership differently when it is used for non-portable property such as a house or car. The appropriate possessive marker is used instead of सँग/सित plus a noun followed by छ/छैन **cha/chaina**, e.g. तपाईंको गाडी छ ? **tapāĩko gāḍī cha?** (Do you have a car?).

3 The conjunction र **ra** is used to join words or clauses together, e.g. तपाईं र म **tapāĩ ra ma**, 'you and me'. But अनि **ani** is used at the beginning of a sentence to give a sense of additionality or of 'after' doing something.

4 The verb थाहा हुनु **thāhā hunu** is used to express knowledge about anything or events. Note that this is an impersonal verb, so the person who has the knowledge takes लाई **lāī** an object marker, e.g. मलाई थाहा छैन **malāī thāhā chaina**, 'I do not know'.

5 आफ्नो **āphno**, a reflexive possessive pronoun, is used in place of other possessive constructions. It functions as an adjective and agrees with the noun it describes in number and gender, e.g. ऊ आफ्नो घरमा बस्छ । **ū āphno gharmā bascha**, 'He lives in his own house'. Note that आफ्ना **āphnā** is for plural and आफ्नी **āphnā** for feminine.

6 The use of कि **ki** in a question to indicate that answering 'no' is an option, as in the example: यो झोला तपाईंको हो कि … ? **yo jholā tapāĩko ho ki** … ? ('Is this your bag or … ?'). There is a blank where होइन **hoina** 'not' is understood.

7 The possessive marker को **ko** can be used with the question words के **ke**, 'what', कहाँ **kahā** 'where' and कहिले **kahile** 'when' to find out about a thing, e.g. केको अचार **keko acār?** 'A pickle from what', कहाँको मान्छे **kahā̃ko mānche?**, 'a person from where', कहिलेको रोटी **kahileko roṭī** 'a bread from when?'.

8 There are certain pronouns in Nepali that appear in special oblique forms when they are followed by postpositions. They are used instead of nouns, e.g. यसको **yasko** 'its', उसको **usko** 'his', कसको **kasko** 'whose', यसमा **yasmā** 'in this', त्यसमा **tyasmā** 'in that'.

5 तपाईं के गर्नुहुन्छ ?
What do you do?

In this unit you will learn:

- ***how to talk about what you and others do normally, habitually or in the near future***
- ***how to use simple adverbs***
- ***how to discuss times, days, and frequency***

11 The cook and the pilot

05.01

Ravi is soon to marry Shailendra's younger sister, and the two men are meeting for the first time. Ravi's job takes him all over South Asia, while Shailendra is tied down to his work in a Kathmandu hotel. Ravi, who is very much Shailendra's elder, feels he knows more about the world than Shailendra, but Shailendra has the last word.

रवि	तिमी शैलेन्द्र, होइनौ ?
शैलेन्द्र	हजुर, म शैलेन्द्र । तपाईं रविज्यू हुनुहुन्छ, होइन ?
रवि	हो, म रवि ।
शैलेन्द्र	तपाईं कहाँ काम गर्नुहुन्छ, रविज्यू ?
रवि	म नेपाल एयरलाइन्समा काम गर्छु । अनि तिमी नि ?
शैलेन्द्र	म साँग्रिला होटेलमा काम गर्छु ।
रवि	तिमी कहिलेकाहीं नेपालबाहिर पनि जान्छौ ?
शैलेन्द्र	अहँ । म कहिल्यै पनि बाहिर जाँदिन । म सधैं यहीं हुन्छु । तर तपाईं सधैं बाहिर जानुहुन्छु, होइन ?
रवि	अँ, अलिअलि घुम्छु । दिल्ली जान्छु, कलकत्ता जान्छु, ढाका जान्छु, कराँची जान्छु । कहिलेकाहीं दुवई पनि जान्छु ।
शैलेन्द्र	तपाईं के काममा बाहिर जानुहुन्छ ?
रवि	म हवाईजहाजको पाइलट हुँ नि !
शैलेन्द्र	लण्डन जानुहुन्न ?
रवि	जाँदिन । धेरैजसो म भारत मात्रै जान्छु । धेरै विदेशी पर्यटकहरू हाम्रो विमानबाट नेपाल आउँछन् ।
शैलेन्द्र	म पनि हाम्रो होटेलमा विदेशी पाहुनाहरूका लागि खाना पकाउँछु नि ।
रवि	ए, तिमी भान्से हौ ?
शैलेन्द्र	हो, म पाँच वर्षदेखि त्यस होटेलको भान्से हुँ ।

रवि	ल, कस्तो राम्रो ! अबदेखि म हरेक शनिवार तिम्रो होटेलमा आउँछु र मीठो खाना खान्छु ।
शैलेन्द्र	तर म यहाँ हुँदिन ! एक हप्तापछि म लण्डन जान्छु । त्यहाँ म एउटा नयाँ रेष्टुराँ खोल्छु ।

Quick vocab

काम गर्नु	to work	लण्डन	London
होटेल	hotel	धेरैजसो	usually
जानु	to go	भारत	India
कहिलेकाहीं	sometimes	पर्यटक	tourist
बाहिर	outside	विमान	flight
कहिल्यै पनि	never	आउनु	to come
यहीं	right here	पाहुना	guest
सधैं	always	-को लागि	for
हुनु	to be	खाना	food
अलिअलि	a little	पकाउनु	to cook
घुम्नु	to travel	भान्से	cook
दिल्ली	Delhi	शनिवार	Saturday
कल्कत्ता	Calcutta	मीठो	tasty
ढाका	Dhaka	खानु	to eat
कराँची	Karachi	हप्ता	week
दुवई	Dubai	पछि	after
हवाईजहाज	aeroplane	रेष्टुराँ	restaurant
पाइलट	pilot	खोल्नु	to open

Ravi	You're Shailendra, aren't you?
Shailendra	Yes, I'm Shailendra. You are Ravi, aren't you?
Ravi	Yes, I'm Ravi.
Shailendra	Where do you work, Ravi?
Ravi	I work at Nepal Airlines. And you?
Shailendra	I work at the Shangri-la Hotel.
Ravi	Do you go outside Nepal sometimes too?
Shailendra	No. I never go outside. I am always here. But you always go outside, don't you?
Ravi	Yes, I travel a little. I go to Delhi, I go to Calcutta, I go to Dhaka, I go to Karachi. Sometimes I go to Dubai as well.
Shailendra	On what work do you go outside?
Ravi	I am an aeroplane pilot, you know!
Shailendra	Don't you go to London?

Ravi	No I don't. Usually I go only to India. Many foreign tourists come to Nepal by our flight.
Shailendra	I too cook food for the foreign guests in our hotel, you know.
Ravi	Oh, you're a cook?
Shailendra	Yes, I've been that hotel's cook for five years.
Ravi	There, how splendid! From now on I will come to your hotel every Saturday and eat good food.
Shailendra	But I shan't be here! After a week I go to London. There I will open a new restaurant.

Grammar

32 THE DICTIONARY FORM OF VERBS

A verb is a word that indicates the performance or occurrence of an action, or the existence of a state or condition. English verbs are words like *see, run, do, eat* and *hear*. So far, you have encountered the various forms of छ and हो that mean *am, is,* and *are*. These are all forms of the Nepali verb हुनु **hunu** *to be*.

The dictionary form of a Nepali verb always ends in -नु **-nu**. This -नु ending is attached to the 'verb base' – the part of the verb that distinguishes it from all other verbs.

For instance,

गर्नु **garnu** *to do* consists of verb base गर्- **gar-** + the dictionary form ending -नु **-nu;**

बस्नु **basnu** *to sit, to reside* consists of verb base बस्- **bas-** + the dictionary form ending -नु **-nu;**

बोल्नु **bolnu** *to speak* consists of verb base बोल्- **bol-** + the dictionary form ending -नु **-nu**, and so on.

> **INSIGHT**
>
> Nepali verb tenses are formed in two ways: (i) by adding suffixes directly to the verb stem and (ii) by using the participles (perfect participle ending in एको and future participle ending in ने) followed by the appropriate paradigms.

33 THE HABITUAL PRESENT TENSE

A tense is a set of forms of a verb which indicates what the relationship is between the time the verb is spoken or written and the time when its action takes place. That is: are you speaking or writing the verb after it has taken place, while it is taking place, or before it takes place? Most Nepali verbs have a full set of past, present and future tenses. The *habitual present* tense is used to make statements about habits or regular occurrences such as *I do, he lives, they eat, she takes*, etc. It can also be used to refer to the future: *I go tomorrow, they come next year, she arrives on Thursday*, etc.

The *habitual present* tense of all Nepali verbs consists of the verb base + a verb ending. (The verb bases introduced here are the present tense verb bases. As will be explained later on, there are also past tense bases.) Nasalization is added between the base and ending of certain verbs. If the verb is affirmative (*I do, I go, I come*), its ending is one of the छ forms of हुनु to be as set out in **Grammar 11**. If the verb is negative (*I do not, I don't go, I don't come*), its ending will be -दैन् **dain** + the same ending taken by छ in the affirmative form of the verb. The only exception to this rule is the form of the verb taken by म, where -छु in the affirmative becomes -दिन **dina** in the negative:

Affirmative		***Negative***		
-छ	**-cha**	-दैन	**-daina**	(with ऊ, यो, त्यो)
-छु	**-chu**	-दिन	**-dina**	(with म)
-छस्	**-chas**	-दैनस्	**-dainas**	(with तँ)
-छौ	**-chau**	-दैनौ	**-dainau**	(with तिमी)
-छौं	**-chaũ**	-दैनौं	**-dainaũ**	(with हामी, हामीहरू)
-छन्	**-chan**	-दैनन्	**-dainan**	(with यी, ती, उनी, यिनी, तिनी, and the plural forms of उनी, यिनी and तिनी)

There are three categories of verb: C-verbs, V-verbs and VV-verbs. If the base of a verb ends in a consonant, it is a C-verb; if it ends in a vowel it is a V-verb and if it ends in two vowels it is a VV-verb:

Dictionary form			***Base***	***Category***	
गर्नु	**garnu**	to do	गर्-	**gar-**	C-verb
बस्नु	**basnu**	to sit, reside	बस्-	**bas-**	C-verb
हुनु	**hunu**	to be	हु-	**hu-**	V-verb
खानु	**khānu**	to eat	खा-	**khā-**	V-verb
लिनु	**linu**	to take	लि-	**li-**	V-verb
आउनु	**āunu**	to come	आउ-	**āu-**	VV-verb
पिउनु	**piunu**	to drink	पिउ-	**piu-**	VV-verb

The way in which the verb base and the ending are joined together depends on which category the verb belongs to. All C-verbs behave in the same way as the verb गर्नु *to do,* in which the final consonant of the base forms a conjunct with the ending:

गर्नु **garnu** *to do*

	Affirmative	***Negative***
singular		
म	गर् + -छु = गर्छु	गर् + -दिन = गर्दिन
हामी, हामीहरू	गर् + -छौं = गर्छौं	गर् + -दैनौं = गर्दैनौं

तँ	गर् + -छस् = गर्छस्	गर् + -दैनस् = गर्दैनस्
तिमी, तिमीहरू	गर् + -छौ = गर्छौ	गर् + -दैनौ = गर्दैनौ
ऊ, यो, त्यो (m.)	गर् + -छ = गर्छ	गर् + -दैन = गर्दैन
उनी, यिनी, तिनी	गर् + -छन् = गर्छन्	गर् + -दैनन् = गर्दैनन्
यी, ती		
उनीहरू, यिनीहरू, तिनीहरू		

In V-verbs, a 'half n' (न्) is infixed between the base and the ending in the affirmative form, and the vowel is nasalized in the negative form. This is an important spelling convention, though both affirmative and negative forms are pronounced as if there is an 'n' in the middle of the word:

जानु **jānu** *to go*

	Affirmative	***Negative***
singular		
म	जा + न् + -छु = जान्छु	जा + ँ + दिन = जाँदिन
हामी, हामीहरू	जा + न् + -छौं = जान्छौं	जा + ँ + -दैनौं = जाँदैनौं
तँ	जा + न् + -छस् = जान्छस्	जा + ँ + दैनस् = जाँदैनस्
तिमी, तिमीहरू	जा + न् + -छौ = जान्छौ	जा + ँ + दैनौ = जाँदैनौ
ऊ, यो, त्यो	जा + न् + -छ = जान्छ	जा + ँ + दैन = जाँदैन
उनी, यिनी, तिनी	जा + न् + -छन् = जान्छन्	जा + ँ + दैनन् = जाँदैनन्
यी, ती		
उनीहरू, यिनीहरू, तिनीहरू		

In VV-verbs, the second of the two vowels is nasalized before the ending is added:

आउनु **āunu** *to come*

	Affirmative	***Negative***
singular		
म	आउ + ँ + -छु = आउँछु	आउ + ँ + -दिन = आउँदिन
हामी, हामीहरू	आउ + ँ + -छौं = आउँछौं	आउ + ँ + -दैनौं = आउँदैनौं
तँ	आउ + ँ + -छस् = आउँछस्	आउ + ँ + -दैनस् = आउँदैनस्
तिमी, तिमीहरू	आउ + ँ + -छौ = आउँछौ	आउ + ँ + -दैनौ = आउँदैनौ
ऊ, यो, त्यो	आउ + ँ + -छ = आउँछ	आउ + ँ + -दैन = आउँदैन
उनी, यिनी, तिनी	आउ + ँ + -छन् = आउँछन्	आउ + ँ + -दैनन् = आउँदैनन्
यी, ती		
उनीहरू, यिनीहरू, तिनीहरू		

With the High pronouns (तपाईं, वहाँ, यहाँ, हजुर) the verbs behave differently. The base is simply the dictionary form ending in -नु, and the affirmative and negative endings are -हुन्छ **huncha** and -हुन्न **hunna** respectively. The verbs remain exactly the same in the singular and the plural.

High forms

गर्नु **garnu** to do

Affirmative	*Negative*
गर्नु + -हुन्छ = गर्नुहुन्छ	गर्नु + -हुन्न = गर्नुहुन्न

आउनु **āunu** to come

Affirmative	*Negative*
आउनु + -हुन्छ = आउनुहुन्छ	आउनु + -हुन्न = आउनुहुन्न

• INSIGHT

हुन्छ is very often used to mean 'okay' and 'yes'. In addition, हुन्छ is also used as the verb at the end of a sentence to indicate a sense of general truth about something, or to refer to events or activities in the near or distant future.

34 USING THE HABITUAL PRESENT TENSE

The habitual present tense is used for habitual actions in the present:

म पोखरामा काम गर्छु ।	I work in Pokhara.
उनीहरू नेपालमा बस्छन् ।	They live in Nepal.

to describe facts or situations that are regularly or generally true:

दार्जीलिङ्गको चिया मीठो हुन्छ ।	Darjeeling tea is good-tasting.
नेपालका धेरै किसानहरू गरीब हुन्छन् ।	Many of Nepal's farmers are poor.

for actions that are going to occur at a specific time, usually in the near future:

भोलि म लण्डन जान्छु ।	Tomorrow I (shall) go to London.
म एक घण्टापछि तपाईंलाई भन्छु ।	After an hour I shall tell you.

The habitual present tense of हुनु can be used in place of the हो and छ forms, in order to create an important difference of meaning. Compare the following four sentences:

म यहाँ छु ।	I am here.

This is a simple statement of fact and therefore it needs nothing more than the simple present tense **छु**.

म यहाँ हुन्छु ।	I am here.

This means *I am here (on a regular basis)* or *I shall be here.*

आज म यहाँ छु ।	I am here today.

Again, this is a simple statement of fact and therefore it needs nothing more than the simple present tense **छु**.

आज म यहाँ हुन्छु ।	I am here today.

This implies that I am regularly here on this particular day: *this is where I am on this day of the week* or that this is a statement about the future: *I shall be here today*.

Any sentence that is in the present tense and uses an adverb such as *usually, always, every day, monthly, often*, etc. must use this tense:

म हरेक दिन अफिसमा हुन्छु ।	I am in the office every day.
ऊ सधैं त्यहाँ हुन्छ ।	He is always there.

35 धेरैजसो USUALLY

धेरैजसो is a combination of **धेरै** *much, many* with **जसो** *similarly.* Therefore the phrase means, literally, *like much* or *like many,* and is used to mean *mostly* or *usually:*

ऊ धेरैजसो कुन रेश्टुराँमा भात खान्छ ?	In which restaurant does he usually eat?*
नेपालीहरू धेरैजसो हिन्दू हुन्छन् ।	Nepalis are mostly Hindus.

* **भात** *rice* is virtually a synonym for *food* in Nepali.

36 मात्रै ONLY, पनि ALSO, TOO, EVEN

मात्रै (and occasionally its non-emphasized form **मात्र**) is used to mean much the same thing as the English word *only,* but it comes after the noun or pronoun it qualifies in a sentence:

म मात्रै भारत जान्छु ।	Only I go to India (I am the only one who goes to India).
म भारत मात्रै जान्छु ।	I go only to India (India is the only place I go to).
ऊ मात्रै भात खान्छ ।	Only he eats rice (he is the only one who eats rice).
ऊ भात मात्रै खान्छ ।	He eats only rice (rice is the only thing he eats).

The first meaning of **पनि** is *too* or *also:*

म पनि भारत जान्छु ।	I too go to India (as well as other people).
म भारत पनि जान्छु ।	I go to India too (as well as to other countries).
ऊ पनि भात खान्छ ।	He too eats rice (as well as other people).
ऊ भात पनि खान्छ ।	He eats rice too (as well as other foods).

The second meaning of **पनि** is *even,* especially when it is used in negative statements:

घरमा भात पनि छैन ।	There isn't even any rice in the house.
मसँग एक रुपियाँ पनि छैन ।	I don't have even one rupee.
तिम्रो घरमा मूसा पनि भोको हुन्छ ।	In your house even a mouse is hungry.

37 कहिले ? WHEN?, कहिलेकाहीं SOMETIMES, कहिल्यै पनि NEVER

कहिले is primarily an interrogative word meaning *when?*

तपाईं भारत कहिले जानुहुन्छ ?	When do you/will you go to India?
उनीहरू बजार कहिले जान्छन् ?	When do they/will they go to the market?

Two very useful two-word phrases that include **कहिले** and its emphasized form **कहिल्यै** are: **कहिलेकाहीं** *sometimes,* and **कहिल्यै पनि** *never.* The first is usually only used in affirmative statements, the second can be used only in negative statements; both can form part of a question:

Q	तिमी कहिलेकाहीं नेपाल जान्छौ ?	Do you go to Nepal sometimes?
A	अहँ, म कहिल्यै पनि जाँदिन ।	No, I never go.
Q	वहाँ कहिल्यै पनि त्यहाँ जानुहुन्न ?	Does he never go there?
A	कहिल्यै पनि जानुहुन्न तर कहिलेकाहीं म जान्छु ।	He never goes, but sometimes I go.

● INSIGHT

Third person subjects (he, she, it, they) of transitive verbs can take ले in the present tense and you will hear this in practice a lot. However, ले is rarely used with first person and second person subjects (I, you) in the present tense. If you hear ले being used with them then it indicates a real emphasis.

38 MODES OF TRANSPORT

The postposition **-बाट**, despite its primary meaning of *from,* is also used to mean *by* in connection with modes of transport:

वहाँ साइकलबाट आउनुहुन्न ।	He does not come by bicycle.
सुरेश ट्याक्सीबाट घर जाँदैन, बसबाट जान्छ ।	Suresh doesn't go home by taxi, he goes by bus.

39 NEW POSTPOSITIONS: –पछि *AFTER;* –सम्म *UP TO, UNTIL;* –को लागि *FOR*

The single-word postpositions **–पछि** *after* and **–सम्म** *up to, until* (pronounced **samma**) are used in exactly the same way as other simple postpositions:

त्यसपछि	after that
दुई बजेपछि	after 2 o'clock
भोलिसम्म	until tomorrow
पोखरासम्म	as far as Pokhara

-सम्म is often used in phrases that also contain either **-बाट** *from* or **-देखि** *from, since* (do not forget that only **-देखि** can be used with expressions of time to mean *since*):

उनी दिल्लीदेखि काठ्माडौंसम्म हवाईजहाजबाट जान्छिन् ।	She goes from Delhi to Kathmandu by plane.
वहाँ दुई बजेदेखि छ बजेसम्म घरमा हुनुहुन्छ ।	From two o'clock until six o'clock he is at home.
तिनीहरु मेरो घरसम्म मात्रै आउँछन् ।	They only come as far as my house.

-को लागि is one of a small number of two-word postpositions that begin with the ownership suffix **-को**. It means *for*, in the sense of *for the sake of* or *intended for:*

ऊ मेरो बुवाको लागि खाना पकाउँछ ।	He cooks food for my father.
यो किताब उसको लागि हो ।	This book is for him.
तिमी मेरो लागि के गर्छौ ?	What do you do for me?

The **-को** of **-को लागि** should be **-का** when the subject is plural:

पाहुनाको लागि ।	for the guest
पाहुनाहरुका लागि ।	for the guests

Exercise 19

Translate into Nepali:

1 We won't go to the market today. There isn't even one rupee in the house.

2 What work does Rāju do? He works in the Nepal Rāṣṭra Bank. His elder brother works there too.

3 Where do you (High) live? Nowadays I live in Kathmandu.

4 Does your (High) younger brother go to the office by taxi? No, he goes by bus.

5 People from Darjeeling usually speak good Nepali.

Exercise 20

Construct sentences along the following lines:

Subject	*Time*	*Place*	*Verb*
1 म	every day	Kathmandu	go.
2 उनीहरु	usually	in Pokhara	live.
3 तिमी	always	in father's shop	speak (**बोल्नु**) Nepali.

4 हामीहरु	nowadays	in Ram's office	work.
5 ऊ	never	in school	speak English.
6 त्यो मान्छे	after one week	London	goes.

12 Women in the villages

05.02

Anne, a Nepali-speaking British woman who works in Kathmandu, is making her first visit to rural Nepal. She is getting to know Shanti, who lives in the village where she is staying. Unusually for a Nepali woman of her age, Shanti is unmarried.

अएन	तिमी धेरैजसो कति बजे उठ्छ्यौ ?
शान्ती	म धेरैजसो छ बजे उठ्छु । तर मेरी भाउज्यू चार बजेतिर उठ्छिन् ।
एन	किन त्यति बिहानै उठ्छिन् ? चार बजेतिर अँध्यारो नै हुन्छ, होइन ?
शान्ती	अँध्यारै हुन्छ, जाडो पनि हुन्छ ! भाउज्यू उठ्छिन् र धारातिर जान्छिन् । त्यसपछि उनी घरका सबै मानिसका लागि चिया पकाउँछिन् ।
एन	तर तिमीलाई सजिलो छ । बिहान काम छैन, होइन ?
शान्ती	म यहाँ बा-आमाको घरमा बस्छु नि, मेरो भागमा घरको काम धेरै हुँदैन ।

एन	अनि तिम्रो दाज्यू कति बजेतिर उठ्नुहुन्छ नि ?

शान्ती	वहाँ सात बजेसम्म सुत्नुहुन्छ । त्यसपछि उठ्नुहुन्छ, हातमुख धुनुहुन्छ, चिया खानुहुन्छ र खेततिर जानुहुन्छ ।
एन	खेतमा तिम्रो दाज्यू एक्लै जानुहुन्छ ?
शान्ती	होइन, वहाँ बुवा र भाइसँग जानुहुन्छ ।
एन	उनीहरु बेलुका मात्रै फर्कन्छन् कि ?
शान्ती	होइन, एघार बजेपछि गाउँका सबै लोग्नेमान्छेहरु खेतबाट फर्कन्छन् । अनि साढे एघार बजेतिर भात खान्छन् ।
एन	सधैं स्वास्नीमान्छेहरू नै भात पकाउँछन् कि ?
शान्ती	भात पकाउनु सधै स्वास्नीमान्छेहरूको काम हुन्छ ।
एन	लोग्नेमान्छेहरू कहिल्यै पनि भात पकाउँदैनन् ?
शान्ती	कहाँ लोग्नेमान्छेहरू भात पकाउँछन् र ? पकाउँदैनन्, हाम्रो घरमा त्यो पनि भाउज्यूको काम हुन्छ !
एन	तिमीहरु बेलुका पनि भात खान्छौ ?
शान्ती	हो । हामीहरू बिहान बेलुका दिनको दुई पटक भात खान्छौं ।
एन	तिम्रो भाउज्यूको जिन्दगी कति गाह्रो छ !
शान्ती	बिहापछि स्वास्नीमान्छेहरूको जिन्दगी गाह्रो हुन्छ ।
एन	अनि तिमी बिहा गर्दिनौ त ?
शान्ती	अहँ, म कहिल्यै पनि बिहा गर्दिन ।

V Quick vocab

कति बजे	at what time?	सजिलो	easy
उठ्नु	to get up	बस्नु	to live, reside
छ बजे	at six o'clock	भाग	share
भाउज्यू	elder brother's wife	सुत्नु	to sleep
-तिर	about	हातमुख	hands and face
त्यति	so, that much	धुनु	to wash
बिहानै	early morning	खेत	wet or irrigated field
अँध्यारो	dark	एक्लै	alone, on one's own
नै	emphasizing word	फर्कनु	to return
जाडो	cold	साढे एघार बजे	at half past eleven
धारा	spring, watersource	पटक	time, turn
त्यसपछि	after that, then	जिन्दगी	life
सबै	all (emphasized)	गाह्रो	hard
चिया	tea	बिहा	marriage

Anne	At what time do you usually get up?
Shanti	I usually get up at 6 o'clock. But my sister-in-law gets up at about 4 o'clock.
Anne	Why does she get up so early in the morning? At about 4 o'clock it is very dark, isn't it?
Shanti	It certainly is dark, and it's cold too. Sister-in-law gets up and goes to the spring. Then she makes tea for everyone in the house.
Anne	But it's easy for you. In the morning you've no work, is that so?
Shanti	I live here in my parents' home you see, I don't have much housework to do.
Anne	And when does your (elder) brother get up then?
Shanti	He sleeps until 7 o'clock. Then he gets up, washes his face and hands, drinks tea and goes to the fields.
Anne	Does your brother go to the fields on his own?
Shanti	No, he goes with Father and younger brother.
Anne	Do they only return in the evening?
Shanti	No, after 11 o'clock all the men of the village return from the fields. And at about half past 11 they eat rice.
Anne	Is it always the women who cook the rice?
Shanti	Cooking the rice is always the women's job.
Anne	Do the men never cook the rice?
Shanti	Where do men ever cook rice?* They do not, in our house that is always sister-in-law's job.
Anne	Do you eat in the evening too?
Shanti	Yes. We eat in the morning and the evening, twice a day.
Anne	How hard your sister-in-law's life is!
Shanti	After marriage women's life is hard.
Anne	And will you not marry then?
Shanti	No, I will never marry.

**Note* This is sarcastic, and should not be taken literally.

Grammar

40 THE HABITUAL PRESENT TENSE: FEMININE FORMS

The छ forms of हुनु have special feminine forms (see **Grammar 11**). These may be used as feminine endings in the habitual present tense:

तँ आउँछेस् ।	You (Low) come.
तिमी गर्छ्यौ ।	You (Middle) do.
ऊ जान्छे ।	She (Low) goes.
उनी सुत्छिन् ।	She (Middle) sleeps.

Each of the four affirmative endings has a negative counterpart. The difference between these and the masculine negative endings is that the -दै- **-dai-** of the masculine becomes -दि- **-di-** in the feminine:

तँ आउँदिनस् ।	You (Low) do not come.
तिमी गर्दिनौ ।	You (Middle) do not do.
ऊ पकाउँदिन ।	She (Low) does not cook.
तिनी रुँदिनन् ।	She (Middle) does not weep.

It is fairly uncommon for speakers of Nepali to use these forms in conversation, and in many contexts they would sound almost pedantically over-correct. They are encountered much more commonly in literary, official, and journalistic language.

41 TIMES OF DAY

The word **बजे** is derived from the verb **बज्नु** which means *to ring, strike*. It translates as *at ... o'clock*:

एक बजे	at 1 o'clock
दुई बजे	at 2 o'clock
तीन बजे	at 3 o'clock

Three further words are of use here: **साढे** plus a half; **सवा** plus a quarter; **पौने** minus a quarter:

सवा तीन बजे	at a quarter past 3
साढे पाँच बजे	at half past 5
पौने चार बजे	at a quarter to 4

This is the general pattern, but there are two exceptions to it:

- Instead of **साढे एक बजे**, it is customary to express half past 1 as **डेढ बजे**;
- Instead of **साढे दुई बजे**, it is customary to express half past 2 as **अढाई बजे**.

To make it clear whether one is talking about a.m. or p.m. (because most Nepalis do not use the 24-hour clock), it is sometimes necessary to specify the time of day when using **बजे**, by using one of the following terms:

बिहान	morning (from dawn to late morning)
दिउँसो	daytime (from late morning to dusk); also used to mean afternoon
बेलुका	evening (after sunset, before night begins)
राति	night
बिहान आठ बजे	at 8 o'clock in the morning
दिउँसो दुई बजे	at 2 o'clock in the afternoon
बेलुका छ बजे	at 6 o'clock in the evening
राति दस बजे	at 10 o'clock at night

Two further times of day are **साँझ** dusk and **मध्यान्न** midday.

• INSIGHT

Nepali speakers from Nepal do not generally use the postposition मा 'in, on, at' with the times of day and the days of the week. For instance, they don't say नौ बजेमा 'at nine o'clock', बिहानमा 'in the morning' or आइतबारमा 'on Sunday'. However, Nepali speakers from Sikkim and Darjeeling in India use मा with बिहान, दिउँसो and बेलुका.

42 DAYS OF THE WEEK

05.03

The word for *day* that is used to denote a day-long period of time is **दिन**, but when it is necessary to specify one particular day of the week, the word used for *day* is **वार** (pronounced **bār**):

आज के वार हो ?	What day (of the week) is it today?

Accordingly, each day of the week has a Nepali name that ends in **वार**, just as the names of English weekdays end in '-day':

Sunday	आइतवार	Thursday	बिहिवार
Monday	सोमवार	Friday	शुक्रवार
Tuesday	मङ्गलवार	Saturday	शनिवार
Wednesday	बुधवार		

In Nepal, Sunday is the first working day of the week, and offices are closed on Saturdays. In India, both Saturday and Sunday are holidays.

In everyday spoken Nepali, the word **अस्ति** *the day before yesterday* is used to denote a day of the previous week, while **अर्को** *other* is used to denote a day of the week to come:

अस्ति षुक्रवार	last Friday
अर्को षनिवार	next Saturday

• INSIGHT

The indefinite future tense, which is conjugated in the same way as the present habitual tense, can be made into a definite future tense if you repeat the verb conjugation, such as म जान्छु जान्छु 'I will go for sure'. The repetition of a word implies an emphasis in Nepali.

43 FREQUENCY: पटक

The word **पटक** can be used in combination with a number to communicate the frequency of an occurrence:

एक पटक	one time, once
दुई पटक	two times, twice
तीन पटक	three times

These phrases can then be joined to a period of time (a week, a day, etc.), using either **-को** or **-मा**, to express how often something happens or is done within that period:

मेरी आमा एक हप्तामा एक पटक बजार जानुहुन्छ ।	My mother goes to the market once a week.
मेरी बहिनी हप्ताको पाँच पटक स्कूल जान्छे ।	My younger sister goes to school five times a week.

Nepali has several words that are near synonyms of **पटक**. These are **चोटि**, **बाजि** and **पल्ट**. For the time being, use **पटक** in preference to these others.

Exercise 21

Construct sentences along the following lines:

Subject	***Time***	***Place***	***Verb***
1 तपाईं	at 7 o'clock	at home	eat rice.
2 त्यो मान्छे	in the evening	in the hotel	drinks tea.
3 वहाँहरू	on Thursday	to my house	come.
4 यिनीहरू	twice a week	to the temple	go.
5 यो केटी	on Saturday	at a friend's house	sleeps.

Exercise 22

Construct sentences along the following lines:

Subject	***from***	***to***	***verb, etc.***
1 म	2 p.m.	6 p.m.	am not at home.
2 तपाईं	Wednesday	Friday	are not in Birāṭanagar.
3 उनीहरू	Tuesday	Thursday	do not work.
4 तिमी	8 a.m.	10.30 a.m.	do not go out.
5 यिनीहरू	1 p.m.	2 p.m.	do not study.

The most important things for the reader to remember

1 The present habitual tense is used to express a regular or usual action in the present tense, often with adverbs of time to denote the frequency of the activity, e.g. **म दिनदिन चिया पिउँछु**, 'I drink tea every day'.

2 The same conjugation of the present habitual tense is also used for the simple future tense. It is normally possible to do so only with a future time indicator, e.g. **म भोलि घरमा बस्छु**, 'I will stay home tomorrow'.

3 **हुन्छ** is used to indicate a fact or generalization in Nepali, e.g. **लण्डनमा जाडो हुन्छ** 'It is cold in London'. **हुन्छ** is also used for 'to be' verb in the simple future tense, e.g. **भोलि गर्मी हुन्छ**, 'It will be hot tomorrow'.

4 *The more postpositions you know, the wider is the range of situations in which you can use the Nepali language. They include* **पछि, सम्म** and **को लागि** as in **त्यसपछि, अहिलेसम्म** and **आजको लागि** 'after 'that', 'until now', 'for today'.

6 पाँच सय रुपियाँ दिनुहोस्

Give me 500 rupees

In this unit you will learn:

- *how to ask or tell people to do or not to do things*
- *how to use the postposition* –लाई *with the indirect objects of verbs*
- *how to use the alternative negative forms of the habitual present tense*
- *how to use the postposition* –तिर
- *how to use the words for* **but, why** *and* **because;** *express agreement and assent*

13 Hiring a rickshaw

06.01

It is a late evening in winter. Ashok, a government official, needs to get to his home in Maharajganj, a residential area in north Kathmandu. Ran Bahadur, a rickshaw driver, is not keen to travel out so far at this time of night, but he is prepared to take Ashok part of the way if the price is right.

अशोक	ए रिक्सा ! खाली हो ?
रण बहादुर	खाली छ हजुर । बस्नुहोस् । कहाँ जानुहुन्छ ?
अशोक	महाराजगंज । कति पैसा लिन्छौ ?
रण बहादुर	हेर्नुहोस्, राति म महाराजगंज जान्नँ । टाढा छ, जाडो पनि छ । म तपाईंलाई लाजिम्पाटसम्म मात्रै लान्छु । त्यहाँबाट ट्याक्सी लिनुहोस् न ।
अशोक	हुन्छ, हुन्छ । तर कति लिन्छौ नि ? अनि हेर । मलाई अलि हतार छ । छिटो गर है ।
रण बहादुर	हतार छ हजुर ? ल, पाँच सय रुपियाँ दिनुहोस् ।
अशोक	पाँच सय रुपियाँ ? म त ट्याक्सीलाई पनि पाँच सय रुपियाँ दिन्नँ !
रण बहादुर	ट्याक्सीलाई कति दिनुहुन्छ त ?
अशोक	यो ट्याक्सी होइन, रिक्सा हो । ल, एक सय रुपियाँ लेऊ अनि हिंड !
रण बहादुर	दुई सय रुपियाँ दिनुहोस् साहेब । एक सय रुपियाँमा म राति यस्तो जाडोमा कतै जान्नँ ।
अशोक	ठीकै छ । कतै नजाऊ ! म अर्को रिक्सा लिन्छु ।
रण बहादुर	यो जाडोमा तपाईं अर्को रिक्सा पाउनुहुन्न । म मात्रै छु अहिले ।
अशोक	ठीकै छ । म ट्याक्सीबाट जान्छु । फरक पर्दैन ।

रण बहादुर	ट्याक्सी त झन् महंगो पर्छ हजुर । अनि यतातिर राति ट्याक्सी पाउनुहुन्न । हुन्छ, मलाई एक सय पचास रुपियाँ दिनुहोस् । म छिटै लान्छु ।
अशोक	ल, ल । अब ढिलो नगर है, छिटो चलाऊ ।

Quick vocab

रिक्सा	rickshaw
खाली	empty
बस्नु	to sit down
महाराजगंज	Maharajganj, a suburb of Kathmandu
लिनु	to take
हेर्नु	to look
लानु	to transport, take somewhere
लाजिम्पाट	Lazimpat, a part of Kathmandu
ट्याक्सी	taxi
न	won't you?
हुन्छ	all right
हतार	hurry
छिटो गर्नु	to act quickly, hurry
है	hey! / do you hear?
दिनु	to give
त	though, but, then
हिड्नु	to set out, get going*
कतै	anywhere
पाउनु	to get, find

फरक पर्नु	to make a difference
झन्	even more
महंगो पर्नु	to be expensive
छिटै	quickly
अब	now
ढिलो गर्नु	to act slowly, be late
चलाउनु	to drive, operate

* हिड्‌नु means both *to walk* and *to begin a journey* or *to set out.*

Ashok	Hey rickshaw! Is it empty?
Ran Bahadur	It's empty, sir. Sit down. Where will you go?
Ashok	Maharajganj. How much money will you take?
Ran Bahadur	Look, I won't go to Maharajganj at night. It's a long way, and it's cold too. I will take you only as far as Lazimpat. Please take a taxi from there, won't you?
Ashok	All right, all right. But how much will you take? And look. I'm in a bit of a hurry. Go quickly.
Ran Bahadur	In a hurry sir? Right, give me 500 rupees.
Ashok	500 rupees? But I wouldn't even pay a taxi 100 rupees!
Ran Bahadur	How much would you pay a taxi then?
Ashok	This isn't a taxi, it's a rickshaw. Right, take 100 rupees and get going.
Ran Bahadur	Give me 200 rupees, Saheb. I won't go anywhere at night in this cold for 100 rupees.
Ashok	That's fine. Don't go anywhere! I'll take another rickshaw.
Ran Bahadur	You won't find another rickshaw in this cold. There's only me now.
Ashok	OK then. I'll go by taxi. It makes no difference.
Ran Bahadur	A taxi will be even more expensive, sir. And you won't get a taxi around here at night. All right, give me 150 rupees. I'll take you quickly.
Ashok	Right, right. Now don't be slow, drive quickly.

● INSIGHT

It is always safe for non-Nepalese Nepali speakers to use the polite form of imperatives such as बस्नुहोस् or बस्नुस् 'please have a seat' unless they are dealing with intimate friends or with children.

The verb पाल्नु is a very polite form of आउनु and when the polite imperative suffix होस् is added to this it is a special verb to show special politeness for seniors or officers as guests at home, e.g. घरमा पाल्नुहोस् 'please come to my home'.

Grammar

44 THE IMPERATIVES

An imperative is a form of a verb that is used to give orders or make requests. Imperatives range from peremptory commands to polite requests. In English, the different levels of politeness are usually distinguished by the use or omission of a word such as *please,* or a phrase such as *would you ... ?* but in Nepali levels of politeness are implicit in the grammatical forms of the various imperatives. There are four levels of politeness, corresponding with the Low, Middle and High second-person pronouns plus an extra Super-Polite level. The Low and Super-Polite are not forms that a foreign speaker is likely to use. The four levels are given below, using the verb **गर्नु** *to do.* The English translations are not meant to be literal, but to give a sense of the level of politeness.

LOW	गर्	**gar**	do! (used to give commands or advice to a person you would normally address as **तँ**)
MIDDLE	गर	**gara**	do! (used to instruct a person of lower status than yourself, or a familiar, whom you would address as **तिमी**)
HIGH	गर्नुहोस्	**garnuhos**	please do! (used to ask a request of someone you would address politely as **तपाईं**)
SUPER-POLITE	गर्नुहोला	**garnuholā**	please would you do! (used to ask a request of someone you might address deferentially)

You are advised to use the High imperatives in all contexts, at least until you are sure of your reasons for using another level.

Negative imperatives are exactly the same as positive imperatives, except that they take a negative prefix, **न- na-**.

LOW	नगर्	**nagar**	don't!
MIDDLE	नगर	**nagara**	don't!
HIGH	नगर्नुहोस्	**nagarnuhos**	please don't!
SUPER-POLITE	नगर्नुहोला	**nagarnuholā**	please would you not do!

Clearly, the more polite the imperative is, the longer the word becomes: in its positive form the most polite is a word of four syllables, while the least polite has only one syllable. The High and Super-Polite forms consist of the dictionary form + a suffix (the suffixes are **-होस्** and **-होला** respectively). For C-verbs, the Low and Middle forms are simply the verb base without and with a final **-a** vowel respectively.

Summary of imperative forms: C-VERBS

affirmative

	गर्नु to do	बस्नु to sit
Low	गर्	बस्
Middle	गर	बस
High	गर्नुहोस्	बस्नुहोस्
Super-Polite	गर्नुहोला	बस्नुहोला

negative

Low	नगर्	नबस्
Middle	नगर	नबस
High	नगर्नुहोस्	नबस्नुहोस्
Super-Polite	नगर्नुहोला	नबस्नुहोला

The Middle imperatives of all V- and VV-verbs take the suffix -ऊ **-ū**, which is added to the verb base. At Low and Middle levels, five commonly used V-verbs behave irregularly by adopting special imperative bases. These verbs are:

	Dictionary form	***Imperative base***
to take	लिनु	ले-
to give	दिनु	दे-
to wash	धुनु	धो-
to weep	रुनु	रो-
to be	हुनु	हो-

The second vowel is dropped from the bases of VV-verbs:

to come	आउनु	आ-
to send	पठाउनु	पठा-

Summary of imperative forms: V-VERBS AND VV-VERBS

Affirmative

	जानु to go	*लिनु* to take	*धुनु* to wash	*आउनु* to come	*पठाउनु* to send
Low	जा	ले	धो	आ	पठा
Middle	जाऊ	लेऊ	धोऊ	आऊ	पठाऊ
High	जानुहोस्	लिनुहोस्	धुनुहोस्	आउनुहोस्	पठाउनुहोस्
S-P	जानुहोला	लिनुहोला	धुनुहोला	आउनुहोला	पठाउनुहोला

Negative

Low	नजा	नले	नधो	नआ	नपठा
Middle	नजाऊ	नलेऊ	नधोऊ	नआऊ	नपठाऊ
High	नजानुहोस्	नलिनुहोस्	नधुनुहोस्	नआउनुहोस्	नपठाउनुहोस्
S-P	नजानुहोला	नलिनुहोला	नधुनुहोला	नआउनुहोला	नपठाउनुहोला

One additional form of the imperative is simply the dictionary form of a verb with its final vowel lengthened from उ **u** to ऊ **ū**. This you use to give specific instructions to a person of lower status than yourself, or to a familiar. Again, the negative form has the prefix न-:

अब यो किताब पढ्नू ।	Now read this book.
रातो लुगा तातो पानीमा नधुनू । रङ जान्छ नि ।	Don't wash the red clothes in hot water. They'll fade, you know.

• INSIGHT

A special imperative form is used to give specific instructions to a person of lower status than you. For this the dictionary form of a verb नु changes to a long नू, e.g. पसल जानू र फलफूल किन्नू 'go to the shop and buy fruits'.

Exercise 23

Translate the following commands into Nepali:

a *Addressing the person concerned as* तिमी*:*

1 Hey, don't sit on that chair, sit on this chair.

2 Speak Nepali in Kathmandu, don't speak English.

3 Read the big red book, don't read the newspaper.

4 Give the boy an apple, don't give him an orange.

b *Addressing the person concerned as* तपाईं*:*

5 Please don't come at 6 o'clock, come at about 8 o'clock.

6 Please tell me but don't tell him.

7 Please take this cup and give that cup to him.

8 Please go to Nepal. Please speak Nepali there.

45 THE POSTPOSITION -लाई -LĀĪ AS OBJECT MARKER

All verbs must have a subject: the subject of a verb is the thing or person that is performing the action of the verb. In the sentence *the man eats rice*, the verb is *eats* and its subject is *the man*. Many verbs (those verbs that are called 'transitive verbs', as explained in **Grammar 58**) can also have an object. In the sentence above, the object is *rice*, because that is what is eaten: the rice receives the action of the verb.

● INSIGHT

When any one of the verbs दिनु, बताउनु, भन्नु, सोध्नु, हेर्नु, देख्नु, भेट्नु, पिट्नु, ल्याइदिनु, मदत गर्नु is used in a sentence, the person who receives something as a result of these action verbs will take the object marker लाई because they are the recipient object.

Objects can be of two kinds: *direct* or *indirect*. In Nepali, an indirect object must always carry the postposition **–लाई**, which will often be translatable as *to* or *at:*

म तिमीलाई भन्छु ।	I say to you.
ऊ मलाई दिन्छ ।	He gives to me.
तपाईं उसलाई दिनुहोस् ।	Please give to him.

In sentences that contain only one object, the general rule is that personal names, human nouns and human pronouns (*he, she, we,* etc.) should carry **–लाई** when they are the object of a verb, while inanimate nouns need not:

म भात खान्छु ।	I eat rice.
हामी टी० भी० हेर्छौं ।	We watch television.
उनीहरु गीत गाउँछन् ।	They sing a song.
ऊ चिठी लेख्छ ।	He writes a letter.
म वहाँलाई सोध्छु ।	I'll ask him.
उनीहरु मलाई हेर्छन् ।	They watch me.

However, there are certain situations in which this rule is broken:

- in contexts in which a human being is being treated as a commodity that can be bought or given away (giving a daughter in marriage, for example), in which case it will be treated as an inanimate noun and will not take **–लाई:**

  ऊ धनी मान्छेलाई छोरी दिन्छ । He gives [his] daughter to a rich man.

- when an inanimate noun is being treated like an animate being (a devout person might bow to a book, or offer worship to a sacred rock, for instance), in which case it will be treated as an animate noun and take **–लाई:**

  म किताबलाई ढोग्छु । I bow to the book.

- if the subject carries the subject-marking suffix **-ले** (introduced in **Grammar 59**) and it is obvious what its object is, it is sometimes unnecessary to mark the object with **–लाई**.

More complex sentences may include both a direct and an indirect object. In these the indirect object carries **–लाई** but the direct object does not, and the rules about animate and inanimate nouns become irrelevant:

म तिमीलाई यो कुरा भन्छु ।	I say this thing to you.
ऊ मलाई पैसा दिन्छ ।	He gives money to me.
तपाईं उसलाई त्यो किताब दिनुहोस् ।	Please give that book to him.

This is a complex area of Nepali grammar, and the foreign learner must develop an intuitive sense of when to use and when not to use –लाई.

46 THE HABITUAL PRESENT TENSE: ALTERNATIVE NEGATIVE FORMS

All V- and VV-verbs have a second series of negative endings, which sound more abrupt than the standard –दैन **-daina** range. In this, the दै **dai** or दि **di** syllable is replaced by a half **n** (न्) while the vowel of the verb base is no longer nasalized.

Standard ending		***Alternative ending***	
–दैन	**-daina**	–न्न	**-nna** (with ऊ, यो, त्यो)
–दिन	**-dina**	–न्नँ	**-nnã** (with म)
–दैनस्	**-dainas**	–न्नस्	**-nnas** (with तँ)
–दैनौ	**-dainau**	–न्नौ	**-nnau** (with तिमी)
–दैनौं	**-dainaũ**	–न्नौं	**-nnaũ** (with हामी, हामीहरू)
–दैनन्	**-dainan**	–न्नन्	**-nnan** (with यी, ती, उनी, यिनी, तिनी, and the plural forms of उनी, यिनी and तिनी)

These endings are commonly used with the verbs जानु and खानु:

ऊ जान्न	S/he does not / will not go	ऊ खान्न	S/he does not / will not eat
म जान्नँ	I do not / will not go	म खान्नँ	I do not / will not eat
तँ जान्नस्	You do not / will not go	तँ खान्नस्	You do not / will not eat
तिमी जान्नौ	You do not / will not go	तिमी खान्नौ	You do not / will not eat
हामी जान्नौं	We do not / will not go	हामीहरू खान्नौं	We do not / will not eat
यिनी जान्नन्	S/he does not / will not go	उनीहरू खान्नन्	They do not / will not eat

The use of the alternative negative ending is obligatory in the phrases *I do not/will not give* and *I do not/will not take:*

म तपाईंलाई मेरो साइकल दिन्नँ ।	I shall not give you my bicycle.
म तपाईंको हातबाट पैसा लिन्नँ ।	I will not take money from your hand.

Otherwise, these alternative negative endings are generally interchangeable with the standard forms, but they are most often used with the first person pronoun (म *I*) to convey the sense of *I shall not* or *I will not* rather than *I do not*. That is, they are often used to express refusal to do something:

म भात खाँदिन ।	I do not eat rice.
म भात खान्नँ ।	I will not eat rice.
म स्कूल जाँदिन ।	I do not go to school.
म स्कूल जान्नँ ।	I will not go to school.

● INSIGHT

The present habitual and simple future tenses have alternative negatives for all conjugations of the verbs, but these can only be used if the root of the verb ends with a vowel, e.g. खान्न, जान्न. If the root of a verb ends with a consonant, it cannot take alternative negatives.

Honorific pronouns such as तपाईं and वहाँ always take the alternative negative, i.e., (जानु) हुन्न because the regular negative जानु (हुँदैन) has a prohibitive meaning, 'it is not right to go'.

47 THE POSTPOSITION -तिर TOWARDS

-तिर **-tira** is a postposition used with words that denote a place or location. It means either **(i)** *in the direction of* that place or location, or **(ii)** *in the vicinity of* that place or location. It is also used **(iii)** with times of day to mean *about* or *approximately.*

i When the phrase or sentence involves a verb of movement -**तिर** means literally *in the direction of* (though often it can be translated as *to*):

दिदी दार्जीलिङ्गतिर जान्छिन् ।	Elder sister goes to Darjeeling.
पर्यटकहरू पहाडतिर जान्छन्	Tourists go to the hills.

ii If no verb of movement is involved in the phrase or sentence, -**तिर** means *in the vicinity of* the place or location to which it is added:

दार्जीलिङ्गतिर मान्छेहरू नेपाली बोल्छन् ।	Around Darjeeling, people speak Nepali.
पहाडतिर मौसम अलि चिसो हुन्छ ।	In the hill areas the weather is rather cold.

iii -**तिर** can be added to the word **बजे** *at* ... o'clock to introduce a measure of vagueness to statements of time:

म एक बजेतिर आउँछु ।	I'll come at about 1 o'clock.
हामी दस बजेतिर भात खान्छौं ।	We eat at about 10 o'clock.

● INSIGHT

तिर literally means 'towards', 'side' or 'direction' but it also means 'about' with a point of time, e.g. दस बजेतिर 'about ten o'clock'. With a period of time you need to use जति instead of तिर, e.g. दस घण्टाजति 'about ten hours'.

48 THE NEGATIVE PARTICLE न

न **na** means *do not* before an imperative, but *won't you?* after an imperative:

भात नखानुहोस् ।	Please don't eat the rice.
यहाँ नआउनुहोस् ।	Please don't come here.
भात खानुहोस् न ।	Please eat the rice, won't you?
यहाँ आउनुहोस् न ।	Please come here, won't you?

It also means both *neither* and *nor:*

यहाँ न पसल छ न स्कूल ।	Here there is neither a shop nor a school.
मसँग न पैसा छ न चुरोट ।	I have neither any money nor any cigarettes.

● INSIGHT

There is a difference between the regular negative and the alternative negative in the present tense. If I say म मन्दिर जान्नँ this indicates that I won't go to the temple *now*, whereas म मन्दिर जाँदिन has the sense of 'I never go'.

49 तर BUT, त THOUGH

There are two ways of saying *but* in Nepali. तर is pretty well an exact translation of *but* and can be used in much the same way as *but* at the beginning of or in the middle of a sentence:

किताब राम्रो छ, तर अलि छोटो छ ।	The book is good, but it's rather short.
भोलि म बिराटनगर जान्छु तर राति बस्दिन ।	Tomorrow I shall go to Biratnagar but I shall not stay the night.

त can never be the first word in a sentence. It can follow a time, or a subject, or something else, which it qualifies. When used in statements, it means *as for, though, but* or *however.*

म त शाकाहारी हुँ । म मासु खाँदिन ।	I am a vegetarian. I do not eat meat.
काठ्माडौं त नेपालको राजधानी हो, भारतको राजधानी होइन ।	But Kathmandu is the capital of Nepal, not the capital of India.
नेपाली भाषा त सजिलै छ, किन बुझ्नुहुन्न ?	But the Nepali language is quite easy, why don't you understand?

त may also end a question or a command, in which case it translates as *then* or *in that case:*

तपाईंकी आमा नेपालमा हुनुहुन्छ ?	Is your mother in Nepal?
हुनुहुन्न ।	No.
कहाँ हुनुहुन्छ त ?	Where is she then?
भारतमा हुनुहुन्छ ।	She's in India.
तपाईं तीन बजेतिर मेरो घर आउनुहुन्छ ?	Will you come to my house at about three o'clock?
होइन, त्यो बेला फुर्सद हुँदैन ।	No, I don't have the time then.
कति बजे आउनुहुन्छ त ?	At what time will you come, then?
यो तिम्रो झोला हो ?	Is that your bag?
होइन ।	No.
कसको हो त ?	Whose is it then?
मेरो साथीको ।	My friend's.

50 हवस् AND हुन्छ: OK, ALL RIGHT

If a Nepali speaker is asked or told to do something, and s/he agrees to do it, the response given is commonly either **हवस् havas** or **हुन्छ huncha**. These words are both derived from the verb **हुनु** *to be*. **हवस्** (sometimes also written **हस्**) translates as *may it be so*, and is a polite word that indicates assent. It is also often said by someone as they depart, almost to mean 'goodbye'. The middle **व** of **हवस्** is pronounced as if it were a vowel, and the word is pronounced **'haus'**:

ए धने, तिमी पाहुनाहरूका लागि चिया पकाऊ है ।	Hey Dhane, make tea for the guests!
हवस् हजुर ।	Certainly, sir.
हस् त, फेरि भेटौंला ।	OK, we'll meet again.

हुन्छ means something like *it is good* or *OK;* it has much the same meaning as **हवस्**, but is rather less deferential.

Exercise 24

Translate into Nepali:

1 Those women never come to the bazaar on Thursday. When do they come, then? They usually come on Tuesday.

2 Foreigners go from Kathmandu to Lukla by plane. Nepalis usually go by bus up to Jiri. From Jiri they walk to Lukla.

3 At what time do those men go to the fields? They go at about 8 o'clock and they come home after three hours.

4 I will stay in Nepal only until tomorrow. At 10.30 tomorrow morning I go to Delhi. After that I go to London.

5 After 8 o'clock at night all the shops are shut. I won't go to the market for you now. I will go tomorrow morning.

6 What work will you (Middle) do for me? I'll go to the market for you (High), OK?

7 My younger sister never cooks food for the family. Sometimes elder sister cooks, sometimes mother cooks.

8 She (Low) goes to school every day, and so does he (Low). But their little brother doesn't go.

The most important things for the reader to remember

1 Nepali has different forms of imperative, which are used to give orders or to appeal or request. Which one you use depends on the politeness with which you need to address a particular person because of his/her position or status, e.g. आ, आऊ, आउनुहोस्, आउनुहोला, आइस्योस् 'Come/please come'.

2 The postposition लाई is used with a person or pronoun (i) when it is used as an object and (ii) when the verb is impersonal, e.g. म तिमीलाई उपहार दिन्छु, 'I will give you a gift' and मलाई नेपाल मनपर्छ, 'I like Nepal'.

3 An alternative negative form is used in the simple present tense with particular verbs. This form of the negative is more commonly used by these verbs in spoken Nepali, e.g. ऊ जान्न रे । 'I heard that he wouldn't go'.

4 Although the postposition तिर literally means 'direction' or 'side' it is also used to denote a particular place. In this context, you can translate it as 'towards' such as दार्जिलिङ्गतिर 'Towards Darjeeling'.

5 The particle न is used as a prefix to create a negative imperative, e.g. नआउनुहोस् 'Please don't come'. But when it comes after an imperative it adds emphasis to it, e.g. आउनुहोस् न, 'Please come, won't you'.

6 हवस् or हुन्छ are used as a response to a request to do something. हवस् is more polite, meaning 'Yes sir I will'. हुन्छ is more informal.

7 सबभन्दा राम्रो

The best

In this unit you will learn:

- *how to make comparisons*
- *how to express likes and dislikes*

14 Towns and villages

07.01

Bimla is doing her homework. She has to write an essay about the differences between life in a city and life in a village. Her younger brother and her parents are helping her out.

बिमला	आज अलिकति स्कूलको काम छ । मलाई सहयोग गर्नुहोस् है बुवा ।
बुवा	हुन्छ, म सहयोग गर्छु ।
बिमला	सँसारको सबैभन्दा ठूलो शहर कुन हो, थाहा छ ?
सुरेश	थाहा छ । काठ्माडौं हो ।
बिमला	सँसारको सबैभन्दा ठूलो शहर काठ्माडौं हो ? कहाँको काठ्माडौं हुनु ? काठ्माडौंभन्दा त दिल्ली ठूलो छ, होइन आमा ?
आमा	हो, दिल्ली, लण्डन, टोक्यो सँसारका ठूला शहरहरू हुन् ।
बुवा	तर टोक्योभन्दा ठूलो शहर छैन यो सँसारमा । टोक्यो सँसारको सबैभन्दा ठूलो शहर हो ।
बिमला	ठीक छ । तपाईंलाई ठूलो शहर मन पर्छ ? मलाई त मन पर्दैन ।
सुरेश	किन मन पर्दैन ?
बिमला	किनभने शहरको जीवन जटिल हुन्छ । गाउँको जीवन सजिलो हुन्छ ।
सुरेश	कहाँको सजिलो हुनु ? शहरको जीवनभन्दा गाउँको जीवन बढी गाह्रो हुन्छ नि । गाउँमा न ठूला पसलहरू हुन्छन् न सिनेमा-घरहरू हुन्छन् न त राम्रा स्कूलहरू हुन्छन् । मलाई त शहर नै मन पर्छ ।
बिमला	कुरा त ठीकै हो । तर गाउँमा हावा सफा हुन्छ, पानी पनि मीठो हुन्छ । गाउँमा दालभात स्वादिलो हुन्छ । होइन त आमा ?

आमा	हो, तिम्रो कुरा साँचो हो । तर शहरमा यातायात, अस्पताल, स्कूल, बजारहरूका सुविधा हुन्छन् । धेरै मान्छेहरू शहरको जीवन मन पराउँछन् ।
बुवा	बिमला, अब तिमीलाई गाउँ र शहरको जीवनमा फरक त थाहा छ । अब भन, तिमीलाई शहर र गाउँमा कुन मन पर्छ ?
बिमला	शहरको जिन्दगी मलाई मन पर्दैन । मलाई गाउँको जीवन देऊ !

V Quick vocab

सहयोग गर्नु	to assist, help
सँसार	the world
सबैभन्दा ठूलो	biggest
-भन्दा	than
टोक्यो	Tokyo
मन पर्नु	to be liked
कि	why?
किनभने	because
जीवन	life
जटिल	complicated, difficult
हावा	air
सफा	clean
स्वादिलो	tasty, flavoursome
कुरा	thing, matter
साँचो	true
यातायात	transport
अस्पताल	hospital
सुविधा	facility, convenience
मन पराउनु	to like

Bimala	Today I have some school work. Please help me, Father.
Father	All right, I'll help.
Bimala	Which is the world's biggest city, do you know?
Suresh	I know. It's Kathmandu.
Bimala	The world's biggest city is Kathmandu? How can it be Kathmandu? Delhi is bigger than Kathmandu, isn't it Mother?
Mother	Yes, Delhi, London, Tokyo are the world's big cities.
Father	But there is no city bigger than Tokyo in this world. Tokyo is the world's biggest city.

Bimala	OK. Do you like big towns? I don't like them.
Suresh	Why don't you like them?
Bimala	Because town life is complicated. Village life is easy.
Suresh	How can it be easy? Village life is much harder than town life. In a village there are neither big shops nor cinemas, nor are there good schools. The town is what I like.
Bimala	What you say is true enough. But in a village the air is clean, and the water tastes good too. In a village the food is flavoursome. Isn't that so, Mother?
Mother	Yes, what you say is true. But in a town there are the facilities of transport, hospitals, schools and marketplaces. Many people like town life.
Father	Bimala, now you know the difference between village and town life. Tell me now, out of the town and the village, which do you prefer?
Bimala	I don't like town life. Give me village life!

Grammar

51 COMPARATIVES AND SUPERLATIVES

When you compare things in English, you say that something is *bigger than* or *better than* something else. Much the same convention exists in Nepali, where the equivalent of the English preposition *than* is a postposition, **-भन्दा**. But in Nepali the adjective remains the same as it would if you were simply describing what you are talking about, e.g., **राम्रो** *good* remains as **राम्रो** *good*, and there is no single Nepali word that means *better*. Comparative sentences can be cast either way:

मेरो घर तिम्रो घरभन्दा ठूलो छ ।	My house is bigger than your house.
तिम्रो घरभन्दा मेरो घर ठूलो छ ।	Than your house my house is bigger.
त्यो दाल यो दालभन्दा मीठो हुन्छ ।	That **dāl** is tastier than this **dāl**.
यो दालभन्दा त्यो दाल मीठो हुन्छ ।	Than this **dāl** that **dāl** is tastier.

The words **बढी** or **ज्यादा** *more*, or the emphatic **ज्यादै** *much more*, are often put in front of the adjective to make it absolutely clear that a comparison is being made:

मेरो गाउँ तिम्रो गाउँभन्दा बढी ठूलो छ ।	My village is bigger than yours.
जुम्लाका स्याउ ज्यादै मीठा हुन्छन् ।	Apples from Jumla are much tastier.

To express a superlative – that is, to say that something is the *best* or the *cheapest* – the same construction is used, except that instead of comparing something to one or a number of other things you simply compare it to **सब**, *all*, or to **सबै**, *absolutely all:*

मेरो गाउँ सबभन्दा ठूलो छ ।	My village is the biggest (of all).
तातोपानीका सुन्तला सबैभन्दा मीठा हुन्छन् ।	Oranges from Tatopani are the tastiest (of all).

Since all of these examples have been descriptive, they have used either छ or हुन्छ. However, it is possible to define something as *the biggest village* or *the cheapest rice:* in these cases the noun may be mentioned twice (though it need not be), and the हो form of the verb can be used:

मेरो घर सबभन्दा ठूलो (घर) हो ।	My house is the biggest (house).
त्यो आँप सबभन्दा मीठो (आँप) हो ।	That mango is the tastiest (mango).
अमेरिकालीहरू सँसारका सबैभन्दा धनी मानिसहरू हुन् ।	Americans are the world's richest people.

Exercise 25

Translate into Nepali:

1. London is bigger than Kathmandu.
2. American people are usually richer than English people.
3. Kathmandu is further from England than Delhi.
4. Kathmandu is Nepal's biggest city.
5. Which is the world's poorest country?
6. There is no language easier than Nepali.

52 LIKES AND DISLIKES USING मन पर्नु

The simplest way of expressing a like or a dislike of something is to use the verb phrase मन पर्नु which literally means *mind* (मन) *to fall* (पर्नु) but translates as *to be liked*. The subject of this verb phrase is not the person who is doing the liking, but the thing that is being liked.

If no person is mentioned in a statement that uses मन पर्नु, then the person who is doing the liking is most probably the person who is making the statement:

त्यो गीत मन पर्छ ।	That song is liked. ('I like that song.')
लण्डन मन पर्दैन ।	London is not liked. ('I do not like London.')
यो पत्रिका मनै पर्दैन ।	This magazine is not liked at all. ('I do not like this magazine at all.')

If no person is mentioned in a question that uses मन पर्नु, then the person who is doing the liking is most probably the person to whom the question is being addressed:

नीलो रङ मन पर्छ ?	Is blue colour liked? ('do you like blue?')
रातो रङ मन पर्छ कि मन पर्दैन ?	Is red colour liked or not? ('do you like red or don't you?')

If it is necessary to state *by whom* a thing is liked or disliked, then the person who likes, or the pronoun that stands for that person, must take the postposition -लाई:

मलाई पहेंलो रङ मन पर्छ ।	I like the colour yellow.
सुशीललाई हरियो रङ मन पर्छ ।	Sushil likes the colour green.
तपाईंलाई कालो रङ मन पर्दैन ?	Do you not like the colour black?
उसलाई यो सेतो कपडा मन पर्दैन ।	He does not like this white cloth.

Less commonly, the liker of something can become the subject of this kind of sentence by using the verb **मन पराउनु**, in which case the postposition **-लाई** is sometimes added to the thing that is liked.

म खैरो रङ मन पराउँछु ।	I like the colour brown.
तपाईं प्याजी रङलाई मन पराउनुहुन्छ ?	Do you like the colour purple?

● INSIGHT

मनपर्छ literally means 'mind/heart falls'. So when you say मलाई नेपाल मनपर्छ it sounds like 'My heart falls on Nepal'. Or you can also translate it as 'Nepal is pleasing to me'. That's why you need to add लाई to the person. However, मन पराउनु, a causative verb, can also be used in conjugation instead: म नेपाल मन पराउँछु ।

Exercise 26

Construct sentences about likes and dislikes along the following lines:

	Person	*Colour*	*likes?*
Example:			
	my mother	red	× = मेरी आमालाई रातो रङ मन पर्दैन । ✓ = मेरी आमालाई रातो रङ मन पर्छ ।
1	grandfather	blue	✓
2	my elder sisters	black	×
3	you (High)	green	✓
4	his younger brothers	yellow	×
5	they	purple	✓

53 किन WHY, किनभने BECAUSE

किन ? *why?* can be used on its own to ask a question:

A आज म अफिस जान्छु ।	Today I shall go to the office.
B किन ?	Why?
A उसलाई त्यो पसल मन पर्छ ।	He likes that shop.
B किन ?	Why?

More commonly, however, **किन ?** *why?* is part of a longer question:

आज तपाईं किन छिटै अफिस जानुहुन्छ ?	Why will you go to the office early today?
उसलाई त्यो पसल किन मन पर्छ ?	Why does he like that shop?

In such questions, the position of **किन ?** depends on what the question asked actually focuses on. In these examples, it focuses on *going to the office* and on *liking*, so it is positioned immediately before them in the sentence. Nepali questions very rarely begin with **किन ?** The replies to such questions generally, however, do begin with **किनभने,** *because*:

किनभने अफिसमा धेरै काम छ ।	Because there is a lot of work at the office.
किनभने त्यो पसल अलि सस्तो हुन्छ ।	Because that shop is quite cheap.

किनभने *because* can of course be used in a sentence to link a cause and its effect:

म गाईको मासु खाँदिन किनभने म हिन्दू हुँ ।	I do not eat beef because I am a Hindu.
ऊ नेपाली बोल्दैन किनभने ऊ हिन्दीभाषी हो ।	He does not speak Nepali because he is a Hindi speaker.

Exercise 27

पढेर बुझ्नुहोस् (Read and understand)

The following is your first encounter with a passage of connected prose. Look up any unfamiliar words in the Nepali–English glossary at the back of the book, and then answer the questions that follow in Nepali.

हामी नेवार हौं । हाम्रो घर एउटा सानो शहरमा छ । शहरको नाम साँखु हो । काठ्माडौंदेखि हाम्रो घर अलि टाढा छ । तर बा हरेक दिन काठ्माडौं जानुहुन्छ । वहाँको अफिस त्यहाँ छ । कहिलेकाहीं म बासँग जान्छु । म हरेक दिन जान्नँ । भोलि म बासँग जान्छु किनभने भोलि धेरै किनमेल छ । म बालाई मदत गर्छु । मा कहिल्यै पनि काठ्माडौं जानुहुन्न । वहाँ घरै बस्नुहुन्छ र घरको काम गर्नुहुन्छ । हामीहरूका लागि वहाँ भात पकाउनुहुन्छ । मालाई दुईजना बहिनी मदत गर्छन् । हाम्रो घरनजिक एउटा धारा छ । हरेक दिन बेलुकातिर कान्छी बहिनी गाग्री लिन्छे र धारा जान्छे । गाग्री भर्छे र घर ल्याउँछे । बारीमा इनार छ, तर हामीहरू कहिल्यै पनि इनारको पानी खान्नौं । अर्को शहरका मान्छेहरू धेरैजसो बिरामी हुन्छन् किनभने उनीहरू इनारको पानी खान्छन् ।

प्रश्नहरू **(QUESTIONS)**

१ हामी कहाँ बस्छौं ?

२ भोलि म बासँग किन शहर जान्छु ?

३ मा काठ्माडौं जानुहुन्छ ?

४ घरमा मा के गर्नुहुन्छ ?

५ बेलुका को धारा जान्छ ?

६ अर्को शहरका मान्छेहरू किन धेरैजसो बिरामी हुन्छन् ?

The most important things for the reader to remember

1 The comparative term **भन्दा** is used as a postposition to compare two entities but Nepali speakers use it in two different ways. The first example is **नेपालभन्दा युके ठूलो छ** 'compared to Nepal the UK is big' and the second example is **युके नेपालभन्दा ठूलो छ** 'The UK is bigger than Nepal'.

2 The Nepali superlative is **सबभन्दा,** which means 'compared to all' or 'the most' followed by adjectives, e.g. **सगरमाथा सबभन्दा अग्लो पहाड हो** 'Everest is the highest mountain'.

3 Likes and dislikes in Nepali are expressed by the impersonal verb **मन पर्नु** or **मन नपर्नु.** Note that the person or subject who likes or dislikes takes **लाई**, an object marker, e.g. **मलाई नेपाल मन पर्छ** 'I like Nepal'.

8 म हिजो आएँ

I came yesterday

In this unit you will learn:

- ***how to use the simple past tense of verbs***
- ***how to use the agentive suffix** -le*
- ***how to name the parts of the body***

15 Sandhya drops by

08.01

Sandhya has come to call on her friend Asha. She had also called at the house the morning before, but had been surprised to find it deserted. She asks Asha where she was. Asha explains.

सन्ध्या	हिजो तपाईं कहाँ जानुभयो ?
आशा	हिजो म कतै गइनँ । घरै बसें ।
सन्ध्या	तर हिजो बिहान म तपाईंकहाँ आएँ । घरमा कोही पनि थिएन ।
आशा	तपाईं मकहाँ कति बजे आउनुभयो ?
सन्ध्या	म सात, होइन, साढे सात बजेतिर आएँ । म अलि ढिलो भएँ ।
आशा	अब सम्झें ! अस्ति बुवा, आमा र भाइहरू केही दिनका लागि नेपालगंज गए । हिजो शनिवार थियो, होइन ?
सन्ध्या	हो, शनिवार थियो ।
आशा	शनिवार बिहान म सधैं मन्दिर जान्छु । अनि हिजो बिहान हामीहरू साढे पाँच बजेतिर पशुपतिनाथको मन्दिर गयौं । घरमा कोही थिएन ।
सन्ध्या	तपाईं हरेक शनिवार पशुपतिनाथ जानुहुन्छ ?
आशा	होइन । अस्ति शनिवार म वज्रयोगिनीको मन्दिर गएँ । कहिलेकाहीं म चाँगुनारायण पनि जान्छु ।
सन्ध्या	हिजो कोसँग जानुभयो ?
आशा	म धेरैजसो एक्लै जान्छु तर अस्ति मेरी दिदी बाग्लुङ्बाट आइन् । अब केही दिनसम्म हाम्रो घरमा बस्छिन् । हामी सँगसँगै मन्दिर गयौं । निक्कै रमाइलो भयो नि ।
सन्ध्या	मन्दिरमा भीड थियो ?
आशा	थिएन । शनिवार सात बजेपछि मात्र त्यहाँ भीड हुन्छ । हामीहरू त बिहानै गयौं अनि भीड थिएन ।

सन्ध्या	तर तपाईंहरू पशुपतिबाट सीधै फर्कनुभएन, होइन ? म तपाईंको ढोकामा आधा घण्टासम्म पर्खें तर पनि तपाईंहरू आउनुभएन । आखिर म निराश भएँ अनि घर फर्कें।
आशा	बीचबाटोमा ठूलो पानी पऱ्यो । हामीहरूसँग छाता थिएन । हामी केही बेरसम्म एउटा रूखको ओतमा बस्यौं । तपाईं भिज्नुभयो ? माफ गर्नुहोला ?
सन्ध्या	होइन, केही छैन । मसँग छाता थियो । यतातिर आकाश अँध्यारो भयो र सिमसिमे पानी मात्रै पऱ्यो ।
आशा	हवस् त दिदी । आज त भेट भयो नि । बस्नुहोस्, चिया लिनुहोस्, सबै खबर सुनाउनुहोस् ।

Quick vocab

हिजो	yesterday
कतै	anywhere
घरै	at home
मकहाँ	my place, my home
तपाईंकहाँ	your place, your home
कोही	someone
सम्झनु	to remember
तर पनि	but even so
आखिर	in the end
निराश	without hope
बीचबाटोमा	on the way
ठूलो पानी	heavy rain
बेर	time (a quantity of)
रूख	tree
अस्ति	day before yesterday
केही	a few, some
पशुपतिनाथको मन्दिर	Pashupatinath temple
वज्रयोगिनीको मन्दिर	Bajra Yogini temple
चाँगुनारायण	Changu Narayan (a temple)
सँगसँगै	together, each with the other
रमाइलो	enjoyable
सीधै	directly, straight
आधा	half
पर्खुन	to wait
ओत	shelter*
भिज्नु	to get wet
माफ गर्नु	to forgive

छाता	umbrella
आकाश	sky
सिमसिमे पानी	light rain
भेट हुनु	to meet up
खबर	news
सुनाउनु	to tell, relate

* Nepali has two words for shelter: **ओत** means *shelter from the rain*, while **छायाँ** means *shelter from the sun*.

Sandhya	Where did you go yesterday?
Asha	I didn't go anywhere yesterday. I stayed at home.
Sandhya	But I came to your place yesterday morning. There was no one in the house.
Asha	What time did you come to my place?
Sandhya	I came at seven, no, at about half past 7. I was a bit late.
Asha	Now I've remembered! The day before yesterday Father, Mother and my younger brothers went to Nepalganj for a few days. Yesterday was Saturday, wasn't it?
Sandhya	Yes, it was Saturday.
Asha	On Saturday morning I always go to the temple. And yesterday morning we went to Pashupatinath temple at about half past 5. There was no one at home.
Sandhya	Do you go to Pashupatinath every Saturday?
Asha	No. Last Saturday I went to Bajra Yogini temple. Sometimes I go to Changu Narayan temple too.
Sandhya	Who did you go with yesterday?
Asha	I usually go alone but the day before yesterday my elder sister came from Baglung. Now she will stay a few days in our house. We went to the temple together. It was very enjoyable, you know.
Sandhya	Was there a crowd at the temple?
Asha	No. There's a crowd there only after 7 o'clock on a Saturday. We went very early, so there wasn't a crowd.
Sandhya	But you didn't come straight back from Pashupati, did you? I waited at your door for half an hour but even so you did not come. In the end I lost hope and I went back home.
Asha	On the way back it rained heavily. We didn't have an umbrella. We sat in the shelter of a tree for a while. Did you get wet? Will you forgive me?

Sandhya	No, it doesn't matter. I had an umbrella. Over here the sky became dark and only light rain fell.
Asha	All right then sister. Today we have met up anyway. Please sit down, have some tea, tell me all the news.

Grammar

54 THE SIMPLE PAST TENSE

The *simple past* tense refers to actions and events that happened in the past, or describes situations and conditions that were true in the past. It usually corresponds with the English *I went, you came, he said, they were, it was*, etc., but can also sometimes be similar to the English present perfect: *I've gone, the rain has come.*

● INSIGHT

Learn and use the expressions बुझ्नुभयो ? 'Did you understand?', बुझें 'I understood' or बुझिनँ 'I did not understand' in class. This will help you learn the past tense conjugation without any difficulty.

Past tense verb bases

The past tense bases of all C-verbs and most V-verbs are the same as the present tense bases (that is, they are formed by taking the dictionary form and dropping the ending -नु – see **Grammar 33**). However, there are four particular V-verbs which form their past tense bases differently. These are:

Verb	Present tense base	Past tense base
धुनु to wash	धु-	धो-
रुनु to weep	रु-	रो-
जानु to go	जा-	ग-
हुनु to be	हु-	थि- or भ-

These four verbs take the same endings as all other verbs. It should also be noted that the final -**a** of the present tense base of the V-verb बिर्सनु *to forget* is dropped before the past tense ending is added:

Verb	Present tense base	Past tense base
बिर्सनु to forget	बिर्स- **birsa-**	बिर्स्- **birs-**

The bases of VV-verbs in past tenses are shortened forms of the present tense verb bases (see **Grammar 33**). The second vowel of the present tense base is dropped to form the past tense base:

VV-verb	Present tense base	Past tense base
आउनु to come	आउ–	आ–
पकाउनु to cook	पकाउ–	पका–
पिउनु to drink	पिउ–	पि–

Past tense verb endings

The simple past tense is formed by taking the past tense base of a verb and adding an ending to it. As always, the choice of ending depends upon what or who the subject of the verb is, and the endings must be learned by heart. They are:

	Affirmative		Negative	
Singular				
म	–एँ	**-ã**	–इनँ	**-inã**
हामी, हामीहरू	–यौं	**-yaũ**	–एनौं	**-enaũ**
तँ	–इस्	**-is**	–इनस्	**-inas**
तिमी, तिमीहरू	–यौ	**-yau**	–एनौ	**-enau**
ऊ, यो, त्यो (m.)	–यो	**-yo**	–एन	**-ena**
ऊ, यो, त्यो (f.)	–ई	**-ī**	–इन	**-ina**
उनी, यिनी, तिनी (m.)	–ए	**-e**	–एनन्	**-enan**
उनी, यिनी, तिनी (f.)	–इन्	**-in**	–इनन्	**-inan**
यी, ती, उनीहरू etc.	–ए	**-e**	–एनन्	**-enan**

The boxes that follow contain the simple past tense forms of the VV-verb आउनु *to come* and the irregular V-verb जानु *to go*.

आउनु ***to come***

	Affirmative (I came, you came, etc.)	*Negative (I did not come, you did not come, etc.)*
म	आ + -एँ = आएँ	आ + -इनँ = आइनँ
हामी, हामीहरू	आ + -यौं = आयौं	आ + -एनौं = आएनौं
तँ	आ + -इस् = आइस्	आ + -इनस् = आइनस्
तिमी, तिमीहरू	आ + -यौ = आयौ	आ + -एनौ = आएनौ
ऊ, यो, त्यो (m.)	आ + -यो = आयो	आ + -एन = आएन
ऊ, यो, त्यो (f.)	आ + -ई = आई	आ + -इन = आइन
उनी, यिनी, तिनी (m.)	आ + -ए = आए	आ + -एनन् = आएनन्
उनी, यिनी, तिनी (f.)	आ + -इन् = आइन्	आ + -इनन् = आइनन्
यी, ती, उनीहरू etc.	आ + -ए = आए	आ + -एनन् = आएनन्

जानु *to go*

	Affirmative (I went, you went, etc.)	*Negative (I did not go, you did not go, etc.)*
म	ग + -एँ = गएँ	ग + -इनँ = गइनँ
हामी, हामीहरू	ग + -यौं = गयौं	ग + -एनौं = गएनौं
तँ	ग + -इस् = गइस्	ग + -इनस् = गइनस्
तिमी, तिमीहरू	ग + -यौ = गयौ	ग + -एनौ = गएनौ
ऊ, यो, त्यो (m.)	ग + -यो = गयो	ग + -एन = गएन
ऊ, यो, त्यो (f.)	ग + -ई = गई	ग + -इन = गइन
उनी, यिनी, तिनी (m.)	ग + -ए = गए	ग + -एनन् = गएनन्
उनी, यिनी, तिनी (f.)	ग + -इन् = गइन्	ग + -इनन् = गइनन्
उनी, यिनी, तिनी (f.)	ग + -इन् = गइन्	ग + -इनन् = गइनन्
यी, ती, उनीहरू etc.	ग + -ए = गए	ग + -एनन् = गएनन्

The High forms of the simple past tense consist of the dictionary form of a verb (हुनु, आउनु, जानु etc.), combined with:

– the suffix -भयो in the affirmative

– the suffix -भएन in the negative.

These forms are always the same, regardless of the number and gender of their subject.

High forms

आउनु to come

Affirmative	*Negative*
आउनु + -भयो = आउनुभयो	आउनु + -भएन = आउनुभएन

जानु to go

Affirmative	*Negative*
जानु + -भयो = जानुभयो	जानु + -भएन = जानुभएन

Note the following examples in which the Nepali simple past tense must be translated with the English present perfect tense:

पानी आयो !	It has begun to rain!
गुरुजी आउनुभयो ?	Has Guruji arrived?
बत्ती गयो !	Power cut!*

Note *Power cuts are an unfortunate feature of daily life in Nepal. बत्ती means *lamp* but by extension it is also used to mean *electric light*. When power is restored after a power cut, the cry is बत्ती आयो !

55 THE SIMPLE PAST FORMS OF हुनु TO BE: थियो AND भयो

	थि-		*भ-*	
	Affirmative	*Negative*	*Affirmative*	*Negative*
म	थिएँ	थिइनँ	भएँ	भइनँ
हामी, हामीहरू	थियौं	थिएनौं	भयौं	भएनौं
तँ	थिइस्	थिइनस्	भइस्	भइनस्
तिमी, तिमीहरू	थियौ	थिएनौ	भयौ	भएनौ
ऊ, यो, त्यो (m.)	थियो	थिएन	भयो	भएन
ऊ, यो, त्यो (f.)	थिई	थिइन	भई	भइन
उनी, यिनी, तिनी (m.)	थिए	थिएनन्	भए	भएनन्
उनी, यिनी, तिनी (f.)	थिइन्	थिइनन्	भइन्	भइनन्
यी, ती, उनीहरू etc.	थिए	थिएनन्	भए	भएनन्
High forms				
तपाईं, तपाईंहरू etc.	हुनुहुन्थ्यो	हुनुहुन्नथ्यो	हुनुभयो	हुनुभएन

The simple past tense of the verb **हुनु** *to be* has two forms. The **थियो** form translates as *was* or *were*, and this form of the verb is used to talk about situations and conditions in the past:

हिजो म नेपालमा थिइनँ, अमेरिकामा थिएँ ।	Yesterday I was not in Nepal, I was in America.
भात जूठो थिएन, चोखो थियो ।	The food was not polluted, it was pure.*

* The word **जूठो** is loosely translated as *polluted*. Any food that has come into contact with someone's mouth – either directly, or indirectly via a hand or a utensil – is considered **जूठो** and therefore may not be eaten by any other person. This everyday concern about cleanliness and hygiene is given a deeper meaning by notions of caste and ritual purity. The observance of this rule is traditionally stricter among higher Hindu castes such as the Bahuns than among, for instance, the various Tibeto-Burman-speaking ethnic groups, and it also varies between families and social classes. While parents and elder siblings may share food with the younger children of a family, as an outsider you should observe these rules unless and until you know for sure that the people with whom you are eating do not observe them so strictly themselves. Food should be touched only with the right hand, because the left hand is used for ablutions.

हिजोको मौसम असाध्है नराम्रो थियो ।	Yesterday's weather was very bad.
धन बहादुरका दुईजना छोरा थिए ।	Dhan Bahadur had two sons.

The **भयो** form refers to changes, events and transformations in the past and may often be translated as *happened* or *became:*

ऊ लाटो थियो, पछि त पण्डित भयो ।	He was stupid, but later he became a Pandit.
खाना तातो थियो, पछि त चिसो भयो ।	The food was hot, but then it became cold.

ऊ सुखी थियो, पछि त दुखी भयो ।	He was happy, but later he became sad.
कोठा फोहोर थियो, पछि पनि सफा भएन ।	The room was dirty, and later it didn't become clean either.
ओहो गोविन्दजी, तपाईंलाई के भयो ? मलाई त केही भएन ।	Oho Govindajī, what happened to you? Nothing has happened to me.

The following pairs of statements illustrate the difference in the meaning of the two forms:

मेरी बहिनी बिरामी थिइन् ।	My sister was ill.
मेरी बहिनी बिरामी भइन् ।	My sister became ill.
कोठामा गर्मी थियो ।	It was hot in the room.
कोठामा गर्मी भयो ।	It became hot in the room.
पसलहरू बन्द थिए ।	The shops were shut.
पसलहरू बन्द भए ।	The shops became shut.

भयो and भएन are commonly used on their own to tell someone that something has or has not been done or completed, when both speakers know what it is that they are talking about. For instance, **A** and **B**, who are both staying in the same hotel, had previously been discussing **B**'s difficulty in getting an air ticket. **A** sees **B** coming back to the hotel, and he knows that he has been to the airline office. Instead of asking him *did you succeed in booking your ticket?* all he needs to say is:

A भयो ? Did it happen?/Any luck?

to which **B** will give one of the following replies:

B भयो ! Yes, it's done! or **B** भएन ! No, no luck!

56 LOCATION AND MOVEMENT

Nepali has two sets of words that mean *here, there,* and *where*. The first, ending in -हाँ, refers mainly to static locations, while the second, ending in -ता, is most commonly used with verbs of motion:

यहाँ	here, in this place	यता	over here, in this direction, hither
त्यहाँ	there, in that place	उता	over there, in that direction, thither
कहाँ	where, in which place	कता	in which direction? whither?
कहीं	somewhere, in any place	कतै	to somewhere, in any direction

57 SOMETHING AND SOMEONE: THE USES OF केही AND कोही

As an adjective, केही means *some* or *a few:*

केही दिन	a few days	केही पैसा	some money
केही मान्छेहरू	some people	केही न केही	something or other

As an adjective, **कोही** also means *some*, but can only be used with human nouns, and usually in the singular:

कोही मान्छे	some man (whom I do not know)
कोही न कोही	someone or other

Much more commonly, these two words are used as third person pronouns, and they can be understood to have the following meanings, depending on the kind of sentence they occur in:

	Affirmative statement	***Negative statement***	***Question***
केही	something	nothing	anything
कोही	someone	no one	anyone

घरमा कोही छ ? घरमा कोही छैन । उनीहरू बगैंचामा छन् ।	Is there anyone in the house? There is no one in the house. They are in the garden.
तिम्रो हातमा के छ ? मेरो हातमा केही छैन आमा ।	What do you have in your hand? I don't have anything in my hand, mother.

In negative sentences **पनि** *even,* also can be added to both **केही** and **कोही** to heighten the negativity of the sentence: *nothing at all, nobody whatsoever:*

मेरो हातमा केही पनि छैन ।	I don't have anything at all in my hand.
घरमा कोही पनि छैन ।	There is no one at all in the house.

Exercise 28

Translate into Nepali:

1 Please open the window, it has become very hot in this room.

2 Yesterday morning the children were all here. But today no one came to school at all.

3 Last Wednesday it rained heavily. I didn't have an umbrella, and I got soaked.

4 Grandfather had two sons. One was called Prakash and one was called Niroj. Prakash became very rich but Niroj was very poor.

5 The people of that country were very poor and there was nothing at all in their houses.

6 Yesterday many people went to Paśupatināth temple, because yesterday was a full moon day **(pūrṇimā)**.

16 A visit from Shankarprasad

08.02

Shankarprasad Acharya is a priest and teacher of high social status. Motilal phoned Shankarprasad Acharya a little earlier, to invite him to his house. He is anxious to cultivate good relations with such a man. Shankarprasad Acharya has just arrived, but the domestic arrangements are not running smoothly.

मोतीलाल	आचार्यजी, नमस्कार । आरामै हुनुहुन्छ ?
शंकरप्रसाद	आराम । तपाईं नि ?
मोतीलाल	मलाई राम्रो छ । बस्नुहोस्, के लिनुहुन्छ तपाईं ?
शंकरप्रसाद	तपाईं जे लिनुहुन्छ म त्यही नै लिन्छु नि ।
मोतीलाल	हवस् त । एकै छिन । म श्रीमतीलाई खबर गर्छु । आज उनले के के पकाइन् मलाई थाहा भएन । म सोध्छु, है ?... ए, अंजु, अंजु, तिमी कता गयौ हँ ? खाना तयार भएन ?
अंजु	हजुर ? म भरखरै बजारबाट आएँ । के गर्नु र, काम धेरै छ । म एक्लै छु । म पहिला चिया तयार गर्छु नि । तपाईंहरू बस्नुहोला ।
मोतीलाल	ओहो कस्तो ढिलो भयो आज । मैले वहाँलाई घरमा बोलाएँ । वहाँ टाढाबाट आउनुभयो, तर तिमीले खाना पकाएनौ ।
अंजु	सुन्नुहोस् । मलाई गाली नगर्नुहोस् । घरमा अरू पनि धेरै काम थियो ।
मोतीलाल	ठीक छ, ठीक छ, अब चाँडै गर । ... आचार्यजी, माफ गर्नुहोला । पहिला चिया लिनुहुन्छ कि ?
शंकरप्रसाद	हुन्छ, हुन्छ । केही छैन ।
मोतीलाल	ए ल चिया पनि आइपुग्यो । बिस्कुट पनि लिनुहुन्छ कि ?
शंकरप्रसाद	हुन्छ । एउटा दिनुहोस् न ।

Quick vocab

आचार्यजी	a respectful title for a religious teacher or a learned man
आरामै	in good health (polite)
जे	that which
त्यही	that same (emphasized form of **त्यो** that)
एकै	just one
खबर गर्नु	to inform

सोध्नु	to ask
तयार	ready
भरखरै	recently, just now
बोलाउनु	to call, invite
गाली गर्नु	to tell off, abuse
अरू	other, additional
चाँडै गर्नु	to do immediately
माफ गर्नु	to forgive
पहिला	firstly
आइपुग्नु	to arrive
बिस्कुट	biscuit

Motilal	Acharyaji, greetings. Are you well?
Shankarprasad	I am well. And you?
Motilal	I am well. Please sit down, what would you like?*1
Shankarprasad	I will have whatever you are going to have.
Motilal	That's fine then. Just one moment. I will tell my wife. I don't know what*2 she has cooked today. I'll ask her, all right? … Oh, Anju, Anju, where have you gone, huh?*3 Isn't the food ready?
Anju	What? I have only just come from the market. What to do, indeed, there's lots of work. I am all alone. I'll prepare tea first, for sure. You people please sit down.
Motilal	Oh, how late things are today! I invited him to our home. He came from far away, but you didn't cook any food.
Anju	Listen. Don't tell me off. There was a lot of other work in the house.
Motilal	OK, OK, now do it immediately … Acharyaji, please forgive (me). Will you first take tea?
Shankarprasad	Yes, yes. It doesn't matter.
Motilal	There now, the tea has arrived too. Would you like a biscuit as well?
Shankarprasad	Yes. Please give me one, would you?

*1 के लिनुहुन्छ ? *what will you take?* is a more polite way of asking someone what they would like to eat or drink than के खानुहुन्छ *what will you eat?*

*2 के is repeated because Motilal expects his wife to have cooked a number of different things.

*3 Motilal and his wife Anju are a traditional couple in that their use of pronouns is asymmetical: he addresses her as **तिमी**, while she calls him **तपाईं**. Less traditional couples nowadays address one another as **तिमी**.

Grammar

58 TRANSITIVE AND INTRANSITIVE VERBS

All Nepali verbs are either transitive or intransitive. When using the simple past tense of any verb it is important to know which category the verb belongs to.

A transitive verb is a verb that must have an object. For instance, we cannot *see* without seeing *something*, and that something is the object of our seeing: it receives the action of our seeing. We cannot *eat*, or *do*, or *make*, or *look*, without something being *eaten, done, made* or *looked at*: therefore, all of these verbs, plus many others, are said to be 'transitive' because they act upon something, which is their object.

An intransitive verb is a verb that cannot have an object. For instance, all verbs of motion are intransitive: we may go *to* a place, or come *from* a place, but these places are not receivers of the action of motion; they are simply destinations or sources.

> **● INSIGHT**
>
> **If you are not sure whether a Nepali verb is transitive or intransitive, think about whether you can use the word 'what' with it. A verb that you can use with 'what' is always transitive and one which you can't use with 'what' is an intransitive verb. भेट्नु 'to meet' is an exception because it takes 'who' not 'what'.**

59 TRANSITIVE VERBS AND THE SUFFIX –ले

The subject of a transitive verb in the simple past tense must take the agentive (or 'subject-marking') suffix –ले. Linguistically, –ले is a relic of an old passive construction, and it has the original meaning of *by*. Because –ले is a postposition, the subject word must change to the oblique case when –ले is added to it. म and तँ take special forms when –ले is added to them:

म	becomes	मै	producing	मैले
तँ	becomes	तैँ	producing	तैँले

All of the other pronouns change in exactly the same way as they do with other postpositions:

ऊ	becomes	उस	producing	उसले	(often pronounced **ulle**)
यो	becomes	यस	producing	यसले	(often pronounced **elle**)
त्यो	becomes	त्यस	producing	त्यसले	(often pronounced **telle**)
को	becomes	कस	producing	कसले	(often pronounced **kalle**)
उनी	becomes	उन	producing	उनले	
यिनी	becomes	यिन	producing	यिनले	
तिनी	becomes	तिन	producing	तिनले	

मैले काम गरें ।	I worked.
हामीले फिलिम हेऱ्यौं ।	We watched a film.

उसले मलाई नमस्ते गरेन ।	He did not greet me.
उनीहरूले एउटा चिठी पनि लेखेनन् ।	They did not write even one letter.
तपाईंले उनलाई उपहार दिनुभयो ?	Did you give her a present?

Some commonly used verbs are a combination of a noun with either the verb **गर्नु** *to do* or the verb **हुनु** *to be*. Such a verb is transitive with **गर्नु** but intransitive with **हुनु**:

उनीहरूले सिनेमा-घर बन्द गरे ।	They shut the cinema.
सिनेमा-घर बन्द भयो ।	The cinema closed.
हामीहरूले काम शुरु गर्‍यौं ।	We started work.
काम शुरु भयो ।	The work began.
सरकारले हडताल खतम गर्‍यो ।	The government stopped the strike.
हडताल खतम भयो ।	The strike ended.

• INSIGHT

ले is also used with animals for their transitive verb actions even when it is in the present or future tense, e.g. गाईले दूध दिन्छ 'The cow gives milk'.

Exercise 29

Put the following sentences into the simple past tense, beginning each new sentence with the word **हिजो** *yesterday* and removing the word **आज** *today*:

१ आज तपाईं चिया खानुहुन्न ?

२ आज म एउटा किताब किन्छु ।

३ आज हामीहरू मासु खाँदैनौं ।

४ आज उनीहरू भात खाँदैनन् । उनीहरूको घरमा चामल छैन ।

५ आज तिमी रेडियो किन सुन्दैनौ ? आज अम्बर गुरुङ्ग गीत गाउनुहुन्छ ।

६ आज आमा उठ्नुहुन्न । वहाँ बिरामी हुनुहुन्छ ।

60 FURTHER USES OF -ले

a With the subject of a transitive verb in tenses other than the past

-ले must always be affixed to the subject of a transitive verb in the simple past tense, but it can also be used to emphasize the subject of a transitive verb in the habitual present tense in the following circumstances:

- if the sentence says that it is part of the natural order of things for the subject to perform the verb, and therefore states that this is a role that is specific to the subject:

कुखुराले फुल पार्छ ।	A chicken lays eggs.
बाघले बाखा खान्छ ।	A tiger eats goats.

घामले न्यानो दिन्छ । Sunshine gives warmth.

पक्का बाहुनले रक्सी खाँदैन । A proper Brahmin does not drink alcohol.

- if the sentence is a question asking who or what is the subject of a transitive verb:

कसले त्यो कुरा भन्छ ? Who says that?

आज कसले चिया बनाउँछ ? Who will make the tea today?

- if the sentence is a response to a question such as those above, or focuses in any way upon the subject of the verb:

आमाले भन्नुहुन्छ नि । Mother says so, you know!

आज भाइले चिया बनाउँछ । Today younger brother will make the tea.

b To denote the use of faculties or instruments

हामी कानले सुन्छौं । We hear with (our) ears.

हामी दाँतले टोक्छौं । We bite with (our) teeth.

हामी आँखाले हेर्छौं । We look with (our) eyes.

हामी मुखले बोल्छौं । We speak with (our) mouths.

हामी नाकले सुँघ्छौं । We smell with (our) noses.

नेपालीहरू दाहिने हातले भात खान्छन् । Nepalis eat rice with (the) right hand.

नेपालीहरू देब्रे हातले भात खाँदैनन् । Nepalis do not eat rice with (the) left hand.

c With nouns to mark a causal function

यस कारणले because of this

त्यस कारणले because of that

के कारणले ? because of what?

The phrases **त्यस कारणले** and **यस कारणले** mean *due to that cause* and *due to this cause* respectively, and they are commonly used to mean *so* or *thus:*

ऊ कलिलो उमेरको केटा हो । यस कारणले उसलाई चुरोट नदिनुहोला । He is a boy of a tender age. So please do not give him a cigarette.

पोहोर साल कम पानी पऱ्यो । त्यस कारणले बजारमा चामल साह्रै महंगो भयो । Last year little rain fell. Therefore rice became very expensive in the market.

The abbreviated forms of this phrase, **त्यस कारण** and **त्यसैले,** are very commonly used.

Other nouns can take **–ले** when they are the cause of an event or a condition, regardless of whether the main verb of the sentence is transitive or not:

अनिकालको बेलामा धेरै मानिसहरू भोकले मर्छन् । In time of famine, many people die of hunger.

मेरा लुगा पानीले भिज्यो । My clothes were made wet by rain.

• INSIGHT

भयो can be translated in English as 'was' to mark a process or change from one state to another as opposed to थियो, which marks a state of being. Also भयो as a verb is used with age and marriage as well as an expression for 'it is fine' or 'it is enough'.

Exercise 30

पढेर बुझ्नुहोस्

अस्ति शनिवार थियो । नेपालमा शनिवार बिदा हुन्छ र अस्ति सबै पसल र अफिसहरू बन्द थिए । त्यो दिन ठूलो पानी पनि पऱ्यो । रामसँग छाता थिएन, ऊ बाहिर गएन । उसले एउटा किताब पढ्यो । हिजो आइतवार थियो । नेपालमा आइतवार बिदाको दिन हुँदैन । हिजो पानी परेन र राम अफिस गयो । रामको बुवा पनि अफिस जानुभयो । रामकी आमा बिहानै मन्दिर जानुभयो । मन्दिरमा वहाँले पूजा गर्नुभयो र आठ बजेतिर घर फर्कनुभयो । राम र रामकी बहिनी माया साढे छ बजे उठे । उनीहरूले चिया र रोटी खाए । "अब म अफिस जान्छु र बाटोमा म एउटा छाता किन्छु" रामले भन्यो ।

प्रश्नहरू

१ अस्ति के वार थियो ?

२ अस्तिको मौसम कस्तो थियो ?

३ अस्ति रामले के गऱ्यो ?

४ हिजो के वार थियो ?

५ हिजो राम कता गयो ?

६ हिजो रामकी आमा कहाँ जानुभयो ?

७ राम र माया कति बजेसम्म सुते ?

61 PARTS OF THE BODY

HEAD

टाउको	head
मुख, अनुहार	face
आँखा	eye
नाक	nose
मुख	mouth
कान	ear
कपाल	hair
दाँत	tooth
जिब्रो	tongue
घाँटी	neck/throat

ARMS

पाखुरा	upper arm
हात	hand/forearm
औंला	finger
कुहिनो	elbow
नङ	fingernail
बूढी औंला	thumb

LEGS

खुट्टा	leg
खुट्टा	foot

चिउँडो	chin
दाह्री	beard

घुँडा	knee
कुर्कुच्चा	heel
औंला	toe

BODY

शरीर	body
पिठ्यूँ	back
पेट	stomach
छाती	breast/chest
काँध	shoulder
कम्मर	waist
मुटु	heart
फोक्सो	lung

OTHER

रगत	blood
छाला	skin
हाड	bone

The most important things for the reader to remember

1 The simple past tense is used to refer to actions or events that happened in the past but there is a different tense to express actions or events that take place even further back in the past. It is called the past perfect or pluperfect tense (see Unit 12).

2 The conjugation of the simple past tense is formed by adding the past markers to the verb stem except for polite form of pronouns that take the whole infinitive plus **भयो** or **भएन**, e.g. **म गएँ-गइनँ** 'I went – I did not go', **तपाईं जानुभयो-जानुभएन** 'you went – you did not go'.

3 The suffix **ले** is used with the subjects of transitive verbs in the past tense, but never with the subjects of intransitive verbs, e.g. **मैले खाएँ** 'I ate' and **म गएँ** 'I went'. **खानु** is a transitive verb and **जानु** is an intransitive verb.

4 **ले** is also used to mark the instrument or body part with which an action is done, e.g. **कलमले लेख्नु** 'to write with a pen' or **हातले खानु** 'to eat with (one's) hand'.

5 **थियो** is used to indicate the condition of something in the past but Hk;ks indicates a process or a change from one condition to another in the past, e.g. **बीस बर्ष अघि ऊ जवान थियो, अहिले बूढो भयो** 'He was young 20 years ago, now he has become old'.

6 Although they may be classified as portable items, Nepali uses the same pattern for the ownership of parts of the body as it does for non-portable items such as houses or cars, e.g. **मेरो एउटा नाक छ ।** 'I have one nose'. This is presumably because one's ownership of one's body is a lifelong proposition!

9 म भात खाएर जान्छु
I'll go when I've eaten

In this unit you will learn:

- ▶ *how to use two verbs in one sentence*
- ▶ *how to report information from other sources*
- ▶ *how to use the continuous tenses of verbs*
- ▶ *how to discuss people's ages*

17 A day off work

09.01

Rajiv has just completed his first week at the office. He and Keshav discuss plans for their day off.

राजीव	भोलि हाम्रो छुट्टी होइन र ?
केशव	हो । भोलि त शनिवारै हो नि ! शनिवार हरेक अफिसको लागि छुट्टीको दिन हुन्छ । तपाईं छुट्टी लिनुहुन्न कि कसो ?
राजीव	लिन्छु नि ! तपाईं धेरैजसो छुट्टीको दिन कसरी बिताउनुहुन्छ ? दिनभरि सुत्नुहुन्छ ?
केशव	दिनभरि सुत्दिन । जिन्दगी त्यति लामो हुँदैन ! म छुट्टीका दिनहरू धेरैजसो केही-न-केही गरेर अथवा कतै-न-कतै गएर बिताउँछु । कहिलेकाहीं म अफिसका केही साथीहरूलाई भेटेर बाहिर जान्छु । आज बिहान मैले दौलतजीसँग कुरा गरें । भोलि पनि यस्तै कार्यक्रम छ रे ।
राजीव	भोलिको कार्यक्रम कहाँ छ नि ?

केशव	उनीहरू गोदावरी जान्छन् रे ।
राजीव	तपाईं पनि जानुहुन्छ कि ?
केशव	म कोसिस गर्छु । भोलि बिहान मेरी श्रीमती बजार जान्छिन् रे । त्यसैले भोलि बिहान म घरै बसेर नानीहरूलाई हेर्छु ।
राजीव	तपाईंका साथीहरू हिंडेरै जान्छन् ? अलि टाढा छ, होइन ?
केशव	हो, टाढै छ । उनीहरू बस चढेर जान्छन् रे । गोदावरीका बसहरू घण्टा-घण्टामा पाटन भएर जान्छन् रे ।
राजीव	गोदावरी पुगेर उनीहरू के गर्छन् ?
केशव	उनीहरू यहाँबाट केही खाने कुरा लिएर जान्छन् रे । केही हप्ता अधि हामीहरू पिकनिकको लागि सुन्दरीजल पनि गयौं । सुन्दरीजल पुगेर हामीहरूले खोलाको बगरमा बसेर खाना खायौं अनि रमाइलो गऱ्यौं । केही साथीहरूले रूखको छायाँमा बसेर ताश खेले अथवा गफ गरे । केही साथीहरू भुईंमा पल्टेर निदाए । त्यस्तै हो । भोलि तपाईं पनि गोदावरी जानुहुन्छ कि ?
राजीव	भोलि बिहान ससुरालीमा निम्तो छ । त्यस कारणले अप्ठ्यारो छ । उनीहरू कति बजेतिर हिंड्छन् ?
केशव	त्यो त अहिलेसम्म पक्का भएन । बेलुकातिर म दौलतजीलाई फोन गरेर पता लगाउँछु ।
राजीव	थाहा पाएर मलाई पनि फोन गर्नुहोस्, है त । भरे बेलुका म घरै हुन्छु ।
केशव	हवस् । भरे बेलुका म तपाईंलाई फोन गर्छु । अब त अबेर भयो । आज छुट्टीको दिन होइन, हाकिम रिसाएर हामीलाई गाली गर्नुहुन्छ ।

Quick vocab

छुट्टी	day off, holiday
कसो ?	how? in what manner?
बिताउनु	to spend time
दिनभरि	all day
लामो	long
केही-न-केही	something or other
अथवा	or
कतै-न-कतै	somewhere or other
भेट्नु	to meet
कुरा गर्नु	to talk, converse
कार्यक्रम	programme
रे	a word marking information gathered elsewhere
कोसिस गर्नु	to try

त्यसैले	therefore
नानी	small child
हिँडेरै	on foot
बस चढ्नु	to board a bus
पाटन	the second largest city of the Kathmandu valley
भएर	via
पुग्नु	to reach, arrive
खाने कुरा	things to eat; food
अघि	ago
पिकनिक	picnic
खोला	river
बगर	bank of a river
रमाइलो गर्नु	to enjoy oneself
छायाँ	shade
ताश	cards
खेल्नु	to play
गफ गर्नु	to chat
भुईं	ground
पल्टनु	to lie down
निदाउनु	to fall asleep
ससुराली	the home of a man's parents-in-law
निम्तो	invitation
अप्ठ्यारो	difficult, awkward
फोन गर्नु	to phone
पक्का	decided
पता लगाउनु	to find out
थाहा पाउनु	to find out
है त	OK then?
भरे बेलुका	this evening
हाकिम	boss
रिसाउनु	to become angry

Rajiv	Tomorrow's our day off, isn't it?
Keshav	Yes. Tomorrow *is* Saturday, you know! Saturday is a day off for every office. Won't you take the day off, or what?
Rajiv	I certainly will, you know! How do you usually spend a day off? Do you sleep all day?
Keshav	I do not sleep all day. Life isn't that long! I usually spend my days off doing something or other or going somewhere or other. Sometimes I meet up with

	some office friends and go out. This morning I talked to Daulatji. He says there is just such a programme tomorrow too.
Rajiv	Where is tomorrow's programme then?
Keshav	He says they will go to Godavari.*[1]
Rajiv	Will you go too?
Keshav	I shall try. My wife says she will go to the market tomorrow morning. So tomorrow morning I will stay at home and look after the children.
Rajiv	Will your friends go on foot? It's quite far, isn't it?
Keshav	Yes, it is rather far. They say they will go by bus. Apparently buses for Godavari go every hour, via Patan.
Rajiv	What will they do when they have reached Godavari?
Keshav	They say they will take some food from here. A few weeks ago we took a picnic to Sundarijal too.*[2] When we reached Sundarijal we sat on the riverbank and ate and enjoyed ourselves. Some friends sat in the shade of a tree and played cards or chatted. Some friends lay down on the ground and went to sleep. That's how it is. Will you also go to Godavari tomorrow?
Rajiv	Tomorrow morning we are invited to my in-laws' house. So it's difficult. At about what time will they leave?
Keshav	That has not been decided yet. This evening I'll phone Daulatji and find out.
Rajiv	When you find out please phone me too, OK? I'll be at home this evening.
Keshav	Sure. I'll phone you this evening. But now it's late. Today isn't a day off, the boss will get angry and tell us off.

Notes *[1]A popular picnicking spot in the south of the Kathmandu Valley where there are botanical gardens.

*[2]A beauty spot to the northeast of Kathmandu.

Grammar

62 TWO VERBS WITH THE SAME SUBJECT: THE -एर PARTICIPLE

In English, if a sentence or a part of a sentence (a clause) contains two verbs performed by the same person, both of the verbs take the same tense and the word 'and' is used to link them, e.g. *I came and (I) sat down, I ate the rice and went out.* In Nepali, the first of the two

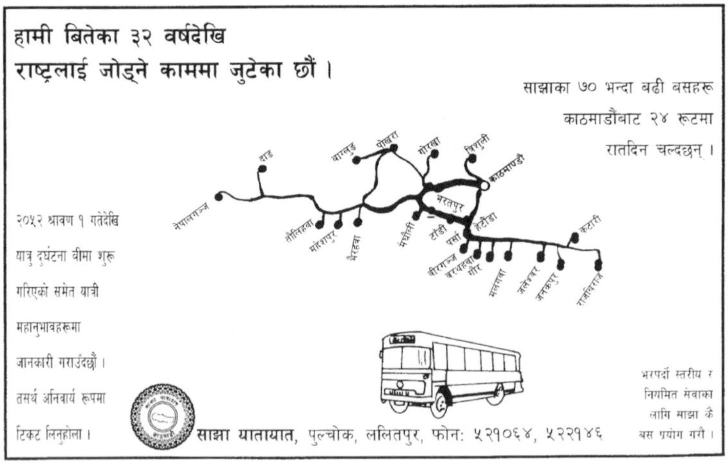

Sājhā bus network map, Nepal

verbs almost always takes a special form (called the 'conjunctive participle'), and the literal translation of the same sentences in Nepali becomes *having come in I sat down* and *having eaten the rice I went out.*

A participle is a form of a verb that may be used adjectivally (to describe nouns) or as one part of a verb phrase in certain tenses. Nepali has a variety of different participles, each with a different ending and its own technical name. In this book, each participle will be referred to by the ending that distinguishes it from all the others.

The conjunctive participle of a Nepali verb is most commonly formed by taking its past tense base and adding the ending -एर **-era** to it. Therefore, we will call it the '**-era** participle':

Verb	***Past tense base***	***-era participle***	
गर्नु	गर-	गरेर	having done
हिँड्नु	हिँड-	हिँडेर	having walked
लिनु	लि-	लिएर	having taken
जानु	ग-	गएर	having gone
आउनु	आ-	आएर	having come
हुनु	भ-	भएर	having become, having been*

Note *The base of हुनु is always भ- for a participle. थि- is never used as the base for a participle.

The **-era** participle refers to an action that takes place *before* the action of the main verb – that is, the final verb – of the sentence. But other than that it does not really have a tense of its own: the tense of the sentence is the tense that is given by the verb at the end. Therefore, the action described by the **-era** participle can be in any tense: past, present or future:

Nepali	***English***
म आएर बसें ।	I came and sat down.
म आएर बस्छु ।	I come and sit down.

म भोलि आएर बस्छु ।	I shall come and sit down tomorrow.
म भात खाएर बाहिर गएँ ।	I ate rice and went out.
म भात खाएर बाहिर जान्छु ।	I eat rice and go out.
भोलि म भात खाएर बाहिर जान्छु ।	Tomorrow I shall eat rice and go out.

In the English sentences, both verbs are in the same tense; in the Nepali versions only the main final verb has a tense. The subject of the Nepali sentence is usually stated at the very beginning of the sentence, as in these examples, but sometimes it is not mentioned until after the **-era** participle:

भात खाएर म बाहिर जान्छु ।	Having eaten rice I go out.

The **-era** participle is formed in exactly the same way, no matter what or who the subject of the sentence is: the level of politeness is indicated by the main verb of the sentence. If the main verb is transitive and in a past tense, the subject must take -**ले**.

उसले झ्यालनेर बसेर एउटा केरा खायो ।	He sat near the window and ate a banana.
म उसको लुगा धोएर तपाईंलाई दिन्छु ।	I shall wash his clothes and give them to you.
हिजो किशनजीले हाम्रो पसलमा आएर एक जोर जुत्ता किन्नुभयो ।	Yesterday Kishanji came into our shop and bought a pair of shoes.
उनीहरू खुम्बु गएर सगरमाथा चढ़े ।	They went to Khumbu and climbed Mount Everest.

भएर, the **-era** participle of **हुनु** *to be*, is also used to mean *via:*

त्यो विमान दिल्ली भएर जान्छ ।	That flight goes via Delhi.
उनीहरूको बस पोखरा भएर काठ्माडौं गयो ।	Their bus went to Kathmandu via Pokhara.

● INSIGHT

A sentence formed by using the conjunctive participle **एर** has two verbal activities sharing the same subject. The subject may appear at the beginning of a sentence or at the beginning of a subsequent clause, e.g. **म केही खाएर जान्छु** or **केही खाएर म जान्छु** 'I will eat something and go'.

The conjunctive participle **एर** also indicates a sense of cause and effect if the sentence is made of two different subjects with a final verb in the past tense, e.g. **तपाई आएर राम्रो भयो** 'It went well because you came'.

63 THE REPORTED SPEECH MARKER रे

रे can only be used as an appendage to a sentence, and never on its own. When it is added to the end of a statement, the word **रे** indicates that the person speaking has been told what s/he has just said by someone else. It is usually possible to ascertain who or what the source of the information is, but sometimes it is left quite vague, just as in English one reports a rumour by beginning 'I hear that ...' or 'they say that ...'

If someone says:

तपाईंको छोरालाई भोक लाग्यो रे ।	Your son is hungry (+ reported speechmarker)

the presence of **तपाईंको छोरा** *your son* in the sentence means that the person speaking has probably been told by your son that he is hungry, in which case the sentence could be translated *your son says he's hungry*. However, it could also mean that someone else has informed the speaker of this fact: one can only be sure if one knows the context in which the statement is made.

Similarly, a sentence such as:

आज आफिस जाँदैन रे ।	(He) won't go to the office today (+ reported speech marker)

could mean *he says he won't go to the office today* or *she says he won't go to the office today* or *they say he won't go to the office today*. Without knowing the context in which the statement is made you really cannot choose between these translations.

This kind of confusion should not occur during a conversation, because the meaning is always clear in its context. Sometimes, however, a speaker will add **रे** to the end of a statement in order to disown responsibility for its truth or falsity. The following statements suggest that the speaker has heard the news s/he reports on the radio, or has read them in a newspaper:

आज पानी पर्दैन रे ।	They say it will not rain today.
भारतको राष्ट्रपति आज नेपाल आउँछ रे ।	The Indian president comes to Nepal today, I hear.

If someone said something but you did not hear what they said, you might wish to ask someone else what was said. A quick way of doing this is simply to say:

के रे ?	What was said?

Exercise 31

Convert the following pairs of sentences into one sentence by changing the first verb into the -**era** participle.

Example

म घर जान्छु । त्यसपछि म खाना खान्छु ।	=	**म घर गएर खाना खान्छु ।**
I shall go home. After that I shall eat.		I shall go home and eat.

१ म नेपाल जान्छु । त्यसपछि म तपाईंलाई चिठी लेख्छु ।

२ म विचार गर्छु । म तपाईंलाई भन्छु ।

३ उनीहरू किताब किन्छन् । त्यसपछि तपाईंकहाँ आउँछन् ।

४ यो केटी स्कूल जान्छे । त्यहाँ अँग्रेजी सिक्छे ।

५ म अफिस जान्छु । म तपाईंलाई फोन गर्छु ।

६ वहाँ झापा जानुभयो । वहाँ मेरो दाइको घरमा बस्नुभयो ।

Exercise 32

Construct sentences that tell someone to do two things, one after the other, along the following lines:

तपाईं/भात खानु/सुत्नु	=	तपाईं भात खाएर सुत्नुहोस् ।
you/eat rice/sleep		You please eat the rice and go to sleep.

१ तिमी/घर जानु/काम गर्नु

२ तपाईं/रेडियो सुन्नु/घर जानु

३ तिमी/चुरोट लिनु/आउनु

४ तपाईं/यो किताब पढ्नु/मलाई दिनु

५ तिमी/लण्डन पुग्नु/मकहाँ आउनु

६ तपाईं/झापा जानु/मेरो दाइको घरमा बस्नु

18 A chance encounter in Darjeeling

09.02

Subir is a resident of Darjeeling, and Ashesh lives in Kathmandu. Some two months ago the two men met while Subir was visiting Kathmandu. Now Subir is surprised to meet Ashesh unexpectedly in Darjeeling.

सुबीर	अहो! तपाईं यहाँ के गर्दै हुनुहुन्छ ? तपाईंलाई देखेर म छक्क परें नि ! तपाईंहरू दार्जीलिङ्गमा बसाइँ सर्नुभयो कि क्या हो ?
अशेष	होइन, म एक हप्तादेखि यहाँको वन संरक्षण विभागमा काम गर्दै छु । पोहोर साल पनि म नेपालमा यस्तै काम गर्दै थिएँ नि ।
सुबीर	अनि कति बस्नुहुन्छ दार्जीलिङ्गमा ? परिवार पनि सँगै छन् ?
अशेष	श्रीमती र छोरीहरू मसँग छन् तर छोराहरूलाई छाडेर आयौं यसपालि । कान्छो छोराको उमेर अहिले तेह्र भयो, जेठो छोरा चाहिं सोह्र वर्ष लाग्यो । स्कूल नगई उनीहरूको प्रगति हुँदैन । त्यस कारणले उनीहरू उतै पढ्दै छन् ।
सुबीर	हो, तपाईंका तीनजना छोरीहरू छन्, अब याद आयो । कान्छी छोरीको नामचाहिं लक्ष्मी अनि जेठी छोरीकोचाहिं सरस्वती, होइन ? तर माहिली छोरीको नाम के हो ? मैले बिर्सें ।
अशेष	माहिली छोरीको नाम राधिका हो । अहिले लक्ष्मी र राधिका एभरेष्ट होटेलमा पौडी खेल्दै छन् । सरस्वती र मेरी श्रीमती बजारमा किनमेल गर्दै छन् । स्कूलहरू भोलिदेखि खुल्छन् नि, आज छुट्टीको अन्तिम दिन हो ।

सुबीर	उनीहरू भोलिदेखि कुनचाहिं स्कूल जान्छन् ? लोरेटो कलेज ?
अशेष	हो, लोरेटो कलेज जान्छन् । स्कूल असाध्धे राम्रो छ रे । त्यो कुरा थाहा पाएर उनीहरूलाई त्यही स्कूलमा राख्यौं हामीहरूले । उनीहरू दुई महिनासम्म त्यहाँ पढ्छन् । दुई महिनापछि हामी काठ्माडौं फर्कन्छौं ।
सुबीर	ठीक गर्नुभयो तपाईंले । अब तपाईं एभेरेष्ट होटेलसम्म हिंडेरै जानुहुन्छ ? निकै माथि छ नि, उकालो पनि छ ।
अशेष	म बिर्सेर घरबाट पैसा नलिईकन निस्कें । त्यस कारणले हिडेर जाँदै छु । तपाईं कता जाँदै हुनुहुन्छ ?
सुबीर	मेरो अफिसको काम पाँच बजे सिद्धियो, अनि म ऊ त्यो चियापसलमा बसेर साथीहरूसँग गफ गर्दै थिएँ । अलिपछि घर जान्छु । मेरो घर पनि उतै छ नि । तर यो बाटोचाहिं अलि घुमाउरो छ । म तपाईंसँग अलि माथिसम्म गएर तपाईंलाई अर्को बाटो देखाउँछु, हुन्न ? त्यो बाटो नघुमीकन सीधै होटेलमा पुग्छ ।
अशेष	बिस्तारै चिया खाएर आउनुहोस् न त । केही हतार छैन ।
सुबीर	भैगो, चिया चिसो भयो । चिया नखाईकन आउँछु । अबेर भयो, श्रीमती रिसाउँछिन् । ल, साहूजी, म गएँ, नमस्कार ।

Quick vocab

छक्क पर्नु	to be surprised
देख्नु	to see
बसाइँ सर्नु	to move house
क्या	what?
वन	forest
संरक्षण	conservation
विभाग	department
छाड्नु	to leave, quit
यसपालि	this time
कान्छो	youngest
जेठो	eldest
लाग्नु	to begin to be, tend towards
प्रगति	progress
उतै	there (emphasized form of उता)
पढ्नु	to study
याद	memory
माहिलो	second eldest
बिर्सनु	to forget

पौडी खेल्नु	to swim
किनमेल	shopping
खुल्नु	to open
अन्तिम	last, final
कुनचाहिं	which?
असाध्दै	extremely
राख्नु	to put, place
माथि	up, above
उकालो	steep, uphill
निस्कनु	to come out
सिद्धिनु	to end
ऊ त्यो	that one, over there
-चाहिं	as for
घुमाउरो	indirect
देखाउनु	to show
घुम्नु	to circle, wander
सीधै	directly
बिस्तारै	slowly, gently
भैगो	never mind!
चिसो	cold
अबेर	lateness
साहूजी	shopkeeper

Subir	Oho! What are you doing here? I was surprised to see you, you know! Have you moved to Darjeeling or what?
Ashesh	No, I've been working in the Forest Conservation Department since one week ago. Last year too I was doing the same kind of work in Nepal, you know.
Subir	And how long will you stay in Darjeeling? Are the family with you too?
Ashesh	My wife and daughters are with me but this time we came without our sons. The younger son is 13 years old now, the elder is just 14. If they don't go to school they won't make progress. So they are studying there.
Subir	Yes, you have three daughters, now I remember. The youngest is called Lakshmi and the eldest Sarasvati, is that not right? But what is the middle daughter's name? I have forgotten.
Ashesh	The middle daughter's name is Radhika. Now Lakshmi and Radhika are swimming at the Everest Hotel. Sarasvati and my wife are shopping in the market.

	The schools open from tomorrow, you know, today is the last day of the holiday.
Subir	Which school will they go to from tomorrow? Loretto College?
Ashesh	Yes, they will go to Loretto College. I hear the school is extremely good. When we got to know that we put them in that school. They will study there for two months. After two months we will return to Kathmandu.
Subir	You did the right thing. Are you going to walk to the Everest Hotel now? It's a long way up, you know, and it's steep too.
Ashesh	I forgot and I came out of the house without any money. That's why I'm walking. Where are you going?
Subir	My office work finished at 5 o'clock, and I was sitting in that teashop over there, chatting with my friends. I'll go home in a little while. My house is in the same direction, you know. But this path is rather indirect. I'll come a little way up with you and show you another path, no? That path goes straight to the hotel without any diversions.
Ashesh	But please drink your tea slowly and then come, won't you? There's no hurry.
Subir	Never mind,* the tea's gone cold. I'll come without drinking the tea. It's late, my wife will be cross. Here, shopkeeper, I'm off, goodbye.

Note *भैगो is a colloquial expression meaning *that's over and done with* or *that's not something that need detain us further.*

Grammar

64 THE CONTINUOUS TENSES IN -दै छ

The *continuous present* tense refers to actions that are occurring even as the verb is being stated, and is the exact equivalent of English verb phrases such as *I am going, they are watching, we are eating*. Just as in English, the tense can also be used to talk about the future, so long as something else in the sentence makes this clear: *I am going tomorrow, we are eating out next Sunday*. This tense of a verb consists of a word that is the Nepali equivalent of *going / watching / eating*, followed by the appropriate form of छ *is* or *are*. To form the first word, the ending -दै is added to the present tense base of the verb.

If the base ends in a vowel, this vowel must be nasalized. The ending is invariable: that is, it is always the same no matter what or who the subject of the verb may be. छ is the verb that must change according to number, gender and level of politeness.

गर्नु **garnu** to do

म	गर् + -दै छु = गर्दै छु	I am doing
हामी, हामीहरू	गर् + -दै छौं = गर्दै छौं	we are doing
तँ	गर् + -दै छस् = गर्दै छस्	you are doing
तिमी, तिमीहरू	गर् + -दै छौ = गर्दै छौ	you are doing
ऊ, यो, त्यो (m.)	गर् + -दै छ = गर्दै छ	he is doing
ऊ, यो, त्यो (f.)	गर् + -दै छे = गर्दै छे	she is doing
उनी, यिनी, तिनी (m.)	गर् + -दै छन् = गर्दै छन्	he is doing
उनी, यिनी, तिनी (f.)	गर् + -दै छिन् = गर्दै छिन्	she is doing
यी, ती, उनीहरू etc.	गर् + -दै छन् = गर्दै छन्	they are doing

जानु **jānu** to go

म	जा + ँ + -दै छु = जाँदै छु	I am going
हामी, हामीहरू	जा + ँ + -दै छौं = जाँदै छौं	we are going
तँ	जा + ँ + -दै छस् = जाँदै छस्	you are going
तिमी, तिमीहरू	जा + ँ + -दै छौ = जाँदै छौ	you are going
ऊ, यो, त्यो (m.)	जा + ँ + -दै छ = जाँदै छ	he is going
ऊ, यो, त्यो (f.)	जा + ँ + -दै छे = जाँदै छे	she is going
उनी, यिनी, तिनी (m.)	जा + ँ + -दै छन् = जाँदै छन्	he is going
उनी, यिनी, तिनी (f.)	जा + ँ + -दै छिन् = जाँदै छिन्	she is going
यी, ती, उनीहरू etc.	जा + ँ + -दै छन् = जाँदै छन्	they are going

The *continuous past* tense is used to describe what was actually going on at a particular time, and is the exact equivalent of English verb phrases such as *I was going, they were watching, we were eating.* It is formed by adding the invariable ending -दै to the present tense base of a verb to create the Nepali for *going / watching / eating,* just as in the continuous present tense. Instead of ending with छ, however, the verb phrase must end with the थि- form of the past tense of हुनु, meaning *was* or *were.* With High pronouns, these tenses end with हुनुहुन्छ in the present and हुनुहुन्थ्यो in the past.

● INSIGHT

If you know the conjugation of छ and थियो properly, you can create the present and past continuous tenses of every verb without difficulty because you only need to modify the main verb into दै form and then attach the appropriate conjugation of the verbs above.

Continuous present

हाम्रा साथीहरू गीत गाउँदै छन् ।	Our friends are singing a song.
बहिनी कविता पाठ गर्दै छे ।	Younger sister is reading out a poem.
आमा समाचार पत्र हेर्दै हुनुहुन्छ ।	Mother is looking at the newspaper.

Continuous past

हाम्रा साथीहरू ठट्टा गर्दै थिए ।	Our friends were joking.
बहिनी पूजा गर्दै थिई ।	Younger sister was performing puja.
आमा चिया बनाउँदै हुनुहुन्थ्यो ।	Mother was making tea.

Theoretically, the negative form of these tenses should be created by changing **छ** to **छैन**, **थियो** to **थिएन**, and so on. But in real life these forms are very rarely used. For instance, if someone asks: **तपाईं काम गर्दै हुनुहुन्छ ?** *are you working?*, and in fact you are simply reading a book, your answer should be along the lines of **होइन, म किताब पढ्दै छु** *No, I'm reading a book.*

There is a specialized continuous present form of **छ** *is*. This is used to say that something exists in a particular place, contrary to a listener's expectations, or to state or emphasize the fact of its existence plainly. It occurs only in the singular form **छँदै छ:**

आखिर, पोखरामा हाम्रो घर छँदै छ ।	After all, we do have a house in Pokhara.
काठ्माडौंमा विमानस्थल छँदै छ नि !	There is an airport in Kathmandu, you know!

Exercise 33

Change the tense of the verb in the following sentences into the continuous present:

१ तपाईं अखबार पढ्नुहुन्छ ?

२ भाइ किताब पढ्छ ।

३ म बाहिर जान्छु ।

४ उनीहरू नेपाली भाषा बोल्छन् ।

५ अब ऊ त्यही कलमले चिठी लेख्छ ।

Exercise 34

Change the tense of the verb in the following sentences into the continuous past, and make any other changes to the sentences that thus become necessary:

१ बुवाले अखबार पढ्नुभयो ।

२ तिमीले त्यो किताब पढ्यौ ?

३ मैले जापानी भाषा सिकें ।

४ उनीहरूले टी० भी० हेरे ।

५ बुवाले बारीमा के गर्नुभयो ?

65 WHICH ONE? THIS ONE! THE USES OF -चाहि ।

The word **चाहिं** is frequently added to adjectives, or to words such as **यो, त्यो, कुन** to replace a noun. In this context it can be understood to mean *one:*

अग्लोचाहिं	the tall one	त्योचाहिं	that one
रातोचाहिं	the red one	योचाहिं	this one
कुनचाहिं ?	which one?		

तपाईंको घर कुनचाहिं हो ? मेरो घर ऊ त्यो अग्लोचाहिं हो ।	Which one is your house? My house is that tall one over there.
तपाईंले कुनचाहिं किन्नुभयो ? सस्तोचाहिं किनें ।	Which one did you buy? I bought the cheap one.

The second usage of **चाहिं** is contrastive. Here it means *as for:*

म रातो बङ्गला स्कूल जान्छु । दाईचाहिं स्कूल जानुहुन्न, अफिस जानुहुन्छ ।	I go to Rato Bangala School. As for elder brother, (he) does not go to school, he goes to the office.
यो मान्छे बाहुन हो, त्योचाहिं नेवार हो ।	This man is a Brahmin, but that one is a Newar.

66 OTHER FORMS OF THE CONJUNCTIVE PARTICIPLE

There are two other forms of conjunctive participle which mean much the same as, but are used less frequently than, the -**एर** participle. These forms end in **-ई -ī** and **-ईकन -īkana:**

Verb		*cj. ptc. 1*	*cj.ptc.2*	*cj.ptc. 3*	
गर्न	to do	गरेर	गरी	गरीकन	doing, having done
हिंड्नु	to walk	हिंडर	हिंडी	हिंडीकन	walking, having walked
लिनु	to take	लिएर	लिई	लिईकन	taking, having taken
जानु	to go	गएर	गई	गईकन	going, having gone
हुनु	to be	भएर	भई	भईकन	being, having become

The negative forms of all participles are formed simply by adding the prefix **न- na-** to the affirmative form:

cj. ptc. 1	*cj.ptc. 2*	*cj.ptc. 3*	
नगरेर	नगरी	नगरीकन	not doing, not having done
नहिंडेर	नहिंडी	नहिंडीकन	not walking, not having walked
नलिएर	नलिई	नलिईकन	not taking, not having taken
नगएर	नगई	नगईकन	not going, not having gone
नभएर	नभई	नभईकन	not being, not having become

In practice, affirmative forms almost always take the **-एर** ending, while negative forms most usually take the **-ईकन** ending. Because **-ईकन** is the longest of the three possible endings, it is emphatic. Consider the differences between the following pairs of sentences:

म भात खाएर बाहिर गएँ ।	I ate and went out.
म भात नखाईकन बाहिर गएँ ।	I went out without having eaten.

The form ending in **-ī** is less commonly used, though it is obligatory in certain idiomatic expressions:

तपाईंलाई नभेटी हुँदैन ।	I simply have to meet you ('having not met you it will not be all right').
मेरी छोरीलाई सिनेमा नगई सुख छैन !	My daughter simply has to go to the cinema (literally, if my daughter does not go to the cinema there is no happiness).
आयो दसैं ढोल बजाई, गयो दसैं रिन बोकाई ।	Dasain came beating the drum, Dasain left, having given us debts to bear.*

Note *A proverb. **ढोल बजाउनु** *to play a drum;* **बोकाई** is from the verb **बोकाउनु**, which is the causative of **बोक्नु** *to carry.* Dasain is Nepal's most important annual Hindu festival.

Incidentally, Nepali poets are blessed by this wealth of choice, which makes it much easier for them to adjust the number of beats in a line of verse.

मेरा छोराछोरीहरू हात धोएर भात खान्छन् । हात नधोईकन भात खानु ठीक हुँदैन ।	My children wash their hands before they eat. It's not good to eat without washing your hands.
उनी नुहाएर सुत्छिन् । ननुहाईकन कहिल्यै पनि सुत्दिनन् ।	She takes a shower before she goes to bed. She never goes to bed without showering first.

Exercise 35

Construct sentences that state that each of the people in column 1 performed each of the verbs in column 3 *without* performing the verb in column 2, thus producing 12 different sentences:

1	2	3
उनका छोराहरू	भात खानु	चिठी लेख्नु
मेरी आमा		मन्दिर जानु
तिमी		
रामे		
रामेकी दिदी		
म		

● INSIGHT

'Without' is बिना in Nepali, which is used with a noun. It can be used either before or after the noun, e.g. पैसाबिना or बिनापैसा 'without money'. You cannot use this word with a verb.

67 EXPRESSIONS OF AGE

There are several ways in which a person's age is expressed in Nepali. The most straightforward is simply to define a person's age using **हो:**

मेरो छोराको उमेर बीस वर्ष हो ।	My son's age is 20 years.
संजयको बुवाको उमेर असी वर्ष हो ।	Sanjay's father's age is 80 years.

More commonly, however, a person is described as being *of* a certain age, using the possessive **-को**:

मेरी जेठी छोरी बाइस वर्षकी हो ।	My eldest daughter is 22 years old.
म चालीस वर्षको हुँ र मेरी श्रीमती उनन्चालीस वर्षकी हुन् ।	I am 40 years old and my wife is 39.

In all of the above examples, the verb at the end of the sentence is equally likely to be the past tense **भयो,** indicating that this is the age that has been attained or reached by the person concerned:

मेरो छोराको उमेर बीस वर्ष भयो ।

संजयको बुवाको उमेर असी वर्ष भयो ।

मेरी जेठी छोरी बाइस वर्षकी भई ।

म चालीस वर्षको भएँ र मेरी श्रीमती उनन्चालीस वर्षकी भइन् ।

68 FURTHER RELATIONSHIP TERMS

The various offspring of a family each has a title that indicates the relative status in terms of age. As average family size decreases, some of these titles are falling into disuse, but five are still quite common:

Brothers or sons	***Sisters or daughters***	
जेठो	जेठी	eldest
माहिलो	माहिली	second eldest
साहिंलो	साहिंली	third eldest
काहिंलो	काहिंली	fourth eldest
कान्छो	कान्छी	youngest

These terms are primarily adjectives:

मेरो जेठो छोरा केही वर्षसम्म बिराटनगरमा बस्यो ।	My eldest son stayed in Biratnagar for some years.
हिजो उसकी माहिली छोरीको बिहा भयो ।	Yesterday his second daughter was married.
तपाईं मभन्दा तीन वर्ष जेठो हुनुहुन्छ ।	You are three years older than me.

Although जेठो is used to mean *older* or *senior to,* both कान्छो and सानो *small* can be used to mean *younger* or *junior to.*

तिमी मभन्दा तीन वर्ष कान्छो छौ ।	You are three years younger
तिमी मभन्दा तीन वर्ष सानो छौ ।	than me.

कान्छा and जेठा are often used rather like nicknames for children. कान्छा and कान्छी *youngest* can also be used to address or refer to young children whose names one does not know:

ए कान्छी, एक छिन यता आऊ !	Hey girl, come here a minute!
ए कान्छा, चिया ल्याऊ !	Hey boy, bring the tea!

The most important things for the reader to remember

1 A special 'and' construction is often used when two verbs occur in one sentence. It is formed by attaching एर to the stem of the first of the verbs, e.g. म उठेर नुहाउँछु 'I get up and take a shower'. The two actions are both performed by the same person in this construction.

2 Remember that when the same construction एर is used with the 'to be' verb हुनु, it becomes भएर. This can be used to mean 'via' or 'by the way of', e.g. म डोहा भएर नेपाल जान्छु 'I am going to Nepal via Doha'.

3 रे is added like a tail to the end of a sentence to tell someone that the information you are passing on to them comes from a third-party source whether it is another person, the media or just a rumour, e.g. ऊ घरमा छ रे 'I hear that he is at home'.

4 The present continuous tense is used to express an ongoing activity. To form this tense, दै is added to the verb stem, followed by the appropriate conjugation of छ, e.g. म अहिले टिभी हेर्दै छु 'I am watching television now'.

5 The past continuous tense is formed in the same way but the past form of the 'to be' verb is added instead, e.g. म फोनमा कुरा गर्दै थिएँ । 'I was talking on the phone'.

6 There is an alternative to the conjunctive participle एर in Nepali. This is formed by adding इकन to the verb stem, as in खाइकन 'after having eaten'. कन is added for emphasis and it can also be left out, e.g. म खाना खाइ or खाइकन आउँछु ।

7 When न is prefixed to the verb stem + इ or इकन it changes the meaning to a negative with a sense of 'without' doing something, e.g. म नखाइ or नखाइकन काम गर्दिन 'I will not work without eating'.

8 There is more than one way in Nepali to talk about the age of a person, e.g. छोरा कति बर्ष भयो ? छोराको उमेर कति हो ? छोरा कति बर्ष लाग्यो or पुग्यो ? These all mean 'How old is your son?'.

10 बजारमा

In the market

In this unit you will learn:

- ***how to discuss the prices and availability of various foods***
- ***how to declare needs and wants***

19 Out shopping

10.01

Anjali and her younger sister have gone to the vegetable market to buy food for the evening meal. Dil Bahadur, who has a stall at the market, sells them some of the items they need.

अंजली	साहूजी नमस्ते !
दिल बहादुर	नमस्ते दिदी । तपाईंलाई के चाहियो ?
अंजली	यहाँ तरकारी पाइन्छ ?
दिल बहादुर	पाइन्छ दिदी, किन पाइँदैन ? यो तरकारी-पसल हो नि ! मकहाँ हरेक किसिमको तरकारी सस्तोमा पाइन्छ ।
अंजली	आलुको कति पर्छ ?
दिल बहादुर	यो रातो आलु किलोको चालीस रुपियाँ हो, त्यो सेतो आलु किलोको पैंतीस रुपियाँ हो । तपाईंलाई कस्तो आलु चाहियो ?

अंजली	कुनचाहिं मीठो हुन्छ नि ?
दिल बहादुर	रातो आलु मीठो हुन्छ रे तर सेतोचाहिं पनि ठीकै छ । कुनचाहिं लिनुहुन्छ दिदी ?
अंजली	हामीलाई तीन किलो रातो आलु दिनुहोस् । प्याज छ ?
दिल बहादुर	छ । किलोको पैंतालीस रुपियाँ ।
अंजली	एक किलो दिनुहोस् । रायोको साग मुठाको कति हो ?
दिल बहादुर	मुठाको दस रुपियाँ । तपाईंलाई कति चाहियो ?
अंजली	एक मुठा मात्रै दिनुहोस् । अलि महंगो छ । चामल र दाल पनि छ ?
दिल बहादुर	अहँ, छैन । यो तरकारी-पसल हो नि ! चामल र दालको लागि अर्को पसलमा जानुहोस् ।
अंजली	अनि मासु ?
दिल बहादुर	मासु पनि यहाँ पाइँदैन । मासु खिचापोखरीमा पाइन्छ । त्यहाँ माछा पनि पाइन्छ ।
अंजली	हुन्छ । अब हामी उतै जान्छौं । कति भयो ?
दिल बहादुर	एक छिन, म हिसाब मर्छु । ल, एक सय पैंसट्ठी रुपियाँ भयो ।
अंजली	मसँग हजारको नोट मात्रै छ । चानचुन छ ?
दिल बहादुर	छ, त्यो समस्या होइन । तर तपाईंहरूलाई खुर्सानी चाहिंदैन ?
अंजली	अहँ, चाहिंदैन । आजलाई यति हो ।
दिल बहादुर	कस्तो अनौठो कुरा ! सबै नेपालीहरूलाई खुर्सानी मन पर्छ, होइन ? तपाईंहरूलाई पिरो खाना मीठो लाग्दैन ?
अंजली	मीठो त लाग्छ, तर हाम्रो घरमा आजकल अँग्रेज साथीहरू छन् । उनीहरूलाई पिरो खाना मनै पर्दैन ।

V Quick vocab

चाहिनु	to be wanted, needed
तरकारी	vegetables
पाइनु	to be available
किसिम	type, kind
सस्तो	cheap
आलु	potato(es)
दाम	price
प्याज	onion(s)
रायो	mustard
साग	greens
मुठा	bunch
चामल	uncooked rice
दाल	lentils
मासु	meat

खिचापोखरी	Khichapokhari (an area of Kathmandu)
माछा	fish
हिसाब गर्नु	to add up, calculate
नोट	note (of currency)
चानचुन	change
समस्या	problem
खुर्सानी	chilli pepper(s)
यति	this much
अनौठो	strange
पिरो	spicy
आजकल	nowadays

Anjali	Shopkeeper, hello!
Dil Bahadur	Hello sister. What do you want?
Anjali	Are vegetables available here?
Dil Bahadur	Yes they are, sister, why wouldn't they be? This is a vegetable shop, you know! In my shop every kind of vegetable is available cheaply.
Anjali	How much are the potatoes?
Dil Bahadur	These red potatoes are 40 rupees a kilo, those white potatoes are 35 rupees a kilo. Which kind of potatoes would you like?
Anjali	Well, which one tastes good?
Dil Bahadur	They say the red potatoes are tasty, but the white ones are fine as well. Which will you take, sister?
Anjali	Give us three kilos of red potatoes. Do you have any onions?
Dil Bahadur	Yes. 45 rupees a kilo.
Anjali	Give me one kilo. How much are the mustard greens per bunch?
Dil Bahadur	10 rupees a bunch. How much do you want?
Anjali	Just give me one bunch. It's a bit expensive. Do you have rice and lentils too?
Dil Bahadur	No, I don't. This is a vegetable shop, you know! Please go to another shop for rice and lentils.
Anjali	And meat?
Dil Bahadur	You can't get meat here either. You can get meat in Khichapokhari. You can get fish there too.
Anjali	All right. We'll go there now. How much do I owe you?
Dil Bahadur	One moment, I'll add it up. Right, it comes to 175 rupees.
Anjali	I have only a 1000 rupee note. Do you have change?
Dil Bahadur	Yes, that's not a problem. But don't you want any chilli peppers?

Anjali	No, we don't. This is enough for today.
Dil Bahadur	What a strange thing! All Nepalis like chilli, don't they? Don't you like spicy food?
Anjali	Yes we do, but nowadays we have some English friends at our house. They don't like spicy food at all.

Grammar

69 NEEDED AND AVAILABLE: चाहिनु AND पाइन

The passive verbs **पाइनु** *to be obtained/be available* and **चाहिनु** *to be needed/be wanted* belong to a category of verbs called 'i-stem verbs' because a short **i** vowel (इ) is added to the verb base to create them. It is a feature of Nepali, and other related languages, that verbs such as *to want, need, get* are expressed in passive terms: rather than *I need,* Nepali speakers say *is necessary to/for me;* instead of *I got,* they will often say *was obtained to/for me.* The thing that is wanted, needed or obtained is made the subject of the passive verb, while the wanter, needer or obtainer becomes its indirect object, marked by the postposition -**लाई**.

INSIGHT

The past of चाहिन्छ is चाहियो and this is what you hear most often, even in present tense contexts, probably because the state of need has already arisen by the time you express it. चाहिन्छ is used to denote generalizations and the near future.

चाहिनु

चाहिनु *to be needed / wanted* is the passive form of the verb **चाहनु** *to wish.* **चाहनु** is used mostly with other verbs: *I wish to leave, I want to learn English* (see **Grammar 110**), whereas **चाहिनु** is used when some *thing* is needed or wanted.

The habitual present tense of **चाहिनु** is used to denote needs that are regular or habitual:

जिन्दगीमा मान्छेहरूलाई के चाहिन्छ ?	What do people need in life?
मान्छेहरूलाई पानी चाहिन्छ ।	People need water.
मान्छेहरूलाई अरू के चाहिन्छ ?	What else do people need?
मान्छेहरूलाई खाने कुरा पनि चाहिन्छ ।	People also need food.
बिरामीहरूलाई के चाहिन्छ ?	What do sick people need?
बिरामीहरूलाई औषधि चाहिन्छ ।	Sick people need medicine.

To express the sense *I want something,* Nepali uses the simple past tense **चाहियो**, e.g.:

मलाई चिनी चाहियो ।	I want sugar.
उसलाई पैसा चाहियो ।	He wants money.

Such sentences denote a need or desire that is very much in the *present*, despite the *past* tense of the verb. The person who is speaking considers that this need or desire arose immediately *before* s/he gave utterance to it.

The negative form **चाहिंदैन** is grammatically in the present tense, but it is used as the negative form of both **चाहिन्छ** and **चाहियो** to mean *is not wanted* or *is not needed:*

ए दिदी, तपाईंलाई चिनी चाहियो ? अहँ, चाहिंदैन ।	Hey elder sister, do you want some sugar? No, I don't.
स्वस्थ मानिसलाई औषधि पटक्कै चाहिंदैन ।	A healthy person has absolutely no need of medicine.

पाइनु

The passive verb **पाइनु** means *to be obtained/be available,* and it is the passive form of the verb **पाउनु** *to get/obtain.* Its most common use has the sense of *to be available:*

ए दिदी, यहाँ बास पाइन्छ ? यहाँ पाइँदैन हजुर, उता गएर सोध्नुहोस् ।	Hey elder sister, is lodging available here? It is not available here sir, go and ask over there.
नेपालमा गाईको मासु पाइँदैन तर राँगोको मासु पाइन्छ ।	You cannot get beef in Nepal, but you can get buffalo meat.

Sometimes the active and the passive form of the verb are equally appropriate. For instance, if you wish to inform someone that you received the letter they sent you, you can choose between the following:

अस्ति मैले तपाईंको चिठी पाएँ ।	I received your letter the other day.
अस्ति तपाईंको चिठी पाइयो ।	Your letter was received the other day.

If the passive form is used, it is normal to leave out a mention of who received the letter. This will be understood to be the person speaking unless it is stated otherwise.

● INSIGHT

पाइन्छ literally means 'is available' or 'is found' but in English you hear 'you can get' for this. So the subject is already understood in पाइन्छ, e.g. लण्डनमा मोमो कहाँ पाइन्छ ? 'Where can you get momos in London?'

Exercise 36

Answer the following questions about **Dialogue 19**:

१ दिल बहादुरको पसलमा तरकारी पाइन्छ ?

२ रातो आलुको दाम कति हो ?

३ अनि सेतो आलुको दाम नि ?

४ दिल बहादुरको पसलमा मासु पाइन्छ ?

५ मासु कहाँ पाइन्छ त ?

६ अंजलीलाई खुर्सानी चाहिन्छ कि चाहिंदैन ?

70 FOOD VOCABULARY

तरकारी	***Vegetables***	फलफूल	***Fruits***
आलु	potato	अम्बा	guava
काँक्रो	cucumber	आँप	mango
काउली, फूलकोपी	cauliflower	कागती	lime
बन्दा कोपी	cabbage	केरा	banana
गोलभेंडा	tomato	निबुवा	lemon
चना	chickpea	सुन्तला	orange
प्याज	onion	स्याउ	apple
फर्सी	pumpkin		
मूला	radish	मासु	***Meat***
रामतोरियाँ	okra	कुखुराको मासु	chicken meat
साग	greens (of several varieties)	खसीको मासु	goat meat
सिमी	beans	राँगोको मासु	buffalo meat
		सुँगुरको मासु	pig meat

Other foods

अचार	chutney	अदुवा	ginger
कोदो	millet	खुर्सानी	chilli
घिउ	ghee	चामल	rice (uncooked)
दाल	lentils		
फुल	egg	दही	yoghurt
भात	rice (cooked)	भटमास	soybean
माछा	fish	मकै	corn, maize
नौनी	butter	लसून	garlic

71 USING -लाइ INSTEAD OF -को लागि

Although the principal use of **-लाई** is as an 'object marker', it is often interchangeable with the postposition **-को लागि** *for:*

बुवाको लागि	or	बुवालाई	for father
एक महिनाको लागि	or	एक महिनालाई	for a month
मेरो लागि	or	मलाई	for me

यो कोसेली मेरी आमालाई हो ।	This gift is for my mother.
उषालाई ।	For Usha (dedication on the title page of a book of poems).
आजलाई तिमीलाई के के चाहियो ?	What things do you need for today?

● INSIGHT

Nepali has three different meanings of 'for', just as English uses it in three different contexts. 'For' is -सम्म and देखि as in दुई घण्टासम्म काम गर्नु 'to work <u>for</u> two hours' and केही दिनदेखि 'for the last few days', respectively. The other meaning is 'for the sake of' as in तपाईंको लागि 'for you'.

Exercise 37

Create ten sentences using the elements below, first stating whether people need the nouns listed in the middle column, and then whether buffaloes (**भैंसीहरू**) need the same things:

मान्छेहरूलाई	पानी	चाहिन्छ or चाहिंदैन
भैंसीहरूलाई	हावा	
	घाँसपात (fodder)	
	षिक्षा (education)	
	बिजुली (electricity)	

The most important things for the reader to remember

1 **चाहिनु** 'to be needed' is used only with nouns and is conjugated as **चाहिन्छ**. This remains unchanged, regardless of who is in need, because Nepali speakers say a thing is needed 'to' a person who takes **लाई**, the object marker.

2 A sense of 'availability' in Nepali is also expressed in a passive form. **पाइनु**, a passive form of **पाउनु** 'to get, to find' is conjugated as **पाइन्छ** or **पाइयो** in the simple past.

3 There are several ways of asking the price of an item in shops or markets. All of these are commonly used in practice, e.g. **कति हो ? कति पर्छ ? कति पैसा ? कसरी हो ?**

4 The postposition **को लागि** means 'for' or 'for the sake of'. **लाई** can be used instead in some situations, e.g. **यो झोला दिदीलाई (दिदीको लागि) हो** 'This bag is for elder sister'.

11 मलाई ठीक जस्तो लाग्छ
It seems fine to me

In this unit you will learn:

- *how to describe feelings and impressions*
- *how to discuss resemblances*

20 A place to stay in Kathmandu

11.01

Dipak and Mahesh have both come to Kathmandu to study at Trichandra College. Their first need was to find places to stay. They compare how each has fared in the search for accommodation.

दीपक	तपाईंले डेरा सजिलैसँग पाउनुभयो ?
महेश	अहँ, पाइनँ । अलि गाह्रो भयो । बल्ल बल्ल ठमेलमा यो सानो कोठा पाइयो । तपाईंले नि ?
दीपक	मलाई खूब राम्रो भयो । म बागबजारमा एकजना साथीकहाँ बस्छु । उसको घरदेखि त्रिचन्द्र कलेज पाँच मिनेटमा पुगिन्छ । कलेज झ्यालबाट नै देखिन्छ !
महेश	ओहो, मेरो डेरा त अलिक टाढा पऱ्यो । झ्यालबाट कुनै कलेज देखिँदैन । पसल, रेष्टुराँ र टूरिष्टहरू मात्रै देखिन्छन् र पप सँगीत मात्रै सुनिन्छ ।
दीपक	डेरा तपाईंलाई राम्रो लागेन जस्तो छ ।

महेश	कोठा ठीकै छ । तर घरपति काठ्माडौं बाहिरको मान्छे हो । ऊ राम्रोसँग नेपाली बोल्दैन । कहिलेकाहीँ हामी एक अर्काको कुरा गलत रूपमा बुझ्छौं ।
दीपक	कहाँको मान्छे हो ?
महेश	ऊ मनाङ्गको हो । तपाईं पनि एक पटक मनाङ्ग पुग्नुभयो, होइन ?
दीपक	हो, म एक पटक गएँ । उतातिर नेपाली भाषा अलि कम बोलिन्छ किनभने त्यहाँका मानिसहरूको आफ्नै भाषा हुन्छ ।
महेश	ठाउँ कस्तो लाग्यो त ?
दीपक	मनाङ्ग त मलाई एकदम मन पर्‍यो । त्यहाँबाट हिमाल छर्लङ्ग देखिन्छ । हावाको सुइँ-सुइँ र खोला-नालाहरूको कलकल ध्वनी बाहेक अरू केही सुनिँदैन । ठमेल जस्तो होइन । एकदम सुन्दर र शान्त ठाउँ हो ।

V Quick vocab

डेरा	lodgings, rented accommodation
सजिलैसँग	easily
बल्ल बल्ल	eventually, in the end
ठमेल	a locality in north-central Kathmandu where many tourists stay
खूब	really, very
बागबजार	Bagbazaar: a locality in east-central Kathmandu
घरपति	landlord
एक अर्का	one another
मिल्नु	to match, accord, come together
मनाङ्ग	Manang (central Nepal)
कम	little, less
बोलिनु	to be spoken
भाषा	language
त्रिचन्द्र कलेज	Trichandra College
पुगिनु	to be reached
झ्याल	window
देखिनु	to be seen, visible
अलिक	slightly, a little
कुनै	any
टूरिष्ट	tourist
पप	pop
सँगीत	music
सुनिनु	to be heard, audible

लाग्नु	to strike, affect, seem
जस्तो	like, similar to
ठाउँ	place
हिमाल	the Himalayas
छर्लङ्ग	clear, clearly
हावा	wind, air
सुइँ-सुइँ	sighing sound
खोला-नालाहरू	rivers and streams
कलकल	the sound of running water
ध्वनी	sound
बाहेक	except for
सुन्दर	beautiful
शान्त	peaceful

Dipak Did you find lodgings easily?

Mahesh No, I didn't. It was rather difficult. In the end I found this little room in Thamel. What about you?

Dipak It went very well for me. I will stay at a friend's place in Bag Bazaar. From his house you can reach Trichandra College in five minutes. You can even see the college from the window!

Mahesh Oho, my lodgings are rather far away. You can't see any college from the window. You can see only shops, restaurants and tourists, and you can hear only pop music.

Dipak It seems that you don't like the lodgings.

Mahesh The room's OK. But the landlord comes from outside Kathmandu. He doesn't speak Nepali well. Sometimes we misunderstand one another.

Dipak Where is he from?

Mahesh He's from Manang. You once went to Manang too, didn't you?

Dipak Yes, I went once. Over there they don't speak very much Nepali because the people have their own language.

Mahesh But how did you like the place?

Dipak I really liked Manang. You can see the Himalayas clearly from there. You can't hear anything except the sighing of the wind and the sound of running water. It's not like Thamel. It's a really beautiful and peaceful place.

Grammar

72 FEELINGS: THE USE OF NOUNS WITH लाग्नु

In English, people actively experience physical or mental conditions such as hunger, thirst or happiness: *I feel hungry, I am thirsty, I was happy.* In Nepali, however, the relationship between the condition and the person who experiences it is reversed, and the condition (*hunger, thirst, happiness*) becomes an active agent which *affects* the person who experiences it. That person becomes the indirect object of the condition, and is therefore marked by the suffix **-लाई**, while the condition becomes the subject of the verb **लाग्नु** which can be translated in various ways according to context but here means *to affect/be felt*.

As with **चाहिनु**, *to be wanted*, if the person in the sentence is experiencing the condition at the time the sentence is uttered, the verb **लाग्नु** must be in the simple past tense, to show that the condition has *affected* that person or *been felt* by him/her. Thus, an English phrase such as *I feel hungry* becomes in Nepali translation *me+object marker hunger affected:*

मलाई भोक लाग्यो ।	I feel hungry.

If the person in the sentence experienced the condition in the past, the verb **लाग्नु** should be in one of the various past tenses, including the simple past tense. However, if the simple past tense is used, the time needs to be mentioned to avoid ambiguity:

हिजो मलाई भोक लाग्यो ।	I felt hungry yesterday.

If the verb **लाग्नु** is in the habitual present tense, it implies a regular or habitual occurrence:

हरेक दिन पाँच बजेतिर मलाई भोक लाग्छ ।	I feel hungry at about 5 o'clock every day.

In all such sentences, despite the fact that they translate as *I feel, you are*, etc., the grammatical subject of the verb is the condition that is experienced, not the person who experiences it, and so the verb **लाग्नु** *to be felt* can take only third person singular endings (लाग्छ/ लाग्दैन or लाग्यो/लागेन).

हिजो मैले धेरै चिउरा खाएँ र मलाई तिर्खा लाग्यो ।	Yesterday I ate a lot of chiurā and I was thirsty.
तपाईंलाई भेटेर मलाई खुशी लाग्यो ।	I am very pleased to have met you.
राति उसलाई जाडो लाग्यो । केही दिनपछि उसलाई रुघा लाग्यो ।	In the night he felt cold. A few days later he caught a cold.
रामेकी आमा चैतमा खस्नुभयो र सबैजनालाई दुख लाग्यो ।*	Rame's mother died in (the month of) Chait and everyone was sad.
मलाई मध्यराततिर निद्रा लाग्यो ।	I fell asleep around midnight.

Note * **खस्नु**, literally *to fall*, is used as an honorific verb meaning *to die*. The non-honorific verb meaning *to die* is **मर्नु**. **बित्नु**, *to pass away*, is another commonly used expression.

In statements of general fact, the person or people affected need not always be mentioned:

पूस महिनामा जाडो लाग्छ ।	In the month of Pus one feels cold.
यहाँका बसहरूमा कहिलेकाहीं उकुस-मुकुस लाग्छ ।	On the buses here one sometimes feels suffocated.

Another meaning of लाग्नु is *to apply* in a more literal, physical sense:

मेरो कमिजमा हिलो लाग्यो ।	My shirt became muddy.
घरमा आगो लाग्यो ।	The house caught fire.

• INSIGHT

You feel something first and then you express it. That's why Nepali uses the simple past form लाग्यो instead of लाग्छ, even in the present tense. It can also be used in simple past contexts normally with a past time reference. The subject of this verb takes लाई because Nepali speakers say 'Hunger has attached to me'. Although लाग्यो can be used in both present and past tense, the negatives are different for each of them. The present tense uses लागेको छैन, whereas the past tense uses लागेन for negatives of लाग्यो ।

Exercise 38

Construct sentences that say that the following people felt, experienced or contracted the following things:

Example: म	happiness (खुशी)	=	मलाई खुशी लाग्यो ।
१ तपाईं	thirst (तिर्खा)		
२ दिदी	hunger (भोक)		
३ रामेकी बहिनी	sadness (दुख)		
४ मेरो दाइ	diarrhoea (दिसा)		
५ बुवा	tiredness (थकाइ)		
६ तिमी	coldness (जाडो)		
७ हामी	a headcold (रुघा)		
८ म	a cough (खोकी)		
९ केटी	embarrassment (लाज)		
१० छोरा	sleep (निद्रा)		
११ वहाँ	fear (डर)		
१२ रामे	liquor (रक्सी)		

73 HOW DO YOU LIKE NEPAL? USING ADJECTIVES WITH लाग्नु

The verb **लाग्नु** occurs with adjectives with the basic sense of *to strike one as*, or *to seem*, and the person affected by the verb takes the postposition **–लाई**. The question **कस्तो लाग्यो** ? means *what did you think of it?, how did you like it?* or *how did you find it?* with reference to a particular point in time:

(तपाईंलाई) नेपाल कस्तो लाग्यो ?	How did you like Nepal?
नेपाल मलाई धेरै राम्रो लाग्यो ।	I liked Nepal very much.
अँग्रेजी भाषा कस्तो लाग्यो ।	How did you find the English language?
मलाई असाध्धे गाह्रो लाग्यो ।	I found it very difficult indeed.
अनि जापानी भाषा कस्तो लाग्यो ?	And how did you find Japanese?
त्यो भाषा झन् गाह्रो लाग्यो ।	I found that language even harder.

The question **कस्तो लाग्छ** ? with the verb **लाग्नु** in the habitual present tense means *what do you think of it?* or *how do you like it?* in more general terms. Contrast the following pairs:

हिजो रातिको खाना कस्तो लाग्यो ?	How did you find the food last night?
नेपाली खाना कस्तो लाग्छ ?	What do you think of Nepali food?
त्यो उपन्यास कस्तो लाग्यो ?	How did you like that novel?
नेपाली साहित्य तपाईंलाई कस्तो लाग्छ ?	How do you find Nepali literature?

Exercise 39

Construct sentences that say that the people in the left-hand column did **not** find the things in the central column to be as described in the right-hand column.

Example

तपाईं	this food	good tasting = **तपाईंलाई यो खाना मीठो लागेन ।**
१ म	that song	sweet sounding (**मीठो**)
२ रामेकी आमा	his village	strange (**अनौठो**)
३ उनीहरू	Japanese	difficult
४ बुवा	India	nice
५ मेरो भाइ	Nepali	easy

74 MORE PASSIVE VERBS

Every transitive verb in Nepali can, at least in theory, produce a passive 'i-stem' counterpart:

Examples of active and passive verbs

बोल्नु	to speak	बोलिनु	to be spoken
देख्नु	to see	देखिनु	to be seen
सुन्नु	to hear	सुनिनु	to be heard

बुझ्नु	to understand	बुझिनु	to be understood
भन्नु	to say	भनिनु	to be said
खानु	to eat	खाइनु	to be eaten

There are also a few intransitive verbs that can do the same:

पुग्नु	to arrive	पुगिनु	to be reached

जापानमा नेपाली भाषा बुझिंदैन ।	In Japan the Nepali language is not understood.
भनिन्छ एउटा भूत यहाँ हरेक रात आउँछ ।	It is said (that) a ghost comes here every night.
हिन्दूहरू गाईलाई देवता मान्छन् । त्यस कारणले हिन्दू समुदायमा गाईको मासु खाइँदैन ।	Hindus believe that the cow is a deity. For that reason, beef is not eaten in the Hindu community.

Often the passive form of the verb is used instead of the active form to indicate that something is or is not possible: **सुनिन्छ** *can be heard, is audible*, **देखिन्छ** *can be seen, is visible:*

मेरो स्वर त्यहाँबाट सुनिन्छ कि सुनिंदैन ?	Can you or can you not hear my voice from there?
नगरकोटबाट सगरमाथा राम्रोसँग देखिन्छ ।	From Nagarkot, Everest is easily visible.
अब हाम्रो गाउँ एक घण्टाभित्र पुगिन्छ ।	Now our village can be reached within one hour.

75 SIMILAR TO: जस्तो

जस्तो is a member of the group of words that also includes **यस्तो** *like this*, **उस्तो** or **त्यस्तो** *like that*, and **कस्तो** *like what?/how?* It is used in two slightly different ways:

जस्तो can be used as a postposition to mean *similar to or like*:

मजस्तो मान्छे ।	A person like me.
तपाईंको छोरा मेरो भाइजस्तो छ ।	Your son is like my younger brother.
तपाईंहरूको भाषा नेपालीजस्तो सुनिन्छ ।	Your language sounds like Nepali.

The following phrases can also be appended to a statement to make it less categorical:

... जस्तो छ ।	... it seems
... जस्तो मलाई लाग्छ ।	... it seems to me
... जस्तो मलाई लाग्यो ।	... it seemed to me
आज पानी पर्दैन जस्तो छ ।	It looks like it won't rain today.

ऊ आज आउँछ जस्तो मलाई लाग्दैन ।	It doesn't seem to me that he will come today.
नेपाल एउटा भूस्वर्ग हो जस्तो मलाई लाग्यो ।	It seemed to me that Nepal was a heaven on earth.

• INSIGHT

मलाई आज पानी पर्छ जस्तो लाग्छ 'It seems to me that' or 'I have a feeling that' (it is going to rain today). You can transpose this sentence and say it differently such as मलाई लाग्छ कि आज पानी पर्छ । Note that कि, 'that', connects the two clauses and जस्तो has no role in this transformation.

• INSIGHT

जस्तै means 'just like' and is the emphatic form of जस्तो. The emphatic marker नै or its vowel sound ऐ is combined with the last letter of a word to express an emphasis in Nepali, e.g. घरमै 'at home', आजै 'this very day'.

76 MAKING ADJECTIVES INTO ADVERBS

Adjectives (words that describe nouns) can be made into adverbs (words that describe the actions of a verb) in a variety of ways. Some have the postposition **–सँग** added to them:

छिटो	quick	छिटोसँग	quickly
ढिलो	slow	ढिलोसँग	slowly
सजिलो	easy	सजिलोसँग	easily
राम्रो	good	राम्रोसँग	well

Some adjectives can also be made into adverbs simply by emphasizing them:

छिटो	quick	छिटै	quickly

Others can be made into adverbs by adding the postposition -ले to them:

मुष्किल	difficult	मुष्किलले	with difficulty

The two sets of adverbs in the following box are derived from the set of adjectives to their left:

Adjective		***Adverb***		
यस्तो	like this	यसरी or	यसो	in this manner
त्यस्तो or उस्तो	like that	त्यसरी or उसरी	त्यसो or उसो	in that manner
जस्तो	similar to	जसरी or	जसो	similarly
कस्तो	like what?	कसरी or	कसो	how?

The ubiquitous adjective **राम्रो** can also take the adverbial form **राम्ररी**.

त्यो काम मुश्किलले गरियो ।	That work was done with difficulty.
यो अक्षर यसरी लेख्नुहोस् ।	Write this letter like this.
त्यो मान्छे जर्मन हो तर नेपाली राम्ररी बोल्छ ।	That man is German but he speaks Nepali well.

Exercise 40

Insert **–लाई** or **–ले** in the gaps in the following sentences:

१ म _______ तिर्खा लागेन ।

२ मेरो भाइ _______ एउटा किताब किन्यो ।

३ उस _______ मेरो घर राम्रो लाग्यो ।

४ मेरी आमा _______ थकाइ लाग्यो ।

५ हामीहरू _______ गीत गायौं ।

६ उस _______ दाहिने हात _______ भात खायो ।

७ वहाँ _______ चार बजेतिर सधैं निद्रा लाग्छ ।

८ तपाईं _______ पोखरा कस्तो लाग्यो ?

९ म _______ रक्सी लागेन ।

१० हामी _______ धेरै रक्सी खायौं ।

Exercise 41

Translate into Nepali:

1 The Himalayas can be seen from my window.

2 The Magar language is spoken around Pokhara.

3 Your (High) voice cannot be heard from here.

4 Your (Middle) village will not be reached in an hour.

5 It is said (that) there is a witch (**boksī**) in that house.

6 In Tibet the Nepali language is sometimes understood.

7 Please walk slowly (High). We'll reach the village easily now.

8 I am very happy to have met your (High) son. He seemed like a very clever (**calāk**) boy to me.

The most important things for the reader to remember

1 Nepali feelings or impressions are expressed by **लाग्नु**, which is an impersonal verb. The person who feels takes **लाई**. The final verb remains unchanged for any person who feels something, e.g. **मलाई / वहाँलाई भोक लाग्यो** 'I am/he is hungry'. The negative of **लाग्यो** is **लागेको छैन ।**

2 **लाग्नु** is also used to denote physical conditions such as **रुघा, खोकी, दिसा लाग्नु** 'to have cold, cough and diarrhoea'. It also describes the weather such as **घाम/जून/बादल लाग्नु**. **लाग्नु** literally means 'to be attached to'. So **घाम लाग्यो** means 'the sunlight is attached to the land'.

3 However, if the feeling takes place on a regular basis, then **लाग्यो** changes into **लाग्छ** or **लाग्दैन** in the negative, e.g. **मलाई बेलुका सधैं थकाइ लाग्छ** 'I am always tired in the evening'.

4 Passive verbs are formed by adding the suffix **इनु** to the verb stem, e.g. **देख्नु** becomes **देखिनु** 'to be seen' and **देखिन्छ** 'is seen'. The person or pronoun is understood within the verb. The passive verbs can be used in all tenses.

5 **जस्तो** is used as a postposition to show similarities between two entities, e.g. **नेपालजस्तो देस** 'a country like Nepal'. It is also used with passive verbs as in **जस्तो देखिन्छ** 'it looks/seems like' and **जस्तो सुनिन्छ** 'it sounds like'. But when you use **जस्तो** with **लाग्छ** it implies a person who feels it as in 'it seems to me'.

12 ऊ कता गएको छ ?

Where has he gone?

In this unit you will learn:

- *how to use the completed tenses*
- *how to state the time of day*
- *how to report what others have said*
- *how to use verb forms to specify causes*

21 A late start

12.01

The Paudel family have overslept, and to make matters worse Father has lost his watch and they do not know what time it is.

लक्ष्मी	बा, बा, अहिले कति बज्यो ?
बा	थाहा छैन छोरी । सायद आठ बजेको होला । भाइ उठेको छैन ?
लक्ष्मी	उठेको छैन बा । अझ पनि आफ्नै कोठामा छ ।
बा	उसलाई उठाऊ अब । पहिला तिमी छिटो तल गएर पसलको भित्ते-घडी हेरेर आऊ त ।
लक्ष्मी	हवस् । पहिला म घडी हेरेर आउँछु अनि त्यसपछि मात्र भाइलाई उठाउँछु ।
बा	उमा, मेरो घडी कता पऱ्यो ? तिमीले देख्यौ ?
आमा	खै, कुन्नि मैले त देखिनँ । तपाईंले हिजो कुन कोट लाउनुभयो ? ऊ त्यो कालो कोट, होइन ? त्यसको भित्री खल्तीमा छाम्नुहोस् त । त्यहाँ छ कि ?
लक्ष्मी	बा ! बा ! आठ बजेको होइन, पौने नौ बजेको छ ।
बा	अहो आज साह्रै ढिलो भयो । तिम्रो भाइ उठेको छैन अहिलेसम्म ? खोइ चिया बनाएनौ तिमीहरूले ?
लक्ष्मी	पानी भरखर उम्लेको छ । अब म तुरुन्तै बनाउँछु ।
आमा	लक्ष्मी, ए लक्ष्मी ! धोबी आएन अहिलेसम्म ?
लक्ष्मी	आएको छैन, आमा । तपाईंले उसलाई मेरो नयाँ सारी दिनुभएन ?
आमा	दिएकी छैन छोरी, तिम्रो भाइको स्कूलको लुगा मात्रै दिएँ ।

लक्ष्मी	ठीकै छ नि । आज आइतवार हो । भाइको स्कूल छुट्टी छँदै छ । भरेसम्म लुगा ल्याउँछ नि । ल, चिया तयार भयो, आउनुहोस् । बा पनि आउनुहोस् ।
आमा	ल, ल, बाबुछोरी चिया खानुहोस् । म भाइलाई पनि उठाएर ल्याउँछु ।

Quick vocab

बा	father, dad
अहिले	now
बज्नु	to ring, strike
सायद	perhaps
होला	it might be (see **Grammar 92** on होला)
अझ पनि	still, even now
उठाउनु	to rouse, lift up
पहिला	first (adverb)
तल	down, below
भित्ते-घडी	wall clock
खै	well; I don't know
कुन्नि	who knows? search me!
कोट	coat
लाउनु	to wear
भित्री	inner
खल्ती	pocket
छाम्नु	to feel with the hand
पौने	a quarter to
खोइ	well; I don't know
उम्लनु	to come to the boil
तुरुन्त	immediately
धोबी	laundryman
सारी	sari; woman's dress
लुगा	clothes
भरे	this evening
बाबुछोरी	father and daughter

Lakshmi	Father, father, what time is it now?
Father	I don't know, daughter. Perhaps it's 8 o'clock. Is your brother not up yet?
Lakshmi	No he's not. He is still in his own room.
Father	Get him up now. But first go quickly downstairs, look at the wall clock in the shop and come back.
Lakshmi	Very well. First I'll look at the clock, and only after that I'll get brother up.
Father	Uma, where's my watch got to? Have you seen it?
Mother	Well I don't know, I haven't seen it. Which coat did you wear yesterday? It was that black coat over there, wasn't it? Feel inside its inner pocket, then. Is it there?
Lakshmi	Father, father! It's not 8 o'clock, it's a quarter to nine!
Father	Oho, we're really late today. Hasn't your brother got up yet? And haven't you made any tea?
Lakshmi	The water has only just boiled. Now I'll make it right away.
Mother	Lakshmi, oh Lakshmi! Hasn't the washerman come yet?
Lakshmi	No he hasn't, mother. You haven't given him my new sari?
Mother	No I haven't, daughter, I only gave him your brother's school clothes.
Lakshmi	Then that's all right, you know. Today is Sunday. It's brother's school holiday. He'll bring the clothes by this evening, you know. There, the tea's ready, please come. Father please come too.
Mother	There, there, father and daughter drink your tea. I'll get brother up and bring him too.

Grammar

77 THE COMPLETED PRESENT TENSE

This tense describes an event or action that happened in the past but still has some bearing on the present because nothing has happened since to supersede or negate it. It is the equivalent of the English *he has come, she has seen, they have done,* but in Nepali the English *has* is replaced by the Nepali for *is* or *are* (छ, छस्, छौ, etc.)

The tense consists of two words. Technically, the first word is called the 'perfect participle', because it describes an action that has been 'perfected' or 'completed'. We shall see later that this participle can be used on its own and in other tenses too. It is formed very simply by adding the ending -एको **-eko** to the past tense base of the verb or, in the case of the High forms, by adding -भएको **-bhaeko** to the dictionary form of the verb. The -एको participle describes the condition of its subject in terms of something it has done or has been in the past.

High forms						*All other forms*					
गर्नु	+	भएको	=	गर्नुभएको		गर्-	+	एको	=	गरेको	done
बस्नु	+	भएको	=	बस्नुभएको		बस्-	+	एको	=	बसेको	seated
बिर्सनु	+	भएको	=	बिर्सनुभएको		बिर्स्-	+	एको	=	बिर्सेको	forgotten
आउनु	+	भएको	=	आउनुभएको		आ-	+	एको	=	आएको	come
जानु	+	भएको	=	जानुभएको		ग-	+	एको	=	गएको	gone
रुनु	+	भएको	=	रुनुभएको		रो-	+	एको	=	रोएको	cried
हुनु	+	भएको	=	हुनुभएको		भ-	+	एको	=	भएको	been

The second word in the completed present tense is the appropriate form of the verb **छ,** according to the number and gender of the subject of the verb. If the verb is transitive, the subject must take -**ले** because grammatically this is a past tense:

मैले गरेको छु ।	I have done.
तिमी सुतेका छैनौ ।	You are not asleep.
उसले किनेको छ ।	He has bought.
हामीले बिर्सेका छौं ।	We have forgotten.
उनीहरू गएका छैनन् ।	They have not gone.

● INSIGHT

There is a short form of the verb for the present perfect tense. If you say -गएको छु this is often pronounced as गा'को छु or even shorter form गा'छु. This is with the verbal stem that ends with a vowel. Verbs that end with consonants use -या as suffix to the verb stem, e.g. गर्‍या छैन or भन्या छैन.

The -**एको** participle can take feminine and plural endings, just as adjectives do. If the subject of the verb is feminine, the ending should be -**एकी -ekī:**

बहिनी स्कूल गएकी छे । Younger sister has gone to school.

If the subject is plural the ending should change to -**एका -ekā:**

केटाहरूले नमस्ते भनेका छन् । The boys have said hello.

These rules are observed consistently in written Nepali, but less consistently in the spoken language. As always, the High forms are the same regardless of the number and gender of the subject.

Although the completed present tense generally refers to an action that was completed in the past, certain verbs must be translated into the continuous present in English. These verbs should be thought of as verbs that indicate a specific limited action (for instance, **बस्नु** *to sit down* and **सुत्नु** *to go to bed* or *to fall asleep*), or that refer to the *beginning* of an action:

ऊ मेचमा बसेको छ ।	He is sitting on a chair (he has sat down on a chair).
पानी परेको छ ।	It is raining (it has begun to rain).
मेरो टाउको दुखेको छ ।	My head is hurting (my head has begun to hurt).
पानी उम्लेको छ ।	The water is boiling (the water has come to the boil).
ऊ माथिको कोठामा सुतेको छ ।	He is sleeping (he has gone to bed/ fallen asleep) in the upstairs room.

The completed present tense is often used to give negative answers to questions that have been posed in the simple past tense, because the simple past (as explained earlier) does sometimes mean much the same as the completed present:

Q को आयो ?	Who has come?
A कोही आएको छैन ।	No one has come.

In everyday speech, the -**एको -eko** ending is often dropped in the negative, and if the base ends in **-a** or **-ā** the vowel is lengthened:

कोही आ'छैन ।	No one has come.
म गा'छैन ।	I have not gone.

Exercise 42

Translate into Nepali:

1 Elder brother has gone to Darjeeling.

2 Sister-in-law has stayed in Kathmandu.

3 Has anyone come to your (High) house? Your (Middle) younger brother has come, but apart from him nobody has come.

4 The water hasn't boiled yet.

5 I have given your clothes to the washerman.

6 He (Low) has bought five new books.

Exercise 43

Answer the following questions with (a) a simple past affirmative and (b) a completed present negative:

Example

कान्छाले भाँडा माझ्यो ?	**a** अँ, माझ्यो । (Yes he has).
(Has **Kānchā** scrubbed the pots?)	**b** अहँ, माझेको छैन । (No he hasn't).

१ दाइ दार्जीलिङ्ग जानुभयो ?

२ भाउज्यू काठ्माडौं आउनुभयो ?

३ तपाईंको घरमा त्यो मान्छे आयो ?

४ तिमीले भात खायौ ?

78 STATING THE TIME OF DAY USING बज्यो

बज्यो is the simple past tense of the verb **बज्नु**, *to ring* or *to strike*. Literally, **बज्यो** means *it struck* or *it rang*, and its subject is a number: *three rang, half past four rang*, etc. The verb remains singular (that is, it ends in **-यो** in the affirmative) in all instances.

Although it is grammatically in the past tense, **बज्यो** is used to ask or tell the present time. The negative form is usually **बजेको छैन**.

अहिले चार बज्यो ?	Is it 4 o'clock now?
अँ, चार बज्यो ।	Yes, it is 4 o'clock.
or	
अहँ, चार बजेको छैन ।	No, it is not 4 o'clock.

It is very important to distinguish between the verb … बज्यो **… bajyo**, *it is … o'clock now*, and the adverb … बजे **… baje,** *at … o'clock:*

तपाईं कति बजे घर जानुहुन्छ ?	At what time do you go home?
म साढे पाँच बजे जान्छु ।	I go at half past 5.
अहिले सवा पाँच बज्यो, होइन ?	It's a quarter past 5 now, isn't it?
हो, म पन्ध्र मिनेटपछि जान्छु ।	Yes, I'll go in ('after') 15 minutes.

INSIGHT

Remember that बजे is an adverb that is used to indicate the time at which an event or an activity begins or ends whereas बज्यो is simply a past form of बज्नु 'to ring'. However, in rural areas people often say बेला कति भो 'what is the time?' instead of कति बज्यो ?

Stating times that include minutes past or minutes to the hour (other than half and quarter hours) involves the use of two different forms of the verb **बज्नु** *to ring:* these are the **-era** participle **बजेर** and the infinitive form **बज्न** plus the postposition **-लाई**:

पाँच बजेर बीस मिनेट ।	Twenty minutes past 5.
पाँच बज्नलाई बीस मिनेट ।	Twenty minutes to 5.

Exercise 44

Answer the following questions about the clockfaces below:

घडी न० १ मा कति बज्यो ?

घडी न० २ मा कति बज्यो ?

घडी न० ३ मा कति बज्यो ?

घडी न० १ मा साढे दस बज्यो ? कति बज्यो त ?

घडी न० २ बाह्र बज्यो ? कति बज्यो त ?

(I)

(II)

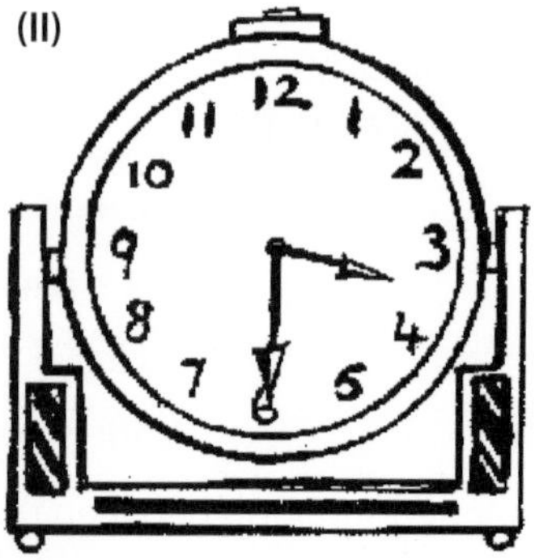

(III)

22 Which countries have you visited?

12.02

Surya Prakash has come to visit Om Bahadur and his son Dhan Bahadur, and the conversation has turned to the subject of foreign travel. Dhan Bahadur relates an unfortunate experience he once had in London.

सूर्य प्रकाश	तपाईं विदेशमा कहाँ कहाँ घुम्नुभएको छ ?
ओम बहादुर	म भारतमा घुमेको छु र बर्मामा पनि । तपाईं नि ?
सूर्य प्रकाश	पोहोर सालसम्म म भारतसम्म मात्रै घुमेको थिएँ तर गएको पूस महिनामा म बेलायत गएँ । तपाईं यूरोप जानुभएको छैन ?

ओम बहादुर	यूरोप त म गएको छैन । मेरो जेठो छोरा धन बहादुर दुई वर्ष अघि लण्डन पुगेको थियो कामको सिलसिलामा । ऊबाहेक हाम्रो परिवारको कोही पनि यूरोप गएको छैन ।
सूर्य प्रकाश	तपाईंको छोरालाई लण्डन मन पऱ्यो त ?
ओम बहादुर	साह्रै रमाइलो छ रे । अस्ति मात्रै म अलिपछि दोस्रो पटक बेलायत जान्छु भनेर भन्दै थियो । लण्डनका रमाइला अनुभवहरू बिर्सेको छैन उसले । तर लण्डन बसेको बेलामा उसलाई एउटा नरमाइलो घटना पनि भयो रे ।
सूर्य प्रकाश	के भयो त ?
ओम बहादुर	ए धने, यता आएर सूर्य प्रकाशजीलाई आफ्नो कथा सुनाऊ न !
धन बहादुर	हवस् त बुवा । एक दिन साँझतिर मेरो काम सिद्धिएको थियो । मेरो डेरा अफिसबाट टाढा भएकोले र पानी परेकोले म बस चढेर त्यसैमा घर गएँ । बस हिंड्ने बेलासम्म खाली सीट नपाएकोले म अर्को मान्छेको छेउमा बसें । बीचबाटोमा छेउमा बसेको मान्छे उठेर गयो र त्यसको अलि बेरपछि बस कण्डक्टर आएर मसँग टिकटको पैसा माग्यो ।
सूर्य प्रकाश	अँ, अनि के भयो ?
धन बहादुर	छेउमा बसेको मानिसले मेरो झोलाबाट वालेट निकालेर भागेको थियो तर मैले केही पनि थाहा पाएको थिइनँ ।
सूर्य प्रकाश	अनि त्यसपछि के भयो ?
धन बहादुर	कण्डक्टर साह्रै असल मानिस थियो । उसले अबदेखि आफ्नो पैसा सुरक्षित ठाउँमा राख्नुहोस् भनेर मलाई सल्लाह दियो ।
सूर्य प्रकाश	पैसाबाहेक अरू थोक त हराएको थिएन ?
धन बहादुर	थिएन । पैसा मात्रै हरायो ।
ओम बहादुर	अनि पैसा यसरी हराएर तिमीले एउटा उपयोगी पाठ सिक्यौ, होइन त ?
धन बहादुर	हजुर ! सिकें ।

Quick vocab

विदेश	abroad
घुम्नु	to travel
बर्मा	Burma
पोहोर साल	last year
गएको	last, previous
पूस	*Pūs* (the name of a month)
यूरोप	Europe
सिलसिला	course, process

अनुभव	experience
घटना	incident
धने	the familiar form of the son's name
कथा	story
बेला	time, occasion
सीट	seat
-को छेउमा	beside
कण्डक्टर	conductor
टिकट	ticket
माग्नु	to ask for
झोला	bag
वालेट	wallet
निकाल्नु	to extract, take out
भाग्नु	to run away
असल	of good character, honest
सुरक्षित	secure
सल्लाह	advice
थोक	thing, item
हराउनु	to be lost
उपयोगी	useful
पाठ	lesson
सिक्नु	to learn

Surya Prakash To which places have you travelled abroad?

Om Bahadur I have travelled in India and in Burma too. What about you?

Surya Prakash Up until last year I had travelled only as far as India, but last Pūs I went to England. Have you not visited Europe?

Om Bahadur Europe is somewhere I haven't visited. My eldest son Dhan Bahadur got to London two years ago in the course of his work. Apart from him, no one in our family has visited Europe.

Surya Prakash Did your son like London then?

Om Bahadur He says it's very pleasant. Just the other day he was saying that after a little while he will go to London a second time. He hasn't forgotten the enjoyable experiences of London. But when he stayed in London one unpleasant incident apparently also occurred.

Surya Prakash What happened?

Om Bahadur	Oh Dhane, come here and tell Surya Prakash your story, won't you?
Dhan Bahadur	Certainly, father. One day my work had finished around dusk. Because my lodgings were far from the office and because it was raining, I boarded a bus and went home in that. Because I couldn't find an empty seat before the bus set off, I sat down beside another man. On the way, the man who was sitting beside me got up and left, and a little while later the bus conductor came and asked me for the money for the ticket.
Surya Prakash	Yes, and then what happened?
Dhan Bahadur	The man who was sitting beside me had taken the wallet out of my bag and run away, but I had not known at all.
Surya Prakash	And what happened after that?
Dhan Bahadur	The conductor was a very good man. He advised me, saying that I should from now on keep my money in a secure place.
Surya Prakash	Apart from the money, no other thing was lost?
Dhan Bahadur	No. Only the money was lost.
Om Bahadur	And, having lost money like this, you learned a useful lesson, didn't you?
Dhan Bahadur	Yes, I did!

Grammar

79 THE COMPLETED PAST TENSE

The -**एको** participle is used with the appropriate form of the verb **थियो** (*was, were*) to describe an action that occurred in the past and does not necessarily tell us anything about the present. The technical name for this tense is the 'pluperfect'. Often, the sense is that the action or event described has been superseded or negated by some other action or event. This tense can usually be translated by using the English word *had,* but in Nepali the tense is used whenever the speaker feels that there is a certain remoteness between the event that is described and the present time. The following examples illustrate the contrast in meaning between the 'completed present' tense that takes **छ** and the 'completed past' tense that takes **थियो**:

म घर फर्केको छु ।	I have returned home (and that is where I am now).
म घर फर्केको थिएँ ।	I had returned home (but I am not necessarily there any more).
उसकी दिदीले बिहा गरेकी छैनन् ।	His elder sister has not married (she is currently unmarried).
उसकी दिदीले बिहा गरेकी थिइनन् ।	His elder sister had not married (but this is not to say that she has not married since).

मेरो छोराले यो किताब पढेको छैन ।	My son has not read this book (and still hasn't read it).
मेरो छोराले यो किताब पढेको थिएन ।	My son had not read this book (but he might have read it by now).
पानी परेको छ ।	It is raining (it has begun to rain).
पानी परेको थियो ।	It was raining (it had begun to rain).
मेरो टाउको दुखेको छ ।	My head is hurting (my head has begun to hurt).
मेरो टाउको दुखेको थियो ।	My head was hurting (my head had begun to hurt).

• INSIGHT

Note that the past particle -एको followed by हुनाले or ले forms a causal construction for the past or present perfect tense. You can't use the same construction for the present habitual or future tenses. किनभने or त्यसकारण are causal conjunctions in any tense, but they require two separate verb conjugations in a sentence.

Exercise 45

Translate into Nepali:

1 My father had never been abroad.

2 In 1978 I went ('had gone') to Nepal for the first time.

3 They (Middle) were sitting in the bus station (**bas bisaunī**) but the bus had not come.

4 It was raining but Rame had not brought his umbrella.

5 His (Low) head was hurting but he had not taken any medicine.

6 They (Middle) had come from Ilām but they had not brought any tea.

80 REPORTING SPEECH USING भनेर

In English, when one reports what someone else has said, the usual construction is 's/he said that' following which one summarizes what was said: 'she said that she was going out'. In Nepali, however, speech is usually reported by quoting the actual words that a person has uttered: 'she said "I am going out"'. If a woman has told you that she will come to visit your mother tomorrow, in Nepali you would report her words verbatim to your mother: 'the woman said "I will come to visit your mother tomorrow"'.

The natural place for a Nepali verb is at the end of a Nepali sentence, and so the Nepali for *said* or *asked* or *told* usually comes after the words that are being quoted. In addition, the word for *said* or *asked* or *told* is usually preceded by the **-एर -era** participle of the verb **भन्नु** *to say* (i.e. **भनेर**, but occasionally **भनी**) which serves the purpose of marking the end of the quotation. Speech marks are not usually used when reported speech is written down. The basic structure of a sentence that reports what someone has said is:

quoted person + -ले – verbatim quote – भनेर – said / told / asked, etc.

उसले तिम्रो नाम के हो भनेर मलाई सोध्यो ।	He asked me what my name was.
उसले टोपी लगाऊ भनेर केटालाई अह्रायो ।	He ordered the boy to put his hat on.
तिम्रो साथीले म आउँछु तर आमा आउनुहुन्न भनेर भनेको छ ।	Your friend has said that he will come but his mother will not.

If the person whose words are being quoted was making an enquiry of any kind, the quotation will end with the interrogative word कि to show that it was a question:

उसले आज तिमी बाहिर गयौ कि भनेर मलाई सोध्यो ।	He asked me whether I had been out today.
मेरो गाइडले तपाईंलाई थकाइ लाग्यो कि भनी सोध्यो ।	My guide asked whether I was tired.

● INSIGHT

भनेर or भनी can be used as reported speech markers, but both of them can also be deleted in practice, as there is a trend in Nepali to use such words less frequently these days.

Exercise 46

Report that the person in column A said the thing in column B to the person or persons in column C:

	A	B	C
1	my younger brother	it won't rain today	said to father
2	that tall man	are you English?	asked me
3	mother	is your friend hungry?	asked my sister
4	the teacher	close your books	told the children
5	father	don't go out tomorrow	advised us

81 BECAUSE IT IS, BECAUSE IT WAS: THE –एकौ PARTICIPLE WITH –लै

The -एको -**eko** participle is used in combination with the word कारण (*cause, reason*) plus -ले (the subject-marking suffix introduced in **Grammar 59**) to show that the action of a verb is the cause of something else:

हिजो पानी परेको कारणले मैले एउटा छाता किनें ।	Because it was raining yesterday I bought an umbrella.
टाउको दुखेको कारणले म दिनभरि घरै बसें ।	Because I had a headache I stayed home all day.

The word **कारण** is very often dropped from this construction, leaving only the -**एको** participle plus -**ले**:

अमेरिकामा नेपाली साथी नभएकोले कृष्णलाई शून्य लाग्यो ।	Because he had no Nepali friend in America, Krishna felt lonely.
तातो चिया खानुभएकोले वहाँको जिब्रो पोल्यो ।	Because he drank hot tea, his tongue got burned.

Exercise 47

Combine the pairs of sentences to produce a single sentence, along the following lines:

Example: खाना चिसो छ । त्यसैले मैले खाइनँ । = खाना चिसो भएकोले मैले खाइनँ ।

१ तपाईंले धेरै पिरो खाना खानुभयो । त्यसैले तपाईंलाई दिसा लाग्यो ।

२ वहाँको पेट दुख्यो । त्यसैले वहाँ स्कूल जानुभएन ।

३ बाहिर गर्मी छ । त्यसैले हामी बाहिर जाँदैनौं ।

४ उसँग कलम छैन । त्यसैले उसले चिठी लेखेन ।

५ उनको श्रीमान बिरामी हुनुभयो । त्यसैले उनलाई दुख लाग्यो ।

82 USING THE -एको PARTICIPLE AS AN ADJECTIVE

In English, sentences containing constructions such as 'the man who …' or 'the house where …' are very common, but in Nepali such constructions are rare. Instead, a phrase such as 'the man who came yesterday' becomes in Nepali 'the yesterday-came man' and 'the house where Ram lives' becomes 'the Ram-lived house':

		Literally:
हिजो आएको मान्छे	the man who came yesterday	yesterday-came man
राम बसेको घर	the house where Ram lives	Ram-lived house
तिमीले भनेका कुराहरू	the things you said	by-you-said things
पोहोर साल परेको पानी	the rain that fell last year	last-year-fallen rain
हामीहरू सुतेको बेला	the time we went to bed	we-slept time
गएको सोमवार	last Monday	gone Monday

In these phrases, the -**एको** participle behaves like an adjective, and its **-o** ending must change according to the number and gender of the nouns it describes:

हिजो आएको लोग्नेमान्छे	the man who came yesterday
हिजो आएकी केटी	the girl who came yesterday
हिजो आएका केटाहरू	the boys who came yesterday
देवकोटाले लेखेको चिठी कुनचाहिं हो ?	Which is the letter that Devkota wrote?
तपाईंलाई भेटेको दिन अस्ति जस्तो लाग्छ ।	The day I met you seems like just the other day.
पढे-लेखेका मान्छेहरू यस्ता किताबहरू पढ्दैनन् ।	Educated people do not read books like this.

• INSIGHT

The subject of an adjectival clause takes ले if the verb is transitive, but not for intransitive verbs. You can make adjectival clauses with a person, place or time, e.g. उसले दिएको उपहार 'the gift he gave' (transitive), ऊ गएको ठाउँ 'the place he went' (intransitive).

83 ORDINAL NUMBERS

The ordinal numbers (*first, second, third*, etc.) function as adjectives, just as they do in English. With five exceptions, they are all formed by adding the suffix -ौं to the number in question. Thus:

चार	four	चारौं	fourth
पाँच	five	पाँचौं	fifth
बीस	20	बीसौं	20th
तेत्तीस	33	तेत्तीसौं	33rd

The following numbers have special forms:

एक	one	पहिलो	first
दुई	two	दोस्रो	second
तीन	three	तेस्रो	third
छ	six	छैटौं	sixth
नौ	nine	नवौं	ninth

यो महाराजाधिराजको आठौं नेपाल-भ्रमण हो । — This is His Majesty's eighth tour of Nepal.

असारको पहिलो दिनमा हाम्रो गाउँमा पहिरो गएको थियो । — On the first day of Asar there had been a landslide in our village.

पहिलो, *first*, can also be used as an adverb to mean *before* or *previously*, by changing its ending from **-o** to **-ā**:

तपाईं पहिला पनि नेपाल आउनुभयो ? होइन, यो मेरो लागि पहिलो पटक हो । — Have you visited Nepal previously as well? No, this is the first time for me.

When it is added to certain large numbers, the suffix -ौं modifies their meanings in a rather different way:

सय	hundred	सयौं	hundreds of
हजार	thousand	हजारौं	thousands of
लाख	hundred thousand	लाखौं	hundreds of thousands of ('lakhs of')
करोड	ten million	करोडौं	tens of millions of ('crores of')

दोस्रो विश्व-युद्धमा लाखौं मान्छेहरू मरे । तीमध्ये हजारौं नेपाली नागरिकहरू पनि थिए । Hundreds of thousands of people died in the Second World War. There were thousands of Nepali citizens among them too.

• INSIGHT

सयौं and हजारौं are really ordinal numbers equivalent to 'hundredth' and 'thousandth', respectively but these words are also used to mean 'hundreds of' or 'thousands of', e.g. सयौं मानिसहरू 'hundreds of people', हजारौं फुलहरू 'thousands of flowers'.

Exercise 48

Translate into Nepali:

1 The guests who came yesterday are all English.

2 It's raining outside. Take that umbrella you (Middle) bought in the bazaar last week.

3 The month when you (Middle) arrived in Nepal is Baisākh.

4 This is the tenth time that I have visited Nepal.

5 The house that you (High, plural) stayed in is very old.

6 Last Friday I had not received the letter you (High) wrote.

7 He (Low) is not the man who came from India.

8 This is not the present you (Middle) gave to mother.

The most important things for the reader to remember

1 The present perfect tense is used to express a completed action without referring to any specific point of time, e.g. **ऊ नेपाल गएको छ** 'He has been to Nepal'. If you used the simple past tense **हिजो** in this sentence, it would be wrong.

2 This tense is used to express the present and ongoing effect of a past action, e.g. **राम आएको छ** 'Ram has come'. The implication is Ram came (past action) and he is still here (present effect). This tense is often used with an action that has been completed a number of times, e.g. **म नेपाल दुई पटक गएको छु** 'I have been to Nepal two times'.

3 Just as the perfect participle and the paradigm **छ** form the present perfect tense, the perfect participle and the paradigm **थियो** form the past perfect tense. The past perfect (pluperfect) tense is used for a situation that takes place in a past more remote than the simple past tense.

4 बज्यो is the past form of बज्नु meaning 'to ring' or 'to strike'. It is used to ask and tell the time of the day, e.g. अहिले कति बज्यो ? 'What time is it now?' Remember the difference between बजे and बज्यो.

5 भनेर is used to report someone's speech to someone else; and the actual words and tense of the person's statement are not changed from their original utterance when it is being reported, e.g. रामले म विरामी छु भनेर भन्यो 'Ram said that he was sick'.

6 The verb stem + एको हुनाले or एकोले is a construction that shows cause and effect. न can be prefixed to the verb to make it negative, e.g. पानी परेको हुनाले जाडो भयो 'It was cold because it rained,' पानी नपरेको हुनाले गर्मी भयो 'It was warm because it did not rain'.

7 The perfect participle can be used as an adjective, e.g. गएको हप्ता 'last week'. You can use the same verb to form an adjectival clause for the past tense, which can be translated by a relative clause in English, e.g. मैले किनेको किताब 'the book I bought', जापानमा किनेको गाडी 'the car bought in Japan'.

8 Memorize the ordinal numbers from पहिलो (first) to छैठौं (sixth) and then just add the suffix औं to each number all the way up to a hundred, e.g. दसौं, बीसौं, सयौं 'tenth, twentieth and hundredth'. A foreigner who can count to 100 in Nepali will never fail to impress.

13 प्रिय राजु ...
Dear Raju ...

In this unit you will learn:
- ***how to say how long ago something happened***
- ***how to talk about seeing or hearing actions performed by others***
- ***how to discuss intentions and the meanings of words***
- ***how to use dates***

23 An exchange of letters

This text is adapted from a passage in TW Clark's *Introduction to Nepali*, first published in 1963.

काठ्माडौं

२०४५/६/६

प्रिय मित्र राजु

भोलिदेखि म स्कूल जाँदिन । आज स्कूलमा मेरो अन्तिम दिन थियो । ढोकानेर उभिएर मैले मभन्दा साना उमेरका केटाहरूले गट्टा खेलेको हेरें । कस्तो रमाइलो ! एउटा मास्टरले मलाई देखेर अबेर भयो किन घर नगएको भनेर सोध्नुभयो । मैले मुख फर्काएँ किनभने मेरा आँखाबाट आँसु बगेको थियो ।

बिस्तारै ढोकासम्म पुगें । ढोकाबाहिर एउटा गाइने उभिएको थियो । मैले बाल्यकालमा धेरै चोटि उसले गाएको र सारङ्गी बजाएको सुनेको थिएँ । मैले उसको हातमा अलिकति पैसा राखेर यतिका दिनसम्म स्कूलमा किन नआएको भनेर सोधें । उसले म बिरामी भएँ, हैजा लागेर झण्डै मरेको हजुर भनेर भन्यो ।

बाले मलाई घरभित्र पसेको देख्नुभयो । किन यस्तो ढिलो भएको भनेर सोध्नुभयो । मैले जवाफ दिइनँ तर वहाँले बुझ्नुभएको जस्तो थियो ।

तपाईंको चिठी नपाएको धेरै भयो । अब चाँडै लेख्नुहोला । तपाईं र तपाईंका प्रियजनलाई प्रेम र शुभकामना ।

तपाईंको मित्र, कुमार

दार्जीलिङ्ग

२५ फेब्रेरी १९८९

प्रिय मित्र कुमार

तिमीले काठ्माडौंबाट पठाएको चिठी पाएर खुशी लाग्यो । गएको महिनादेखि नै अब जवाफ लेख्छु लेख्छु भनेको तर हरेक दिन कुनै न कुनै काम परेकोले लेखिनँ । यति ढिलो गरेकोमा मलाई माफ गर ।

तिमीले लेखेको स्कूलको अन्तिम दिनको बयान मर्मस्पर्शी थियो । मैले एकजना सम्पादक साथीलाई सुनाएँ । उनको नाम कुमार भण्डारी हो । उनले ज्यादै मन पराए । उनले मलाई अलि लामो बयान लेखेर मलाई पठाऊ भनेका छन् । मनमा लागेको जे कुरा पनि लेख्नू भनेका छन् । कुमार भण्डारी तिम्रो दाइले चिनेका मान्छे हुन् क्यारे, होइन ? तर तिम्रो दाइलाई नभेटेको धेरै महिना भयो रे । उनी सिक्किमबाट बसाइँ सरेर आएका हुन् ।

आमालाई मेरो नमस्कार सुनाऊ । चिठी नलेखेकोमा म वहाँसँग क्षमा माग्छु । वहाँको दर्शन नपाएको पनि धेरै वर्ष भयो । कति वर्ष भयो सम्झना छैन ।

तिम्रो हितैषी, राजु

Quick vocab

प्रिय	dear
मित्र	friend
-नेर	near to
उभिनु	to stand upright
गट्टा	a game played with pebbles
मास्टर	schoolmaster
मुख	face
फर्काउनु	to turn
आँसु	tear(s)
बग्नु	to flow
पस्नु	to enter
बुझ्नु	to understand
प्रियजन	loved ones
प्रेम	love
शुभकामना	good wish(es)
फेब्रेरी	February
पठाउनु	to send
जवाफ	reply
लेख्नु	to write
माफी	forgiveness
गाइन	a member of a caste of itinerant village singers or minstrels
बाल्यकाल	childhood
चोटि	time, turn
सारङ्गी	fiddle, Nepali violin
गाउनु	to sing
बजाउनु	to play music
बिरामी	ill
हैजा	cholera
झण्डै	almost
मर्नु	to die
बयान	account, description
मन पराउनु	to like

चिन्नु	to know (a person)
क्यारे	I think
क्षमा	forgiveness
दर्शन पाउनु	to get to see someone (ultra-polite)
सम्झना	memory

Kathmandu, 2045/9/9

Dear friend Raju,

From tomorrow I will not go to school. Today was my last day at school. I stood near the gate and watched boys younger than me playing with pebbles. What fun! A master saw me and asked me why I hadn't gone home, it was late. I turned my face away because tears were flowing from my eyes.

Slowly I reached the gate. A Gaine was standing outside the gate. In my childhood I had heard him singing and playing the fiddle many times. I put a little money in his hand and asked him why he hadn't been to the school for so many days. He said that he had been ill, that he had caught cholera and nearly died.

Father saw me enter the house. He asked me why I was so late. I did not answer him, but Father seemed to understand.

It's been a long time since I received a letter from you. Now please write soon. Love and good wishes to you and your loved ones.

Your friend, Kumar.

Darjeeling, 25 February 1989

Dear friend Kumar,

I was happy when I received the letter you sent from Kathmandu. Since last month I have been intending to write but I didn't write because every day some job or other came my way. Forgive me for being so late.

The description you wrote of your last day at school was very touching. I read it out to an editor friend. His name is Kumar Bhandari. He liked it very much. He says you should write a slightly longer account and send it to him. He says you should write whatever you like. I think Kumar Bhandari is someone your brother knows, is that not so? But he says he hasn't met your brother for many months. He has moved here from Sikkim.

Please convey my greetings to your mother. I ask her forgiveness for not having written a letter. It is many years since I have seen her. I cannot remember how many years it is.

Your well-wisher, Raju.

Grammar

84 USING THE -एको PARTICIPLE AS A VERB

The -**एको** participle is used on its own, without any auxiliary verb, to form an abbreviated completed present tense. In this case, the negative is formed by adding the prefix **न**-:

ऊ कहिले आएको ?	When did he come?
हिजो आएको ।	He came yesterday.
तिमीहरू अघि किन नआएको ?	Why didn't you come before?
खै, कुन्नि किन नआएको हजुर !	Well, who knows why we didn't come sir!
के गरेको तिमीले ?	What have you done?
आफ्नै काम गरेको ।	Just my own work.

● INSIGHT

The एको participle is used to form a colloquial past (not conjugated), which is an alternative to the simple past conjugation. However, if you use the colloquial past all the time just because it is easy it will sound rather strange!

85 HOW LONG IS IT SINCE ... ?

The -**एको** participle is used to express the idea of time having elapsed since something happened. For example, if you wish to ask someone how long they have been in Nepal you can phrase the question 'you Nepal come how much time happened':

तिमी नेपाल आएको कति दिन भयो ?	How many days has it been since you came to Nepal?

The word **दिन** *day(s)* is optional here. It can be left out, or have another word for a period of time (e.g. **हप्ता** *week*, **महिना** *month*, or **वर्ष** *year*) substituted for it. A person who has *not* visited Nepal for a long time might be asked the question

तिमी नेपाल नगएको कति वर्ष भयो ?	How many years is it that you have not gone to Nepal? (i.e. since you last went to Nepal?)
मासु नखाएको दुई महिना भयो ।	It's two months since I ate meat.
हिन्दी फिलिम नहेरेको धेरै भएको छ ।	It's been a long time since I watched a Hindi film.

● INSIGHT

When you ask a question using the colloquial past, e.g. तपाईं कहाँ गएको, it literally means 'where did you go?' but actually it means 'where have you been?' The implication is 'someone was looking for you'.

86 SEEING OR HEARING ANOTHER PERSON'S ACTIONS

The -**एको** participle is used to describe what someone is doing when another person sees or hears them. The sentences on the left-hand side below say that someone saw or heard someone else. The sentences on the right amplify them by noting what the person who is seen or heard was doing at the time.

In such sentences, the **-एको** participle translates as *going, singing, playing, speaking* etc. and in the word order it must follow the person who is being seen or heard. If the person who is seen or heard is performing a transitive verb, then s/he must take the suffix -**ले**

अस्ति मैले तिमीलाई देखें ।	अस्ति मैले तिमीलाई स्कूल गएको देखें ।
I saw you two days ago.	I saw you going to school two days ago.
बुवाले मेरो कुरा सुन्नुभयो ।	बुवाले मैले गीत गाएको सुन्नुभयो ।
Father heard me.	Father heard me singing a song.
आमाले बच्चाहरूलाई हेर्नुभयो ।	आमाले बच्चाहरूले गट्टा खेलेको हेर्नुभयो ।
Mother watched the children.	Mother watched the children playing pebbles.

● INSIGHT

You can construct a complex sentence in the past tense by adding anything you need after the एको participle. But once you end the sentence with the appropriate conjugation of any tense, the sentence is complete and nothing further can be added.

You can use the एको participle to express the elapsing of time since the inception of an action that is still ongoing, e.g. मैले नेपाली सिकेको एक बर्ष भयो. However, there is another construction with the same sense in which the inception time of an action is mentioned in the present perfect tense, e.g. म एक बर्षदेखि नेपाली सिक्दै छु 'I have been learning Nepali for one year'.

Exercise 49

Translate into Nepali:

1 She (Middle) saw him (Low) playing cards yesterday.

2 I heard her (Middle) singing that song last month.

3 He (Low) saw him (High) coming home three days ago.

4 I saw you (Middle) smoking a cigarette last Wednesday.

5 He (High) heard her (Middle) speaking Hindi last week.

6 They (Middle) saw you (Middle) going to school the day before yesterday.

87 THE -एकौ PARTICIPLE WITH हौ OR होइन

The -**एको** participle is also used in combination with the appropriate form of the verb **हो** to form a completed present tense which identifies and emphasizes the subject of the verb (this is less common than the combinations with **छ** and **थियो**):

त्यो काम उसले गरेको हो ।	That job is the one he did.
ऊ मेरी प्रेमिका हो, बिहा गरेको होइन ।	She is my girlfriend, we are not married.

The -**एको** participle is also used with **हो** or **होइन** to form a completed present tense which emphasizes the fact that something is or is not the truth:

मैले माछा किनेको होइन ।	It is not fish that I bought.
उनीहरू मन्दिर गएका होइनन् ।	It is not true that they went to the temple.

● INSIGHT

There is a difference between ऊ गएको छ/छैन and ऊ गएको हो/होइन although English translates both of them as 'he has gone'. The first one is clearly a present perfect tense and the latter is the confirmation of an action.

88 THOUGHTS AND INTENTIONS USING भनेर AND भनेकौ

The primary meaning of the verb **भन्नु** is *to say* or *to tell*, but it also has the important secondary meaning of *to think/to remember*. You might find it helpful to think of the -**एर** participle of **भन्नु**, (i.e., **भनेर**) as meaning *saying to oneself* in the following sentences:

भरे घरमा पाहुनाहरू आउँदै छन् भनेर म बजारतिर लागें ।	Remembering ('saying (to myself)')that guests were coming to my home in the evening, I headed for the market.
जिरीबाट खुम्बु टाढा छ भनेर उनीहरू चामल, दाल, नुन र चिया बोकेर हिँडे ।	They set out carrying rice, dāl, salt and tea, remembering ('saying (to themselves)') that Khumbu is far from Jirī.
भाँडामा कोदो बाँकि छ कि भनेर उसले भित्र हेऱ्यो ।	Wondering ('saying (to himself)') if there was any millet left in the pot, he looked inside.

The -**एको** participle of **भन्नु** followed by **त** or **तर**, (i.e. **भनेको त...** or **भनेको तर...**) means *I intended to but ...* It follows a statement of what the speaker intended to do:

आज बिहान बजार जान्छु भनेको त पैसा नै भएन ।	This morning I thought I'd go tothe market, but I didn't even have any money.
चिठी लेख्छु भनेको त बत्ती नै गयो ।	I thought I'd write a letter, but there was a power cut.

● INSIGHT

When a sentence employing the एर participle involves two different subjects and the final verb is in the present continuous or past tense, this indicates a cause and effect. भनेर in this sentence has a similar sense –तपाईंलाई मनपर्छ भनेर मैले मोमो पकाएको 'I cooked momos because I thought you would like them'.

● INSIGHT

म जान्छु भनेको तर सन्चो भएन can be translated as 'I thought that I would go but I was not well'. When one thinks of doing something Nepali uses भनेको as in this example. Note that the subject (मैले) for भनेको is implicit and unstated.

89 WHAT DOES THIS WORD MEAN?

Another use of the -एको participle of भन्नु is to state or ask the meaning of a word.

अँग्रेजीमा 'किताब' भनेको के हो ? अँग्रेजीमा 'किताब' भनेको book हो ।	What is the meaning of the word 'किताब' in English? In English 'किताब' means 'book'.
नेपालीमा 'book' भनेको के हो ? नेपालीमा 'book' भनेको किताब हो ।	What is the meaning of the word 'book' in Nepali? In Nepali, 'book' means 'किताब'.

A second way of asking the meaning of a word involves the use of the word **अर्थ,** *meaning:*

हिमालयको अर्थ हिउँको घर हो ।	The meaning of **himālaya** is 'home of snow'.
पुस्तकालयको अर्थ पुस्तकहरूको घर हो । पुस्तक भनेको किताब हो ।	The meaning of **'pustakālaya** is home of books'. **pustak** means 'book'.

Exercise 50

Fill in the gaps in the following sentences:

१ अँग्रेजीमा पुल भनेको ____ हो ।

२ अँग्रेजीमा ओरालो भनेको ____ हो ।

३ अँग्रेजीमा हैजा भनेको ____ हो ।

४ नेपालीमा letter भनेको ____ हो ।

५ नेपालीमा face भनेको ____ अथवा ____ हो ।

६ नेपालीमा month भनेको ____ हो ।

90 THE NEPALI YEAR

In Nepal, most people use the traditional Bikram calendar, the विक्रम संवत, instead of the western or Gregorian calendar. The Bikram year begins on the first day of the spring month of बैसाख, which falls sometime around the middle of April (on April 19 in 1998). The months are solar rather than lunar, so the correspondence between western and Bikram dates is slightly different from year to year.

The Bikram calendrical era runs 56 years ahead of the Western calendar from January 1 to the first day of बैसाख, and 57 years ahead from the first day of बैसाख until December 31. Thus, January 1998 begins in the middle of the month of पूस and ends in the middle of the following month of माघ in the Bikram year of 2054, while September 1998 begins in the middle of the month of भदौ and ends in the middle of असोज in the Bikram year of 2055.

Bikram Sambat dates may be expressed in full:

२०५४ साल कात्तिक २२ गते शुक्रवार	Friday, the 22nd day of Kāttik, year 2054 (= 7 November 1997)

or in an abbreviated form:

२०५४ असार ३१ गते	31st day of Asār, 2054 (= 15 July, 1997)

The word गते means *day of the solar month*. Thus, if you want to know the date in the Bikram year it is common to ask

आज कति गते हो ?	What's the date today?
आज एक्काईस गते हो ।	It's the 21st today.

The Bikram Sambat is used less commonly among Nepali speakers outside Nepal itself. In Nepali-speaking communities in northeast India and Bhutan, the western calendar is more generally used, and in this case the word गते is replaced by the word तारीख, *day of a month in the western calendar:*

१९९३ मा मेरी कान्छी छोरीको जन्म भयो । कुन महिनामा ? जून महिनाको तेईस तारीखमा ।	My youngest daughter was born in 1993. In which month? On the 23rd of the month of June.

The word साल is used to refer to particular years, instead of the other word for *year*, वर्ष, which is used for periods of time (तीन वर्ष *three years*, एक सय वर्ष *one hundred years*). Nepali speakers often omit the दुई हजार *two thousand* when mentioning a particular year, just as English speakers might talk about what happened in '97, rather than '1997'. So, instead of saying that something happened in दुई हजार सात साल *the year 2007*, they will often simply refer to that year as सात साल *the year seven.*

तपाईं कुन सालमा पहिलो पटक नेपाल आउनुभयो ?	In which year did you first come to Nepal?
म चार वर्ष अघि, एकाउन्न सालमा आएँ ।	I came four years ago, in the year 51.

The months of the Hindu year have classical Sanskrit names which take slightly different colloquial forms in each of the languages of South Asia. The classical names are used on formal or official documents, the colloquial names in everyday speech and also often in writing.

Exercise 51

Translate the following dates into Nepali:

The months of the Nepali year

	Classical name	*Colloquial name*	
१	वैशाख	बैसाख	mid-April to mid-May
२	ज्येष्ठ	जेठ	mid-May to mid-June
३	आषाढ	असार	mid-June to mid-July
४	श्रावण	साउन	mid-July to mid-August

५	भाद्र	भदौ	mid-August to mid-September
६	आश्विन	असोज	mid-September to mid-October
७	कार्त्तिक	कात्तिक	mid-October to mid-November
८	मार्गशीर्ष	मङ्सीर	mid-November to mid-December
९	पौष	पूस	mid-December to mid-January
१०	माघ	माघ	mid-January to mid-February
११	फाल्गुण	फागुन	mid-February to mid-March
१२	चैत्र	चैत	mid-March to mid-April

1 Thursday 10th January 1921.

2 Tuesday 10th Chaitra 2016.

3 Sunday 26th November 1956.

4 Friday 1st Phalgun 2042.

Exercise 52

पढेर बुझ्नुहोस् ।

सुरेन्द्रको दाइ जापान गएको दुई वर्ष भयो । गएको साल दाइले नेपाल फर्केर सुरेन्द्रलाई एउटा राम्रो क्यामेरा दिनुभयो । दुई हप्ता अघि एउटा राम्रो रेडियो पनि पठाउनुभयो । दाइले दिएका क्यामेरा र रेडियो दुवै जापानमा बनेका हुन् । त्यस

कारणले राम्रा र बलिया छन् । एक हप्ता अघि दार्जीलिङ्गबाट आउनुभएको काकाले पनि सुरेन्द्रलाई एउटा क्यामेरा दिनुभयो । तर काकाले दिएको क्यामेरा दाइले दिएको क्यामेरा जस्तो राम्रो र बलियो देखिएन । सुरेन्द्रलाई दुइटा क्यामेरा चाहिँदैन । उसलाई एउटा क्यामेरा मात्रै चाहिन्छ । गएको सोमवार काका दार्जीलिङ्ग फर्कनुभयो र आज बिहान सुरेन्द्रले काकाले दिएको क्यामेरा एउटा साथीलाई बेच्यो । उसले ठूलो नाफा गरेको छ तर उसकी आमा यो कुरा थाहा पाएर रिसाउनुभएको छ । आमा भन्दै हुनुहुन्छ 'केही दिनपछि तेरो काका फेरि आउनुहुन्छ नि । अनि तँ वहाँलाई के भन्छस् ? 'तपाईंले दिनुभएको क्यामेरा मैले बेचें' भनेर भन्छस् ? तुरुन्तै साथीकहाँ गएर बेचेको क्यामेरा फिर्ता ले र साथीलाई पैसा फिर्ता दे । नातेदारले दिएको कोसेली बेच्नु अपराध हुन्छ, बुझिस् ? ।

प्रश्नहरु

१ सुरेन्द्रको दाइ जापान गएको कति वर्ष भयो ?

२ सुरेन्द्रको दाइले जापानबाट के पठाउनुभयो ?

३ दाइले दिएका क्यामेरा र रेडियो किन बलिया र राम्रा छन् ?

४ सुरेन्द्रको काका कहाँबाट आउनुभएको थियो ?

५ सुरेन्द्रलाई कतिवटा क्यामेरा चाहिन्छ ?

६ आमा सुरेन्द्रसँग किन रिसाउनुभयो ?

The most important things for the reader to remember

1 The colloquial past tense of a verb is formed by attaching the perfect participle **एको** to the verb stem. It is not conjugated; so very commonly used in spoken Nepali. **एको** changes to **एका** for plural and **एकी** for feminine. Add **न** before the verb to negate it.

2 The **एको** participle is used as a connector in sentences that indicate the elapsing of time since the end of a completed action, e.g. **मैले घर किनेको तीन बर्ष भयो** 'It has been three years since I bought the house'.

3 Note that the **एको** participle also indicates the elapsing of time since the inception of an action that is still continuing, e.g. **मैले नेपाली भाशा सिकेको एक बर्ष भयो** 'It has been one year since I have learned Nepali'. The context tells us whether this is an ongoing or a completed act.

4 The perfect participle **एको** is also used with verbs such as 'to see', 'to watch', 'to hear' or 'to dream' to find out if any past activity has been noticed by anybody. Note that the perfect participle has its own subject and it also takes **ले** for a transitive verb, e.g. **मैले उसले गीत गाएको सुनें** 'I heard him singing a song'.

5 The **एको** participle when it is followed by **हो** or **होइन** verifies the fact that something has or hasn't happened, e.g. **राम घर गएको हो कि होइन**? 'Is it or is it not true that Ram has gone home?'

6 **भनेर** is primarily a reported speech marker but it also expresses a sense of 'thinking that', 'wondering if' or 'because I thought', e.g. **पानी पर्छ भनेर मैले छाता बोकेको** 'I have carried an umbrella thinking that it would rain'.

7 When a statement is followed by **भनेको तर** it indicates that the speaker was thinking of doing something but for some reason this did not actually happen, e.g. **म तपाईंकाँ आउँछु भनेको तर पाहुना आयो** 'I thought (I said) I would come to your house, but a guest came'.

14 पानी पऱ्यो भने ...

If it rains ...

In this unit you will learn:

- ***how to construct conditional sentences***
- ***how to express doubt***
- ***how to make suggestions***
- ***how to discuss whether something is enough***

24 Out trekking

14.01

Subhas is leading a group of foreign visitors on a trek from Pokhara to Jomsom. They have just arrived at a lodge after a long wet first day. As they eat their evening meal, served by Dilmaya, Subhas discusses the route for the next day with Bekh Bahadur, the lodgekeeper.

दिलमाया	तपाईंहरू यतातिर बसेर भात खानुहोस् है त ! यति भातले पुग्छ कि पुग्दैन ?
सुभास	यति भातले मलाई सायद पुग्दैन होला दिदी । अरू पनि छ कि ?
दिलमाया	पुगेन भने केही छैन । अरू थुप्रै छ ।
बेख बहादुर	भोलि तपाईंहरू कतातिर लाग्ने नि ?
सुभास	गण्डकी पुल झरेर जोमसोमतिर जाने । बाटो ओरालो छ, होइन ? भोलि मौसम सफा भयो भने हामीहरू साँझतिर तातोपानी पुग्छौं होला । तर आज जस्तो भोलि पनि पानी पऱ्यो भने अलि गाह्रो

	होला । बाटो चिप्लो हुन्छ, बिस्तारै बिस्तारै हिँडेर तातोपानी साँझसम्म पुगिँदैन होला । साँझसम्म तातोपानी पुगिएन भने राति कहाँ बास बस्ने त ?
बेख बहादुर	तातोपानीभन्दा तल अर्को एउटा सानो गाउँ छ । बाटोमा ढिलो भयो भने त्यहाँ बास बस्नुहोस् न । गाउँको नाम त बिर्सें । तर त्यहाँबाट तातोपानी माथितिर पर्छ, बाटो अलि उकालो पनि छ । तपाईंहरू त्यहीं बस्नुभयो भने बेस होला । ए दिलमाया, भात खोइ त !
दिलमाया	अरू केही लिनुहुन्छ कि ?
सुभास	भात अलिकति थप्ने ।
दिलमाया	लौ, लिनुहोस् । तरकारी पनि थप्ने ?
सुभास	हवस्, तरकारी पनि थप्नुहोस् । अलिकति दाल छ कि ?
दिलमाया	दाल त सकियो । साथीहरूलाई भात पुग्यो ?
सुभास	पुग्यो होला । विदेशीहरूले त त्यति धेरै भात खाँदैनन् ।
दिलमाया	हातले पनि खाँदैनन्, होइन ?
सुभास	हो, उनीहरूलाई अलि अप्ठ्यारो हुन्छ ।
बेख बहादुर	भोलि तपाईंहरू घोडेपानी भएर जाँदै हुनुहुन्छ, होइन ?
सुभास	अर्को बाटै छैन । अरू कसरी जाने त ?
बेख बहादुर	यहाँबाट घोडेपानी जाने बाटो र घान्द्रुङ्ग जाने बाटो एउटै हो । तर पल्लो गाउँदेखि बाटो छुट्टिन्छ । तलको बाटोचाहिं घोडेपानी जाने बाटो हो, माथिकोचाहिं घान्द्रुङ्ग जाने बाटो हो । भोलि ठूलो पानी पर्‍यो भने घान्द्रुङ्ग बाटोबाट जानुहोस्, अलि सजिलो होला ।
सुभास	त्यो बाटोबाट धौलागिरी देखिँदैन होला । घोडेपानीबाट राम्रोसँग देखिन्छ रे । हिमाल हेर्ने यिनीहरूको कस्तो रहर हुन्छ, हगि ?
बेख बहादुर	त्यो त हो तर ठूलो पानी परेको बेलामा कतैबाट केही पनि देखिँदैन । आउने हप्ता तपाईंहरू त त्यही बाटोबाट फर्कनुहुन्छ, होइन त ? भोलि पानी परेन भने मात्र घोडेपानी जानुहोस् ।
सुभास	ल त, धन्यवाद । अब त सुत्ने बेला भयो । है त ? भोलि भेटौंला ।

Quick vocab

भात	cooked rice, food, meal
पुग्नु (1)	to be enough
थुप्रै	heaps
गण्डकी	the Gandaki river
पुल	bridge
झर्नु	to descend
जोमसोम	Jomsom (a village)

मौसम	weather
सफा	clear
तातोपानी	Tatopani (a village)
पुग्नु (2)	to reach, arrive
बास बस्नु	to stay for a night
-भन्दा तल	below, lower down than
बेस	best, better
थप्नु	to add, supplement, top up
सकिनु	to be finished
घोडेपानी	Ghorepani (a village)
घान्द्रुङ्ग	Ghandrung (a village)
पल्लो	next, further
छुट्टिनु	to divide, bifurcate
धौलागिरि	Dhaulagiri (a mountain)
रहर	desire
हगि ?	isn't that so?
भेटौंला	we will meet (probable future tense: see **Grammar 96**)

Dilmaya	Please sit over here and eat, do you hear? Will this much rice be enough or not?
Subhas	This much rice might not be enough for me, sister. Is there any more?
Dilmaya	If it's not enough it doesn't matter. There's heaps more.
Bekh Bahadur	Where are you heading tomorrow, eh?
Subhas	We're going down to the Gandaki bridge and then towards Jomsom. The path is downhill, isn't it? If the weather is clear tomorrow we'll probably reach Tatopani around dusk. But if it it also rains tomorrow like it did today it will be rather difficult. The path will be slippery, and walking slowly we probably won't reach Tatopani by dusk. If we don't reach Tatopani by dusk, where shall we lodge for the night?
Bekh Bahadur	Below Tatopani there is another small village. If you are slow on the way stay there. I've forgotten the name of the village, though. But from there Tatopani is higher up, the path is rather steep too. If you stay there that will be better. Oh Dilmaya, where's the rice?
Dilmaya	Will you have something more?
Subhas	A little more rice, please.
Dilmaya	There you are. Shall I put vegetables too?

Subhas	Sure, please put vegetables too. Is there a little bit of **dāl** too?
Dilmaya	I'm afraid the **dāl**'s finished. Have your friends had enough rice?
Subhas	I expect they've had enough. Foreigners don't eat such a lot of rice.
Dilmaya	They don't eat with their hands either, do they?
Subhas	Yes, it's a bit difficult for them.
Bekh Bahadur	Tomorrow you're going via Ghorepani, aren't you?
Subhas	There's no other way. How else can we go?
Bekh Bahadur	From here, the path to Ghorepani and the path to Ghandrung are one and the same. But from the next village the path divides. The lower path is the path going to Ghorepani, the higher one is the path going to Ghandrung. If it rains heavily tomorrow, go by the Ghandrung path, it will be a bit easier.
Subhas	You probably can't see Dhaulagiri from that path. I gather that you can get a good view of it from Ghorepani. How they long to see the Himalayas, right?
Bekh Bahadur	That's true, but when it rains heavily nothing can be seen from anywhere. Next week you will come back by that path, won't you? Only go to Ghorepani if it doesn't rain tomorrow.
Subhas	Right then, thank you. Now it's time for bed. OK? We'll meet tomorrow.

Grammar

91 REAL CONDITIONAL SENTENCES

A real conditional sentence is the equivalent of a sentence in English that begins with *if,* and talks about events that might happen or situations that might exist in the future. It is called a 'real' conditional sentence because it always refers to what will be or what might be, and therefore what it describes is *possible: if it doesn't rain I will go out.* There is another kind of conditional sentence that talks about what might have been, but was not, and is therefore *impossible or unreal: if it hadn't rained I wouldn't have gone out.* This second kind of conditional sentence is introduced in **Grammar 130**.

To form a real conditional sentence in Nepali, you take two sentences and link them together with the word **भने**. **भने** is a participle of the verb **भन्नु** *to say* that is not easily translated when it is used in this way, because it simply marks the end of the 'if' clause of the sentence. The closest English parallel is found in an informal expression such as *say/suppose it doesn't rain* ... The 'if' clause of the sentence usually comes before the main clause. When it is referring to some possibility in the future, its verb must be in the *simple past* tense.

The 'if' clause of a conditional sentence can begin with **यदि** *if*, and in fact it often does, but **यदि** *if* is not essential. **भने** is essential in such sentences whether **यदि** is used or not.

> **• INSIGHT**
>
> **A real conditional sentence is constructed with the simple past conjugation in the first clause, followed by भने at the beginning of the second, in which the likelihood of the condition being fulfilled is considered to be low.**

To construct a Nepali sentence that means *if it doesn't rain I will go out*, begin with the simple past tense of *to rain* as the 'if' clause, then add **भने** to show that the 'if' clause has ended, and then state that you will go out:

(यदि) पानी परेन	भने	म बाहिर जान्छु ।
(If) it didn't rain (condition)	(marks end of 'if' clause)	I will go out. (consequence)

= पानी परेन भने म बाहिर जान्छु ।	If it doesn't rain I will go out.
यदि तिमी आएनौ भने म एक्लै जान्छु ।	If you don't come I will go alone.
यदि आमा रुनुभयो भने दिदी पनि रुनुहुन्छ ।	If mother cries elder sister will cry too.
यदि दालमा खुर्सानी राख्नुभएन भने मीठो हुँदैन ।	If you don't put any chilli in the dāl it won't taste good.

> **• INSIGHT**
>
> **यदि at the beginning of a sentence can be used to add emphasis but this is often not employed in colloquial speech. As long as there is भने at the end of the first clause it is a conditional sentence of 'if … then'.**

The second half of a real conditional sentence can also take the form of a request or a command, instead of a prediction:

यदि तपाईंलाई थकाई लाग्यो भने मेरो कोठामा सुत्नुहोस् ।	If you feel tired, please lie down in my room.
यदि बजारमा लसून पाइएन भने अदुवा मात्रै किन्नू, बुझ्यौ ?	If garlic is not available in the market, just buy ginger, do you understand?

> **• INSIGHT**
>
> **When a person says that he is going to Nepal and you know this as a fact, you can use the conditional marker भने with a present tense verb, e.g. तपाईं जानुहुन्छ भने मेरो परिवारलाई एउटा उपहार लगिदिनुस् 'If you are going, then please take a gift for my family'. This condition is more likely to happen than one in which the first clause uses the simple past tense.**

Exercise 53

Translate into Nepali:

1 If you are tired, please rest.

2 If you are thirsty, please drink this water.

3 If our guests are hungry I will go to the market and buy fruit and vegetables.

4 If you (Middle) do not come tomorrow, mother will stay at home and cry.

5 If I do not come to the office by 5 o'clock, please meet me at the temple.

6 If father does not send me a letter this week I will phone him at home.

92 USING होला TO MEAN PERHAPS, MIGHT BE

होला is the *probable future* tense of the verb **हुनु** *to be*, and means *it (probably) will be*. It can be added to the end of statements, regardless of their tense, to qualify them and make them less categorical.

For instance, shopkeeper A is asked whether there is any rice in his shop, and he is sure that there isn't, so he answers categorically:

Q साहूजी, चामल छ ?	Any rice, shopkeeper?
A छैन !	No!

But shopkeeper B is less certain; he thinks there probably isn't any, but feels he had better check:

Q साहूजी, चामल छ ?	Any rice, shopkeeper?
B छैन होला ।	Probably not …
आज पानी पर्दैन होला ।	It probably won't rain today.
आज गिरीश घरै छ ? **थाहा छैन, घरै छ होला ।**	Is Girish at home? I don't know, he probably is at home.
बजारमा मासु पाइँदैन होला ।	You probably won't get any meat in the market.

The probable future tense is introduced in full in **Grammar 96**.

93 THE -ने -NE PARTICIPLE AS AN ADJECTIVE

This participle is simply the dictionary form of a verb with its ending changed from -नु **-nu** to -ने **-ne**:

dictionary form		**-ne** participle	
जानु	to go (verb)	**जाने**	going (adjective)
खानु	to eat (verb)	**खाने**	eating (adjective)
गर्नु	to do (verb)	**गर्ने**	doing (adjective)

The first use of the -ने **-ne** participle is to describe nouns:

पोखरा जाने बाटो	the road to Pokhara ('Pokhara going road')
खाने कुरा	things to eat ('eating things')
आउने हप्ता	next week ('coming week')
सुत्ने कोठा	bedroom ('sleeping room')
काम गर्ने मान्छे	a working man
नेपाली बोल्ने मानिस	a Nepali-speaking person

● INSIGHT

Just as the एको participle is used to create adjectives and adjectival clauses, the ने participle can also be used to create adjectives and adjectival clauses such as सुत्ने कोठा and म सुत्ने कोठा, which can be translated as 'sleeping room' and 'a room where I sleep', respectively.

It is important to distinguish between the -ने participle and the -एको participle, because both are used to describe nouns. However, the -एको participle always refers to actions or situations that are in the past as compared with the main verb of the sentence, while the -ने participle refers to situations that are either coterminous or in the future as compared with the main verb:

हामी नेपाल बसेको बेलामा ।	When we lived in Nepal.
हामी नेपाल बस्ने बेलामा ।	When we live in Nepal.
सगरमाथा चढेको मान्छे ।	A person who has climbed Everest.
सगरमाथा चढ्ने मान्छे ।	A person who does/will climb Everest.
प्रवचन दिएको मान्छे ।	The person who gave the lecture.
प्रवचन दिने मान्छे ।	The person who gives lectures/will give a lecture.

The negative is formed simply by adding the prefix न- to the verb:

नपाइने	unavailable
नखाने	not eating
नबिर्सिने	unforgettable
रक्सी नखाने मान्छेलाई किन रक्सी दिएको तिमीले ?	Why have you given raksī to a person who does not drink?
अँग्रेजी नबुझ्ने केटालाई अँग्रेजीमा किन गाली गर्छौ ?	Why do you tell off a boy who does not understand English in English?
नेपालमा नपाइने फलफूल अमेरिकामा जतातते पाइन्छ ।	Fruits that are not available in Nepal can be found everywhere in America.
आज बादल लागेकोले सगरमाथा देख्ने कुरै छैन ।	Because it is cloudy today there's no chance of seeing Everest.

94 USING THE -ने PARTICIPLE TO TALK ABOUT FUTURE ACTIONS

The second use of the -ने participle is as a kind of grammatical shortcut to talk about plans and intentions for the near future. It is used frequently in informal conversation, and people who speak Nepali as a second language (both Nepalis and foreigners) find it so convenient (because the verb ending is the same no matter who the subject of the verb is) that they sometimes use it excessively:

तपाईंहरू भोलि जाने ?	Are you leaving tomorrow?
होइन, भोलि बस्ने, पर्सि जाने ।	No, we're staying tomorrow and leaving the day after tomorrow.
तपाईं चिया खाने कि कफी खाने ?	Will you drink tea or coffee?
म चिया खाने ।	I'll drink tea.
चियामा चिनी राख्ने ?	Shall I put sugar in the tea?
चिनी नराख्ने, दूध मात्रै राख्ने ।	Don't put sugar, just put milk.
अब जाने, होइन ?	We're off now, aren't we?
हो, अबेर भयो, अब अलिपछि जाने ।	Yes, it's late, we'll leave in a little while now.

These usages are acceptable, but it is more polite to use the variable verb endings, especially when talking to someone you are addressing as तपाईं.

● INSIGHT

Note that the subject of a transitive verb in an adjectival clause takes ले even when it is in the present habitual or simple future tense, e.g. मैले खाने खाना 'the food I eat' or 'the food that I will eat'.

95 THE VERB पुग्नु TO ARRIVE, SUFFICE

This verb has two different uses. In the first, it is used to mean *to reach/arrive* at a destination and in this context it is intransitive (that is, the subject never needs to take -ले):

यो विमान साढे तीन बजे दिल्ली पुग्छ । This flight reaches Delhi at half past 3.

Although it is an intransitive verb, पुग्नु also has a passive 'i-stem' version, which is पुगिनु *to be reached:*

मेरो गाउँ टाढै छ । साँझसम्म पनि पुगिंदैन होला ।	My village is quite a long way away. We probably won't reach it even by nightfall.

When the subject of the verb *to arrive* is *coming towards* the speaker, rather than going away from him/her, then the compound verb आइपुग्नु (consisting of the 'i-stem' of आउनु + पुग्नु) is commonly used:

ल, हेर त, वाराणसीको विमान आइपुग्यो । There, look, the Varanasi flight has arrived.

The second use of **पुग्नु** is to mean *to suffice/be enough,* and in these contexts the verb is transitive (i.e. its subject must take -**ले** in past tenses, and will most often take -**ले** in the habitual present tense too). The person for whom the commodity mentioned suffices or has sufficed must take the object-marking suffix -**लाई**. For instance, if you wish to say that five rupees will be enough money for you, the sentence will be constructed as follows:

मलाई	पाँच रुपियाँले	पुग्छ ।
for me	five rupees + -ले	suffices.

Exercise 54

Write Nepali sentences stating that the amounts or commodities in the right-hand column were or were not enough for the people in the left-hand column:

1 the tourists who came yesterday	this much food	✓
2 the Sherpa who helped us	ten rupees	✕
3 the woman who cooked the food	a kilo of ghee	✕

Exercise 55

Write Nepali sentences stating that the amounts or commodities in the right-hand column might or might not be enough for the people in the left-hand column:

1 the tourists who are coming tomorrow	this much food	✕
2 the Sherpa who is going to help us	ten rupees	✓
3 the woman who cooks the food	a kilo of ghee	✓

The most important things for the reader to remember

1 भने a conditional marker is used at the end of the simple past conjugation of the first clause of a real conditional sentence in Nepali. Note that the final verb in the second clause is always in the simple future sentence, e.g. म नेपाल गएँ भने हिमाल हेर्छु 'If I go to Nepal I will look at the mountains'.

2 Just like the **एको** participle, the **ने** participle is also used in spoken Nepali to indicate future actions and it is not conjugated. Just add **न** before the verb to negate it, e.g. तपाईं जाने कि नजाने ? 'Are you going or not?'

3 The **ने** participle is also used to form verbal adjectives as well as adjectival clauses in the present or future tenses, e.g. बस्ने कोठा 'sitting room', खाने कोठा 'dining room', म जाने देश नेपाल हो 'The country where I am going is Nepal'.

15 म आउने साल जाउँला

I'll go next year

In this unit you will learn:

- ***how to use the probable future tense***
- ***how to talk about how much time and/or money it takes to do something***

25 Going home for Dasain

15.01

Saroj and Krishna both live and work in London, but as the great annual festival of Dasain approaches they begin to wonder whether they might go home to Nepal to celebrate it.

सरोज	यो साल तपाईं दसैंको लागि घर जानुहुन्छ ?
कृष्ण	अहिलेसम्म निश्चय गरेको छैन । तपाईं नि ?
सरोज	पैसा पाइयो भने जाउँला । तर पैसा मात्रै होइन, छुट्टी पनि चाहिन्छ नि ।
कृष्ण	एक हप्ताको छुट्टी त पाइएला नि । त्यो समस्या नहोला । मेरो लागि मुख्य समस्या पैसा नै हो । आजकाल नेपाल पुग्न कति पैसा लाग्छ ?
सरोज	हवाईजहाजबाट जानुभयो भने पाँच सय पाउण्ड लाग्छ, होइन ?
कृष्ण	हो, पाँच सय जति लाग्ला । अनि हवाईजहाजबाट जानुभएन भने कसरी जानुहुन्छ त ? लण्डनबाट बस अथवा रेल काठ्माडौं जान्छ त ?
सरोज	केही टूरिष्ट बसहरू त जान्छन् । तर बसमा नेपाल पुग्न कम्तिमा दुई हप्ता लाग्ला ।
कृष्ण	अनि हामीलाई साहूजीले चार हप्ताको छुट्टी देला र ? मेरो विचारमा दिंदैन !
सरोज	दिंदैन ! हवाईजहाजबाट जानु बाहेक अर्को उपाय छैन ।
कृष्ण	दसैंको बेलामा तपाईंको घरमा को को होलान् त ?
सरोज	बुवा र आमा हुनुहुन्छ । कान्छा र साहिंला भाइहरू पनि हुन्छन् । अरू नातेदारहरू पनि आउलान् । भगवानको कृपा भयो भने म पनि पुगुँला ।
कृष्ण	अनि दिदी नि ?

सरोज	तीन वर्ष अघि दिदीको बिहा भयो । अहिलेसम्म उनी हरेक साल भाइ टीकाको लागि माइत आएकी छिन् । यो साल पनि आउलिन् ।
कृष्ण	माहिलो भाइचाहिं आउँदैन ?
सरोज	माहिलो भाइ सायद आउँदैन होला यस पालि । ऊ दुई महिनादेखि अरबमा काम गर्दै छ । यो साल छुट्टी लिएन भने सायद अर्को साल पाइएला रे । तर यो साल आउने कुरै छैन रे । एक वर्षपछि अलि सजिलो होला उसलाई ।
कृष्ण	अरबमा नेपालीहरूको जिन्दगी कस्तो हुन्छ ? भाइले लेखेको होला नि ?
सरोज	गाह्रो होला, तर तपाईं हेर्नुहोला । दुई-चार वर्षभित्र ऊ दस लाख कमाएर फर्किन्छ । अनि पोखरा गएर उसले महल जस्तो घर बनाउला र त्यसैमा बसेर हामी धूमधामसित दसैं मनाऔंला । अनि हामी हेरौंला, कसको जिन्दगी गाह्रो छ भनेर !

Quick vocab

दसैं	(the festival of) Dasain
निश्चय गर्नु	to decide
मुख्य	main
पाउण्ड	pound
जति	as much as
कम्तिमा	at least
जानुबाहेक	except for/apart from going
उपाय	means
नातेदार	relative
भगवान	God
कृपा	kindness
टीका	anointing
माइत	a married woman's parents' home; her natal home
अरब	Arabia
कमाउनु	to earn
फर्किनु	to return
महल	palace
धूमधाम	pomp and splendour
मनाउनु	to celebrate

Saroj	Will you go home for Dasain this year?
Krishna	I haven't decided yet. What about you?
Saroj	If I get the money I'll go. But it's not just the money, I need time off too, you know.
Krishna	You'll probably get one week's leave, you know. That won't be a problem. For me the main problem is money. How much does it cost to get to Nepal these days?
Saroj	If you go by air it costs £500, doesn't it?
Krishna	Yes, it probably costs about £500. And if you don't go by air how else will you go? Does a bus or a train go to Kathmandu from London?
Saroj	Some tourist buses do go. But to get to Nepal by bus will probably take at least two weeks.
Krishna	And will the boss give us four weeks' leave, indeed?*[1] I think he won't!
Saroj	He won't! There is no alternative to going by plane.
Krishna	But who will be at your house at Dasain?
Saroj	Father and Mother will be there. Youngest and third eldest brother will also be there. Other relatives will probably come too. If God is kind I'll also get there.
Krishna	And what about your elder sister?
Saroj	Three years ago my sister got married. So far she has come to the natal home every year for Bhai Tika.*[2] She'll probably come this year.
Krishna	Won't your second eldest brother come?
Saroj	My second eldest brother might not come this time. He's been working in Arabia for two months. He says that if he doesn't take leave this year he'll probably get it next year. But this year he says there's no question of coming. After a year it will be a bit easier for him.
Krishna	What is life like for Nepalis in Arabia? Your brother must have written?
Saroj	It's probably hard, but you watch! Within a few years he will earn a million and come back. Then he'll go to Pokhara and build a house like a palace, and we'll stay in it and celebrate Dasain with pomp and splendour. Then we'll look to see whose life is hard!

Notes *[1]The addition of र makes a question rhetorical: the person asking knows that the answer is 'no'.

*[2]भाइ टीका is a day of the Tihar festival when sisters anoint their brothers.

Grammar

96 THE PROBABLE FUTURE TENSE

Nepali has several different ways of expressing the future tense, and the main difference between them lies in their degree of certainty.

The habitual present and continuous present tenses can be used to refer to the future, just as they can in English:

भोलि मेरो भाइ भारत जान्छ ।	Tomorrow my brother goes to India.
भोलि मेरो भाइ भारत जाँदै छ ।	Tomorrow my brother is going to India.

Of course, both of these sentences would be in the present tense if the word **भोलि** were removed from them. The probable future tense, however, is used exclusively to refer to the future, and it contains within it a measure of uncertainty:

भोलि मेरो भाइ भारत जाला ।	Tomorrow my brother will (probably) go to India.

In the affirmative, the probable future tense consists of a verb base plus an ending; the endings are as follows:

Probable future tense: verb endings

म	-उँला
हामी, हामीहरू	-औंला
तँ	-लास्
तिमी, तिमीहरू	-औला
ऊ, यो, त्यो (m.)	-ला
ऊ, यो, त्यो (f.)	-ली
उनी, यिनी, तिनी (m.)	-लान्
उनी, यिनी, तिनी (f.)	-लिन्
यी, ती, उनीहरू etc.	-लान्

Probable future tense: verb bases

The formation of the verb bases for the probable future tense has five rules:

1 The endings are added to the bases of C-verbs in a regular manner (**म गरुँला** *I will do,* **तँ गर्लास्** *you will do,* **तिमी गरौला** *you will do,* etc.).

2 If the base of a V-verb ends in -ā, the endings are added in a regular manner (**म खाउँला** *I will eat,* **ऊ खाला** *he will eat,* **उनी खालान्** *he will eat*, etc.).

3 The V-verbs दिनु *to give,* लिनु *to take,* and हुनु *to be* are irregular:

a दिनु employs the base दि- in first person forms (म दिउँला *I will give,* हामी दिऔंला *we will give*) and दे- in all others (ऊ देला *he will give,* उनीहरू देलान् *they will give,* etc.).

b लिनु employs the base लि- in first person forms (म लिउँला *I will take,* हामी लिऔंला *we will take*) and ले- in all others (ऊ लेला *he will take,* उनीहरू लेलान् *they will take,* etc.).

c हुनु employs the base हो- in all forms except the first person singular; thus म हुँला *I will be,* but उनी होलिन् *she will be.*

4 Verbs other than दिनु and लिनु whose bases end in -i (principally the passive 'i-stem' verbs) take an intervening -e- between base and ending, e.g. बिर्सिएला *it will be forgotten,* पाइएला *it will be obtained,* etc.

5 The base of a VV-verb is usually the normal present tense base (आउ. from आउनुए पिउ. from पिउनु etc.). But for the first person forms the second vowel is dropped. Thus: म आउँला *I will come,* हामी आऔंला *we will come,* but ऊ आउला *he will come,* उनीहरू आउलान् *they will come,* etc.

Probable future tense

	हुनु to be	जानु to go	गर्नु to do	आउनु to come	दिनु to give
म	हुँला	जाउँला	गरुँला	आउँला	दिउँला
हामीहरू	होऔंला	जाऔंला	गरौंला	आऔंला	दिऔंला
तँ	होलास्	जालास्	गर्लास्	आउलास्	देलास्
तिमी, तिमीहरू	होऔला	जाऔला	गरौला	आऔला	देऔला
ऊ (m.)	होला	जाला	गर्ला	आउला	देला
ऊ (f.)	होली	जाली	गर्ली	आउली	देली
उनी (m.)	होलान्	जालान्	गर्लान्	आउलान्	देलान्
उनी (f.)	होलिन्	जालिन्	गर्लिन्	आउलिन्	देलिन्
यी, ती, उनीहरू	होलान्	जालान्	गर्लान्	आउलान्	देलान्

Formally, Nepali grammar contains negative forms of these verbs in which their endings change to -ओइन, -ओइनस्, -ओइनौ, etc. but these are encountered very rarely indeed and there is very little purpose in the foreign learner memorizing them. Generally, the future negative is formed either by adding the prefix न- to the forms listed above, or by using the habitual present tense in the negative and adding होला *perhaps* to the end of the statement. The meaning varies slightly, according to which form is used:

म जाउँला ।	I'll probably go.
म नजाउँला ।	I'll probably not go (with the sense that the person who is being spoken to would prefer the person who is speaking not to go).

म जाँदिन होला ।	I probably won't go.
ऊ एउटा सिपाही होला ।	He may be a soldier.
ऊ सिपाही नहोला ।	He may not be a soldier.
ऊ सिपाही हुँदैन होला ।	He probably won't be a soldier.

● INSIGHT

होला means 'probably' or 'maybe' and is used frequently on its own as an expression. It can also be used at the end of a final verb conjugation to indicate the uncertainty of a future action.

Because of the slightly doubtful tone of this future tense, it *has* to be used in sentences that refer to the future and begin with the word **सायद**, *perhaps:*

आज जाँदिन । सायद भोलि-पर्सि जाउँला ।	I won't go today. Perhaps I'll go tomorrow or the day after.

The following proverb uses the probable future tense of the verb **भर्नु** *to fill:*

तैं रानी मै रानी को भर्ला कुवाको पानी ?	(If) you're a queen and I'm a queen, who will fill water from the well?

The High form of the probable future tense consists of the dictionary form of the verb + **होला**. It is therefore identical to the Super-Polite imperative (see **Grammar 44**) and in fact the two meanings do converge:

बेलायतबाट मलाई चिठी लेख्नुहोला ।	Please write me a letter from England.
बेलायतबाट मलाई चिठी लेख्नुहोला कि ?	Will you write me a letter from England?

97 THE INFINITIVE + लाग्नु: WHAT DOES IT COST TO ... ?, HOW LONG DOES IT TAKE TO ... ?

The verb **लाग्नु** is used to mean:

- *to cost* when it is combined with a sum of money:

कति पैसा लाग्छ ?	How much does it cost?
बीस रुपियाँ लाग्छ ।	It costs 20 rupees.

- *to take* when it is combined with a quantity of time:

कति समय लाग्छ ?	How much time does it take?
तीन घण्टा लाग्छ ।	It takes three hours.

Note: There is no Nepali equivalent of the English 'it' in these sentences; and, although the subject of the verb **लाग्नु** may be plural (e.g. *three hours*), the verb behaves as if it is singular; hence **तीन घण्टा लाग्छ,** not **तीन घण्टा लाग्छन्**.

These sentences may be extended by prefacing them with a verb, which must appear in its infinitive form. This is very simply the dictionary form minus its final **-u**:

Dictionary form	***Infinitive***		
जानु	जान	**jāna**	to go
आउनु	आउन	**āuna**	to come
पुग्नु	पुग्न	**pugna**	to reach

Both forms of the verb (-**नु** and -**न**) can be translated as *to go, to come* and so on, and there is very little difference in their meaning. However, only the form ending in -**न** may be used in this kind of sentence:

गोरखा जान कति पैसा लाग्छ ?	How much does it cost to go to Gorkha?
गोरखा पुग्न तीन घण्टा लाग्छ ।	It takes three hours to reach Gorkha.
गोरखा जान र आउन पूरा एक दिन लाग्छ ।	It takes a whole day to go to Gorkha and come (back).

If the sentence involves nouns or pronouns (e.g. *how long does it take* <u>*you*</u> *…*, or *how much does it cost* <u>*them*</u> *…*) then these must take the postposition -**लाई**:

पोखराबाट मुक्तिनाथ पुग्न उनीहरूलाई एक हप्ता लाग्यो ।	It took them a week to reach Muktinath from Pokhara.
जुम्लाबाट हुम्ला पुग्न हामीलाई एक हप्ता लाग्दैन होला, तीन-चार दिन मात्रै लाग्ला ।	It probably won't take us a week to reach Humla from Jumla, it will probably only take us three or four days.

15.02

Exercise 56

Put the following sentences into the probable future tense, substituting the word **भोलि** for **हिजो** in each:

१ हिजो मौसम साह्रै राम्रो थियो ।

२ हिजो दिल्लीबाट काठ्माडौं पुग्न दुई घण्टा जति लाग्यो ।

३ हिजो नानीहरूले खेतमा फुटबल खेले । उनीहरूको लुगामा हिलो लाग्यो ।

४ हिजो सीताले घर राम्रोसँग सफा गरिन् ।

५ हिजो दिदीले भात पकाइनन्, दाइले पकाए ।

६ हिजो घरमा पाहुनाहरू भएको कारणले उनीहरू स्कूल आएनन् ।

98 WORDS FOR APPROXIMATELY

Nepali has various words that can be used to mean *about* or *approximately:*

-तिर	about (with expressions of time only)
करीब	approximately, roughly
जति	about, as much as
झण्डै	almost, virtually

The postposition -तिर (see **Grammar 47**) is used with expressions of time to mean *at roughly such-and-such a time:*

दस बजेतिर आउनुहोस्	Please come at about 10 o'clock.
छिटो हिँड्यौं भने हामी साँझतिर पुगौंला ।	If we walk quickly we will arrive at around dusk.

The word **करीब** is used before an expression of quantity to mean *about* or *approximately:*

एक महिनाको लागि हामीलाई करीब दुई किलो नुन चाहिन्छ होला ।	We will probably need about two kilos of salt for a month.
यहाँबाट मेरो घर पुग्न करीब दस मिनेट लाग्छ ।	It takes about ten minutes to reach my house from here.

The word **जति** is used after an expression of quantity or time to mean *as much as* or *as many as:*

यस गाउँका बाह्रजना जति मानिसहरू दोस्रो विश्व-युद्धमा मरे ।	As many as 12 people from this village died in the Second World War.

झण्डै has the sense of *almost* or *very nearly:*

यी व्यापारीहरूलाई ल्हासा पुग्न झण्डै एक हप्ता लाग्यो ।	It took these traders almost a week to reach Lhasa.

● INSIGHT

There are several words that mean 'approximately' in Nepali. तिर is used with points of time, e.g. नौ बजेतिर 'about 9 o' clock', जति is used with periods of time, e.g.; एक घण्टाजति. Words such as अन्दाजी and करिब are used before the time word for either situation, e.g. अन्दाजी एक बजे or अन्दाजी एक घण्टा.

Exercise 57

Translate into Nepali:

It costs £500 to go to Nepal by air from London, and it takes 15 hours to reach Kathmandu. I always buy an interesting book at the airport! When I went to Nepal last year I bought a very fat novel and it took me about ten hours to read it. I will probably go to Nepal again next year, and I might buy two novels this time. In Nepal, I went to Bhadrapur. If you go to Bhadrapur by bus from Kathmandu it's quite cheap but it takes a whole day to arrive there. There were a lot of people on the bus going to Bhadrapur and the road leading to Bhadrapur was very bad. I didn't buy a book for that journey, because I was going with one or two Nepali friends. If you go to Bhadrapur by plane it costs a lot of money but it doesn't take much time. A plane going to Bhadrapur flies from the capital every morning at 10 o'clock. If I go to Bhadrapur again next year, I will probably go by plane.

The most important things for the reader to remember

1 The probable future tense shows less certainty that an action will be completed. When it is conjugated, the different forms of **होला** (probably) are attached as a suffix to the verb, e.g. **हामी होटेलमा बसौंला** 'We will probably stay at the hotel'. As for **तपाईं** and **वहाँ** the infinitive verb is followed by **होला,** e.g. **वहाँ भोलि आउनुहोला** 'He will probably come tomorrow'.

2 When **लाग्नु** is used in relation to the price or time of travel and transportation it means 'to cost' or 'to take', e.g. **रेलमा बीस पाउण्ड लाग्छ** or **एक घण्टा लाग्छ** 'It cost 20 pounds by train' or 'it takes one hour'.

16 के गर्नुपर्छ ? *What should I do?*

In this unit you will learn:

▸ *how to use expressions meaning should, ought, must and had to*

26 Arriving at Tribhuvan International Airport

16.01

Harish has returned to Nepal after an absence of 20 years. He finds the airport completely unrecognizable, and he enlists the help of Nirmal, an airport attendant, to see him through the various formalities.

हरिश	नमस्ते !
निर्मल	नमस्ते हजुर । तपाईं लण्डनबाट आउनुभएको हो ?
हरिश	हजुर, भरखरै आइपुगेको नेपाल एयरलाइन्सको विमानमा । सुन्नुहोस् न, म नेपाल नआएको धेरै वर्ष भयो । पहिले विमानस्थल गौचर मात्रै थियो । भन्नुहोस् न, कता जानुपर्छ, के के गर्नुपर्छ ?
निर्मल	ठीक छ, म तपाईंको लागि सबै कुरा मिलाउँछु । तपाईंलाई भिसा चाहियो ? त्यसो हो भने तपाईंलाई ऊ त्यो लाइनमा उभिनुपर्छ ।

हरिश	म त नेपाली नागरिक हुँ नि । भिसा लिनुपर्दैन !
निर्मल	ए, माफ गर्नुहोस् है । ऊ, सामान आइपुग्यो । अब सामान टिप्नुपर्छ ।
हरिश	मेरो सामान त अहिलेसम्म निस्केको छैन । यहाँ धेरै बेरसम्म कुर्नुपर्छ कि के हो ?
निर्मल	पर्दैन होला । धेरैजसो पाँच मिनेट पनि लाग्दैन ।
	(पाँच मिनेटपछि)
हरिश	अझ पनि आएको छैन । बीचबाटोमै हरायो कि के हो ?
निर्मल	चिन्ता गर्नुपर्दैन । म भित्र गएर तपाईंको सामान निकाल्छु । तर तपाईंले मलाई एक सय रुपियाँ दिनुपर्छ ।
हरिश	एक सय रुपियाँ ? मसँग नेपाली पैसा छैन । पैसा साट्नुपर्छ ।
निर्मल	ऊ त्यहाँ बैंक छ । त्यहीं गएर साट्नुहोस् ।
	(पाँच मिनेटपछि)
निर्मल	भयो ? हेर्नुहोस्, तपाईंको सामान आइपुग्यो । अब तपाईं सामान लिएर भन्सारतिर जानुपर्छ ।
	(भन्सारमा)
हरिश	नमस्कार, नमस्कार ।
भन्सार अधिकृत	पासपोर्ट देखाउनुहोस् त । आज कहाँबाट आउनुभएको ?
हरिश	लण्डनबाट । झोला खोल्नुपर्छ ?
भन्सार अधिकृत	खोल्नुपर्छ । हामीले भित्र हेर्नुपर्छ एक चोटि । तपाईंले आफै प्याक गरेको हो ?
हरिश	हो, मैले आफै प्याक गरेको । लुगा-फाटाबाहेक यसमा अरू खास त केही छैन ।
भन्सार अधिकृत	त्यस्तै होला, तर हामीले हेर्नैपर्छ, के गर्ने ? ल, ठीक छ । भयो ।
निर्मल	आउनुहोस् हजुर म तपाईंको लागि ट्याक्सी बोलाउँछु । सामान पनि दिनुहोस्, तपाई त थाक्नुभयो होला, म बोक्छु ।
हरिश	पर्दैन, गह्रुँगो छैन ।
निर्मल	तपाईं कहाँसम्म जाने ? होटेलको रिजर्वेशन भयो ?
हरिश	पर्दैन । दाइको घर छ नक्सालमा ।
निर्मल	लौ त । यहाँबाट नक्साल पुग्न ट्याक्सीमा पाँच सय रुपियाँ जति लाग्छ । अनि तपाईंले मलाई पनि पाँच सय दिनुपर्छ । धन्यवाद । फेरि भेटौंला है ।

Quick vocab

गौचर	cow pasture
भिसा	visa
लाइन	queue, line
नागरिक	citizen
सामान	luggage
टिप्नु	to pick up
कुर्नु	to wait
अझ पनि	still
चिन्ता गर्नु	to worry
साट्नु	to exchange
भन्सार	customs
अधिकृत	official
पासपोर्ट	passport
खोल्नु	to open
आफै	self, oneself
प्याक गर्नु	to pack
लुगा-फाटा	clothes and such like
खास	special, particular
थाक्नु	to be tired
बोक्नु	to carry
गह्रुँगो	heavy
रिजर्वेशन	reservation
नक्साल	Naxal (a district of Kathmandu)

Harish	Hello!
Nirmal	Hello sir. Have you come from London?
Harish	Yes, on the Nepal Airlines flight that has just arrived. Listen, I have not visited Nepal for many years. Before, the airport was just a cow pasture. Tell me, where should I go, what things do I have to do?
Nirmal	OK, I'll organize everything for you. Do you need a visa? If so, you have to stand in that queue over there.
Harish	But I'm a Nepali citizen, you know. I don't need to get a visa.
Nirmal	Oh, please forgive me. Look, the luggage has arrived. Now you must pick up your luggage.
Harish	But my luggage hasn't come out yet. Does one have to wait a long time here, or what?
Nirmal	Probably not. It usually doesn't even take five minutes.

After five minutes:

Harish	It still hasn't come. Has it been lost on the way or something?
Nirmal	No need to worry. I'll go inside and get your luggage out. But you must give me 100 rupees.
Harish	100 rupees? I haven't any Nepali money. I must exchange some money.
Nirmal	There's a bank over there. Go there and exchange it.

After five minutes:

Nirmal	Done? Look, your luggage has arrived. Now you must take the luggage and go towards customs.

At customs …

Harish	Hello, hello.
Customs official	Show me your passport then. Where have you come from today?
Harish	From London. Should I open my bag?
Customs official	Yes. We have to take a look inside. Did you pack it yourself?
Harish	Yes, I packed it myself. There's nothing special in it apart from clothes and such like.
Customs official	That's probably how it is, but we have to look, what to do? There, that's OK. It's done.
Nirmal	Come sir, I'll call a taxi for you. Give me your luggage too, you must be tired, I'll carry it.
Harish	There's no need, it's not heavy.
Nirmal	How far are you going? Have you made a hotel reservation?
Harish	No need. There's my brother's house in Naksal.
Nirmal	That's that then. To get from here to Naksal by taxi costs about 500 rupees. And you must give me 500 too. Thank you. See you again!

Grammar

99 MUST, SHOULD, DON'T HAVE TO

The combination of the dictionary form of a verb with third person singular forms of the verb पर्नु *to fall* (पर्छ and पर्दैन in the present tense, and पर्‍यो and परेन in the past) is used to express meanings such as *must, need to, should, have to,* and *ought to.* The two words are joined together when written:

हुनुपर्छ	must be / should be / has to be / ought to be
बोल्नुपर्छ	must speak / should speak / has to speak / ought to speak
गर्नुपर्छ	must do / should do / has to do / ought to do

● INSIGHT

When पर्छ is used after an infinitive verb, this construction indicates that a person ought to carry out the activity indicated by the infinitive. The helper verb पर्छ remains unchanged, regardless of whether the person is singular or plural.

If the sentence mentions a person upon whom this need or obligation 'falls', s/he must be marked in the sentence – sometimes with the postposition **-लाई** if the verb is intransitive:

तिमीहरू (लाई) भोलि आउनुपर्दैन ।	You do not have to come tomorrow.

– and always with **-ले** if the verb is transitive:

केटा-केटीहरूले साँचो बोल्नुपर्छ	Boys and girls should speak the truth.

The affirmative construction is commonly used to prescribe correct behaviour in general terms:

विद्यार्थीहरूले गुरुलाई आदर गर्नुपर्छ ।	Students should respect their teacher.
सबैले ईश्वरलाई मान्नुपर्छ ।	Everyone should believe in God.
लोग्नेले स्वास्नीलाई माया गर्नुपर्छ ।	A husband should love his wife.

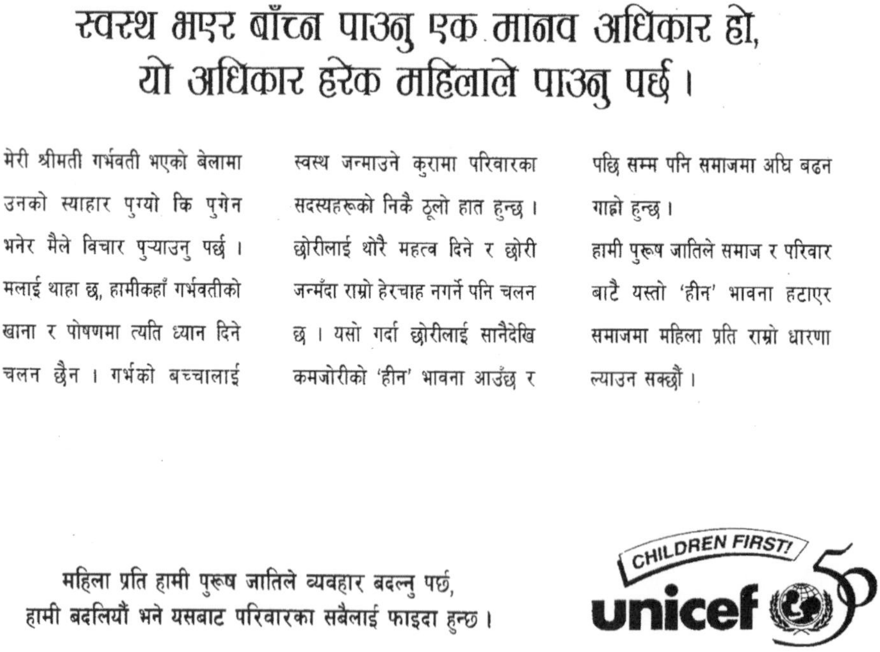
स्वस्थ भएर बाँच्न पाउनु एक मानव अधिकार हो,
यो अधिकार हरेक महिलाले पाउनु पर्छ ।

मेरी श्रीमती गर्भवती भएको बेलामा उनको स्याहार पुग्यो कि पुगेन भनेर मैले विचार पुऱ्याउनु पर्छ । मलाई थाहा छ, हामीकहाँ गर्भवतीको खाना र पोषणमा त्यति ध्यान दिने चलन छैन । गर्भको बच्चालाई स्वस्थ जन्माउने कुरामा परिवारका सदस्यहरूको निकै ठूलो हात हुन्छ । छोरीलाई थोरै महत्व दिने र छोरी जन्मँदा राम्रो हेरचाह नगर्ने पनि चलन छ । यसो गर्दा छोरीलाई सानैदेखि कमजोरीको 'हीन' भावना आउँछ र पछि सम्म पनि समाजमा अघि बढ्न गाह्रो हुन्छ । हामी पुरूष जातिले समाज र परिवार बाटै यस्तो 'हीन' भावना हटाएर समाजमा महिला प्रति राम्रो धारणा ल्याउन सक्छौं ।

महिला प्रति हामी पुरूष जातिले व्यवहार बदल्नु पर्छ,
हामी बदलियौं भने यसबाट परिवारका सबैलाई फाइदा हुन्छ ।

CHILDREN FIRST!
unicef

a UNICEF advertisement in Nepali

The main heading translates 'To be able to live healthily is a human right; every woman should get this right'

The meaning of the negative construction with **पर्दैन** is not exactly the opposite of this. Rather than saying that it is wrong to do something, it simply states that there is no need to do it:

उनीहरूलाई म भन्छु, तपाईंले भन्नुपर्दैन ।	I will tell them, you do not need to.
मसँग दुइटा कलम छ, तपाईंले किन्नुपर्दैन ।	I have two pens, you do not need to buy (one).
सुन्दरी केटीले गहना लाउनुपर्दैन ।	A pretty girl does not need to wear jewellery.

The word **पर्दैन** is commonly used on its own, without being attached to a verb, to mean *no need* or *don't bother:*

म तपाईंको लागि पानी लिएर आउँछु है ?	I'll bring some water for you, OK?
पर्दैन, हामीसँग दुई बोतल पानी छ ।	No need, we have two bottles of water.

If a need or obligation to *be* something or somewhere 'falls' upon an inanimate noun, that noun takes neither **ले** nor **लाई**:

तपाईंको खल्तीमा पैसा त हुनैपर्छ ।	There simply must be money in your pocket.

• INSIGHT

Instead of using पर्छ, you can also use another construction indicating obligation or necessity to carry out any action suggested by the infinitive. आवश्यक छ or जरुरी छ expresses a sense of necessity or obligation, e.g. उसले पढ्नु आवश्यक छ 'it is necessary for him to study'.

Exercise 58

Change the following statements of fact into statements of general obligation.

Example

ऊ हरेक दिन अफिस जान्छ । He goes to the office every day.	=	उसलाई हरेक दिन अफिस जानुपर्छ । He has to go to the office every day.
ऊ हरेक दिन अफिस जाँदैन He doesn't go to the office every day.	=	उसलाई हरेक दिन अफिस जानुपर्दैन He doesn't have to go to the office every day.

१ हामी ईश्वरलाई पूजा गर्छौं ।

२ मेरो भाइ हरेक दिन दाल भात खान्छ ।

३ आज बिदा हो, हामीहरू अफिसमा जाँदैनौं ।

४ उनीहरू हामीलाई त्यो कथा सुनाउँदैनन् ।

५ सीताले घर सफा गर्दिन । त्यो काम एउटा नोकरले गर्छ ।

६ आज म भात पकाउँदिन । मेरो श्रीमानले पकाउनुहुन्छ ।

100 MUST, HAD TO

The obvious meaning of a verb followed by the simple past tense of **पर्नु** *to fall* (**पर्‍यो** or **परेन**) is an obligation in the past:

हिजो घरमा तरकारी नभएर मलाई बजार जानुपर्‍यो ।	Yesterday there were no vegetables in the house and I had to go to the market.
अस्ति अफिस बन्द थियो, त्यस कारण मलाई शहर जानुपरेन ।	The day before yesterday the office was shut, so I did not have to go to town.
हिजो शहरमा मलाई यता-उता धेरै ठाउँ दौड्नुपर्‍यो ।	Yesterday I had to run here and there to many places in town.

However, the same construction may sometimes be used when the speaker is talking about the immediate present, because he considers the obligation that presses upon him as he speaks to have 'fallen' in the past tense. Because the obligation has already 'fallen', the speaker expresses his intention to carry out the action without further delay:

नानीको लुगामा हिलो लाग्यो, अब धुनुपर्‍यो ।	Mud has got on to the child's clothing, now I must wash it.
ल, गुरुजी आउनुभयो । अब किताब खोलेर पढ्नुपर्‍यो ।	Look, teacher has arrived. Now we must open (our) books and read.
रेष्टुराँ पाँच मिनेटपछि बन्द हुन्छ । अब पैसा तिर्नुपर्‍यो ।	The restaurant will close in five minutes. Now I must pay the bill.

● INSIGHT

When Nepali uses a strong sense of obligation (e.g. जानै पर्छ) it implies that if it is not fulfilled an unpleasant situation may occur. The English equivalent for this level of strong obligation is 'must'.

● INSIGHT

पर्छ is also used in a progressive form in any tense, e.g. मैले दिनमा दस घण्टा काम गर्नु परिरहेको छ 'I am having to work ten hours a day'. However, it cannot be used with the दै continuous marker in this way.

Exercise 59

Change the following statements of fact into statements of past or immediate need:

Example अब म जान्छु । = अब मलाई जानुपर्‍यो ।
हिजो म गइनँ । = हिजो मलाई जानुपरेन ।

१ अब बुवा पशुपतिनाथको मन्दिर जानुहुन्छ ।

२ अब तिमी अलिकति भात खान्छौ ।

३ अब म चाँडै सुत्छु ।

४ हिजो मैले धेरै काम गरिनँ ।

५ हिजो किसानहरू खेतमा गएनन् ।

६ हिजो आमा बजार जानुभएन ।

101 THE VERBS मिल्नु AND मिलाउनु

The verb **मिल्नु** is very versatile, and can mean *to come together, match, fit, get along,* etc. It is best explained through examples:

त्यो रङ यो रङसँग पटक्कै मिल्दैन ।	That colour really doesn't match with this colour.
ताल्चामा यो साँचो मिलेको छैन ।	This key hasn't fitted the lock.
उनीहरूको कुरा मिल्यो ।	They came to an agreement.
यस वाक्यमा त्यो शब्द अलि मिल्दैन ।	In this sentence that word is a little unsuitable.
मेरो छोरा आफ्ना साथीहरूसँग रामोसँग मिल्छ ।	My son gets along well with his friends.

The verb **मिलाउनु** is the causative of **मिल्नु**. That is, it causes a coming together, a matching, etc. and translates into English as *to arrange, assemble, adjust, bring together, sort out:*

त्यो त अलि महंगो भयो, साहूजी । दाम मिलाएर दिनुहोस् ।	That's a little expensive, shopkeeper. Please adjust the price for me.
भोलि कति बजे भेट्ने ? समय मिलाउनुपर्छ ।	What time shall we meet tomorrow? We must arrange a time.
एक छिन पर्खनुहोस् है । कपाल मिलाउनुपर्‍यो ।	Wait a moment, won't you. I have to tidy my hair.
अब तपाईंहरूको कुरा मिल्यो । हात मिलाउनुहोस् ।	Now you are in agreement. Please shake hands.

The most important things for the reader to remember

1 The verb stem + नु पर्छ forms an obligatory sentence in Nepali, which is expressed in English as 'should, need to, has to, have to, and ought to', e.g. म पसल (मा) जानुपर्छ 'I need to go to the shop'.

2 No conjugation is required for any obligatory sentence in Nepali. However, the subject takes ले for transitive verbs in all tenses, e.g. मैले काम गर्नुपर्छ 'I have to work'. With intransitive verbs the subject does not take ले but it can take लाई.

3 For a strong obligation a particle नै is added to the infinitive verb; or its vowel sound ऐ can also be added as a suffix to नु changing it into नै. The meaning here is that something simply must be done, no matter what.

4 The past form of पर्छ is पर्‍यो but this is occasionally used in the present context as well, e.g. अब घर जानु पर्‍यो 'I have to go home now'. It shows that the need to go home has already risen.

5 मिल्नु and मिलाउनु have several meanings in different contexts, e.g. कुरा मिल्नु 'to come to an agreement', रङ्ग मिल्नु 'to match with a colour', साथीसँग मिल्नु 'to get along with a friend'. Note that मिल्नु is intransitive and मिलाउनु is a transitive or causative verb, e.g. समय मिलाउनु 'to arrange a time', हात मिलाउनु 'to shake hands'.

17 भित्र जान हुँदैन
You're not allowed in

In this unit you will learn:

- ***how to ask and state what is right and what is wrong***
- ***how to ask and state what one is allowed to do***
- ***how to identify some basic facts about religion in Nepal***

27 Americans at Pashupati temple

17.01

Jim has been living in Nepal for three months, and he is showing some American friends who have come to visit him the sights of the Kathmandu Valley. He wonders if he might take them into Pashupati temple. The policeman at the entrance explains why he cannot.

जिम	हामी मन्दिरभित्र जान हुन्छ ?
प्रहरी	तपाईंहरू कुन देशबाट आउनुभएको ?
जिम	हामीहरू अमेरिकाबाट आएको ।
प्रहरी	हो र ? कति राम्रो नेपाली बोल्नुहुन्छ तपाईं ! तपाईंले नेपाली भाषा कहाँ सिक्नुभयो ?
जिम	वहीं, अमेरिकामा अलिकति सिकें । अहिले नेपाल बसेको तीन महिना भयो हामी मन्दिरभित्र ...

प्रहरी	अहो, अमेरिकामा पनि नेपाली भाषा सिक्न पाइन्छ ? मलाई थाहा थिएन । नेपाली सिकाउने मानिसहरू छन् ?

जिम	प्रशस्त छन् । भन्नुहोस् न, हामी मन्दिरभित्र पस्न हुन्छ कि हुन्न ?
प्रहरी	तपाईं हिन्दू धर्मावलम्बी हुनुहुन्छ ?
जिम	धर्मावलम्बी भनेको के हो ? मैले बुझिनँ ।
प्रहरी	भनाइको मतलब, तपाईं हिन्दू हुनुहुन्छ ?
जिम	अहँ, म हिन्दू होइन । हामीहरू हिन्दू नभएको कारणले तपाईं हामीलाई भित्र पस्न दिनुहुन्न ?
प्रहरी	अलि मिल्दैन । यो पशुपतिनाथको मन्दिर नेपालको सबैभन्दा प्राचीन तीर्थस्थल हो । त्यो तपाईंलाई थाहा हुनुपर्छ । त्यसैले यहाँ विशेष नियमहरू लाग्छन् । पुजारीहरूले हिन्दूहरूलाई मात्र भित्र पस्न दिन्छन् । अनि हिन्दू भएर पनि कसैले छालाबाट बनेको कुनै चिज लाउन हुँदैन ।
जिम	केही छैन । हामी हिन्दू नभएकोले भित्र पस्ने कुरै छैन जस्तो छ । तर मन्दिरको चोक हेर्न पाइन्छ कि ?
प्रहरी	बाग्मती नदीभन्दा पर ऊ त्यो रूखै रूखले ढाकेको थुम्को छ नि । त्यसलाई मृगस्थली भन्छन् । तपाईंहरू बाग्मती खोला ऊ त्यो पुरानो पुलबाट तर्नुहोस् । पुलबाट राजराजेश्वरी घाट देखिन्छ । त्यहाँ काठ्माडौंका हिन्दूहरूले आफ्ना मृतहरू जलाउँछन् । त्यसको फोटो खिच्न हुँदैन । साह्रै अनुचित हुन्छ ।
जिम	बुझें । तर मृगस्थलीमा के छ ? रूखहरू मात्रै ?
प्रहरी	होइन, मृगस्थलीमा पुराना शिवालयहरू धेरै छन् । बाँदरहरू पनि थुप्रै छन् । त्यहाँ घाममा बसेर पशुपतिनाथको मन्दिरको साह्रै राम्रो दृश्य हेर्न पाइन्छ ।
जिम	त्यहाँबाट मन्दिरको फोटो खिच्न हुन्छ ?
प्रहरी	हुन्छ, एकदमै ठीक छ । तर बाँदरहरूसँग होस् गर्नुहोस् । बाँदरहरूलाई फलफूल दिन हुँदैन । तिनीहरूले दुख दिन्छन् ।

V Quick vocab

वहीं	there; in that very place
सिकाउनु	to teach
धर्मावलम्बी	a follower of a religion
भनाइ	utterance, something said
मतलब	meaning
प्राचीन	ancient
तीर्थस्थल	place of pilgrimage
विशेष	special
नियम	rule
छाला	leather

बन्नु	to be made
आँगन	courtyard, compound
बाग्मती नदी	the Bagmati river
-भन्दा पर	the other side of
ढाक्नु	to be covered
थुम्को	hillock
तर्नु	to cross
मृत	dead person
जलाउनु	to burn, cremate
फोटो खिच्नु	to take a photograph
अनुचित	improper
शिवालय	Shiva temple
दृश्य	view
होस् गर्नु	to be careful
दुख	trouble

Jim	Is it all right for us to go into the temple?
Policeman	Which country have you come from?
Jim	We have come from America.
Policeman	Is that so? What good Nepali you speak! Where did you learn the Nepali language?
Jim	Right there in America I learned a little. Now I have lived in Nepal for three months. Can we …
Policeman	Aho, can you learn Nepali language in America too? I didn't know. Are there people who teach Nepali?
Jim	There are plenty. Tell me, is it or isn't it all right for us to enter the temple?
Policeman	Are you a follower of Hinduism?
Jim	What does **dharmāvalambī** mean? I didn't understand.
Policeman	What I mean is, are you a Hindu?
Jim	No, I am not a Hindu. Will you not allow us into the temple because we are not Hindus?
Policeman	It's a bit inappropriate. This temple of Pashupatinath is Nepal's most ancient pilgrimage place. That you should know. So special rules apply here. The priests only allow Hindus to enter. And even if they are Hindus, no one is supposed to wear anything made from leather.
Jim	It doesn't matter. It seems that because we are not Hindus there is no question of going inside. But can one get to look at the temple courtyard?
Policeman	On the far side of the Bagmati river over there, the hillock covered by trees, right? They call that Mrigasthali.

	Cross the Bagmati river by that old bridge over there. From the bridge you can see Rajarajeshwari Ghat.* There, Kathmandu's Hindus burn their dead. It is not right to take a photo of that. It is extremely improper.
Jim	I've understood. But what is there at Mrigasthali? Just trees?
Policeman	No, at Mrigasthali there are many old Shiva shrines. There are lots of monkeys too. You can sit in the sun there and look at a very fine view of Pashupatinath temple.
Jim	Is it all right to take a photo of the temple from there?
Policeman	Yes, that's absolutely fine. But be careful with the monkeys. You shouldn't give the monkeys any fruit. They'll give you trouble.

Note *A **ghāṭ** is a stepped platform leading down to a river. **Ghāṭs** are often used for the performance of religious devotions and as cremation sites.

Grammar

102 IS IT ALL RIGHT TO ... ? USING THE INFINITIVE WITH हुन्छ/हुँदैन

The combination of the infinitive of a verb + **हुन्छ/हुँदैन** expresses meanings such as *should/should not, is/is not permitted, is/is not advisable, is/is not all right.* Often, no subject is mentioned in these sentences, which are often general statements about what is and what is not correct behaviour: in such cases it can be understood to mean *one should ...* or *one should not ...*

मन्दिरमा जुत्ता लाउन हुँदैन ।	One should not wear shoes in a temple.*
हिन्दू धर्म अनुसार गाई काट्न हुँदैन ।	According to Hindu religion, it is wrong to kill a cow.
इस्लामी धर्म अनुसार सुँगूरको मासु खान हुँदैन ।	According to Islamic religion, it is wrong to eat pork.

Note *The soles of the feet or shoes are unclean, and shoes should be removed before entering the interiors of houses, temples, etc. It is also insulting to sit with one's legs crossed in such a way that the sole of one's shoe is in front of another person's face. Similarly, care should be taken not to let one's feet pass above any part of a Nepali person's body, nor should one touch another person on the crown of the head.

The alternative negative form of हुनु (हुन्न instead of हुँदैन) is also frequently used in these contexts. The subject of a verb in a sentence of this type must take **-ले** if the verb is transitive:

तिमीले पिरो धेरै खान हुन्न, अलिकति खान त हुन्छ ।	You should not eat too much spicy (food), but it's OK to eat a little.

103 THEY DON'T ALLOW YOU TO ...

Nepali uses the verb दिनु *to give* to mean *to let* or *to allow*. The subject of दिनु will usually take -ले in all tenses, to make it absolutely clear who the subject is. When one of the first person pronouns (म or हामी) is the subject, however, it is unlikely to take -ले except in past tenses. The structure of such a sentence is typically:

Allower + -ले   Person allowed + -लाई   Infinitive   दिनु (to allow)

मैले घरमा उसलाई चुरोट खान दिइनँ ।	I did not allow him to smoke a cigarette in the house.
प्रहरीले तिमीलाई मन्दिरमा जुत्ता लाउन दिंदैन होला ।	The policeman probably won't allow you to wear shoes in the temple.
बत्ती किन निभायौ तिमीले ? बत्ती बालेर मलाई अखबार पढ्न देऊ न ।	Why have you switched off the light? Switch it on and let me read the newspaper, won't you!*
यहाँभन्दा माथि जान दिंदैनन् । त्यहाँ पहिरो जाने खतरा छ ।	(They) don't let you go higher than this. There is a danger of landslides there.

Note *The Nepali equivalent of *to switch on* is खोल्नु *to open*, while *to switch off* is बन्द गर्नु, *to shut*.

● INSIGHT

In order to say 'you are allowed to go', you must use verb stem + न हुन्छ but not verb stem + नु हुन्छ. This is because + नु हुन्छ is a present tense conjugation for तपाई or वहाँ and this would therefore create confusion. But in the negative, either form of infinitive (नु or न) can be used because हुँदैन denotes only a prohibition and this confusion does not arise.

● INSIGHT

If you say 'I let you go' in Nepali, it is म तपाईंलाई जान दिन्छु. This actually means 'I give you permission to go'. There is a word understood but unstated in this Nepali sentence, which is 'permission'.

Exercise 60

Create five sentences along the following lines:

allower	*allowee*	*place/time*	*verb*	*allow?*
I	people	in my house	smoke	X

= म मान्छेहरूलाई मेरो घरमा चुरोट खान दिन्नँ ।

	allower	*allowee*	*place/time*	*verb*	*allow?*
1	mother	my friends	in our house	drink alcohol	X
2	they	us	into the temple	go	✓

3 elder brother	children	in the morning	watch TV	✓
4 father	us	in the evening	go out	X
5 you (High)	tourists	in the temple	wear shoes	✓ ?

104 भएर BEING AND भएर पनि DESPITE BEING

भएर, the **-एर** participle of **हुनु,** is commonly used to point out the cause of something, in much the same way that the **-एको** participle is used in combination with **-ले** to create a part of a sentence beginning with *because*. When **भएर** is used, however, the cause is stated less emphatically:

नेवार भएर उनीहरू नेपाली मात्रै होइन नेपाल भाषा पनि बोल्छन् ।	Being Newars, they speak not only Nepali but Nepal Bhasha too.*
मेरी हजुरआमा बूढी भएर घरबाट धेरै कम निस्कनुहुन्छ ।	Being old, my grandmother very seldom comes out of the house.

Note *The official name for the Newari language is **नेपाल भाषा**. The Kathmandu Valley, where it is the indigenous language, was known as **नेपाल** until the present century.

The English translation of each of the above sentences could equally begin *because they are Newars ...* and *because she is old ...*

The addition of **पनि** (*even, also*) to **भएर** makes the sentence mean that although what is stated is indeed the case, other things are not as might be expected:

नेवार भएर पनि उनीहरू नेपाली मात्रै बोल्छन् ।	Despite being Newars, they speak only Nepali.
बूढी भएर पनि मेरी हजुरआमा हरेक दिन मन्दिर जानुहुन्छ ।	Despite being old, my grandmother goes to the temple every day.

● INSIGHT

When the verb stem + एर is followed by पनि it forms a new construction in the first clause that has the sense 'despite of' or 'in spite of'. A sense of 'still' अझै is understood in the second clause of this sentence although sometimes it is not used.

105 RELIGION IN NEPAL

Religion is an integral part of traditional life in Nepal, which was the only country in the world with Hinduism as its official religion until 2006, when it became a secular state. The concept of **धर्म** (*righteousness, duty, morality, religion*) pervades many activities, and religious concepts have played an important role in the shaping of society. Most Nepali-speaking people are Hindus, though there are many Buddhist Newars and Buddhism is also prevalent among the people of the high mountain regions. Islam is represented in most Tarai towns, and there is a Muslim community in Kathmandu. The Christian community is very small.

For Hindus, religion consists in the worship (पूजा) of special beings (*gods:* **देव, देवता**) at particular times (certain times of the day, holy days of the week or month, annual festivals, etc.), in particular holy places (at a family altar, at a temple, etc.). They share a belief in the principle of rebirth, the consequence of actions (कर्म), and the illusory nature of the material world (सँसार). The ultimate aim of religious practice is deliverance (मोक्ष) from the endless cycle of birth and rebirth, but most Hindus simply hope for a better rebirth through the accumulation of merit (पुण्य).

Buddhism and Hinduism are closely intertwined in the Kathmandu Valley cities and sometimes it is difficult to decide whether a particular temple has a Buddhist or a Hindu dedication. For many Nepalis, the distinction is meaningless. However, Buddhism is a distinct religion which, unlike Hinduism, has a founder, the historical Buddha called Gautama, who is also given the title Shakyamuni. Buddhism shares many beliefs in common with Hinduism, but it has a different understanding of the concept of deliverance, which is **निर्वाण,** the 'snuffing out' of desire. Unlike Hinduism, Buddhism is also practised by monastic communities. The religion has its own pantheon of deities. Of these, the Bodhisattvas (beings who have delayed their own attainment of **निर्वाण** and have vowed to work for the enlightenment of all sentient beings) are widely worshipped.

To state that a particular deity is worshipped at a particular place or time, use the verb phrase **-को पूजा हुनु**

यो मन्दिरमा महादेवको पूजा हुन्छ ।	Mahādev is worshipped at this temple.
दसैंको ठूलो पर्वमा दुर्गा देवीको पूजा हुन्छ ।	The goddess Durga is worshipped in the great festival of Dasain.

Exercise 61

Translate into Nepali:

A	Which god does this temple belong to? Is it all right to go inside?
B	This is the temple of Ganesh. Yes, it is all right for you to go inside, but you must take your shoes off.
A	Is this a very old temple?
B	Yes, it is very ancient. People come here every morning and do **pūjā** of Ganesh.
A	Why do they have to come here every morning?
B	They do not have to come, but it is good to come here every day. If you do **pūjā** of Ganesh every morning your day will be successful. That is a belief of ours.
A	What should I do now?
B	You have done **darśan** of the god, and that is good. Please give a little money for the temple.

A	I do not have very much money on me. But perhaps it will be all right to give ten rupees?
B	Yes, that is fine. Please come, it is late. Now we must go to Paśupati temple. It is not so far. If we walk there we can reach it in half an hour.
A	Which deity is worshipped at Paśupati temple?
B	Shivajī is worshipped there.

● INSIGHT

मध्ये is a postposition meaning 'among', e.g. दस जनामध्ये 'among ten people' or 'out of ten people'. You can also say दस जनामा to mean the same thing in spoken Nepali, but remember that मध्ये and मा are interchangeable only in this context.

The most important things for the reader to remember

1 हुन्छ means 'it is okay' as an expression in Nepali. When हुन्छ is used with an infinite verb, it gives a sense that it is okay to do it or that one is allowed to do it, e.g. **मन्दिरमा जान हुन्छ** 'It is okay to go into the temple'.

2 When हुँदैन, a negative of हुन्छ, is used with an infinitive verb it means 'prohibited' or 'not allowed' to do. The subject takes ले if the verb is transitive and the verb does not change whatever the subject, e.g. **तपाईंले गाँजा खानुहुँदैन** – 'You should not smoke ganja'.

3 दिनु is used as an auxiliary with other verbs to mean 'to let' or 'to allow to'. The main verb ends with न and दिनु is conjugated according to the person or pronoun that is its subject, e.g. **म तिमीलाई जान दिन्छु** 'I will let you go'.

4 When the conjunctive participle एर is used with पनि (even) it has the sense 'despite' or 'in spite of being or doing something', e.g. **बूढो भएर पनि ऊ बलियो देखिन्छ** 'He looks strong despite being old'.

18 म नेपाली सिक्न सक्छु
I can learn Nepali

In this unit you will learn:

- *how to use the Nepali verbs that mean can*
- *how to describe verbs*
- *how to talk about learning and teaching*
- *how to talk about wanting to do something*

28 How many languages can you speak?

18.01

हर्षराज	तपाईं कतिवटा भाषा बोल्न सक्नुहुन्छ ?
तिलविक्रम	म बाल्यकालदेखि नै लिम्बू भाषा बोल्छु । लिम्बू भाषा मेरो मातृभाषा नै हो । मेरो लागि लिम्बू भाषा आमाको दूध जस्तै हो ।
हर्षराज	लिम्बू भाषा तपाईंको मातृभाषा नै होला, तर तपाईंको लागि नेपाली पनि दोस्रो मातृभाषा जस्तो छ, होइन ?
तिलविक्रम	लिम्बू भाषा मैले आमाबाट सिकेको भाषा हो, तर सानो उमेरदेखि नै म नेपाली भाषा पनि बोल्छु । वास्तवमा मातृभाषा भनेको के हो ? आफूले जन्मदेखि बोलेको भाषा हो कि आमाबाट सिकेको भाषा हो ?
हर्षराज	मेरो विचारमा तपाईं मातृभाषा भन्ने शब्दलाई ती दुवै अर्थ दिन सक्नुहुन्छ । तपाईंकी आमा पनि नेपाली भाषा बोल्न सक्नुहुन्छ ?
तिलविक्रम	वहाँलाई नेपाली बोल्न आउँदैन ।
हर्षराज	पटक्कै आउँदैन ?
तिलविक्रम	त्यसो त होइन, तर धेरै कम आउँछ वहाँलाई । बुवा त नेपालीमा काम चलाउन सक्नुहुन्छ । हाम्रो गाउँका लोग्नेमान्छेहरू गाउँभन्दा बाहिर व्यापारको लागि घुम्छन् अथवा काम गर्छन् तर स्वास्नीमानिसहरू प्रायजसो गाउँभित्र नै बस्छन् । त्यसै कारणले उनीहरू लिम्बूबाहेक अन्य भाषाहरू सिक्न पाउँदैनन् । अनि बूढा बूढीहरू धेरैजसो कुनै पनि भाषा लेख्न पढ्न सक्दैनन् ।
हर्षराज	लिम्बू र नेपालीबाहेक तपाईंलाई कुन कुन भाषाहरू बोल्न आउँछ ?

तिलविक्रम	म हिन्दी बुझ्न सक्छु र अलिअलि बोल्न पनि सक्छु । नेपालीभाषीहरूलाई हिन्दी बुझ्न त्यति गाह्रो हुँदैन । युवा-युवतीहरू सिनेमा घरमा हिन्दी फिलिमहरू हेर्छन् । आजकाल नेपालमा हिन्दी टीभीका कार्यक्रमहरू पनि हेर्न पाइन्छ । हिन्दी बुझ्न नसक्ने युवा-युवती अब बिरलै पाइन्छन् नेपालमा ।
हर्षराज	त्यो त हो । अनि नयाँ पुस्ताका केटाकेटीहरू आफ्ना पुर्खाहरू जस्ता अपढ हुँदैनन्, होइन त ? उनीहरू स्कूलहरूमा नेपाली मात्रै होइन, अँग्रेजी पनि लेख्न पढ्न सिक्छन् ।
तिलविक्रम	तर केटाकेटीहरू मात्रै होइन, अँग्रेजी भाषा बोल्न सक्ने केही बूढाहरू पनि छन् हाम्रो गाउँमा । उनीहरू धेरैजसो ब्रिटिश आर्मीको पिन्सेन खान्छन् । बोल्न मात्रै होइन, कोही-कोही बूढाहरू त अँग्रेजी भाषा पढ्न पनि सक्छन् । गजबको कुरा हो नि । एक समयमा मलाई पनि अँग्रेजी सिक्न मन लागेको थियो । तपाईंलाई कहिल्यै अँग्रेजी सिक्न मन लागेन ?
हर्षराज	अँग्रेजी त म पढ्न सक्छु तर बोल्न सक्दिन । अभ्यास गर्न त मन लाग्छ तर अँग्रेजी जान्ने साथी छैन । के गर्ने ?

Quick vocab

भाषा	language
बोल्नु	to speak
सक्नु	to be able to
दूध	milk
मातृभाषा	mother tongue
वास्तव	reality
आफू	one's self
जन्म	birth
शब्द	word
अन्य	other
पाउनु	to get to, manage to
बूढा	old man
बूढी	old woman
युवा-युवतीहरू	young men and women
हिन्दी टीभीका कार्यक्रमहरू	Hindi TV programmes
बिरलै	rarely
पुर्खा	ancestor
दुवै	both

काम चलाउनु	to get by, function
पटक्कै	at all
प्रायजसो	usually, mostly
ब्रिटिश आर्मी	British Army
पिन्सेन खानु	to receive ('consume') a pension
गजब	surprise, amazement
जान्नु	to know

Harsharaj	How many languages can you speak?
Tilbikram	I speak the Limbu language ever since childhood. The Limbu language is my mother tongue, in fact. For me the Limbu language is like mother's milk.
Harsharaj	The Limbu language might well be your mother tongue, but for you Nepali too is like a second mother tongue, isn't it?
Tilbikram	The Limbu language is the language I learned from my mother, but I also speak Nepali from a young age. In reality, what does 'mother tongue' mean? Is it the language spoken from birth or the language learned from your mother?
Harsharaj	I think you can give both those meanings to the word 'mother tongue'. Can your mother speak Nepali too?
Tilbikram	She can't speak Nepali.
Harsharaj	Not at all?
Tilbikram	It's not quite like that, but she knows very little. Father can get by in Nepali. The men of our village travel for trade or they work outside the village, but the women generally stay right in the village. So they don't get to learn any languages other than Limbu. And the old men and women usually can't read or write any language.
Harsharaj	What languages can you speak except for Limbu and Nepali?
Tilbikram	I can understand Hindi and I can speak just a little as well. It's not so hard for Nepali speakers to understand Hindi. The young men and women watch Hindi films at the cinema. Nowadays you can get to watch Hindi TV programmes in Nepal as well. It's rare to find young people who cannot understand Hindi in Nepal today.
Harsharaj	That's true. And the children of the new generation are not illiterate like their ancestors, are they? In schools they learn to write and read not only Nepali but English too.

Tilbikram	But it's not just children, there are also some old men in our village who can speak English. Most of them receive British Army pensions. And there are some old men who can not only speak but can also read English. It's amazing, you know. At one time I wanted to learn English too. Did you never want to learn English?
Harsharaj	I can read English but I can't speak it. I'd like to practise it but I don't have a friend who knows English. What to do?

Grammar

106 TO BE ABLE TO ...

Nepali has two verbs that mean *can*. They are each used in combination with the infinitive of a verb. सक्नु means *can* in a way that refers to the inherent or physical capability of its subject to perform the verb in question:

ऊ सगरमाथा चढ्न सक्छ । — He can climb (is capable of climbing) Everest.

ऊ सगरमाथा चढ्न सक्दैन । — He cannot climb (is not capable of climbing) Everest.

● INSIGHT

सक्नु 'to be able to' can also be used in a progressive form in any tense but not with a normal continuous marker दै, e.g. हामी अहिलेसम्म खर्च गर्न सकिरहेका छौं 'So far we are managing to spend'.

सक्नु has more than one meaning, depending on the context. It is also used to give permission to do something such as म मन्दिरमा जान सक्छु ? 'May I go to the temple?'

In sentences in past tenses, the subject will take -ले if the verb that it was able or unable to perform is transitive:

Present tense	***Past tense***
ऊ तपाईंको कुरा बुझ्न सक्दैन । He can't understand what you say.	उसले तपाईंको कुरा बुझ्न सकेन । He couldn't understand what you said.
म त्यो किताब पढ्न सक्दिन । I can't read that book.	मैले त्यो किताब पढ्न सकिनँ । I couldn't read that book.

When discussing a person's ability to speak a language, a common construction has it that the language *comes* to that person:

मलाई नेपाली अलिअलि आउँछ । — I know just a little Nepali.

मलाई अँग्रेजी बोल्न आउँछ तर लेख्न आउँदैन । — I can speak English but I cannot write it.

Exercise 62

Write nine short Nepali sentences stating that each of the persons on the left is able to perform each of the verbs on the right:

I	speak Nepali
she (Middle)	cook Nepali food
you (High)	understand this book

107 TO GET TO, MANAGE TO

पाउनु means *can* in the sense of *getting the opportunity to/managing to.* It suggests that permission has been granted, or that circumstances are in some other way favourable. The difference in meaning between **पाउनु** and **सक्नु** is particularly marked in negative sentences:

लण्डनमा म नेपाली बोल्न पाउँदिन ।	In London I can't (don't get the chance to) speak Nepali.
नेपालमा मैले अँग्रेजी सिक्न पाइनँ ।	In Nepal I couldn't (didn't get the chance to) learn English.
उसले सगरमाथा चढ्न पाएन ।	He could not (did not get a chance to) climb Everest.
लण्डनमा तपाईं गुन्द्रुक खान पाउनुहुन्न ।	You won't be able to (won't get the chance to) eat gundruk in London.

The passive form of **पाउनु**, i.e. **पाइनु**, can also be used impersonally to state that something is permitted, or that the opportunity exists to do something:

लण्डनमा नेपाली बोल्न पाइँदैन ।	In London one doesn't get to speak Nepali.
जाडो मौसममा सगरमाथा चढ्न पाइँदैन ।	One cannot (get permission to) climb Everest during the cold weather.
हेलम्बुतिर गुन्द्रुक खान पाइन्छ ।	One gets (the chance) to eat gundruk in the Helambu area.

Exercise 63

Write nine short Nepali sentences stating that each of the persons on the left managed to perform each of the verbs on the right yesterday:

he (Low)	climb Everest
they (Middle)	make a phone call
you (Middle)	eat **gundruk**

108 DESCRIBING A VERB

Nepali usually uses the infinitive of the verb (e.g. **सिक्न** *to learn, learning*) when that verb is being described with an adjective. If you wish to celebrate the ease with which you have mastered Nepali so far, you might like to declare:

नेपाली सिक्न सजिलो हुन्छ ।	To learn Nepali is easy.
उसको उच्चारण अलि अनौठो छ । त्यस कारणले उसको नेपाली बुझ्न गाह्रो छ ।	His pronunciation is a little odd. So it is difficult to understand his Nepali.
नातेदारसँग पैसा माग्न अप्ठ्यारो हुन्छ ।	It is awkward to ask a relative for money.

अप्ठ्यारो and गाह्रो can both be translated as *difficult*, but they have slightly different connotations. गाह्रो means *difficult* in the sense of something being hard or tough, while अप्ठ्यारो means that something is problematic, awkward or tricky.

109 TO LEARN TO, TEACH TO

सिक्नु means *to learn*. It is used with both nouns and verbs; when combined with another verb in a phrase meaning *to learn to ...*, the verb that is learned takes its infinitive form:

म नेपाली भाषा सिक्दै छु ।	I am learning Nepali.
म नेपाली भाषा पढ्न सिक्दै छु ।	I am learning <u>to read</u> Nepali.
म चिनियाँ भाषा सिक्दै थिएँ ।	I was learning Chinese.
म चिनियाँ भाषा लेख्न सिक्दै थिएँ ।	I was learning <u>to write</u> Chinese.
अब रामे गाडी हाँक्न सिक्दै छ ।	Now Rame is learning to drive a car.
मेरी छोरीले अहिलेसम्म साइकल चढ्न सिकेकी छैन ।	My daughter has not learned to ride a bicycle yet.

सिकाउनु is the causative of सिक्नु and it therefore means *to cause to learn* or *to teach*.

गाउँको एउटा बूढाले मलाई यो गीत गाउन सिकाएको थियो ।	An old man in the village taught me to sing this song.
वहाँ यी साना बच्चाहरूलाई अक्षर पढ्न सिकाउँदै हुनुहुन्छ ।	She is teaching these small children to read the alphabet.

A second verb that means *to teach* is पढाउनु, which is actually the causative of पढ्नु *to read, to study*. Therefore, पढाउनु is only used in more academic contexts, and only सिकाउनु is used in combination with the infinitive of a verb to mean *to teach to ...*

तपाईं यो स्कूलमा के पढाउनुहुन्छ ?	What do you teach at this school?
म गणित पढाउँछु यहाँ ।	I teach mathematics here.
आज तपाईं बच्चाहरूलाई के गर्न सिकाउनुहुन्छ ?	What will you teach the children to do today?
आज म उनीहरूलाई हिसाब गर्न सिकाउँछु ।	Today I shall teach them to add up.

School subjects

इतिहास	History	विज्ञान	Science
गणित	Mathematics	अँग्रेजी	English
भूगोल	Geography	नेपाली	Nepali

● INSIGHT

Verb stem + न आउनु and verb stem + न सक्नु express two different meanings but they are sometimes interchangeable if you are not very precise, e.g. तपाईंलाई गर्न आउँछ ? 'Do you know how to do it?' is interchangeable with तपाईं गर्न सक्नुहुन्छ ? 'Can you do it?'

But there is a difference between these two sentences. Even if you know how to do something, you can still say that you can't do it, perhaps for physical reasons.

110 TO WANT TO ...

There are several ways of expressing a wish to do something. The first is to use the verb **चाहनु** *to want to* in combination with the infinitive form of a verb:

गुरुजी नानीहरूलाई एउटा कुरा भन्न चाहनुहुन्छ ।	Guruji wants to tell the children something.
नेपालमा तपाईं आफ्नो परिवारको लागि कस्ता उपहारहरू किन्न चाहनुहुन्छ ?	What sort of presents do you want to buy for your family in Nepal?

The second way of expressing a wish to do something is to use the past tense of the verb phrase **मन लाग्नु**, which is **मन लाग्यो**. This is perhaps a more typically Nepali way of expressing the same idea. **मन लाग्यो** means something like *mind struck* or *mind tended.* It is in the past tense because the person in question has in the very recent past conceived the wish to perform whatever the verb might be: the wish has just 'struck' him/her. In their simplest form, such sentences are structured as follows:

subject + **लाई** – infinitive verb – **मन लाग्यो**

मलाई रुन मन लाग्यो ।	I want to cry.
उसलाई घर जान मन लाग्यो ।	He wants to go home.

The negative form is **मन लागेन**:

तपाईंलाई हामीकहाँ बस्न मन लागेन ?	Don't you want to stay at our place?
खै, तिमीलाई गीत गाउन किन मन लागेन ?	Well, why don't you want to sing a song?

If the sentence is about a wish that was conceived in the past but is no longer entertained, **मन लाग्नु** must take the completed past tense:

मलाई अमेरिकाको कुनै यूनिभर्सिटीमा पढ्न मन लागेको थियो, तर सकिनँ ।	I wanted to study in some American university, but I could not.
मलाई नेपाल पुगेर तपाईंको परिवारलाई फोन गर्न मन लागेको थियो, तर नम्बर फेला परेन ।	I wanted to phone your family when I reached Nepal, but I could not find the number.

● INSIGHT

पाउनु as an auxiliary verb is more commonly used in negative constructions, although it can be used in positive constructions too. You use it in negative sentences when an external circumstance prevents you from carrying out the action you wish to do, e.g. माफ गर्नुहोस्, म आउन पाइनँ. 'I am sorry I could not manage to come'.

111 VERBS MEANING TO BELIEVE

The English verb *to believe* translates into Nepali in several different ways, and the question of which verb to use depends very much on context. The three main verbs are:

(-लाई) मान्नु	to accept, regard well, respect
(-मा) विश्वास गर्नु	to trust in, have faith in
पत्याउनु	to accept as a factual truth
म तपाईंको दाईलाई धेरै मान्छु ।	I respect your elder brother a lot.
म हिन्दू धर्मलाई पनि मान्छु, बौद्ध धर्मलाई पनि मान्छु ।	I believe in both Hinduism and Buddhism.
म उनीहरूको कुरामा विश्वास गर्दिन ।	I don't trust in what they say.
देवी-देवताहरूमा म धेरै विश्वास गर्छु ।	I believe strongly in the gods and goddesses.
उनीहरूले भनेको कुरा पत्याउन गाह्रो छ ।	It is difficult to believe what they say.

The most important things for the reader to remember

1 सक्नु is used as an auxiliary verb to indicate the capability of carrying out an action. The main verb ends with न and the auxiliary verb is conjugated according to its subject, e.g. म घोडा चढ्न सक्छु 'I can ride a horse'.

2 Nepali uses आउनु 'to come' with other verbs to express an ability or skill. आउनु is used as an impersonal verb so the verb remains unchanged whatever the subject, e.g. मलाई नेपाली बोल्न आउँछ 'I know how to speak Nepali'. The verb 'speak' can be omitted here.

3 पाउनु (to get, find, receive) can also be used as an auxiliary verb. It indicates that the subject wishes to carry out the action of the main verb and the circumstances help him to complete this. The English equivalents to this are 'to manage to' or 'to get a chance to' do something, e.g. बल्ल बल्ल उसले कलेजमा पढ्न पायो 'Finally he got a chance to study at the college'.

4 पाइन्छ, the passive form of पाउनु, is also used with infinitive verbs for similar reasons. The subject (person) is understood in the passive form; and therefore the verb remains unchanged, e.g. लण्डनमा बस्न पाइन्छ 'You can stay in London' or 'you are allowed to stay in London'.

5 When a verb is being described by using an adjective, the verbal stem should end with न. However, you may often hear नु instead of न in spoken Nepali, e.g. हिँड्न or हिँड्नु राम्रो हुन्छ 'Walking/to walk is good'.

6 चाहनु is used with an action verb that its subject wants or desires to carry out and it is appropriately conjugated in all tenses, e.g. म नेपाली सिक्न चाहन्छु 'I want to learn Nepali'.

7 मन लाग्नु is used in spoken Nepali to express a sense of 'to want to' in which the verb remains unchanged regardless of what the subject is. It is an impersonal verb so the subject takes लाई, e.g. मलाई मोमो खान मन लाग्यो 'I want to eat momos'; or 'I feel like eating momos'.

19 डाक्टरकहाँ
At the doctor's

In this unit you will learn:

- *how to talk about purpose and beginning to do something*
- *how to talk about remembering and forgetting*

29 Kalyani visits the doctor

19.01

Jivan takes his daughter Kalyani to see Dr Shrestha because she has been complaining of sore eyes.

जीवन	नमस्ते डाक्टर साहेब ।
डा० श्रेष्ठ	नमस्ते । बस्नुहोस् । भन्नुहोस् त, के भयो ?
जीवन	डाक्टर साहेबलाई मेरी छोरी बिरामी भएर देखाउन आएको । बिसन्चो भएको दुई-चार दिन भयो । आज बिहान टाउको दुखेको कुरा गर्न थाली । अनि त्यो सुनेपछि डाक्टरलाई देखाउनुपर्‍यो भनेर हामीहरू हतार हतार आयौं ।
डा० श्रेष्ठ	ए, ठीक गर्नुभयो तपाईंले... नानी, तिम्रो नाम के हो त ?
कल्याणी	कल्याणी, डाक्टर साहेब ।
डा० श्रेष्ठ	अनि तिम्रो उमेर ?
कल्याणी	सात वर्ष, डाक्टर साहेब ।
डा० श्रेष्ठ	यिनको टाउको आज मात्र दुख्न थालेको ? यसभन्दा अघि बिरामी थिइनन् ?
जीवन	केही दिनदेखि आँखा दुखेको कुरा गर्दै थिई । हिजो हेरेर थाहा पाएँ दुवै आँखा राता भएका थिए ।
डा० श्रेष्ठ	भन त नानी, तिमीलाई कस्तो छ ?
कल्याणी	आँखा दुख्यो डाक्टर साहेब ।
डा० श्रेष्ठ	एक चोटि जिब्रो देखाऊ त । कुनचाहिं आँखा दुख्यो नि ?
कल्याणी	दुवै आँखा दुख्छ डाक्टर साहेब ।
डा० श्रेष्ठ	आँखा कहिले दुख्न थाल्यो ?
कल्याणी	बुधवार स्कूल पुगेपछि दुख्न थाल्यो डाक्टर साहेब । म किताब पढ्न बसें अनि त्यही बेला मेरो आँखा दुख्न थाल्यो ।
डा० श्रेष्ठ	टाउको पनि दुख्छ ?
कल्याणी	आज बिहान दुखेको थियो, डाक्टर साहेब । अब त निको भयो ।

डा० श्रेष्ठ	अनि पेट नि ?
कल्याणी	दुख्दैन डाक्टर साहेब ।
डा० श्रेष्ठ	तपाईंकी छोरीको स्वास्थ्य धेरैजसो कस्तो हुन्छ ?
जीवन	केही महिना अघि यसलाई दिसा लागेको थियो डाक्टर साहेब । दिसा लागेपछि हामीले जीवन-जल दियौं अनि चाँडै निको भयो । त्यसबाहेक केही त भएको छैन ।
डा० श्रेष्ठ	घरमा तपाईंहरू केमा भात पकाउनुहुन्छ ?
जीवन	चूल्होमा डाक्टर साहेब ।
डा० श्रेष्ठ	मट्टीतेलको चूल्हो ?
जीवन	होइन, डाक्टर साहेब, हामी दाउरामा पकाउँछौं । हामी गरीब मान्छे, मट्टीतेल किन्न सकिँदैन ।
डा० श्रेष्ठ	घरभित्रको धुवाँले यिनका आँखालाई अलि बिगारेको हुन सक्छ । म तपाईंलाई यसको औषधि दिन्छु । अनि केही दिनसम्म बिहान र बेलुका दिनको दुई पटक उमालेर सेलाएको पानीले सफा गर्न नबिर्सनू, है त ?
जीवन	हवस् डाक्टर साहेब, धन्यवाद । औषधि किन्न कता जानुपर्छ ?
डा० श्रेष्ठ	कुनै पनि औषधि पसलमा पाइन्छ । ल, बिस्तारै जानुहोस् । चार दिनभित्र निको भएन भने मलाई देखाउन फेरि आउनुहोस् ।

V Quick vocab

डा०	Dr
बिरामी	ill
बिसन्चो	unwell (opposite of सन्चो)
टाउको	head
दुख्नु	to hurt
थाल्नु	to start, begin
-पछि	after
नानी	child, little one
जिब्रो	tongue
दिसा	to have diarrhoea
जीवन-जल	life-water: a diarrhoea remedy
चूल्हो	cooker, stove, cooking hearth
दाउरा	firewood
धुवाँ	smoke
बिगार्नु	to spoil, pollute, cause harm to
उमाल्नु	to boil

सेलाउनु	to cool
औषधि	medicine
किन्नु	to buy
फेरि	again

Jivan	Hello Doctor Saheb.
Dr Shrestha	Hello. Sit down, Tell me then, what's happened?
Jivan	My daughter's become ill and I have come to show her to Doctor Saheb. She's been unwell for several days. This morning she began to say that her head hurt. And when we heard that we thought we should show her to Doctor Saheb and we came in a hurry.
Dr Shrestha	Oh, you did the right thing … Child, what is your name?
Kalyani	Kalyani, Doctor Saheb.
Dr Shrestha	And your age?
Kalyani	Seven years, Doctor Saheb.
Dr Shrestha	Did her head only begin to hurt today? She wasn't ill before this?
Jivan	For several days she was saying that her eyes hurt. Yesterday I looked and discovered that both eyes had become red.
Dr Shrestha	Tell me child, how are you?
Kalyani	My eyes hurt, Doctor Saheb.
Dr Shrestha	Just show me your tongue then. Which eye hurts?
Kalyani	Both eyes hurt, Doctor Saheb.
Dr Shrestha	When did your eyes begin to hurt?
Kalyani	My eyes began to hurt after I got to school on Wednesday, Doctor Saheb. I sat down to read a book and at that moment my eyes started to hurt.
Dr Shrestha	Does your head hurt too?
Kalyani	It was hurting this morning, Doctor Saheb. But now it's better.
Dr Shrestha	And what about your stomach?
Kalyani	It doesn't hurt, Doctor Saheb.
Dr Shrestha	How is your daughter's health usually?
Jivan	A few months ago she had diarrhoea, Doctor Saheb. When she got diarrhoea we gave her 'Jivan-Jal' and she got better quickly. Apart from that, nothing has happened.
Dr Shrestha	What do you cook your food on at home?
Jivan	On a cooker, Doctor Saheb.
Dr Shrestha	A kerosene cooker?
Jivan	No, Doctor Saheb, we cook on firewood. We are poor people, kerosene cannot be afforded.

Dr Shrestha	The smoke inside the house might have harmed her eyes a little. I will give you medicine for this. And for a few days do not forget to wash her eyes twice a day, morning and evening, with water that has been boiled and cooled, OK?
Jivan	Very well, Doctor Saheb, thank you. Where should I go to buy the medicine?
Dr Shrestha	You can get it in any medicine shop. There, take care. If she is not better within four days come to show (her to) me again.

Grammar

112 EXPRESSING PURPOSE

The infinitive of a verb can be used in combination with verbs such as **जानु** *to go,* **आउनु** *to come,* and also with other verbs, to express purpose. In these contexts, the infinitive of the verb means *in order to* do whatever the verb might be:

हेर्न जानु	to go (in order) to watch
लिन पठाउनु	to send (in order) to get
गर्न आउनु	to come (in order) to do
हामीहरू दाउरा काट्न वनतिर जाँदै छौं ।	We are going to the forest to cut firewood.
आज दिउँसो पल्लो गाउँको मान्छे हाम्रो गाई हेर्न आउँदै छ ।	This afternoon a man from the next village is coming to look at our cow.

● INSIGHT

An infinitive verb in combination with a motion verb expresses the purpose of doing something in any tense. The infinitive verb with को लागि or भनेर can also express the similar idea.

Sometimes, the postposition **-लाई** is added to the infinitive of the verb to emphasize the sense of purpose. This is especially necessary in spoken Nepali, when purpose is often expressed outside the framework of a full sentence:

उनीहरू किन पोखरा जाँदै छन् ? सिनेमा हेर्नलाई ?	Why are they going to Pokhara. To watch a film?
तिमीहरू किन वनभित्र पसेको ? दाउरा काट्नलाई ?	Why have you entered the forest? To cut firewood?

Another context in which purpose is expressed is one in which you wish to say that something is needed in order for a particular verb to happen. In this case, the postposition **-को लागि** *for* is added to the infinitive of the verb:

फोटो खिच्नको लागि के चाहिन्छ ? फोटो खिच्नको लागि क्यामेरा चाहिन्छ ।	What does one need to take a photograph? To take a photograph you need a camera.
यो रेडियो बजाउनको लागि मैले एउटा ब्याटरी किन्नुपऱ्यो ।	In order to play this radio I had to buy a battery.

113 BEGINNING TO DO SOMETHING

Nepali has four verbs that mean *to begin*. These are: **शुरु हुनु, शुरु गर्नु, थाल्नु,** and **लाग्नु.**

(i) शुरु हुनु and शुरु गर्नु

शुरु is a noun meaning *beginning*. Thus, **शुरुमा** means *in the beginning*. **शुरु हुनु** is intransitive, while **शुरु गर्नु** is transitive; they have the sense of *to commence* and *to start* respectively. They are both used as the main verb of a sentence and cannot be combined with any other verb:

आजको कार्यक्रम कति बजे शुरु हुन्छ ?	At what time does today's programme begin?
काम साह्रै ढिलो भयो । अब हामीले शुरु गर्नुपर्छ ।	The work is very overdue. We must start now.

> **● INSIGHT**
>
> **When लाग्नु is conjugated to show the imminence of an activity, it is always used in the simple past tense although it is meant to be in the present tense, e.g. म जान लागेँ. It indicates that the preparation for doing something has already taken place.**

(ii) थाल्नु

थाल्नु and **लाग्नु** can both be used with the infinitive of a verb to indicate the beginning of an event or action. Although **थाल्नु** and **लाग्नु** both mean *to begin*, there are certain tenses and contexts in which one should be used instead of the other, and in some contexts there is some difference in meaning between the two verbs. Nepali speakers use these two verbs rather more than English speakers use the English verb *to begin*.

थाल्नु has the sense *to start to …* In the past tense, it means that the subject began to perform the verb with which **थाल्नु** is combined, but it does not imply that the verb is still being performed:

ऊ मन्दिर जान थाल्यो ।	He started to go to the temple.
मेरी बहिनी रुन थाली ।	My younger sister started to cry.

थाल्नु is transitive when it is used with transitive verbs, so the subject must take -ले in the past tense:

मैले अस्ति बुधवारदेखि अफिसमा काम गर्न थालें ।	I started to work at the office from last Wednesday.
बाले भरखरै अखबार पढ्न थाल्नुभएको थियो ।	Father had just started to read the newspaper.

थाल्नु is used in the present tense in situations where the subject makes a voluntary choice to perform the verb:

म आजै गर्न थाल्छु ।	I shall start to do it today.
भोलिदेखि ऊ अँग्रेजी सिक्न थाल्छ रे ।	He says he will start to learn English from tomorrow.

(iii) लाग्नु

लाग्नु has the sense *to begin to* ... It is very rarely used in the present tense, where it gives way to थाल्नु. In the past tense, it often means that the verb has begun to happen or be performed, but is still ongoing. For instance, the sentences म घर जान लागें and म घर जान लागेको छु might be taken literally to mean *I began to go home* and *I have begun to go home* but in fact they can both mean *I am going home* or *I am on my way home*:

ए भाइ, तिमी कता जान लागेको ?	Hey, brother, where are you off to?
म ठमेल जान लागेको । तिमी नि ?	I'm going to Thamel. What about you?
म भोटाहिटी जान लागेको ।	I'm on my way to Bhotahiti.

Compare the translations of the following sentences, one of which uses लाग्नु and the other थाल्नु:

ऊ मन्दिर जान लागेको छ ।	He is on his way to the temple/he is about to set out for the temple.
ऊ मन्दिर जान थालेको छ ।	He has started going to the temple.

The first sentence means that he has *begun to go* to the temple, and is currently headed in that direction. The second sentence suggests that he was not previously in the habit of visiting the temple, but has *started to go* recently.

लाग्नु is more suited than थाल्नु to casual or involuntary actions or events. It never takes -ले, even in the past tense when the verb it is linked with is transitive.

Further examples of लाग्नु and थाल्नु

ए दीपक, तिमी के गर्न लाग्यौ ?	Hey Deepak, what are you doing?
म भात खान लागेको, आमा !	I'm eating rice, mother!
पानी पर्न लाग्यो । अब छाता खोल्नुपर्छ ।	It's started to rain. Now we must open the umbrella.
कार्त्तिक महिनादेखि मौसम अलि चिसो हुन थाल्छ ।	From the month of Karttik the weather starts to be rather cold.

114 AFTER DOING SOMETHING

The postposition -**पछि** *after* is added to the past tense base of verbs, with the **-e-** vowel forming a junction between them, to mean:

खाएपछि	after eating
गएपछि	after going
भनेपछि	after saying
उठेपछि	after getting up
भएपछि	after being /becoming
रातमा नराम्रो सपना देखेपछि ऊ फेरि निदाउन सकेन ।	After he had a nightmare in the night, he could not sleep again.*
बा-आमा मरेपछि साना बच्चाहरूलाई कसले हेर्छ ?	After mother and father have died, who will look after the small children?
झिसमिसे बिहान उठेर हातमुख धोएर दाँत माझेपछि म बाहिर निस्कें ।	I went out after I had got up in the pale early dawn, washed my hands and face, and brushed my teeth.

Note *In Nepali, one 'sees' a dream or nightmare.

● INSIGHT

When an 'after doing' construction such as खाएपछि 'after eating' is used in the negative by prefixing न as in नखाएपछि, the English translation for that is 'when', e.g. नखाएपछि कमजोर हुन्छ 'When you do not eat you become weak'.

115 REMEMBERING AND FORGETTING

The verb **बिर्सनु** means *to forget:*

हामीलाई नबिर्सनुहोस् !*	Don't forget us!
माफ गर्नुहोस् है, मैले तपाईंको नाम बिर्सें ।	Please forgive me, I have forgotten your name.
आज तिमी स्कूलबाट किन ढिलो आयौ ? बाटो बिर्सेर हो कि क्या हो ?	Why did you come home late from school today? Did you forget the way or what?

Note *also the expression **माया नमार्नुहोस्** ! literally, *don't kill affection*, which means 'don't forget me/us' or 'keep in touch'.

बिर्सनु is also combined with the infinitive of a verb to mean *to forget to ...*

क्षमा गर्नुहोला, मैले तपाईंको ठेगाना टिप्न बिर्सें ।	Please forgive me, I forgot to take a note of your address.

बिहा गर्ने हतपतले उसले केटी माग्न बिर्स्यो ।	Because of (his) hurry to get married he forgot to ask for a girl.*

Note *A proverb which describes how in one's rush to get something done one can often forget some crucial ingredient.

● INSIGHT

When Nepali speakers forget something or forget to do something they often use भुसुक्क to add an emphasis to this. This is a Nepali onomatopoeic word that is collocated with the verb बिर्सनु 'to forget', e.g. मैले खान भुसुक्क बिर्सें 'I completely forgot to eat'.

If you wish to tell someone to remember to do something, you should tell them *not to forget* to do it, using **बिर्सनु**:

बेलायत फर्केपछि हामीलाई चिठी लेख्न नबिर्स है त !	After you return to England, remember (don't forget) to write us a letter, OK?
भरे बेलुका रेडियोमा समाचार सुन्न नबिर्सनुहोस् ।	Please remember (don't forget) to listen to the news on the radio this evening.

There are two verbs that mean *to remember* –**याद हुनु** and **सम्झनु**. These are used in slightly different ways.

याद is a noun meaning *memory* or *recollection*. One way of saying that you do or do not remember something is simply to state:

मलाई याद छ ।	I remember ('to me there is memory').
मलाई याद छैन ।	I don't remember ('to me there is not memory').

In practice, this construction is used most commonly in the negative to state that someone has no recollection of some fact or event from the past:

यो धेरै अघिको कुरा हो । तपाईंलाई याद छैन होला ।	This is something that happened a long time ago. Perhaps you don't remember.

In the constructions that use **याद**, the person who is or is not remembering is passive. S/he is not actively remembering or forgetting the matter in question. But the verb **सम्झनु** is used to mean *to remember/recall* in a more active sense. As explained above, it rarely occurs in the negative, because the verb **बिर्सनु** *to forget* fulfils that role.

बल्ल सम्झें । तपाईंले छ बजे आउनू भनेर भन्नुभएको थियो, होइन ?	At last I've remembered. You said to come at 6 o'clock, didn't you?
कहिलेकाहीं म आफ्नो बिहाको दिन सम्झेर हाँस्छु ।	Sometimes I recall my wedding day and I smile.

The causative of **सम्झनु** is **सम्झाउनु**, which literally means *to remind*. However, it is most commonly used to mean *to explain/counsel:*

मेरा छोरा बिहा गर्न मान्दैन । उसलाई अलि सम्झाउनुहोस् न ।	My son refuses to marry. Just explain things to him, would you?

116 BEFORE DOING SOMETHING: POSTPOSITIONS BEGINNING WITH -भन्दा

There is a set of two-word postpositions of which the first word is -**भन्दा**. Because -**भन्दा** is also used to make comparisons (see **Grammar 51**), these postpositions have at least a vaguely comparative sense to them. Three of them mean *before*, and can be used with nouns or verbs:

-भन्दा पहिले	before, previous to, ago
-भन्दा अघि	before, previous to, ago
-भन्दा अगाडि	before, previous to, ago
आजभन्दा दस वर्ष अघि यस टोलमा एउटा चियापसल पनि थिएन ।	Ten years ago there wasn't even a teashop in this part of town.
सन् १९६९ भन्दा पहिले कसैले चन्द्रमामा पाइला टेकेको थिएन ।	Before 1969 no one had set foot on the moon.

These three postpositions are also used with verbs to mean *before*. In such constructions, -**भन्दा** must be added to the dictionary form of the verb:

मन्दिरभित्र पस्नुभन्दा पहिले जुत्ता खोल्न नबिर्सनुहोस् ।	Please remember (don't forget) to take off your shoes before going into the temple.
घर जानुभन्दा अगाडि म तपाईंलाई यो कोसेली दिन चाहन्छु ।	Before going home I want to give you this gift.
सुत्नुभन्दा अघि तिमीहरूले हात खुट्टा किन नधोएको ?	Why didn't you wash your hands and feet before going to bed?

● INSIGHT

In spoken Nepali, you hear पहिला more than पहिले. Nepali uses a phrase like तपाईं पहिले/पहिला to indicate 'you first', which is the same as 'after you' in English. Phrases like धेरै पहिले or धेरै अघि 'long ago' are used to relate a story or episodes from history.

● INSIGHT

भन्दा अघि/अगाडि/पहिले or पहिला all mean 'earlier than' and these are used with verbs to indicate 'prior to' or 'before'. When they are used with nouns they mean 'previous to' or 'ago'. You can still express the same sense even without using भन्दा.

Exercise 64

Translate into Nepali:

My elder sister got married two weeks ago. Now she lives in Dhulikhel (**dhulikhel**). Dhulikel is nearly ten miles from Bhaktapur. Last Sunday we went there to meet her husband and her new family.

To get to Dhulikhel we had to take a taxi as far as Ratna Park. At Ratna Park we had to board a bus that was going to Panchkhal (**pā̃cakhāl**). Dhulikel is on the way to Panchkhal.

After we arrived at Ratna Park father had to go into a shop. He had forgotten to buy any presents (**upahār**). Father had to go into three shops to buy cloth (**kapaḍā**), sweets (**miṭhāī**) and bangles (**curā**). Mother began to feel worried because it had begun to get rather late. But it takes only one hour to reach Dhulikhel and buses leave (**chuṭnu**) every hour.

After father had bought the gifts we began to search for the Dhulikhel bus. A man standing beside a new blue bus had begun to shout (**karāunu**) 'Panchkhal! Panchkhal!' Father went to the office to buy our tickets. Before father returned with the tickets I asked the driver (**cālak**) if the bus would also go to Dhulikhel. He said that it would. He also said that there was no question of not going to Dhulikhel because there is a good hotel there. Before the bus sets out from Dhulikhel for Panchkhal all the passengers (**yātruharū**) eat their morning meal there, he said. Suddenly it began to rain, so we all found a place to sit on the bus. After a few minutes our journey (**yātrā**) began.

The most important things for the reader to remember

1 A sense of 'in order to' or 'expressing purpose of doing something' in Nepali is formed by using **जानु** or **आउनु** as an auxiliary, usually with motion verbs, e.g. **म पसलमा किताब किन्न जान्छु** 'I am going to the shop to buy a book'.

2 In Nepali, the inception of an action or state of affairs is normally expressed by using **थाल्नु** (to begin) with infinitive verbs, e.g. **मैले पढ्न थालें** 'I began to read'. **सुरु गर्नु** is occasionally used instead of **थाल्नु** but it is more common with nouns, e.g. **तपाईं कार्यक्रम कतिबजे सुरु गर्नुहुन्छ ?** 'What time do you start the programme?'

3 Verb stem + **न लाग्नु** is used to indicate the imminence of a verbal activity. The English equivalent to this is 'to be about to' or 'almost happening', e.g. **म निस्कन लागें, एकछिन पर्खनुहोस्** 'I am about to leave, wait a minute'. Note that this is the only usage in which **लाग्नु** is conjugated according to its person or pronoun subject.

4 The verb stem + **एपछि** indicates two actions done one after another in a complex sentence, e.g. **खाएपछि म अफिस गएँ** 'I went to the office after eating'.

5 **बिर्सनु** means 'to forget' something and it is also used with other infinitive verbs to say 'to forget to do something' such as **खान बिर्सनु** 'to forget to eat'. **भुसुक्क**, an onomatopoeic word, is used to say 'to forget completely'. **बिर्सनु** is conjugated in all tenses.

6 When an infinitive verb such as **जानु** or **खानु** is followed by **भन्दा पहिले** or **भन्दा अघि/अगाडि** it implies that you do something before doing something else, e.g. **सुत्नुभन्दा पहिले म टिभी हेर्छु** 'I watch television before going to bed'.

7 You can also use this construction with nouns, e.g. **तपाईंभन्दा पहिले** 'before you', **दुई बर्ष अघि/अगाडि** 'two years ago'. If you want to use a comparative phrase to say 'ten years ago', you need to compare this with 'today' as in **आजभन्दा दस बर्ष अघि.**

20 नेपालको नक्सा
The map of Nepal

In this unit you will learn:
- *about the geography of Nepal*
- *how to use bhanne to mean called and that*
- *how to discuss physical locations*

30 The map of Nepal

नेपालको नक्सा हेर्नुहोस् । यसबाट तपाईं नेपालको बारेमा धेरै कुरा थाहा पाउन सक्नुहुन्छ । यसलाई हेरेपछि नेपालको भौगोलिक स्थिति पनि बुझिन्छ ।

नेपालका दुइटा छिमेकी राष्ट्रहरू छन् । उत्तरमा भोट छ । भोट चालीस वर्षदेखि चीनको एउटा प्रान्त भएको छ । दक्षिणमा भारतका उत्तर प्रदेश, बिहार, र पश्चिम बंगाल भन्ने प्रदेशहरू छन् । पूर्वतिर सिक्किम छ, अनि सिक्किमभन्दा पर भूटान पनि छ । तर भूटान चीन र भारतजस्तो नेपालको छिमेकी राष्ट्र होइन ।

तपाईं दक्षिण नेपालको सिमानादेखि उत्तरतिर चढ्नुभयो भने तपाईंले तीनवटा भोगौलिक क्षेत्रहरू पार गर्नुपर्छ । दक्षिणमा तराई क्षेत्र छ । यसलाई नेपालीहरू मदेस पनि भन्छन् । तराईको जमीन समतल छ अनि त्यहाँ उत्तर भारतको जस्तो गर्मी हुन्छ । पहिला पहिला यहाँ जंगल थियो तर करीब दुई सय वर्ष अघि किसानहरू यहाँ खेतीपाती गर्न आए । उनीहरूले जङ्गल फाँडेर खेती गर्न थाले । अहिले अलिकति जङ्गल मात्रै बाँकि छ । नेपालगंज, वीरगंज, जनकपुर र विराटनगर तराईका षहरहरू हुन् । तराईमा नेपाली मात्रै होइन, मैथिली, भोजपुरी, अवधी, थारु र अन्य भाषाहरू पनि बोलिन्छन् ।

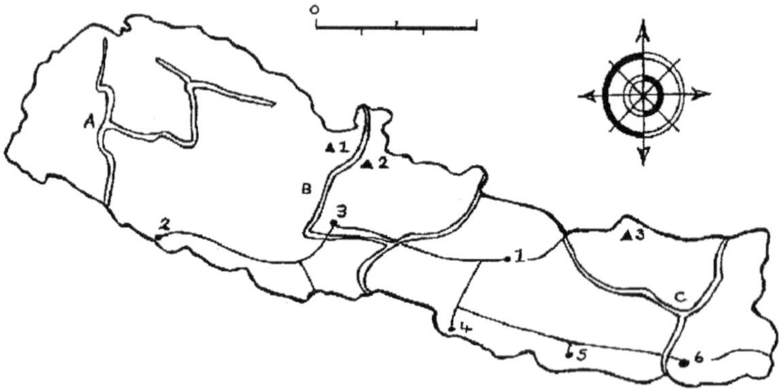

[Mountain] 1	धवलागिरी	[Town] 4	वीरगंज
[Mountain] 2	अन्नपूर्ण	[Town] 5	जनकपुर
[Mountain] 3	सगरमाथा	[Town] 6	विराटनगर
[Town] 1	काठ्माडौं	[River] A	कर्णाली
[Town] 2	नेपालगंज	[River] B	गण्डकी
[Town] 3	पोखरा	[River] C	कोशी

तराई क्षेत्रभन्दा माथि पहाडी क्षेत्र छ । यहाँको जमीन प्रायजसो उकालो र ओरालो हुन्छ । किसानहरू बेंसीहरूमा धान रोप्न तल झर्छन्, पाखाहरूमा मकै रोप्न माथि चढ्छन् । उनीहरू भैंसी, बाखा र अन्य पशुहरू पनि पाल्छन् । काठ्माडौंको ठूलो उपत्यका पहाडी क्षेत्रमा पर्छ । यो नेपाल राज्यको राजनैतिक र साँस्कृतिक केन्द्र हो । पहाडी क्षेत्रमा जनसंख्या ज्यादै बढेको कारणले खेतीपातीको लागि जमीनको अभाव छ । त्यस कारणले पहाडका मानिसहरू हिजोआज कामको खोजीमा विदेशिन लागेका छन् । नेपाली भाषाको जन्मस्थल सुदूर पश्चिम नेपालमा पर्छ, तर मध्य र पूर्वी नेपालमा नेवारी, गुरुङ्ग, मगर, लिम्बू, तामाङ्ग र राई जस्ता भोट-बर्मेली भाषाहरू पनि बोलिन्छन् ।

पहाडी क्षेत्रभन्दा माथि हिमाली क्षेत्र छ । यहाँ सगरमाथा, मकालु, अन्नपूर्ण, धौलागिरी जस्ता सँसारका सबैभन्दा अग्ला शिखरहरू पाइन्छन् । यहाँको जनसंख्या तराई र पहाड़को जनसंख्याको दाँजोमा सानो छ । यस क्षेत्रमा बस्ने मानिसहरूको भाषा भोटको भाषासँग मिल्छ । उनीहरू बौद्ध धर्म मान्छन् अनि उनीहरूको मुख्य व्यवसाय व्यापार हो ।

भोटको सिमानाबाट अनेकौं नदीहरू निस्केर भारततिर बग्छन् । तीमध्ये कर्णाली, गण्डकी र कोशी नदीहरू धेरै महत्त्वपूर्ण छन् । जाडोमा पानी कम पर्छ । त्यस कारणले यी खोलाहरू जाडोमा साना हुन्छन् । तर बर्सातमा पानी परेपछि सबै खोला-नालाहरू बढ्छन् । त्यो खेतीपातीको लागि साह्रै आवश्यक हुन्छ ।

नेपालमा बाटाहरू धेरै कम छन् भन्ने कुरा यो नक्सालाई हेरेर तपाईं थाहा पाउन सक्नुहुन्छ । ती बाटाहरूमा बस, ट्रक र गाडीहरू प्रशस्त चल्छन् । तर पनि आ-आफ्ना घर पुग्न धेरैजसो नेपालीहरूलाई अझै पनि हिँड्नैपर्छ ।

Quick vocab

नक्सा	map
-को बारेमा	about
भौगोलिक	geographical
स्थिति	situation
छिमेकी	neighbour
राष्ट्र	nation
उत्तर	north
प्रान्त	province
प्रदेश	state
पूर्वी	eastern
दक्षिण	south
सिमाना	border
क्षेत्र	region
पार गर्नु	to cross, traverse
जमीन	land
समतल	level, flat
गर्मी	heat
पहिला पहिला	long ago
जंगल	jungle, uninhabited place
खेतीपाती	agriculture, farming
फाँड्नु	to cut down
खेती	agriculture, farming

बाँकि	remaining
पहाडी क्षेत्र	the hill region
धान	growing rice, paddy
रोप्नु	to plant
झर्नु	to descend
मकै	maize
भैंसी	buffalo
बाखा	goat
पशु	animal, livestock
पाल्नु	to rear
उपत्यका	valley
पर्नु	to be located
राज्य	country, state
राजनैतिक	political
साँस्कृतिक	cultural
केन्द्र	centre
जनसंख्या	population
बढ्नु	to increase, grow
खोजी	search
विदेशिनु	to go abroad
जन्मस्थल	birthplace
सुदूर	remote, far
पश्चिम	west
मध्य	mid-
भोट-बर्मेली	Tibeto-Burman
शिखर	peak
-को दाँजोमा	compared to
व्यवसाय	occupation
अनेकौं	many
मध्ये	among
नदी	river
महत्त्वपूर्ण	important
जाडो	the cold season
बर्सात	the rainy season
आवश्यक	necessary
ट्रक	truck
गाडी	car
तर पनि	none the less

Look at the map of Nepal. From this you can discover many things about Nepal. After looking at this Nepal's geographical situation can be understood.

Nepal has two neighbour nations. In the north is Tibet. Tibet has been a province of China for 40 years. In the south are the states of India called Uttar Pradesh, Bihar and West Bengal. To the east is Sikkim and beyond Sikkim there is Bhutan too. But Bhutan is not a neighbour nation of Nepal as China and India (are).

If you climb from the border of southern Nepal towards the north you have to cross three geographical regions. In the south is the Tarai region. Nepalis also call this Mades. The land of the Tarai is flat and there there is heat like northern India's. Long ago there was jungle here but about 200 years ago farmers came here to do agriculture. They cut down the jungle and began to farm. Now there is only a little jungle left. Nepalganj, Birganj, Janakpur and Biratnagar are towns of the Tarai. In the Tarai not only Nepali but also Maithili, Bhojpuri, Awadhi, Tharu and other languages are spoken.

Above the Tarai region is the Hill region. Here the land is mostly uphill and downhill. The farmers go down to plant paddy rice in the valleys, and climb up to plant maize on the hillsides. They also rear buffaloes, goats and other animals. The large valley of Kathmandu is located in the Hill region. This is Nepal's political and cultural centre. Because the population has increased greatly in the Hill region there is a shortage of land for agriculture. For that reason the people of the hills have begun nowadays to go abroad in search of work. The birthplace of the Nepali language is in far west Nepal, but in middle and east Nepal Tibeto-Burman languages such as Newari, Gurung, Magar, Limbu, Tamang and Rai are also spoken.

Above the Hill region is the Himalayan region. Here one finds the world's highest peaks, such as Sagarmatha, Makalu, Annapurna, Dhaulagiri. The population here is small compared to the population of the Tarai and the Hills. The language of the people who live in this region is similar to the language of Tibet. They are Buddhists? and their main occupation is trade.

Many rivers emerge from the Tibetan border and flow toward India. Among them, the Karnali, Gandaki and Koshi are very important. In the winter little rain falls. Therefore these rivers are small in the winter. But after rain falls in the rainy season all the rivers and streams grow. That is very necessary for agriculture.

You can discover that there are very few roads in Nepal by looking at this map. Many buses, trucks and cars run on those roads. None the less, most Nepalis still have to walk to reach their homes.

Exercise 65

Answer the following questions about the geography of Nepal:

१ नेपालीहरू तराई क्षेत्रलाई के भन्छन् ?

२ नेपाली भाषाबाहेक तराई क्षेत्रमा अरू कुन कुन भाषाहरू बोलिन्छन् ?

३ पहाडी क्षेत्रको जमीन प्रायजसो कस्तो हुन्छ ?

४ नेपाली भाषाबाहेक पहाडी क्षेत्रमा अरू कुन कुन भाषाहरू बोलिन्छन् ?

५ नेपालका नदीहरूमध्ये कुन कुनचाहिं महत्त्वपूर्ण छन् ?

६ घर पुग्नलाई धेरैजसो नेपालीहरूले के गर्नुपर्छ ?

● INSIGHT

पर्छ is generally used as an auxiliary to indicate the direction or side of a particular place. But it is also used to show the location of a particular place, e.g. काठमाडौं वाग्मती अञ्चलमा पर्छ 'Kathmandu is in Bagmati zone'.

Grammar

117 USING पर्नु WITH LOCATIONS

The simplest way to state the location of something is to use the verb **हुनु to be**, which in the present tense must take its छ form. However, the verb पर्नु, literally *to fall*, is often used when the discussion of a location involves some sense of direction:

तपाईंको गाउँ कतातिर पर्छ ?	Where (in which direction) is your village located?

It is also used to locate places within countries, districts or zones, in which case it can be thought of as meaning *falls within:*

ललितपुर शहर बागमती अञ्चलमा पर्छ ।	The city of Lalitpur falls within the Bagmati zone.

118 ABOVE, BELOW, BEYOND: MORE POSTPOSITIONS BEGINNING WITH -भन्दा

A set of two-word postpositions, of which the first word is **-भन्दा**, deals with the physical locations of things, in terms of height, distance and so on:

-भन्दा माथि	above
-भन्दा तल	below
-भन्दा पर	beyond, on the far side of
हाम्रो गाउँभन्दा माथि बस्ती छैन । गाउँभन्दा माथि वनै वन छ । तर गाउँभन्दा तल त धेरै खेतहरू छन् । गाउँभन्दा तलका खेतहरूमा हामी धान रोप्छौं ।	There are no settlements above our village. Above our village there is nothing but forest. But below the village there are many fields. We plant rice in the fields below our village.

● INSIGHT

If you use the comparative term भन्दा to indicate 'above', 'below' or 'beyond', you need to mention what you are comparing that with, e.g. योभन्दा माथि, योभन्दा तल, योभन्दा पर etc. Note that you do not have to use भन्दा just to say 'There are two rooms above or upstairs': माथि दुईवटा कोठा छन् ।

Of course, both माथि and तल are also used as adverbs to describe the up-and-down way in which much human movement must take place in the Himalayas:

मिरमिरे बिहान हामी गाई–बाखा चराउन माथि चढ्यौं । साँझ पर्नुभन्दा अघि हामी तल गाउँतिर झर्‍यौं	In the pale early dawn we climbed up to graze the cows and goats. Before dusk fell we came down to the village.

119 THE USE OF भन्ने TO MEAN NAMED

भन्ने is the -ने participle of the verb भन्नु *to say.* It can often be translated as *called* or *named:*

पूर्वी नेपालको इलाम भन्ने सानो शहर	a small town called Ilam in east Nepal
यती भन्ने अनौठो प्राणी	a strange creature called the Yeti
गीता खड्का भन्ने नयाँ विद्यार्थी	a new student named Gita Khadka

Note the word order of the phrases above. Instead of 'a new student named Gita Khadka', Nepali has *Gita-Khadka-named new student.*

● INSIGHT

भन्ने is used in two ways in Nepali. First, it is used with nouns to denote 'named' or 'called' as in जोमसोम भन्ने ठाउँ 'a place called Jomsom'. Second, it is used with conjugated verbs such as सुन्नु 'to hear', थाहा हुनु 'to know' etc. to connect with a first clause, e.g. मैले ऊ बिरामी छ भन्ने सुनें.

120 THE USE OF भन्नै TO MEAN THAT

भन्ने is also used to link a question, a fact, etc. with its content:

कुनचाहिं होटेल सबभन्दा राम्रो होला भन्ने प्रश्न उठ्यो ।	The question arose as to which hotel would be the best.
तपाईं नेपाल आउनुभएको थियो भन्ने मलाई थाहा थिएन ।	I did not know that you had come to Nepal.
तपाईं चाँडै निको हुनुहुन्छ भन्ने म आशा गर्छु ।	I hope that you will be well soon.

● INSIGHT

Keep it in mind that the pronunciation of भन्ने sometimes gets mixed up with the pronunciation of भने, which is a conditional marker. You need to give a slight pause with half न before you say ने, otherwise it would sound like भने 'if'.

It is perhaps useful to think of the sentences given above as containing a question or an item of knowledge that is described by **भन्ने**, *saying:*

the 'which hotel will be the best'-saying question

the 'you had come to Nepal'-saying knowledge

a 'you will be well soon'-saying hope

Nepali is rich in proverbs (**उखान**), which might also be quoted using **भन्ने**:

बालुवा निचोरेर तेल आउन्न भन्ने उखान ।	The proverb that says that oil does not come from squeezing sand.
इमान भनेको लाख हो, धन भनेको खाक हो भन्ने उखान ।	The proverb that says that honesty means a great deal (but) wealth means ashes.
हीराको मोल कीराले जान्दैन भन्ने उखान ।	The proverb that says that an insect doesn't know the value of diamonds.

The most important things for the reader to remember

1 In order to indicate the direction of a particular place, Nepali uses **पर्छ** followed by **तिर,** which is a postposition, e.g. **काठमाडौँबाट लाङ्टाङ् हिमाल उत्तरतिर पर्छ ।** 'Mt Langtang lies to the north of Kathmandu'.

2 The English words 'above', 'below' or 'beyond' are relative terms in Nepali; therefore Nepali uses a comparative term **भन्दा** to indicate them properly, e.g. **योभन्दा माथि** or **तल दुईटा कोठा छन् ।** 'There are two rooms above (or below) this. However, you can simply say' **माथि** or **तल दुईटा कोठा छन्** by deleting **योभन्दा** a relative term.

3 **भन्ने** which comes from **भन्नु** 'to say' can be translated as 'called, or named' and it is often used with nouns, e.g. **लण्डन भन्ने शहर** 'the city called London', **पिटर भन्ने मान्छे** 'a person named Peter'.

4 When the same **भन्ने** is used with verbs, it changes its role into a conjunction, which is often translated as 'that', e.g. **मैले भोलि पानी पर्छ भन्ने सुनेँ** 'I heard that it would rain tomorrow'. The full form of **भन्ने** is **भन्ने कुरा. कुरा** is understood in this sentence.

21 म चुरोट खान्थें
I used to smoke

In this unit you will learn:
- ***how to use the habitual past tense***
- ***how to use expressions meaning while and as soon as***
- ***how to talk about hopes and desires***

31 Bad habits

21.01

An old man tells his grandson about how he decided to give up smoking.

नाति	तपाईं कुनै बेला चुरोट खानुहुन्थ्यो, हजुरबा ?
हजुरबा	पहिला खान्थें, अब खाँदिन । करीब बीस वर्ष अघि मैले चुरोट खान छाडें ।
नाति	तपाईं धेरै चुरोट खानुहुन्थ्यो ?
हजुरबा	अँ, थुप्रै खान्थें । बिहान उठ्नेबित्तिकै एउटा चुरोट झिकेर सल्काउँथें । अनि चिया खान्थें । तर चिया खाँदाखेरि पनि चुरोट खानुपर्थ्यो ।
नाति	एक दिनमा तपाईं कति खिल्ली चुरोट खानुहुन्थ्यो, हजुरबा ?
हजुरबा	खै, अहिले सम्झनै छैन ! हिँड्दाखेरि खान्थें, बस्दाखेरि खान्थें, खेतमा काम गर्दाखेरि खान्थें, भात खानुभन्दा अघि खान्थें, भात खाएपछि खान्थें । धेरै खान्थें !
नाति	अनि सुत्दाखेरि नि ?
हजुरबा	सुत्न गएपछि एक-दुई वटा खान्थें तर निदाएपछि चुरोट खान अलि अप्ठ्यारो हुन्छ, कान्छा । सायद सपनामा पनि खान्थें कि ? खै, थाहा छैन !
नाति	अनि छाड्ने निधो कसरी गर्नुभयो ?
हजुरबा	सानो उमेरदेखि नै तेरो बाले डाक्टर बन्ने आकाँक्षा राखेको थियो । उसले कलकत्ता विश्वविद्यालयमा ठाउँ पायो अनि पढ्न गयो । डाक्टर बन्न उसले धेरै वर्षसम्म पढ्नुपर्‍यो त्यहाँ, तर बल्ल-बल्ल डाक्टर भयो । घर फर्केपछि उसले मलाई बा किन चुरोट खानुहुन्छ भनेर गाली गर्न थाल्यो ।
नाति	डाक्टर भएपछि त वहाँले भन्नैपर्‍यो नि, हजुरबा !
हजुरबा	हो, चुरोट खाने बानी स्वास्थ्यलाई हानीकारक छ भनेर भन्थ्यो, बारम्बार । कुनै दिन छाड्नैपर्ला भन्थ्यो । अनि ऊ

	कलकत्ताबाट फर्केको केही दिनभित्र नै मलाई रुघा-खोकी लाग्यो । अनि छाती दुख्न थाल्यो । त्यही बेला उसकी आमाले पनि मलाई गाली गर्न थाली तिमी किन चाँडै मर्न चाहन्छौ भनेर ।
नाति	अनि चुरोट खान छाड्नुभएको, हो ?
हजुरबा	हो, छाड्नैपऱ्यो नि । अनि चुरोट नखाएको दुई-चार हप्तापछि मलाई केही फाइदा भएको थाहा पाएँ ।
नाति	कस्तो फाइदा ?
हजुरबा	रुचि बढ्यो । पहिला म भात अलि कम खान्थें किनभने भात खाँदाखेरि चुरोटको तलतल लाग्थ्यो । तर चुरोट छाडेको केही दिनभित्र त्यो पुरानो तलतल हरायो अनि मैले राम्ररी खान थालें ।
नाति	तपाईं त रक्सी खानुहुन्न, हो ?
हजुरबा	म रक्सी खाँदिन । कहिले पनि खाएको छैन । यस जिल्लाका गाउँहरूमा धेरैजसो बाहुनहरू बस्छन् नि । यहाँका मानिसहरूले केही वर्ष अघिसम्म पुराना परम्पराहरूको पालन गर्थे । रक्सी खाँदैनथे, मासु पनि खाँदैनथे, जिल्लाबाहिरका केटीहरू ल्याउँदैनथे, तर ...
नाति	तर तपाईं जस्तै उनीहरू पनि चुरोट खान्थे, होइन ?
हजुरबा	अहँ, खाँदैनथे । म र एउटा पसलको साहूजी मात्रै खान्थ्यौं । हामीहरूबाहेक कसैले खाँदैनथ्यो । छिमेकीहरू मलाई बिग्रेको भन्थे !

Quick vocab

कुनै	any, some
चुरोट खानु	to smoke cigarettes
छाड्नु	to give up, quit
झिक्नु	to take out
हानीकारक	harmful
चाहनु	to want to
फाइदा	benefit
रुचि	appetite
सल्काउनु	to set light to
-दाखेरि	while
सपना	dream
निधो	decision
आकाँक्षा	ambition
बानी	habit

स्वास्थ्य	health
तलतल	craving
परम्परा	tradition
पालन गर्नु	to maintain, foster
जिल्ला	district
ल्याउनु	to bring
बिग्रनु	to go wrong, be corrupted

Grandson	Did you smoke at any time, grandfather?
Grandfather	I used to smoke before, now I don't. I quit smoking about 20 years ago.
Grandson	Did you smoke a lot?
Grandfather	Yes, I smoked heaps. As soon as I got up in the morning I would take out a cigarette and light it. Then I would drink tea. But even while I was drinking the tea I had to smoke a cigarette as well.
Grandson	In one day how many cigarettes did you smoke, grandfather?
Grandfather	Well, I don't even remember now! I smoked while I was walking, I smoked while I was sitting down, I smoked while I was working in the field, I smoked before meals, I smoked after meals. I smoked a lot!
Grandson	And what about while you were sleeping?
Grandfather	After I had gone to bed I would smoke one or two but after you have fallen asleep it's a bit difficult to smoke a cigarette, boy! Perhaps I smoked in my dreams? Well, I don't know!
Grandson	And how did you decide to give up?
Grandfather	Your father had had an ambition to become a doctor from a very young age. He got a place at Calcutta University and he went to study. To become a doctor he had to study for many years there, but in the end he became a doctor. After he came home he began to tell me off saying 'Why does Father smoke cigarettes?'
Grandson	But after he became a doctor he had to say that, you know, grandfather!
Grandfather	Yes, he used to say again and again that the habit of smoking cigarettes is harmful to health. He used to say that I'd have to quit some day. And within a very few days after he returned from Calcutta I caught a cough and cold. And my lungs began to hurt. At that very time his mother also began to tell me off, saying 'Why do you want to die soon?'*

Grandson	And you quit smoking, right?
Grandfather	Yes, I had to quit, you know! And a few weeks after I quit I realized that I had had some benefit.
Grandson	What sort of benefit?
Grandfather	My appetite increased. Before, I used to eat rather little rice because while I was eating I would crave a cigarette. But within a few days of quitting cigarettes that old craving was lost and I began to eat well.
Grandson	But you don't drink alcohol, right?
Grandfather	I don't drink alcohol. I never have. It's mostly Brahmins who live in the villages of this district. Up until a few years ago the people here maintained old traditions. They didn't drink alcohol, they didn't eat meat either, they didn't bring girls from outside the district (as brides), but …
Grandson	But like you they also smoked cigarettes, no?
Grandfather	No, they didn't. Only I and one shopkeeper smoked. Apart from us no one smoked. The neighbours said I was corrupted!

Note *When quoting what someone actually said to them, Nepali speakers will usually refer to themselves using the Low or Middle pronoun (**तँ** or **तिमी**).

Grammar

121 THE HABITUAL PAST TENSE

The habitual past tense is used to describe an event or action that happened repeatedly or as a matter of habit or custom in the past: *I used to eat, he used to drink, they used to smoke.*

● INSIGHT

The present habitual tense and past habitual tense look very much the same except for the past marker of the 'to be' verb. Use the short form of the थियो conjugation in place of the present tense marker and then just add the short form of the थियो conjugation next to the negative verb conjugation of the present habitual tense.

Bases and endings

The habitual past tense of a verb in the affirmative is formed in a similar way to the habitual present tense, as set out in **Grammar 33**. The verb base is exactly the same as it is in the habitual present, but in the habitual past tense the ending is simply the **थियो** form of the verb **हुनु** *to be,* minus its **'i'** vowel:

Pronoun	थियो *form*		*Habitual past ending*
म	थिएँ	becomes	-थें
हामी, हामीहरू	थियौं	becomes	-थ्यौं
तँ	थिइस्	becomes	-थिस्
तिमी, तिमीहरू	थियौ	becomes	-थ्यौ
ऊ (m.)	थियो	becomes	-थ्यो
ऊ (f.)	थिई	becomes	-थी
उनी (m.)	थिए	becomes	-थे
उनी (f.)	थिइन्	becomes	-थिन्
यी, ती, उनीहरू	थिए	becomes	-थे

Affirmative forms in गर्नु

	Habitual present		*Habitual past*	
म	गर्छु	I do	गर्थें	I used to do
हामी, हामीहरू	गर्छौं	we do	गर्थ्यौं	we used to do
तँ	गर्छस्	you do	गर्थिस्	you used to do
तिमी, तिमीहरू	गर्छौ	you do	गर्थ्यौं	you used to do
ऊ (m)	गर्छ	he does	गर्थ्यो	he used to do
ऊ (f)	गर्छे	she does	गर्थी	she used to do
उनी (m)	गर्छन्	he does	गर्थे	he used to do
उनी (f)	गर्छिन्	she does	गर्थिन्	she used to do
यी, ती, उनीहरू	गर्छन्	they do	गर्थे	they used to do

The negative form of the habitual past tense is very simply the third person singular negative form of the habitual present (गर्दैन, हुँदैन, आउँदैन etc.) + the appropriate ending, taken from the list above. The one exception to this rule is the form that is used with म *I*, which takes the ending on to the first person form (that is, आउँदिन instead of आउँदैन).

Negative forms

		Habitual present		*Habitual past*
म	आउँदिन	I do not come	आउँदिनथें	I used not to come
हामी, हामीहरू	पकाउँदैनौं	we do not cook	पकाउँदैनथ्यौं	we used not to cook
तँ	खाँदैनस्	you do not eat	खाँदैनथिस्	you used not to eat
तिमी, तिमीहरू	सुत्दैनौ	you don't sleep	सुत्दैनथ्यौ	you used not to sleep
ऊ (m)	हुँदैन	he is not	हुँदैनथ्यो	he used not to be
ऊ (f)	गर्दिन	she does not	गर्दैनथी	she used not to do

उनी (m)	जाँदैनन्	they do not go	जाँदैनथे	they used not to go
उनी (f)	रुँदिनन्	she does not cry	रुँदैनथिन्	she used not to cry
उनीहरू	दिँदैनन्	they do not give	दिँदैनथे	they used not to give

Alternative negative forms

The same endings may also be added to the alternative negative forms of the habitual present (for which, see **Grammar 46**):

Habitual present		***Habitual past***	
म जान्नँ	I do not go	म जान्नथेँ	I used not to go
ऊ खान्न	he does not eat	ऊ खान्नथ्यो	he used not to eat
तिमी आउन्नौ	you do not come	तिमी आउन्नथ्यौ	you used not to come

High forms

The High forms of the habitual past tense are simply adapted forms of the habitual present tense:

- In the affirmative, the habitual present ending -**हुन्छ** becomes the habitual past ending -**हुन्थ्यो**.
- In the negative, the habitual present ending -**हुन्न** becomes the habitual past ending -**हुन्नथ्यो**.

High forms

Habitual present		***Habitual past***	
तपाईं हेर्नुहुन्छ	you watch	तपाईं हेर्नुहुन्थ्यो	you used to watch
तपाईं हेर्नुहुन्न	you do not watch	तपाईं हेर्नुहुन्नथ्यो	you used not to watch
वहाँ आउनुहुन्छ	s/he comes	वहाँ आउनुहुन्थ्यो	s/he used to come
वहाँ आउनुहुन्न	s/he does not come	वहाँ आउनुहुन्नथ्यो	s/he used not to come

The habitual past tense may often be translated as *used to go, used to eat, used to watch, used to say* and so on. It cannot express an action or an event that has happened only once or is part of a discrete series, because this is the function of the simple past tense. For instance, **ऊ काठ्माडौं गयो** means *he went to Kathmandu*, with the sense that this was a one-time action, whereas **ऊ काठ्माडौं जान्थ्यो** means *he used to go to Kathmandu*, indicating that this was his regular routine at some time in the past.

The following sentences illustrate this difference further. Those on the left-hand side refer to a specific event or action, those on the right describe a regular habit or truth:

मैले साथीको घरमा भात खाएँ । I ate at a friend's house.	म साथीको घरमा भात खान्थेँ । I used to eat at a friend's house.
उसले गाउँ गएर रक्सी खायो । He went to the village and drank raksī.	ऊ गाउँ गएर रक्सी खान्थ्यो । He used to go to the village and drink raksī.

Although the habitual past is obviously a past tense, the subject of a transitive verb need not take -ले in this tense unless it is being emphasized: this is the same rule that applies to the habitual present tense.

गर्मीमा घाँस काट्न चमेली कहाँ जान्थी ?	Where used Chameli to go to cut grass during the summer?
पहिले हामीलाई बिजुली चाहिँदैनथ्यो, अहिले सधैँ चाहिन्छ ।	We didn't need electricity before, now we need it all of the time.
तीस वर्ष अघिसम्म तराई क्षेत्रमा धेरै मान्छेहरू औलोले मर्थे ।	Up until 30 years ago many people used to die of malaria in the Tarai region.
काठ्माडौंको वातावरण बिग्रेको छ । पहिला पहिला यहाँ साह्रै राम्रो हुन्थ्यो रे ।	Kathmandu's environment has been spoiled. Long ago it used to be very good here, they say.

Exercise 66

Change the following sentences into the habitual past tense:

१ यस गाउँका किसानहरू धान रोप्दैनन् । उनीहरू मकै रोप्छन् ।

२ भात खाएपछि हामीले हात-मुख धुनुपर्छ ।

३ चियापसलमा चिया पनि पाइन्छ, खाने कुरा पनि पाइन्छ ।

४ तिमी भारत गएर के काम गर्छौ ? म चौकिदारको काम गर्छु ।

५ दाइहरू जुम्लामा बस्नुहुन्न, दैलेखमा बस्नुहुन्छ ।

६ म हरेक हप्ता उसलाई एउटा लामो चिठी लेख्छु ।

122 FINISHING, STOPPING, QUITTING

Nepali has a number of verbs that mean *to end, finish, be completed, stop,* that can be used only with nouns:

Intransitive		***Transitive***	
खतम हुनु	to end	खतम गर्नु	to finish
टुङ्गिनु	to come to an end	टुङ्ग्याउनु	to bring to an end
समाप्त हुनु	to conclude	समाप्त गर्नु	to bring to a conclusion
सिद्धिनु	to be finished	सिद्ध्याउनु	to finish off
रुक्नु	to stop, cease moving	रोक्नु	to stop, prevent
सकिनु	to be finished		

२००७ सालमा राणाहरूको षासन खतम भयो र नेपालमा प्रजातन्त्रको स्थापना भयो ।	In the year 2007 the Ranas' regime ended and democracy was established in Nepal.
आजको समाचार समाप्त भयो । तपाईं रेडियो नेपाल सुन्दै हुनुहुन्छ ।	That is the end of today's news. You are listening to Radio Nepal.

यति शब्दहरू बोलेपछि प्रधानमन्त्रीको भाषण टुङ्गियो ।	When he had spoken this many words, the Prime Minister's speech came to an end.
भक्तपुर जाने बस त ठिमीमा रुक्दैन भाइ !	But the Bhaktapur bus doesn't stop at Thimi, brother!

The verb **छाड्नु** *to stop, leave off, quit,* is used with the infinitive of a verb to show that the subject has stopped performing that verb. In past tenses the subject of **छाड्नु** must take -**ले** if the verb is transitive.

आफ्नो स्वास्थ्य बिग्रिन थालेको देखेर बुवाले चुरोट खान छाड्नुभयो ।	Seeing his health declining, Father gave up smoking cigarettes.
आमालाई घरको काममा सघाउनुपरेकोले चमेली स्कूल जान छाडी ।	Because she had to help Mother out at home, Chameli stopped going to school.
छोरालाई औषधि खान छाड्न नदिनुहोस् नत्र निको हुँदैन ।	Don't let your son stop taking the medicine, or else he won't get well.

123 WHILE DOING, IMMEDIATELY AFTER DOING

Every complete Nepali sentence must contain a verb, whose normal place is at the end of the sentence. This is the main verb of a sentence, and it provides the sentence with a tense (past, present or future). Sentences may contain other words which are derived from a verb but have no tense of their own. So far we have met two of these:

i the past tense base of a verb plus -**एर** (or -**ई** or -**ईकन**):

ii the past tense base of a verb plus -**एपछि**:

Two new words of this type are introduced here.

a Present tense verb base + -**दाखेरि** *while …*

The suffix -**दाखेरि** is added to the present tense base of a verb to mean that the rest of the sentence happens/happened/will happen at the same time as that verb. It can often be translated as *while doing, while going, while eating,* etc.

> **● INSIGHT**
>
> The verb stem + दाखेरि means 'when', 'while', 'during' or 'at the time of' any event. Note that खेरि is optional and often deleted in practice, e.g. बस्दाखेरि becomes बस्दा, which means the same. This construction also indicates cause and effect, e.g. पानी नपर्दा गर्मी भयो 'it is hot because it did not rain'.

The ending is added to verb bases in exactly the same way as the -दै ending is added to bases to form the continuous present tense (see **Grammar 64**): it is added directly to the bases of C-verbs, but when a base ends in a vowel that vowel must be nasalized:

Verb	***Base***		***Suffix***			
गर्नु	गर्		+ दाखेरि	=	गर्दाखेरि	while doing
बोल्नु	बोल्		+ दाखेरि	=	बोल्दाखेरि	while speaking
आउनु	आउ	+ँ	+ दाखेरि	=	आउँदाखेरि	while coming
जानु	जा	+ँ	+ दाखेरि	=	जाँदाखेरि	while going

भक्तपुर जाँदाखेरि म तिम्रो दाइलाई भेटुँला ।	On my way to Bhaktapur I'll (probably) meet your elder brother.
बच्चाहरू बारीमा खेल्दाखेरि घरभित्र शान्ति हुन्छ ।	While the children are playing in the field there is peace in the house.
भात खाँदाखेरि गफ गर्न हुँदैन ।	It is not good to talk while eating.

This suffix can be added to the हुँ- base of the verb *to be*, and also to its छ form; there is a slight difference in meaning between the two:

हुँदाखेरि	while becoming/being (in a defining sense)
छँदाखेरि	while being (in a describing or locating sense)
मानिसहरू बूढो हुँदाखेरि धर्म मान्न थाल्छन् ।	When people are becoming old they begin to believe in religion.
त्यो केटा सानो छँदाखेरि उसको बा बित्नुभयो ।	When that boy was small his father passed away.

The -दाखेरि suffix is often shortened to -दा, with no change in meaning:

भक्तपुर जाँदा ...	While going to Bhaktapur ...
मानिसहरू बूढो हुँदा ...	When people are becoming old ...

b The -ने participle + -बित्तिकै *as soon as*

This suffix is added to the -ने participle of a verb to mean that something else happened immediately after it. If the verb is transitive, its subject must take -ले.

मैले भात खानुहोस् भन्नेबित्तिकै सबैजनाले खपाखप खान थाले ।	As soon as I said 'please eat', everyone began to eat voraciously.
सिपाहीले खुकुरी टिप्नेबित्तिकै सबैजना भागे	As soon as the soldier picked up the kukri, everyone ran away.
मदनलाई देख्नेबित्तिकै मुनालाई उसको माया लाग्यो ।	As soon as she saw Madan, Muna fell in love with him.*

Note *Muna and Madan are the eponymous hero and heroine of a narrative poem by Lakshmi Prasad Devkota (1905–59), first published in the 1930s, which is the most popular book ever written in Nepali.

INSIGHT

Nepali expresses a sense of 'as soon as' or 'immediately after' in several different ways, but two ways are very important to remember. They are: verb stem + नेबित्तिकै and verb stem + नासाथ, e.g. मोमो खानेबित्तिकै or खानासाथ ऊ सुत्यो. 'He slept as soon as he ate momos'.

124 WILL HAVE TO, USED TO HAVE TO

Combinations of पर्छ/पर्दैन and पऱ्यो/परेन with the dictionary form of a verb to mean *must, should, have to* and *had to* are introduced in **Grammar 99** and **100**. It is of course sometimes necessary to talk about what someone used to have to do in the past or what someone might have to do in the future. In such cases पर्नु takes the habitual past tense forms पर्थ्यो/ पर्दैनथ्यो and the probable future tense form पर्ला respectively:

ब्रिटिश आर्मीमा हुँदाखेरि मैले चक्कु, काँटा र चम्चाले खाना खानुपर्थ्यो । तिमीले पनि भर्तिमा गएपछि त्यसरी नै खानुपर्ला ।	While I was a soldier in the British Army, I used to have to eat with knife, fork and spoon. After you have enlisted you will probably have to eat in exactly the same way.
यहाँ बिजुली आउनुभन्दा अगाडि दिदी-बहिनीहरूलाई पानी लिन खोलासम्म झर्नुपर्थ्यो ।	Before the electricity (supply) came here, the young women used to have to go down to the river to fetch water.

125 WISHING, HOPING AND DECIDING

In English, you say that someone wishes, hopes or decides *to do* something. In Nepali, desires, hopes or decisions to do something are often expressed passively, using the expression मन लाग्नु, or actively by using the verb चाहनु *to want to* (**Grammar 110**). However, there is one other way of expressing these ideas in Nepali, and this uses the -ने participle of a verb to describe the wish, hope, etc.:

जाने इच्छा गर्नु	to wish to go ('to do a going wish')
हेर्ने रहर हुनु	to have a desire to see ('a seeing desire')
लेख्ने निधो गर्नु	to decide to write ('to do a writing decision')
बस्ने विचार गर्नु	to consider staying ('to do a staying thought')
पाउने आशा गर्नु	to hope to get ('to do a getting hope')
बन्ने आकाँक्षा राख्नु	to have an ambition to become ('a becoming ambition')
हाम्रो घरमा बस्दाखेरि उनीहरूले बिहा गर्ने निधो गरेका थिए ।	While they were living in our house they decided to get married.

सानै उमेरदेखि नै मैले काठ्माडौं जाने इच्छा गरेको थिएँ, आखिर म जान पाएँ ।	Right from a young age I wanted to go to Kathmandu, eventually I managed to go.
म केही दिनभित्र उसको चिठी पाउने आशा गर्दै छु ।	I am hoping to receive a letter from him within a few days.

Note also the construction with -पर्ने:

पढ्नुपर्ने किताब	a book one should read
भेट्नुपर्ने मान्छे	a person one should meet
अँग्रेजी सिक्न मन लाग्यो भने तपाईंले पढ्नपर्ने किताब यही हो ।	If you want to learn English this is the book you should read.
तपाईंलाई मुस्ताङ्ग जान अनुमति चाहियो भने भेट्नपर्ने मान्छे लोबासाङ्ग नामग्याल हुन् ।	If you need permission to go to Mustang, the man you should meet is Lobsang Namgyal.

● INSIGHT

A very large number of Nepali conjunct verbs consist of a noun or an adjective followed by गर्नु and हुनु. When the verbs made from nouns such as विचार गर्नु 'to think', आशा गर्नु 'to hope' इच्छा गर्नु 'to wish' are used with other verbs, the main verb is changed with ने as a modifier, e.g. मैले नेपाली सिक्ने विचार गरेको छु.

Exercise 67

Translate into Nepali:

I used to live with my mother and father in a small town called Panauti. Panauti is in the south-east corner of the Kathmandu Valley. I used to study in a small school there. As soon as my age reached 11 years I had to quit that small school. From that time on I had to study in a big school in a city called Bhaktapur. I used to have to take a bus every morning at seven o'clock. Many of my friends used to go on that bus too. While we were returning in the evening we used to sing songs and when we reached Panauti we were very happy.

Below my house there was a big river. In the summer months we used to go to swim in the river as soon as we got home. Sometimes my school clothes were all wet and Mother used to be angry. She would have to wash them as soon as I came home and it was difficult to dry (**sukāunu**) them. But because Saturday was a holiday she used to let me swim on Fridays.

While I was studying in the big school at Bhaktapur I decided to become a teacher when I was big. Because I hoped to become a teacher I studied well. As soon as I left that school I went to Tribhuvan University and nowadays I live in Kathmandu. After a few days I will have to give my final exams (**parikṣā**). I am still hoping to become a teacher. If I am successful in my exams I will have to seek (**khojnu**) a job (**jāgir**).

The most important things for the reader to remember

1 Any action that is repeatedly done on a regular basis in the past is called the past habitual or historic tense and this is conjugated. The English uses 'used to' to express this idea. An alternative negative is very commonly used with this tense, e.g. **म पहिले रक्सी पिउँथें** 'I used to drink alcohol before'.

2 The verb stem + **दाखेरि** is a construction for 'when' or 'while', which is used to express an action occurring while another action is taking place, e.g. **घरमा बस्दाखेरि म आराम गर्छु** 'I take a rest when I am staying at home'.

3 A sense of 'as soon as' or 'immediately after' is expressed by the verb stem + **नेबित्तिकै** in Nepali, e.g. **उठ्नेबित्तिकै म नुहाउँछु** 'I take a shower as soon as I get up'.

4 **पर्ला,** which is the combination of **पर्छ** + **होला,** is used to mean 'will have to' and it is not conjugated, e.g. **म जानु पर्ला** 'I will have to go'.

5 There are many verbs that consist of a noun plus **गर्नु** 'to do', e.g. **विचार गर्नु** 'to think', **आशा गर्नु** 'to hope', **इच्छा गर्नु** 'to wish'. When they are used with other verbs to say to 'think of doing' or 'hope to do' etc., the other verb is modified with the **ने** participle to describe the nouns, e.g. **म नेपालमा हिमाल चढ्ने विचार गर्दै छु** 'I am thinking of climbing mountains in Nepal'.

22 म चिया पकाऊँ ?

Shall I make tea?

In this unit you will learn:

- *how to use the subjunctive forms of verbs*
- *how to use compound verbs with दिनु*
- *how to talk about trying and searching*

32 Cancelling the tea party

22.01

Like many middle-class urban Nepali housewives, Parvati has an older woman to help her with her chores. On this particular Wednesday the weather is against them.

जाई	आज के काम छ ? पहिले चिया पकाऊँ ?
पार्वती	हुन्छ दिदी, पकाउनुहोस् न । चिया खाएर म तपाईंलाई भनुँला ।
जाई	चियामा चिनी र दूध राखिदिऊँ ?
पार्वती	एक चम्चा चिनी र अलिकति दूध राखिदिनुहोस् ।
जाई	चिनी कता पर्‍यो ?
पार्वती	दराजभित्र खोज्नुहोस् । त्यहाँ हुनुपर्छ ।
जाई	हवस् ... । ल, चिया कहाँ राखूँ ? टेबुलमा राखिदिऊँ ?

पार्वती	टेबुलमा दाग लाग्ला कि ? ऊ त्यो कपडामाथि राखिदिनुहोस् ।
जाई	हवस् । आज के के गर्नुपर्छ ? म थाहा पाऊँ न ?
पार्वती	आज दिउँसो श्रीमान अफिसका साथीहरू लिएर आउँदै हुनुहुन्छ ।
जाई	उनीहरू बेलुकासम्म बस्ने कि ? म भरे भात पकाइदिऊँ ?
पार्वती	आज बुधवार भएकोले भान्से आउँदैन । त्यस कारण भात पकाउनु नपरोस् भनेर मैले चिया-सियाको लागि मात्रै निम्त्याउनू भनेको छु वहाँलाई । वहाँ सम्झनुहुन्छ कि बिर्सनुहुन्छ म भन्न सक्दिन । तपाईंलाई थाहै छ नि दिदी, लोग्नेमान्छेको जात !
जाई	हेरौं न । बिर्सनुहुन्न क्यारे । कतिजना आउँदै छन् ?
पार्वती	मैले उनीहरूका लागि बगैंचामा दुइटा टेबुल राखेको छु । पछि तपाईं आठवटा मेचहरू मिलाइदिनुहोस् । आज पानी नपरोस् । घरभित्र आठजना अटाउने ठाउँ नै छैन !
जाई	हवस् त । एक छिनपछि बजार जानुपर्ला, बिस्कुट-सिस्कुट किन्नलाई, होइन ?
पार्वती	हो, जानुपर्छ । मलाई पनि उता जानुपर्छ दिउँसो । सँगै जाऔं ।
जाई	हवस् । अब म घर सफा गर्न थाल्छु ।
पार्वती	हुन्छ । एक पटक चर्पी र नुहाउने कोठामा पनि हेर्नुहोस् । भरसक पाहुनाहरूलाई असुविधा नहोस् न । म भान्सा-कोठामा हुन्छु ।
जाई	सुत्ने कोठा पनि मिलाइदिऊँ ?
पार्वती	पर्दैन दिदी । सबै अलपत्र छ । म पछि आफै मिलाउँला ।
जाई	आम्मै ! पानी आयो ! सर्वनाश भयो !
पार्वती	धन्दा नमान्नुहोस् । म अफिसमा फोन गरेर एक पटक सम्झाउन कोसिस गर्छु । अब उनीहरू आऊन् कि नआऊन् हामी त घरभित्रै बस्नुपर्छ नि ।

Quick vocab

पहिले	first
चम्चा	spoon
दराज	drawer
खोज्नु	to search, look for
धाग लाग्नु	to make a mark or stain
चिया-सिया	tea and snacks
निम्त्याउनु	to invite
जात	species, type
बगैंचा	garden

अटाउनु	to fit, be accommodated
बिस्कुट-सिस्कुट	biscuits and such like
चर्पी	lavatory
नुहाउने कोठा	bathroom
भरसक	as much as possible
असुविधा	inconvenience
भान्सा-कोठा	kitchen
सुत्ने कोठा	bedroom
अलपत्र	untidy
आम्मै	mother! (an exclamation of alarm)
सर्वनाश	disaster
धन्दा मान्नु	to worry

Jai	What work is there today? Shall I make tea first?
Parvati	OK sister, please do make some. I'll tell you while we drink tea.
Jai	Should I put sugar and milk in the tea?
Parvati	Please put one spoonful of sugar and a little milk.
Jai	Where has the sugar got to?
Parvati	Search in the drawer. It should be there.
Jai	Very well … Now, where shall I put the tea? Shall I put it on the table?
Parvati	Might the table be marked? Put it on that cloth over there.
Jai	Very well. What things do we have to do today? May I know?
Parvati	This afternoon my husband is bringing some office friends.
Jai	Will they stay until the evening? Shall I cook rice this evening?
Parvati	Because it's Wednesday today the cook won't come. For that reason, so that we wouldn't have to cook food, I have told him to invite them only for tea and snacks.* Whether he will remember or forget I cannot say. You know, don't you sister, what men are like!
Jai	Well, let's see. Perhaps he won't forget. How many are coming?
Parvati	I have put two tables for them in the garden. Later, please arrange eight chairs. I hope it won't rain today. There really isn't room in the house for eight people!
Jai	Certainly. In a moment I'll have to go to the market to buy biscuits and such like, no?

Parvati	Yes, you will. I have to go that way too this afternoon. Let's go together.
Jai	Of course. Now I'll start cleaning the house.
Parvati	Fine. Take a look in the lavatory and the bathroom too. As far as possible let there be no inconvenience for the guests. I'll be in the kitchen.
Jai	Shall I tidy the bedroom too?
Parvati	It's not necessary sister. Everything's untidy. I'll tidy it myself later.
Jai	Oh mother! It's raining. It's a disaster!
Parvati	Don't worry. I'll phone the office and try to explain. Now, whether they come or they don't, we have to sit inside the house.

Note ***चिया-सिया** tea and snacks. It is possible to add a meaningless rhyming word to certain words to mean *and things associated with it.*

● INSIGHT

Note that the suffix to the verb stem for the first person singular म is उँ and for plural हामी it is औँ in order to create a subjunctive form of a verb, e.g. म जाऊँ ? 'Shall I go?', हामी खाऔँ 'Let's eat'. Note that some people (especially Bahuns and Chettris) may say जाम् or खाम् 'Let's go or eat' instead.

Grammar

126 MAY I? VERBS IN THE SUBJUNCTIVE

The subjunctive form of a Nepali verb is used in three contexts:

A Nepali AIDS warning

- **i** to ask whether or suggest that you might do something: *may I come in? let's wash these clothes!*
- **ii** to express a wish that something might happen: *may the weather be good today! May you all be successful in your examination!*
- **iii** in phrases along the lines of *whether it does or it doesn't.*

Nepali grammar provides subjunctive forms of the verb for all possible subjects, but in practice you rarely need to know more than the four that are set out below.

Subject	*ending*	*गर्नु*	*हुनु*	*आउनु*	*दिनु*
म	-ũ	गरूँ	होऊँ	आऊँ	दिऊँ
ऊ, त्यो, यो	-os	गरोस्	होओस्	आओस्	देओस्
हामी	-aũ	गरौं	होऔं	आऔं	दिऔं
उनीहरू	-ūn	गरून्	होऊन्	आऊन्	दिऊन्

With म *I* and हामी *we,* the subjunctive is very similar to the probable future tense minus its -ला ending (see **Grammar 96**), except that हुनु *to be* keeps the base हो- in every instance, even with म *I*.

म तपाईंलाई एउटा गुनासो सुनाऊँ ? तपाईं रिसाउनुहुन्न ?	May I tell you of a complaint? You won't be angry?
ऊ ठीक समयमा आइपुगोस् ।	He'd better arrive on time.
नेपाली साहित्य फलोस् फुलोस् !	May Nepali literature fruit and bloom!
बाहुनले न च्याउ खाओस् न च्याउको स्वाद पाओस् ।	A Brahman shall neither eat a mushroom nor know its taste.*

Note *A proverb. Certain Brahmans follow a strict dietary code, and avoid garlic, onions, mushrooms and many other foods. *The negative form of the subjunctive is formed simply by adding the prefix* न- *to the affirmative form:*

आज पानी नपरोस्, भोलि परोस् !	May it not rain today, [but] rain tomorrow!

The sense of the proverb is that actual experience is of greater value than mere theoretical knowledge.

● INSIGHT

For the subjunctive, you can just say ऊ जावस्, which simply translates as 'Let him go'. You can also use चाहनु 'to want' with conjugations to express a stronger meaning, e.g. म ऊ जावस् भन्ने चाहन्छु 'I want him to go'. You can also say the other way: म चाहन्छु कि ऊ जावस् ।

Exercise 68

Finish the following sentences with a subjunctive verb:

१ तपाईंको छोरा चाँडै निको (be).

२ भोलि हामीहरू फिलिम हेर्न पोखरा (go)?

३ हामीहरू तपाईंकी आमालाई के (say)?

४ तपाईंको जिन्दगी सुखी (be).

५ आजको बस ढिलो (not be).

६ म तपाईंकहाँ कति बजे (come)?

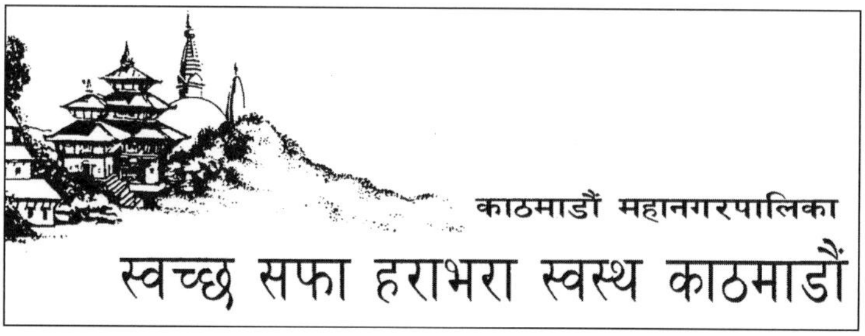

An environmental message from Kathmandu Municipal Council

127 DOING SOMETHING FOR ANOTHER PERSON: COMPOUND VERBS WITH दिनु

Any transitive verb may be combined with the verb **दिनु** *to give*, producing what is called a 'compound verb', when the action of the verb is being referred away from the person who performs the action. Often this means that the verb is being performed for someone else's benefit, or on someone else's behalf. In this context, the verb in question must take its 'i-stem', in which a short **i** vowel is attached to its past tense base:

verb	*base*	*i-stem*	*compound verb*	
गर्नु	गर-	गरि	गरिदिनु	to do for someone else
भन्नु	भन-	भनि	भनिदिनु	to inform
लेख्नु	लेख-	लेखि	लेखिदिनु	to write for

Because the meaning of a compound verb focuses very much on its positive aspect, it rarely occurs in the negative.

डाक्टर साहेबले हाम्रो लागि औषधि लेखिदिनुभयो ।	The doctor wrote out a prescription for us.
चिठी चाँडै पठाइदिनुहुन्छ कि ?	Will you send the letter immediately?
अलि पर्खनुपर्ला । थाहा पाउनेबित्तिकै म तपाईंलाई भनिदिन्छु ।	You might have to wait a while. As soon as I find out I will tell you.

● INSIGHT

When the compound verb stem + इदिनु is used in the imperative form it adds more politeness to the request, e.g. एउटा चिट्ठी लेखिदिनुहोस् न. There are some compound verbs in Nepali that are mostly used in a short form. गरिदिनु and भनिदिनु are shortened to गर्दिनु and भन्दिनु.

128 TRYING AND SEEKING

The verb **खोज्नु** has two meanings:

खोज्नु means *to search for* when it is associated with a noun or pronoun:

घरको साँचो कता पऱ्यो ? दिनभरि खोजेर पनि भेट्टाउन सकिनँ ।	Where has the house key got to? Despite searching all day I could not find it.
म उनीहरूको घर खोज्दै थिएँ । त्यो बेला उनीहरू पनि त्यहाँ टुप्लुक्क आइपुगे ।	I was looking for their house. Then they suddenly arrived there too.

खोज्नु means *to try to* when it is associated with the infinitive of a verb:

मैले बारम्बार सरकारी जागिर पाउन खोजें तर म हरेक पटक असफल भएँ ।	I tried again and again to get a government job, but I was unsuccessful every time.
मैले तपाईंलाई फोन गर्न खोजें तर लाइन एकदम बिजी थियो ।	I tried to phone you but the line was really busy.

An alternative to **खोज्नु** is the verb **कोसिस गर्नु**, which can be used in combination with the infinitive of a verb in much the same way as **खोज्नु**, or on its own:

मैले भोटिया भाषा पनि सिक्न कोसिस त गरेको थिएँ, तर पढ्ने फुर्सद नभएको कारणले असफल भएँ ।	I did try to learn Tibetan, but I failed because I didn't have the time to study.
हामीलाई भोलि आउन अलि अप्ठ्यारो होला, तर कोसिस गरौंला ।	It might be a bit difficult for us to come tomorrow, but we will try.

The most important things for the reader to remember

1 Nepali uses different subjunctive forms according to the subject pronoun to express a wish that something will happen, e.g. **म जाऊँ ?** 'Shall I come?' **ऊ जावस्** 'I wish he would go'.

2 When the verb stem is combined with **-इदिनु** it forms a compound verb to imply a sense of doing something for the sake of somebody else, e.g. **म गरिदिन्छु** 'I will do it for you'. So this is another way of showing your desire to help someone.

3 If you use **खोज्नु** with other infinitive verbs it gives a sense of 'to try/seek to do something', although **खोज्नु** means 'to look for or search' when it is used with nouns, e.g. **मैले नेपाली बोल्न खोजें** 'I tried to speak Nepali'.

23 उसले औषधि खाएको भए

If he'd taken the medicine

In this unit you will learn:

- *how to say that things have already happened*
- *how to construct unreal conditional sentences*
- *how to convey the sense that something has just been realized*

33 A death in the neighbourhood

23.01

One of Sita's neighbours has died. She tells Manju how it happened.

मंजु	हिजो मैले तपाईंलाई अस्पताल जान लागेको देखेको थिएँ, हो ? बिरामी हुनुहुन्छ कि के हो ?
सीता	होइन, म छिमेकको एउटा चिनेको मान्छेलाई भेट्न गएको थिएँ । अस्ति उसको छोरालाई बजारमा भेट्दा उसले बा कमलपित्त भएर अस्पताल जानुभएको छ भन्यो ।
मंजु	ए, सिकिस्त बिरामी भएको रहेछ तपाईंको छिमेकी ? अहिले कस्तो छ रे ?
सीता	अस्पताल पुग्नेबित्तिकै मैले उसलाई जाँच्ने डाक्टरसँग सोधें । तर बिचरा दुई घण्टा अघि नै मरिसकेको रहेछ ।
मंजु	ए । तपाईं अस्ति जानुभएको भए भेट हुन्थ्यो, हगि ?
सीता	हो नि, तर के गर्ने र ? ऊ त्यति छिटै मर्छ भन्ने कुरा मैले कल्पना पनि गरेको थिइनँ । त्यस्तो थाहा भएको भए त म चाँडै जान्थें नि । यस्तो उमेरमा नमरेको भए हुन्थ्यो । उसको आत्माले शान्ति पाओस् भन्नुपर्‍यो, अरू के भन्ने र ?
मंजु	मान्छे त्यति बूढो होइन, क्यारे ?
सीता	बूढो भएको भए त त्यति दुखको कुरा पनि हुँदैनथ्यो नि । तर मान्छे पैंतीस वर्षको मात्रै रहेछ ! डाक्टरको भनाइ अनुसार रक्सी धेरै खान्थ्यो रे । रक्सी नखाइकन औषधि खाएको भए त यसरी अकालै मर्ने नै थिएन नि ।
मंजु	दाह-सँस्कार भइसक्यो ?
सीता	आज बिहानै पशुपतिमा भइसक्यो नि । कति चाँडै भएछ ! अफिसमा काम नभएको भए मेरो श्रीमान जानुहुन्थ्यो । तर मिलेन । भरे बेलुका उसकी स्वास्नीलाई भेट्न जानुपर्ला ।

मंजु	छोराछोरी कत्रा रहेछन् नि ?
सीता	छोराको बिहा भइसक्यो क्यारे । छोरी पनि तरुनी भइसकेको छ । अब बिचरा त्यो आइमाईले एक्लै छोरीको बिहाको कुरा मिलाउनुपर्छ ।
मंजु	तर सन्तान नभएको भए उसलाई झन् गाह्रो हुन्थ्यो नि । छोरा ठूलो भइसकेको रहेछ नि, केही छैन, उसले आमालाई सघाइदिन्छ ।

V Quick vocab

चिन्नु	to know, be acquainted with
कमलपित्त	jaundice
सिकिस्त	gravely, seriously (ill)
रहनु	to remain, be
जाँच्नु	to examine
भेट	meeting
कल्पना गर्नु	to imagine
हुन्थ्यो	it would have been all right
आत्मा	soul
शान्ति	peace
अनुसार	according to
अकालै	early, untimely
दाह-सँस्कार	cremation rite
कत्रो	how big?
तरुनी	young woman
सन्तान	offspring
सघाउनु	to help

Manju	I saw you going to the hospital yesterday, did I? Are you ill, or what is it?
Sita	No, I went to see a man I know from the neighbourhood. The other day when I met his son in the market he said his father had contracted jaundice and had gone to hospital.
Manju	Oh is he seriously ill, your neighbour? How do they say he is now?
Sita	As soon as I reached the hospital I asked the doctor who examined him. But the poor man had already died just two hours earlier.
Manju	Oh. If you had gone two days ago you'd have seen him, no?

Sita	That's right, but what to do, indeed? I had never even imagined that he would die quickly like that. If I'd known that I'd have gone right away. It would have been better if he hadn't died at such an age. We must say 'may his soul find peace', what else can we say, after all?
Manju	So the man wasn't so old, eh?
Sita	If he'd been old then it wouldn't have been such a sad affair either, you know. But the man is only 35 years old! According to the doctor, he used to drink a lot. If he had taken his medicine and hadn't drunk alcohol he wouldn't have died such an untimely death, you know.
Manju	Has the funeral ceremony taken place?
Sita	It took place at Pashupati early this morning. How quickly it has happened! If there hadn't been work at the office my husband would have gone. But it wasn't convenient. This evening I'll have to go and see his wife.*
Manju	How big are the children?
Sita	I think the son's already married. The daughter's a young woman already too. Now, poor thing, that woman has to arrange her daughter's marriage alone.
Manju	But if she didn't have children it would be even harder for her, you know. The son's grown up already you know, it doesn't matter, he will help his mother.

Note *Among Nepali Hindus, it is unusual for a woman to attend a funeral.

Grammar

129 ALREADY DONE: COMPOUND VERBS WITH सक्नु

The verb सक्नु has been encountered before, in combination with the infinitive of a verb, where it means *can/be able*. However, the same verb has the second meaning of *to finish/be completed*. Its i-stem form सकिनु can therefore be used interchangeably with the verb सिद्धिनु to mean *to finish:*

आजको काम सकियो ।	Today's work is finished.
हिजोको पाठ अझै पनि सिद्धिएको छैन ।	Yesterday's lesson is still not finished.

• INSIGHT

सक्नु with an infinitive verb means 'to be able to' but with nouns it means 'to finish' in spoken Nepali, e.g. काम सक्यो 'The work is finished'. When it is combined with a verb such as खाइसक्नु (verb stem + इसक्नु) it means 'to finish eating' or the English translates it as 'to have already eaten'.

The i-stem form of any verb (see **Grammar 69**), whether transitive or intransitive, may also be combined with **सक्नु** to emphasize that its action has already been completed. The compound verb consists of the i-stem of the verb + **सक्नु**, written as a single word:

मैले पढिसकें ।	I have already read.
तिमी आइसकेका थियौ ।	You had already come.
ऊ सुतिसकेको छ ।	He is already asleep.
वहाँ बितिसक्नुभयो ।	He has already passed away.

Because it serves to emphasize that something is over and done with when it is the second part of a compound verb, the verb **सक्नु** almost always takes a past tense in this context – usually this is the simple past or the completed past. For the same reason, it is rarely used in the negative. The completed present tense is also sometimes used, but often its meaning (*has already ...*) is conveyed by the shorter simple past tense.

In Nepali, compound verbs with **सक्नु** are used much more commonly than the English translation *already* might suggest. In a context where an English speaker might say *it's become dark* or *he has left*, a Nepali speaker will often say **अँध्यारो भइसक्यो** *it's already become dark* and **ऊ गइसक्यो** *he's already left.*

मेरो त बिहा भइसक्यो नि । मेरो लागि दुलही खोज्नुपर्दैन ।	But I am already married, you know. You don't need to seek for a bride for me.
आज म मन्त्रालय दुई पटक गइसकें । अब तेस्रो पटक जानु नपरोस् !	I've already been to the ministry twice today. Let me not have to go a third time now!
त्यो उपन्यास त मैले धेरै अघि पढिसकें ।	I read that novel a long time ago.
कुनै पनि उपन्यास एक पटक पढिसकेपछि दोस्रो पटक पढ्न मनै लाग्दैन ।	After I have read any novel once I really don't wish to read it a second time.

130 UNREAL CONDITIONAL SENTENCES

Unreal conditional sentences state that if something *had been* the case in the past something else *would have* happened: *if it had rained I wouldn't have gone out; if it hadn't rained I would have gone out.* Such sentences are 'unreal' because anyone who utters, hears, reads or writes them knows that in fact the reality turned out differently.

• INSIGHT

Note that the appropriate conjugation of verb stem + ने थियो in the unreal conditional sentence is often abbreviated and conjugated exactly as the past habitual tense, e.g. ऊ आएको भए म खुशी हुने थिएँ or हुन्थें 'I would have been happy if he had come'.

The 'if' clause must end with a combination of the **.एको** participle of whichever verb is involved, followed by the short **-e** participle of the verb **हुनु** *to be*, i.e. -**एको भए**. If the verb is negative it takes the prefix **न**-.

Real condition	**Unreal condition**
पानी पऱ्यो भने ...	पानी परेको भए ...
If it rains ...	If it had rained ...
ऊ आएन भने ...	ऊ नआएको भए ...
If he doesn't come ...	If he hadn't come ...

In general, the form -**एको भए** is used no matter who or what the subject is, regardless of number, gender, or level of politeness. But occasionally, if the subject is felt to deserve especial deference or politeness, the High form consisting of the dictionary form + **भएको भए** is used instead:

तपाईं जानुभयो भने ...	तपाईं जानुभएको भए ...
If you go ...	If you had gone ...
तपाईं जानुभएन भने ...	तपाईं नजानुभएको भए ...
If you don't go ...	If you hadn't gone ...

The second part of an unreal conditional sentence usually ends with a verb that is exactly the same as the habitual past tense. However, the meaning of this tense when it is the conclusion of an unreal conditional sentence is very different:

त्यो रेश्टुराँमा हामीहरू गुन्द्रुक खान्थ्यौं । We <u>used to eat</u> gundruk in that restaurant.

त्यो रेश्टुराँमा गएको भए हामीहरू गुन्द्रुक खान्थ्यौं । If we had gone into that restaurant we <u>would have eaten</u> gundruk.

In fact, the final verb of an unreal conditional sentence is actually a shortened form of a tense that consists of the -**ने** participle + **थियो**.

हिउँ नपरेको भए म सगरमाथा चढ्ने थिएँ । If it had not snowed I would have climbed Everest.

The meaning remains exactly the same when the shorter form of the verb (the habitual past) is used instead:

हिउँ नपरेको भए म सगरमाथा चढ्थें । If it had not snowed I'd have climbed Everest.

मसँग पैसा भएको भए म परिवारको लागि कोसेलीहरू किन्थें । If I'd had any money on me I'd have bought presents for the family.

तपाईंले त्यो कुरा अँग्रेजीमा भन्नुभएको भए ऊ बुझ्थ्यो । If you had said that thing in English he would have understood.

घाम लागेको भए बच्चाहरू बाहिर खेल्थे ।	If the sun had shone the children would have played outside.
बासी भात नखाएको भए तिम्रो पेट दुख्दैनथ्यो ।	If you hadn't eaten stale rice your stomach wouldn't be hurting.

● INSIGHT

The unknown past tense does not really exist in English. However, this is used to relate any event or activity unbeknown to you, e.g. ऊ घरमा जान्छु भनेर गएको तर भट्टिमा पुगेछ. 'He left saying he would go home, but arrived at an inn.' This tense is more common in telling stories.

Exercise 69

Match up the beginnings and ends below to create five unreal conditional sentences. Translate the five sentences into English.

१ मलाई भोक लागेको भए ...	... त्यो मान्छे अकालै मर्दैनथ्यो ।
२ पानी नपरेको भए ...	... हाम्रो घरमा बिजुली हुँदैनथ्यो ।
३ पहाडमा खोलाहरू नभएको भए ...	... बेलुका झन रमाइलो हुन्थ्यो ।
४ बेलामा औषधि खाएको भए ...	... उनीहरू भात खान आउँथे ।
५ साथीले गीत गाएको भए ...	... म खपाखप भात खान्थें ।

131 THE SHORT COMPLETED PRESENT TENSE

The completed present tense is explained in **Grammar 77**. In everyday spoken Nepali, this tense may take a shortened form, partly because it is rather longwinded. After all, why use five syllables to say 'I've done' in Nepali when you need only use three? The short forms of the completed present tense are also used to imply that something happened suddenly or unexpectedly.

The short form of the completed present tense is simply the full form minus the final -को of the -एको participle that is the first word of the pair. The two words of the full form become a single word in the short form:

Full form	**Short form**
म गएको छु	म गा'छु ।
उनीहरू आएका छन्	उनीहरू आ'छन् ।
तपाईंले गर्नुभएको छ	तपाईंले गर्नुभा'छ ।

132 REALIZATION: USING रहेछ AT THE END OF SENTENCES

रहेछ is the short form of **रहेको छ**, the completed present tense of the verb **रहनु** *to remain/continue to be*. **रहेछ** can be thought of as an add-on word similar to **होला** (**Grammar 92**), although there is a difference in that **रहेछ** must take the place of another verb, and cannot simply be appended to any statement. **रहेछ** or its negative form **रहेनछ** may be used instead of **छ, छैन, हो** or **होइन** at the end of a sentence to indicate that the speaker has just realized what s/he is saying. It has no real equivalent in English, unless it be the exclamation mark, or the old-fashioned exclamation 'why!' with which an observation can begin in English.

> **• INSIGHT**
>
> The meaning of रहेछ is similar to that of एछ (seen earlier). However, रहेछ can be used in all tenses and it replaces the verb 'to be' completely. Note that रहेछ is often shortened to रैछ, रे'छ or र'छ in spoken Nepali.

Simple statements	**Realizations**
तपाईंको घर राम्रो छ । Your house is nice.	तपाईंको घर राम्रो रहेछ ! Why, your house is nice!
उसको हातमा बन्दूक छ । There is a gun in his hand.	उसको हातमा बन्दूक रहेछ ! Hey, he's got a gun in his hand!
तपाईंको छोरा अग्लो भइसक्यो । Your son has become tall.	तपाईंको छोरा अग्लो भइसकेको रहेछ ! Why, your son has become tall!
मेरो खल्तीमा पैसा छैन । There is no money in my pocket.	मेरो खल्तीमा पैसा रहेनछ ! Why, there's no money in my pocket!

133 THE VERB चिन्नु TO KNOW/RECOGNIZE

This verb is used exclusively with human nouns as indirect objects. In the habitual present tense it means *to recognize* while in past tenses it means *to be acquainted with.*

तपाईं त्यस मान्छेलाई चिन्नुहुन्छ ? अहँ, चिन्दिन । वहाँ को हुनुहुन्छ ?	Do you recognize that person? No, I don't. Who is he?
त्यहाँ कोही चिनेको मान्छे भएको भए म उसैलाई भन्थें ।	If there had been anyone there that I knew, I'd have told him/her.
खबरदार, मैले तिमीलाई राम्रोसँग चिनेको छु !	Beware, I know you very well!

Exercise 70

Translate into Nepali:

Today some people we know are coming to our house for dinner at 6 o'clock. I return home from the university at 4 o'clock, but the house is empty! And I look in my bag to see if the key is there and the bag is empty too! Where might it have gone? I search in every place but I cannot find the key.

The cook should have come at half past 3 but he has not come yet. Perhaps he has already come to the house but then gone to the market. If he had stayed in the house until 4 o'clock this problem would not have occurred. Should I break a window to get in? Or shall I go back to the university and search for the key in my office? I don't know, what shall I do?

Oh, now the cook has arrived and he has the key in his hand! If I had broken (फोड्नु *to break*) a window my husband would have really told me off!

It is already a quarter past 4. He opens the door for me. Shall I phone my husband and tell him to come home soon? No, there's probably no need. The cook has already bought all the food and now he will cook it for us.

The most important things for the reader to remember

1. When सक्नु is used with other verbs it forms a compound verb and indicates that the activity of the main verb has been completed. The sense of सक्नु in this construction is often best translated in English as 'already', e.g. मैले खाइसकें 'I have already eaten'.
2. An unreal conditional sentence contains two clauses of which the first clause ends with the conjunction एको भए and the second clause of which the final verb is conjugated by the verb stem + ने थियो appropriately. The probability of this condition being fulfilled is zero because it is contrary to what actually happened.
3. When an activity or an event takes place unbeknown to you, then the verb stem + एछ with the appropriate conjugation is used to express a sense of surprise that it has happened. This might be called the unknown past tense, e.g. गएको राति पानी परेछ 'Oh, it rained last night'.
4. रहेछ expresses a sense of discovery or surprise in any tense, because of a new situation or new information that you have discovered. So the auxiliary verbs हो, छ and थियो change to रहेछ automatically to indicate this realization, e.g. ऊ बिरामी रहेछ 'Oh, he is/was sick!' or 'I found out that he is/was sick' depending on the present or past context.

24 त्यसो भए ...

If that's how it is...

In this unit you will learn:

- *some verses of a Nepali folksong*
- *how to intensify the action of a verb*
- *the longer continuous tenses*
- *the short real conditional sentence*

34 Two porters and a folksong

24.01

Mahila works as a porter in the hills. On his way home one day he meets another porter, and they agree to keep each other company along the way.

भरिया	ए भाइ, आज कतातिर ?
माहिला	आज घरतिर जाने ।
भरिया	कहाँ हो घर ?
माहिला	त्रिसुली नदीपारि, फेदी गाउँ ।
भरिया	आज कहाँबाट हिँडेको ?
माहिला	आज नुवाकोटबाट बिहानै हिँडेको ।
भरिया	एक्लै हिँड्दाखेरि अलि डर हुन्छ नि । साथी छैन ?

माहिला	साथी–भाइहरूसँग हिँडेको थिएँ उनीहरू त धादिङ्गतिर गएछन् । उनीहरूको बाटो उता पर्‍यो, मेरो बाटो यता पर्‍यो । के गर्ने ?
भरिया	ल, त्यसो भए तपाईंको र मेरो बाटो यहाँदेखि एउटै भयो । यहाँबाट सँगै जाऔं ।
माहिला	हुन्छ, रमाइलो हुन्छ । तपाईंको भारी ठूलो रहेछ । के छ त्यसमा ?
भरिया	यसमा नुन, तेल र कपडा छ । देउरालीको एउटा साहूको भारी हो यो ।
माहिला	मलाई थकाइ लाग्यो । कस्तो चर्को घाम लागेको, हगि ? ऊ त्यो पीपलको बोटमुनि एक छिन थकाइ मारौं न ।
भरिया	हुन्छ, बसौं । कस्तो तिर्खा लाग्यो ! यतातिर पानी पाइन्छ कि ?
माहिला	हेर्नुहोस्, ऊ त्यहाँ तलबाट एउटा केटा आइरहेको छ । घर नजिकै होला उसको । म सोध्छु, है ... ए कान्छा, तिम्रो घर कहाँ हो ?
केटा	यहींनेर छ, दाइ । किन र ?
माहिला	त्यसो भए एक अङ्खोरा पानी ल्याउन सक्छौ ? चर्को घाम लागेको छ, हामीलाई तिर्खा लाग्यो ।
केटा	भइहाल्छ नि दाइ, म लिएर आउँछु । (पाँच मिनेटपछि)
केटा	ल, पानी लिनुहोस् । ए तपाईंको साथी त सुतिहाल्नुभएछ ।
माहिला	ल, उसलाई उठाउन एउटा गीत गाउनुपर्छ । तिमीलाई गीत गाउन आउँछ ?
केटा	आउँछ दाइ । गाऊँ त ? ल, सुन्नुहोस् है त । रेसम फिरिरि, रेसम फिरिरि उडेर जाऊँ कि डाँडामा भन्ज्याङ्ग, रेसम फिरिरि कुकुरलाई कुतीमा कुती, बिरालोलाई सुरी तिम्रो हाम्रो माया प्रीति दोबाटोमा कुरी रेसम फिरिरि, रेसम फिरिरि उडेर जाऊँ कि डाँडामा भन्ज्याङ्ग, रेसम फिरिरि एकनाले बन्दुक दुईनाले बन्दुक मृगलाई ताकेको मृगलाई मैले ताकेको होइन मायालाई डाकेको रेसम फिरिरि, रेसम फिरिरि उडेर जाऊँ कि डाँडामा भन्ज्याङ्ग, रेसम फिरिरि
माहिला	ए यो भाइले पानी ल्याइदिएको छ । मैले त खाएँ । तिमी सुतिरहेका थियौ । खाने हो ?

Quick vocab

-पारि	on the far side of
डर	fear
चर्को	hot, sharp
थकाइ मार्नु	to rest ('to kill weariness')
यहीं	right here
-नेर	near
अङ्खोरा	jug, steel cup
रेसम	silk (handkerchief)
फिरिरि	rippling (in the breeze)
उड्नु	to fly
डाँडा	hill, ridge
भन्ज्याङ्ग	pass
कुकुर	dog
बिरालो	cat
माया	love, affection
प्रीति	love, affection
दोबाटो	crossroads
एकनाले	single-barrelled
बन्दुक	gun
दुईनाले	double-barrelled
मृग	deer
ताक्नु	to aim
डाक्नु	to call, invite

Porter Oh brother, where are you going today?
Mahila I'm going home today.
Porter Where's home?
Mahila The other side of the Trisuli river, Phedi village.
Porter Where did you start from today?
Mahila Early this morning I set out from Nuwakot.
Porter It's a bit frightening when you walk alone, you know. Have you no companions?
Mahila I set out with some friends, but they have gone to Dhading. Their path was in that direction, mine in this. What to do?
Porter Well, if that's how it is your path and mine are the same from here. Let's go together from here.
Mahila OK, it will be pleasant. Your load is big. What is in it?
Porter There's salt, oil and cloth in this. This is a load for a businessman in Deurali.

Mahila	I'm tired. How hot the sun is, don't you think? Let's rest beneath that pipal tree for a moment.
Porter	Yes, let's sit down. How thirsty I am! Can we get some water somewhere here?
Mahila	Look, there's a boy coming from lower down. His house will be nearby. I'll ask ... Hey Kancha, where's your house?
Boy	It's just near here. Why do you ask?
Mahila	If that's so, can you bring a jug of water? The sun is hot, we are thirsty.
Boy	No problem brother, I'll bring it.
	After five minutes:
Boy	Here, take the water. Oh, your friend has gone to sleep.
Mahila	Right, we'll have to sing a song to wake him up. Can you sing?
Boy	Yes I can, brother. Shall I sing then? Right, listen to me.*[1] *Silk (handkerchief) rippling (in the breeze), Silk (handkerchief) rippling (in the breeze),* *[2] *Shall I go flying (over the) hills and passes? Silk (handkerchief) rippling (in the breeze).* *(Saying) 'kuti kuti' to a chicken, (saying) 'suri' to a cat* *Your love and my love, waiting at the crossroads.* *Silk (handkerchief) rippling ...* *One-barrelled gun, two-barrelled gun, aiming at a deer,* *It's not a deer that I am aiming at, it's love that I am calling.* *Silk (handkerchief) rippling ...*
Mahila	Oh, this brother has brought some water. *I* have drunk some. You were sleeping. Will you drink?

Note *[1]The boy sings a few verses of one of the most famous Nepali folksongs, रेसम फिरिरि. Like many folksongs, रेसम फिरिरि contains a lot of wordplay that is difficult to translate.

*[2]It is an old tradition for young men and women to exchange handkerchiefs as love tokens.

Grammar

134 COMPOUND VERBS WITH हाल्नु

When used on its own, the verb हाल्नु means *to insert, put in*. It may be compared to the verb राख्नु *to place upon, keep*. In fact, राख्नु is felt by some Nepali speakers to be a more polite way of saying *to put in*, so that one will hear some speakers saying म चियामा चिनी हालिदिऊँ ? *shall I put sugar in the tea?* and others saying म चियामा चिनी राखिदिऊँ ?

When it is combined with the i-stem of a verb to form a compound verb, however, **हाल्नु** simply reinforces and underlines the sense of that verb without changing its essential meaning.

ऊ गयो	he went
भयो	it's happened
तपाईंले देख्नुभयो	you saw
ऊ गइहाल्यो	he's gone away
भइहाल्यो	it's over and done with
तपाईंले देखिहाल्नुभयो	you have surely seen
ऊ धेरै दिन बसेन । तीन दिनपछि त गइहाल्यो नि ।	He didn't stay long. After three days he was gone, you know.
तपाईंले देखिहाल्नुभयो यहाँ दिन दिनै बत्ती जान्छ ।	You have seen very well that there is a power cut here every day.
तीनवटा उदाहरण भएपछि त भइहाल्यो नि ।	After three examples it's over and done, you know.

● INSIGHT

हाल्नु by itself means 'to put' and when it is used with other verbs it means 'to put oneself into action'. It indicates the immediacy of an action that is often used with construction such as verb stem + ने बित्तिकै.

135 CONTINUOUS TENSES USING रहनु

When used on its own, the verb **रहनु** means *to remain, continue*. It is frequently combined with the i-stem of a verb to form a compound verb that emphasizes the continuous nature of an action. The -**एको** participle of such a compound verb is used to form a continuous tense:

अब हेर्नुहोस् नगरपालिकालाई आज म यो सुझाव लेखिरहेको छु । यस्तै सुझाव	Look now, today I am writing this suggestion for the municipality.
पोहोर साल पनि यही बेला लेखिरहेको थिएँ । तर कसैले पनि ध्यान दिइरहेका छैनन् ।	Last year too I was writing the same kind of suggestion at exactly this time. But no one is giving this matter any attention.
म एउटा नेपाली भाषाको पाठ्यपुस्तक लेख्न सोचिरहेको थिएँ । साथीहरू नलेख भनिरहेका थिए । तर लेख्न शुरु गरिहालें । अहिलेसम्म पनि लेखिरहेको छु ।	I was thinking of writing a textbook of the Nepali language. (My) friends were telling me not to write (it). Even so I began to write. I am still writing it now.

Because of the greater length of these verbs, they are used instead of the other continuous tenses (गर्दै छ, गर्दै थियो etc.) when there is a need to stress the continuous nature of an activity.

Exercise 71

Convert the tense of the following sentences from an habitual tense to a continuous tense with रहनु:

Examples

म अफिसमा काम गर्छु ।	म अफिसमा काम गरिरहेको छु ।
म अफिसमा काम गर्थें ।	म अफिसमा काम गरिरेहको थिएँ ।

१ उनीहरू जाँड-रक्सी धेरै पिउँथे ।

२ गोपाल राम्रा राम्रा गीत गाउँथ्यो ।

३ मेरो भाइ टाढाको एउटा स्कूलमा जान्छ ।

४ खैरेनीबाट काठ्माडौंमा धेरै तरकारी आउँछ ।

५ म यहाँबाट कीर्तिपुरसम्म हिँडेर जान्थें ।

• INSIGHT

The alternative continuous tense formed by रहनु is more commonly used in spoken Nepali. Note that this alternative continuous tense is often used in short form, e.g. ऊ के गरिरहेको छ ? This sentence is shortened to के गरिरा' को or के गरिरा' ? It means 'what is he doing?'.

136 SHORT REAL CONDITIONAL SENTENCES

The **-e** participle consists of a verb's past tense base + the vowel **e** or (another way of looking at it) the -**एको** participle minus its -**को**.

Grammar 91 explained how to construct a real conditional sentence by using the simple past tense of a verb followed by **भने** for the 'if' clause, and a present or future tense (or an imperative) for the 'then' clause. A second, quicker way of expressing the same meaning replaces the verb of the 'if' clause with the short **-e** participle of the verb, and leaves out the word **भने**. For example, compare the long and short versions of the sentences *if it rains I won't go out* and *if it doesn't rain I will probably go out:*

Long version	**Short version**
पानी पर्‍यो भने म बाहिर जाँदिन ।	पानी परे म बाहिर जाँदिन ।
पानी परेन भने म बाहिर जाउँला ।	पानी नपरे म बाहिर जाउँला ।

Often, the **-e** participle will be followed by त, *though, but,* to underline the conditional nature of the sentence.

अलिकति भात भए पुग्छ ।	A little rice will be enough *('if there is a little rice it will suffice').*
भोक लागे त भात खाऊ न भाइ ।	If you're hungry just eat, younger brother.
पैसा नभए त बिल कसरी तिर्ने ?	But if there is no money how will we pay the bill?
अँग्रेजी बोले पनि हुन्छ, नेपाली बोले पनि हुन्छ ।	It is OK if you speak English, and it's OK if you speak Nepali too.

Exercise 72

Create one short real conditional sentence from each pair of sentences:

Example

पानी पर्दैन । म बाहिर जाउँला । = पानी नपरे म बाहिर जाउँला ।

१ भोक लाग्दैन । म खाजा नखाउँला ।

२ थकाइ लाग्यो । म आराम गरुँला ।

३ काठ्माडौं छाडेर जान मन लाग्दैन । काठ्माडौंमै बसुँला ।

४ नेपाली सिक्न गाह्रो लाग्यो । हिन्दी सिक्न पनि गाह्रो लाग्यो । जापानी सिकुँला ।

५ गुन्द्रुक मीठो लागेन र आलु-तामा पनि मीठो लागेन । कालो दाल खाउँला ।

● INSIGHT

Note that the short form of the conditional is very commonly used with हुन्छ 'It is okay'. In that case the meaning slightly changes, e.g. म भित्र आए हुन्छ ? Literally, it means 'is it okay if I come in?' or 'May I come in?' in which a sense of permission is understood.

Exercise 73

Translate into Nepali:

I went with elder brother to the airport yesterday. Some guests were coming from Delhi to stay with us. Early in the morning we had phoned the Nepal Airlines office and a woman had said that the Delhi flight would arrive at 3 o'clock in the afternoon. 'If that's the case then we must set out from home at 2.30', said elder brother. As soon as we arrived at the airport elder brother asked an official (**कर्मचारी**) about the flight. The official told him that it had left Delhi only recently because the weather had been very bad. 'In that case how long will we have to wait here?', elder brother asked. 'It is flying (**uḍnu**) towards Nepal now', the official said, 'it will arrive within one hour.' 'The aeroplane is late and we will have to wait here', elder brother said. 'But mother and father are waiting at home', I told him, 'They do not know that the plane is coming late.' 'You go and phone them', elder brother said. 'Tell them that we will come straight home after the plane arrives.'

The most important things for the reader to remember

1 In order to show the immediacy of an action, Nepali combines the verb stem with -इहाल्नु and uses the appropriate conjugation, e.g. औषधी खाएपछि वहाँ सुतिहाल्नुभयो 'He slept immediately after taking medicine'.

2 इरहनु is used as a suffix with other verbs to indicate the sustained continuity of an action that would be expressed in English as 'to remain doing something', 'to continue to do something', e.g. बस् + इ + रहनु = बसिरहनु 'to continue to stay'.

3 If this compound verb is changed into a perfect participle with एको followed by a conjugated form of छ, थियो or हुन्छ it forms present, past and future perfect continuous tenses as in म बसिरहेको छु, म बसिरहेको थिएँ, म बसिरहेको हुन्छु or हुनेछु respectively.

4 A conditional sentence can also be formed in Nepali by attaching the suffix ए directly to the verb stem instead of using भने. This is a short conditional form without any conjugation, e.g. मन परे खानुहोस्, मन नपरे नखानुहोस् 'If you like it please eat it, if you don't like it, don't eat it'.

Appendices

Cardinal numbers

० शून्य

१ एक	११ एघार	२१ एक्काइस	३१ एकतीस	४१ एकचालीस
२ दुई	१२ बाह्र	२२ बाईस	३२ बत्तीस	४२ बयालीस
३ तीन	१३ तेह्र	२३ तेईस	३३ तेत्तीस	४३ त्रिचालीस
४ चार	१४ चौध	२४ चौबीस	३४ चौंतीस	४४ चवालीस
५ पाँच	१५ पन्ध	२५ पच्चीस	३५ पैंतीस	४५ पैंतालीस
६ छ	१६ सोह्र	२६ छब्बीस	३६ छत्तीस	४६ छयालीस
७ सात	१७ सत्र	२७ सत्ताईस	३७ सैंतीस	४७ सतचालीस
८ आठ	१८ अठार	२८ अट्ठाइस	३८ अठ्तीस	४८ अठचालीस
९ नौ	१९ उन्नाईस	२९ उन्तीस	३९ उनन्चालीस	४९ उनन्चास
१० दस	२० बीस	३० तीस	४० चालीस	५० पचास

५१ एकाउन्न	६१ एकसट्ठी	७१ एकहत्तर	८१ एकासी	९१ एकानब्बे
५२ बाउन्न	६२ बैंसट्ठी	७२ बहत्तर	८२ बयासी	९२ बयानब्बे
५३ त्रिपन्न	६३ त्रिसट्ठी	७३ त्रिहत्तर	८३ त्रियासी	९३ त्रियानब्बे
५४ चउन्न	६४ चौंसट्ठी	७४ चौहत्तर	८४ चौरासी	९४ चौरानब्बे
५५ पचपन्न	६५ पैंसट्ठी	७५ पचहत्तर	८५ पचासी	९५ पच्चानब्बे
५६ छपन्न	६६ छैंसट्ठी	७६ छहत्तर	८६ छयासी	९६ छयानब्बे
५७ सन्ताउन्न	६७ सतसट्ठी	७७ सतहत्तर	८७ सतासी	९७ सन्तानब्बे
५८ अन्ठाउन्न	६८ अठसट्ठी	७८ अठहत्तर	८८ अठासी	९८ अन्ठानब्बे
५९ उनन्साठी	६९ उनहत्तर	७९ उनासी	८९ उनानब्बे	९९ उनान्सय
६० साठी	७० सत्तरी	८० असी	९० नब्बे	१०० सय

Above 100, the numbers proceed as they do in English, but omitting the English 'and':

१०१	एक सय एक
२६२	दुई सय बैंसट्ठी
१०००	एक हजार or हजार
१४२३	एक हजार चार सय तेईस
२५१०८	पच्चीस हजार एक सय आठ
१०००००	एक लाख
११३४३३	एक लाख तेह्र हजार चार सय तेत्तीस
३७०००००	सैंतीस लाख
१०००००००	एक करोड

If commas are used to split up large numbers, the placing of the commas reflects the system of **हजार**, **लाख**, and **करोड**, rather than thousands and millions. For example, the number 31,350,226 will appear as:

३,१३,५०,२२६	तीन करोड तेह्र लाख पचास हजार दुई सय छब्बीस

Kinship terms

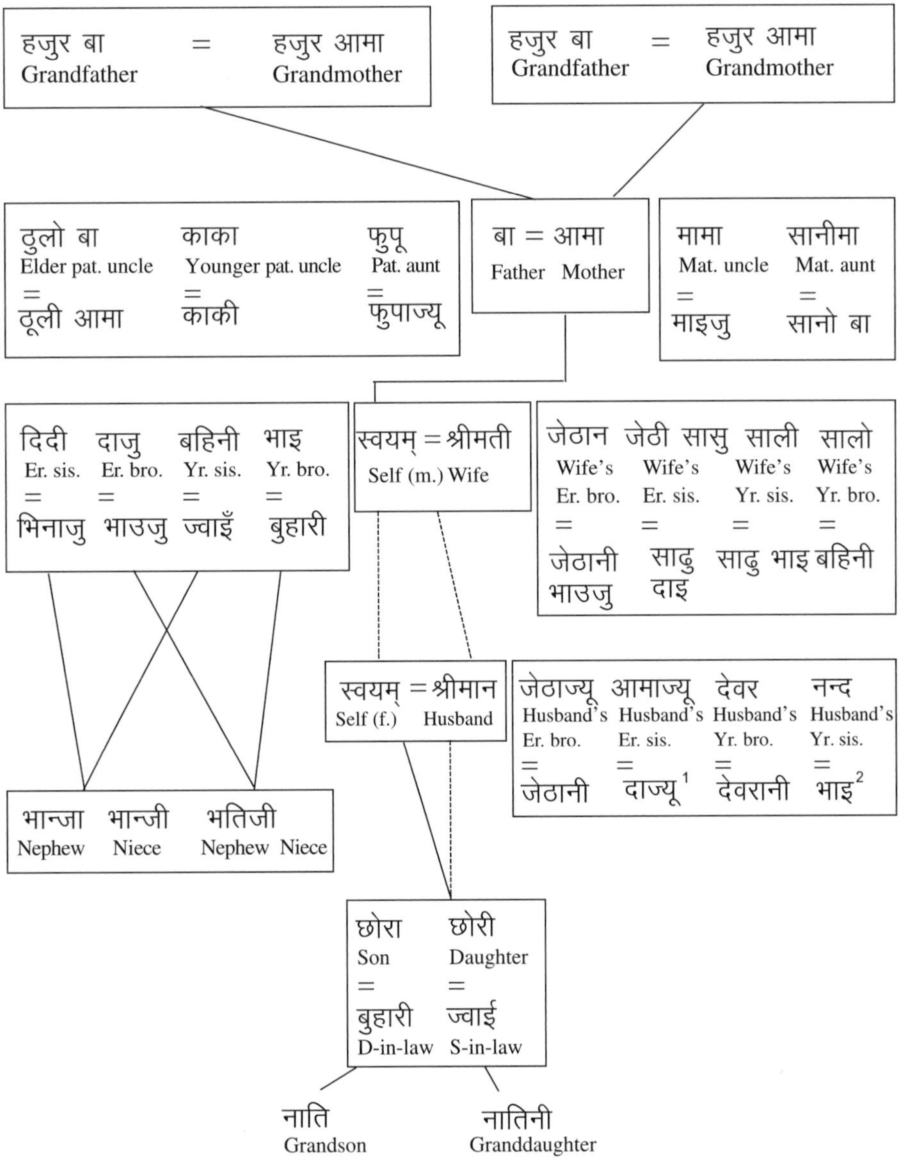

[1] more formally, आमाज्यू दाज्यू
[2] more formally, नन्दे भाई

Key to exercises

1

1	होइन, म बिमल कुमार होइन ।	**hoina, ma Bimal Kumār hoina.**
2	हो, म विद्यार्थी हुँ ।	**ho, ma vidyārthī hũ.**
		or
	होइन, म विद्यार्थी होइन ।	**hoina, ma vidyārthī hoina.**
3	हो, म नेपाली हुँ ।	**ho, ma nepālī hũ.**
		or
	होइन, म नेपाली होइन ।	**hoina, ma nepālī hoina.**

2

1	म अँग्रेज हुँ ।	**ma ãgrej hũ.**
2	हामी विद्यार्थी हौं ।	**hāmī vidyārthī haũ.**
3	तिमी हिन्दुस्तानी हौ ।	**timī hindustānī hau.**
4	तिमीहरू किसान हौ ।	**timīharū kisān hau.**
5	तपाईं शिक्षक हुनुहुन्छ ।	**tapāī̃ sikṣak hunuhuncha.**
6	ऊ शिक्षक हो ।	**ū śikṣak ho.**
7	उनी धनी मान्छे हुन् ।	**unī dhanī mānche hun.**
8	ती मान्छेहरू प्रहरी हुन् ।	**tī mānche harū praharī hun.**
9	वहाँ नेपाली हुनुहुन्छ ।	**vahā̃ nepālī hunuhuncha.**
10	यहाँहरू भारतीय हुनुहुन्छ ।	**yahā̃harū bhāratīya hunuhuncha.**

3

1	... होइन ।	**... hoina.**	6	... होइन ।	**... hoina.**
2	... होइनौं ।	**... hoinaũ.**	7	... होइनन् ।	**... hoinan.**
3	... होइनौ ।	**... hoinau.**	8	... होइनन् ।	**... hoinan.**
4	... होइनौ ।	**... hoinau.**	9	... हुनुहुन्न ।	**... hunuhunna.**
5	... हुनुहुन्न ।	**... hunuhunna.**	10	... हुनुहुन्न ।	**... hunuhunna.**

4

1	राम्रो किसान	**rāmro kisān**	6	धनी किसानहरू	**dhanī kisānharū**
2	ठूलो किताब	**ṭhūlo kitāb**	7	राम्रा किताबहरू	**rāmrā kitābharū**
3	धनी केटी	**dhanī keṭī**	8	साना केटीहरू	**sānā keṭīharū**

4	नयाँ केटा	**nayā̃ keṭā**	9	गरीब केटाहरू	**garīb keṭāharū**
5	राम्रो राजा	**rāmro rājā**	10	धनी राजाहरू	**dhanī rājāharū**

5

१ हो, काठ्माडौं ठूलो छ ।	**ho, kāṭhmāḍaū̃ ṭhūlo cha.**
२ होइन, भक्तपुर गाउँ होइन, शहर हो ।	**hoina, bhaktapur gaū̃ hoina, śahar ho.**
३ हो, काठ्माडौं राम्रै छ ।	**ho, kāṭhmāḍaū̃ rāmrai cha.**
४ हो, काठ्माडौं ठूलो शहर हो ।	**ho, kāṭhmāḍaū̃ ṭhūlo śahar ho.**
५ हो, भक्तपुर पुरानो छ ।	**ho, bhaktapur purāno cha.**
६ होइन, भक्तपुर नयाँ शहर होइन, पुरानो शहर हो ।	**hoina, bhaktapur nayā̃ śahar hoina, purāno śahar ho.**

6

१ भाइ स्कूलमा छ ।	**bhāi skūlmā cha.**
२ दाजु दार्जीलिङ्गमा हुनुहुन्छ ।	**dāju dārjīliṅgmā hunuhuncha.**
३ दिदी महेन्द्र महाविद्यालयमा हुनुहुन्छ ।	**didī mahendra mahāvidyālaymā hunuhuncha.**
४ भोलि आमा र बुवा घरमा हुनुहुन्छ ।	**bholi āmā ra buvā gharmā hunuhuncha.**
५ परिवारमा दाजु-भाइ र दिदी-बहिनीहरू धेरै छन् ।	**parivārmā dāju-bhāi ra didī-bahinīharū dherai chan.**

7

१ … छैन ।	**… chaina.**
२ … हुनुहुन्न ।	**… hunuhunna.**
३ … हुनुहुन्न ।	**… hunuhunna.**
४ … हुनुहुन्न ।	**… hunuhunna.**
५ … छैनन् ।	**… chainan.**

8

१ प्रहरी थाना नजिक छैन, अलि टाढा छ ।	**praharī thāna najik chaina, ali ṭāḍhā cha.**
२ हो, हुलाक घर अलि टाढा छ ।	**ho, hulāk ghar ali ṭāḍhā cha.**
३ लजबाट बजार तीन किलोमीटर टाढा छ ।	**lajbāṭa bajār tīn kilomīṭar ṭāḍhā cha.**
४ बजारमा प्रहरी थाना, पसलहरू, हुलाक घर र बैंक छ ।	**bajārmā praharī thānā, pasalharū, hulāk ghar ra baĩk cha.**
५ प्रहरी थाना बजारमा छ ।	**praharī thānā bajārmā cha.**
६ सरस्वती मन्दिर बजारबाट तीन किलोमीटर टाढा छ ।	**sarasvatī mandir bajārbāṭa tīn kilomīṭar ṭāḍhā cha.**

9

नेपाली कक्षामाः	**nepālī kakṣāmā:**
१ दसजना विद्यार्थीहरू छन् ।	**dasjanā vidyārthīharū chan.**
२ पाँचजना अँग्रेजहरू छन् ।	**pā̃cjanā āgrejharū chan.**
३ दुईजना जर्मनहरू छन् ।	**duījanā jarmanharū chan.**
अँग्रेजी कक्षामाः	**āgrejṣ kakṣāmā:**
४ उन्नाइसजना विद्यार्थीहरू छन् ।	**unnāisjanā vidyārthīharū chan.**
५ नौजना केटाहरू छन् ।	**naujanā keṭāharū chan.**
६ दसजना केटीहरू छन् ।	**dasjanā keṭīharū chan.**

10

१ मसँग दस रुपियाँ र एक बट्टा चुरोट छ ।	**masāga das rupiyā̃ ra ek baṭṭā curoṭ cha.**
२ हामीहरू तीन हप्तादेखि नेपालमा छौं ।	**hāmīharū tīn haptādekhi nepālmā chaū̃.**
३ हुलाक घरमा दसजना लोग्ने-मान्छे, तीनजना आइमाई र पाँचजना केटा छन् ।	**hulāk gharmā dasjanā logne-mānche, tīnjanā āimaī ra pā̃cjanā keṭā chan.**
४ तपाईंसँग कति पैसा छ ?	**tapā̃īsāga kati paisā cha?**
५ त्यो भारतीय मान्छेसँग पैसा छैन, तर नेपाली केटासँग दस रुपियाँ छ ।	**tyo bhāratīya mānchesāga paisā chaina, tara nepālī keṭāsāga das rupiyā̃ cha.**
६ धनी किसानसँग दस पाथी चामल र दस किलो आलु छ ।	**dhanī kisānsāga das pāthī cāmal ra das kilo ālu cha.**
७ हरेक टेबुलमा दुई कप चिया छ ।	**harek ṭebulmā duī kap ciyā cha.**
८ शिक्षकसँग किताब छैन र विद्यार्थीहरूसँग कलम छैन ।	**śikṣaksāga kitāb chaina ra vidyārthīharūsāga kalam chaina.**

11

भाइ शिक्षक हो ।	**bhāi śikṣak ho.**	भाइ घरमा छ ।	**bhāi gharmā cha.**
दिदी शिक्षक हुन् ।	**didī śikṣak hun.**	दिदी घरमा छिन् ।	**didī gharmā chin.**
भाइहरू शिक्षक हुन ।	**bhāiharū śikṣak hun.**	भाइहरू घरमा छन् ।	**bhāiharū harmā chan.**
दाज्यू शिक्षक हुनुहुन्छ ।	**dājyū śikṣak hunuhuncha.**	दाज्यू घरमा हुनुहुन्छ ।	**dājyū gharmā hunuhuncṣa.**
आमा शिक्षक हुनुहुन्छ ।	**āmā śikṣak hunuhunṣha.**	आमा घरमा हुनुहुन्छ ।	**āmā gharmā hunuhuncha.**
म शिक्षक हुँ ।	**ma śikṣak hũ.**	म घरमा छु ।	**ma gharmā chu.**

12

1	एक हप्ता	**ek haptā**
2	दुईजना मान्छे	**duījanā mānche**
3	तीनवटा किताब	**tīnvaṭā kitāb**
4	चारजना केटा	**cārjanā keṭā**
5	पाँच रुपियाँ	**pā̃c rupiyā̃**
6	छवटा मेच	**chavaṭā mec**
7	सातजना आइमाई	**sātjanā āimāī**
8	आठवटा कक्षा	**āṭhvaṭā kakṣā**
9	नौ किलो	**nau kilo**
10	दसजना विदेशी	**dasjanā videśī**
11	दुई किलो	**duī kilo**
12	साढे सात किलो	**sāḍhe sāt kilo**
13	तीन पाथी	**tīn pāthī**
14	अढाई माना	**aḍhāī mānā**
15	तीन रुपियाँ पचहत्तर पैसा	**tīn rupiyā̃ pacahattar paisā**
16	साढे नौ रुपियाँ	**sāḍhe nau rupiyā̃**

13

१ रतनजीको आफ्नो मोटर छैन ।	**Ratanjīko āphno moṭar chaina.**
२ रातो मोटर रतनको होइन । रतनको साथीको हो ।	**rāto moṭar Ratanko hoina. Ratanko sāthīko ho.**
३ सुबीरको आफ्नो मोटर छैन ।	**Subīrko āphno moṭar chaina.**
४ सुबीरको दाज्यूको एउटा मोटर छ ।	**Subīrko dājyūko euṭā moṭar cha.**

14

१ धन बहादुरकी श्रीमतीका दुईजना दिदी छन् ।	**Dhan Bahādurkī śrīmatīkā duījanā didī chan.**
२ मेरो बुवा-आमा छैन ।	**mero buvā-āmā chaina.**
३ मेरी आमाका चारजना नाति-नातिनी छन् ।	**merī āmākā cārjanā nāti-nātinī chan.**
४ उनीहरूको छोराछोरी छैनन् ।	**unīharūko chorāchorī chainan.**
५ वहाँका नौवटा गाई छन् ।	**vahā̃kā nauvaṭā gāī chan.**
६ हाम्रा पाँचवटा मोटा भैंसी छन् ।	**hāmrā pā̃cvaṭā moṭā bhaĩsī chan.**

15

१ तिमी मेरो छोराको साथी हौ, होइन ? तिम्रो नाम गौतम हो ?	timī mero chorāko sāthī hau, hoina? timro nām Gautam ho?
२ तिम्रो साथीको बुवाको नाम गणेश मान हो ? थाहा छ कि छैन ?	timro sāthīko buvāko nām Gaṇeś Mān ho? thāhā cha ki chaina?
३ वहाँको नाम लक्ष्मी नाथ हो । त्यो मलाई थाहा छ ।	vahā̃ko nām Lakṣmī Nāth ho. tyo malāī thāhā cha.
४ मेरो घर यहाँबाट टाढा छैन । तिम्रो घर कहाँ छ ?	mero ghar yahā̃bāṭa ṭāḍhā chaina. timro ghar kahā̃ cha?
५ तपाईंको बुवा बैंकमा हुनुहुन्छ । तपाईंकी आमालाई थाहा छ ?	tapāī̃ko buvā baīkmā hunuhuncha. tapāī̃kī āmālāī thāhā cha?
६ उनीहरूका गाईहरू हाम्रो खेतमा छन् । उनीहरूलाई थाहा छैन ?	unīharūkā gāīharū hāmro khetmā chan. unīharūlāī thāhā chaina?
७ हाम्रो थर पोखरेल हो । हामी बाहुन हौं ।	hāmro thar pokharel ho. hāmī bāhun haũ.
८ यो तिम्रो घडी होइन । मेरी आमाको हो ।	yo timro ghaḍī hoina. merī āmāko ho.

16

मेरो नाम … हो । मेरो घर … मा छ । मेरो परिवारमा हामी … जना हौं … … … र … ।	mero nām … ho. mero ghar … mā cha. mero parivārmā hāmī … janā haũ: … … … ra …
मेरी दिदीको नाम … हो । वहाँ … मा हुनुहुन्छ ।	merī didīko nām … ho. vahā̃ … mā hunuhuncha.
मेरी दिदीको श्रीमानको नाम … हो ।	merī didīko śrīmānko nām … ho.

17

१ सूर्यका एकजना छोरा र एकजना छोरी छन् ।	sūryakā ekjanā chorā ra ekjanā chorī chan.
२ प्रीतिको विचारमा सूर्यकी छोरी छ ।	Prītiko vicārmā Sūryakī chorī cha.
३ सूर्यको छोराको नाम गिरीश हो ।	Sūryako chorāko nām Girīś ho.
४ किताबमा गिरीशको नाम छ ।	kitābmā Girīśko nām cha.

18

१ त्यस केटाका दुइटा घर छन् ।	tyas keṭākā duiṭā ghar chan.
२ यस ठूलो गाउँमा एउटा चियापसल मात्रै छ ।	yas ṭhūlo gāũmā euṭā ciyāpasal mātrai cha.
३ उसका आठजना छोरी छन् ।	uskā āṭhjanā chorī chan.
४ उनका चारजना छोरा छन् ।	unkā cārjanā chorā chan.
५ यस मान्छेका धेरै साथीहरू छन् ।	yas mānchekā dherai sāthīharū chan.
६ कसको साथी छैन ?	kasko sāthī chaina?

19

१ आज हामी बजार जाँदैनौं । घरमा एक रुपियाँ पनि छैन ।

२ राजु के काम गर्छ ? ऊ नेपाल राष्ट्र बैंकमा काम गर्छ । उसको दाजु पनि त्यहाँ काम गर्छ ।

३ तपाईं कहाँ बस्नुहुन्छ ? हिजोआज म काठ्माडौंमा बस्छु ।

४ तपाईंको भाइ ट्याक्सीबाट अफिस जान्छ ? होइन, ऊ बसबाट जान्छ ।

५ दार्जीलिङ्गका मान्छेहरू धेरैजसो राम्रो नेपाली बोल्छन् ।

20

१ म हरेक दिन काठ्माडौं जान्छु ।

२ उनीहरू धेरैजसो पोखरामा बस्छन् ।

३ तिमी सधैं बुवाको पसलमा नेपाली बोल्छौ ।

४ हामीहरू हिजोआज रामको अफिसमा काम गर्छौं ।

५ ऊ कहिल्यै स्कूलमा अँग्रेजी बोल्दैन ।

६ त्यो मान्छे एक हप्तापछि लण्डन जान्छ ।

21

१ तपाईं सात बजे घरमा भात खानुहुन्छ ।

२ त्यो मान्छे बेलुका होटेलमा चिया खान्छ ।

३ वहाँहरू बिहिवार मकहाँ (मेरो घर) आउनुहुन्छ ।

४ यिनीहरू हप्ताको दुई पटक मन्दिर जान्छन् ।

५ यो केटी शनिवार साथीकहाँ (साथीको घरमा) सुन्छे ।

22

१ म दिउँसो दुई बजेदेखि छ बजेसम्म घरमा हुँदिन ।

२ तपाईं बुधवारदेखि शुक्रवारसम्म बिराटनगरमा हुनुहुन्न ।

३ उनीहरू मङ्गलवारदेखि बिहिवारसम्म काम गर्दैनन् ।

४ तिमी आठ बजेदेखि साढे दस बजेसम्म बाहिर जाँदैनौ ।

५ यिनीहरू दिउँसो एक बजेदेखि दुई बजेसम्म पढ्दैनन् ।

23

(a) १ ए, त्यो मेचमा नबस, यो मेचमा बस ।

२ काठ्माडौंमा नेपाली बोल, अँग्रेजी नबोल ।

३ ठूलो रातो किताब पढ, अखबार नपढ ।

४ केटालाई एउटा स्याऊ देऊ, सुन्तला नदेऊ ।

(b) ५ छ बजे नआउनुहोस्, आठ बजेतिर आउनुहोस् ।

६ मलाई भन्नुहोस् तर उसलाई नभन्नुहोस् ।

७ यो कप लिनुहोस् र त्यो कप उसलाई दिनुहोस् ।

८ नेपाल जानुहोस् । त्यहाँ नेपाली बोल्नुहोस् ।

24

१ ती आइमाईहरू बिहिवार कहिल्यै बजारमा आउँदैनन् । कहिले आउँछन् त ? उनीहरू धेरै जसो मङ्गलवार आउँछन् ।

२ विदेशीहरू काठ्माडौंबाट लुक्लासम्म हवाईजहाजमा जान्छन् । नेपालीहरू धेरैजसो बसबाट जिरीसम्म जान्छन् । जिरीबाट उनीहरू लुक्लासम्म हिँड्छन् ।

३ ती लोग्ने-मान्छेहरू कति बजे खेतमा जान्छन् ? उनीहरू आठ बजेतिर जान्छन् अनि तीन घण्टापछि फर्किन्छन् ।

४ म भोलिसम्म मात्रै नेपालमा बस्छु । भोलि बिहान साढे दस बजे म दिल्ली जान्छु । त्यसपछि म लण्डन जान्छु ।

५ राति आठ बजेपछि सबै पसल बन्द हुन्छन् । म तपाईंको लागि अहिले बजार जान्नँ । म भोलि बिहान जान्छु, हुन्छ ?

६ तिमी मेरो लागि के काम गर्छौ ? म तपाईंको लागि बजार जान्छु, हुन्छ ?

७ मेरी बहिनी कहिल्यै पनि परिवारको लागि खाना पकाउँदिनन् । कहिलेकाहीं दिदी पकाउनुहुन्छ, कहिलेकाहीं आमा पकाउनुहुन्छ ।

८ ऊ हरेक दिन स्कूल जान्छे, ऊ पनि जान्छ । तर उनीहरूको भाइ जाँदैन ।

25

१ लण्डन काठ्माडौंभन्दा ठूलो छ ।

२ अमेरिकालीहरू धेरैजसो अँग्रेजहरूभन्दा धनी हुन्छन् ।

३ काठ्माडौं बेलायतबाट दिल्लीभन्दा टाढा छ ।

४ काठ्माडौं नेपालको सबभन्दा ठूलो शहर हो ।

५ सँसारको सबभन्दा गरीब देश कुन हो ?

६ नेपाली भाषाभन्दा सजिलो भाषा छैन ।

26

१ हजुरबालाई नीलो रङ मन पर्छ ।

२ मेरा दिदीहरूलाई कालो रङ मन पर्दैन ।

३ तपाईंलाई हरियो रङ मन पर्छ ।

४ उसका भाइहरूलाई पहेंलो रङ मन पर्दैन ।

५ उनीहरूलाई प्याजी रङ-मन पर्छ ।

27

१ तपाईंहरू साँखुमा बस्नुहुन्छ ।

२ किनभने भोलि धेरै किनमेल छ अनि तपाईं बालाई मदत गर्नुहुन्छ ।

३ मा कहिल्यै काठ्माडौं जानुहुन्न ।

४ घरमा मा घरको काम गर्नुहुन्छ र भात पकाउनुहुन्छ ।

५ बेलुका तपाईंकी कान्छी बहिनी धारा जान्छे ।

६ किनभने उनीहरू इनारको पानी खान्छन् ।

28

१ झ्याल खोल्नुहोस्, यस कोठामा, धेरै गर्मी भयो ।

२ हिजो बिहान बच्चाहरू सबै यहाँ थिए । तर आज कोही पनि स्कूल आएन ।

३ अस्ति बुधवार ठूलो पानी पर्‍यो । मसँग छाता थिएन अनि म भिजें ।

४ हजुरबाका दुईजना छोरा थिए । एकजनाको नाम प्रकाश थियो, र एकजनाको नाम निरोज थियो । प्रकाश धेरै धनी हुनुभयो तर निरोज धेरै गरीब हुनुहुन्थ्यो ।

५ त्यो देशका मानिसहरू धेरै गरीब थिए अनि उनीहरूका घरहरूमा केही पनि थिएन ।

६ हिजो धेरै मानिसहरू पशुपतिनाथको मन्दिर गए, किनभने हिजो पूर्णिमा थियो ।

29

१ हिजो तपाईंले चिया खानुभएन ?

२ हिजो मैले एउटा किताब किनें ।

३ हिजो हामीहरूले मासु खाएनौं ।

४ हिजो उनीहरूले भात खाएनन् । उनीहरूको घरमा चामल थिएन ।

५ हिजो तिमीले रेडियो किन सुनेनौ ? हिजो अम्बर गुरुङगले गीत गाउनुभयो ।

६ हिजो आमा उठ्नुभएन । वहाँ बिरामी हुनुहुन्थ्यो ।

30

१ अस्ति शनिवार थियो ।

२ अस्ति ठूलो पानी पर्‍यो ।

३ उसले एउटा किताब पढ्यो ।

४ हिजो आइतबार थियो ।

५ हिजो राम अफिस गयो ।

६ हिजो रामकी आमा मन्दिर जानुभयो ।

७ राम र माया साढे छ बजेसम्म सुते ।

31

१ म नेपाल गएर तपाईंलाई चिठी लेख्छु ।

२ म विचार गरेर तपाईंलाई भन्छु ।

३ उनीहरू किताब किनेर तपाईंकहाँ आउँछन् ।

४ यो केटी स्कूल गएर अँग्रेजी सिक्छे ।

५ म अफिस गएर तपाईंलाई फोन गर्छु ।

६ वहाँ झापा गएर मेरो दाइको घरमा बस्नुभयो ।

32

१ तिमी घर गएर काम गर ।

२ तपाईं रेडियो सुनेर घर जानुहोस् ।

३ तिमी चुरोट लिएर आऊ ।

४ तपाईं यो किताब पढेर मलाई दिनुहोस् ।

५ तिमी लण्डन पुगेर मकहाँ आऊ ।

६ तपाईं झापा गएर मेरो दाइको घरमा बस्नुहोस् ।

33

१ तपाईं अखबार पढ्दै हुनुहुन्छ ?

२ भाइ किताब पढ्दै छ ।

३ म बाहिर जाँदै छु ।

४ उनीहरू नेपाली भाषा बोल्दै छन् ।

५ अब ऊ त्यही कलमले चिठी लेख्दै छ ।

34

१ बुवा अखबार पढ्दै हुनुहुन्थ्यो ।

२ तिमी त्यो किताब पढ्दै थियौ ?

३ म जापानी भाषा सिक्दै थिएँ ।

४ उनीहरू टी० भी० हेर्दै थिए ।

५ बुवा बारीमा के गर्दै हुनुहुन्थ्यो ?

35

उनका छोराहरूले भात नखाईकन चिठी लेखे ।

मेरी आमाले भात नखाईकन चिठी लेख्नुभयो ।

तिमीले भात नखाईकन चिठी लेख्यौ ।

रामेले भात नखाईकन चिठी लेख्यो ।

रामेकी दिदीले भात नखाईकन चिठी लेखिन् ।

मैले भात नखाईकन चिठी लेखें ।

उनका छोराहरू भात नखाईकन मन्दिर गए ।

मेरी आमा भात नखाईकन मन्दिर जानुभयो ।

तिमी भात नखाईकन मन्दिर गयौ ।

रामे भात नखाईकन मन्दिर गयो ।

रामेकी दिदी भात नखाईकन मन्दिर गइन् ।

म भात नखाईकन मन्दिर गएँ ।

36

१ पाइन्छ । दिल बहादुरको पसलमा तरकारी पाइन्छ ।

२ रातो आलुको दाम किलोको आठ रुपियाँ हो ।

३ सेतो आलुको दाम किलोको छ रुपियाँ हो ।

४ पाइँदैन । दिल बहादुरको पसलमा मासु पाइँदैन ।

५ मासु खिचापोखरीमा पाइन्छ ।

६ अञ्जलीलाई खुर्सानी चाहिँदैन ।

37

मान्छेहरूलाई पानी चाहिन्छ ।

मान्छेहरूलाई हावा चाहिन्छ ।

मान्छेहरूलाई घाँसपात चाहिँदैन ।

मान्छेहरूलाई शिक्षा चाहिन्छ ।

मान्छेहरूलाई बिजुली चाहिन्छ ।

भैंसीहरूलाई पानी चाहिन्छ ।

भैंसीहरूलाई हावा चाहिन्छ ।

भैंसीहरूलाई घाँसपात चाहिन्छ ।

भैंसीहरूलाई शिक्षा चाहिँदैन ।

भैंसीहरूलाई बिजुली चाहिँदैन ।

38

१ तपाईंलाई तिर्खा लाग्यो ।

२ दिदीलाई भोक लाग्यो ।

३ रामेकी बहिनीलाई दुःख लाग्यो ।

४ मेरो दाइलाई दिसा लाग्यो ।

५ बुवालाई थकाइ लाग्यो ।

६ तिमीलाई जाडो लाग्यो ।

७ हामीलाई रुघा लाग्यो ।

८ रामेलाई रक्सी लाग्यो ।

९ वहाँलाई डर लाग्यो

१० छोरालाई निद्रा लाग्यो ।

११ केटीलाई लाज लाग्यो ।

१२ मलाई खोकी लाग्यो ।

39

१ मलाई त्यो गीत मीठो लागेन ।

२ रामेकी आमालाई उसको गाउँ अनौठो लागेन ।

३ उनीहरूलाई जापानी भाषा गाह्रो लागेन ।

४ बुवालाई भारत राम्रो लागेन ।

५ मेरो भाइलाई नेपाली भाषा सजिलो लागेन ।

40

१ मलाई तिर्खा लागेन ।

२ मेरो भाइले एउटा किताब किन्यो ।

३ उसलाई मेरो घर राम्रो लाग्यो ।

४ मेरी आमालाई थकाइ लाग्यो ।

५ हामीहरूले गीत गायौं ।

६ उसले दाहिने हातले भात खायो ।

७ वहाँलाई चार बजेतिर सधैं निद्रा लाग्छ ।

८ तपाईलाई पोखरा कस्तो लाग्यो ?

९ मलाई रक्सी लागेन ।

१० हामीले धेरै रक्सी खायौं ।

41

१ मेरो झ्यालबाट हिमालय देखिन्छ ।

२ मगर भाषा पोखरातिर बोलिन्छ ।

३ तपाईंको स्वर यहाँ सुनिंदैन ।

४ तिम्रो गाउँ एक घण्टामा पुगिंदैन ।

५ भनिन्छ त्यो घरमा बोक्सी छ ।

६ भोटमा नेपाली भाषा कहिलेकाहीं बुझिन्छ ।

७ बिस्तारै हिँड्नुहोस् है । अब गाउँ सजिलै पुगिन्छ ।

८ तपाईंको छोरालाई भेटेर मलाई खुशी लाग्यो । मलाई त्यो धेरै चलाक केटा जस्तो लाग्यो ।

42

१ दाजु दार्जीलिङ्ग जानुभएको छ ।

२ भाउज्यु काठ्माडौंमा बस्नुभएको छ ।

३ तपाईंको घरमा कोही आयो ? तिम्रो भाइ आएको छ, तर ऊबाहेक कोही आएको छैन ।

४ पानी अहिलेसम्म उम्लेको छैन ।

५ मैले तिम्रो लुगा धोबीलाई दिएको छु ।

६ उसले पाँचवटा नयाँ किताब किनेको छ ।

43

१ अँ, जानुभयो ।	अहँ, जानुभएको छैन ।
२ अँ, आउनुभयो ।	अहँ, आउनुभएको छैन ।
३ अँ, आयो ।	अहँ, आएको छैन ।
४ अँ, खाएँ ।	अहँ, खाएको छैन ।

44

घडी न० १ मा एघार बज्यो ।

घडी न० २ मा साढे तीन बज्यो ।

घडी न० ३ मा पौने आठ बज्यो ।

घडी न० १ मा साढे दस बजेको छैन । एघार बजेको छ ।

घडी न० २ बाह्र बजेको छैन । साढे तीन बजेको छ ।

45

१ मेरो बुवा कहिल्यै विदेश जानुभएको थिएन ।

२ १९७८ मा म पहिलो पटक नेपाल गएको थिएँ ।

३ उनीहरू बस बिसौनीमा बसेका थिए तर बस आएको थिएन ।

४ पानी परेको थियो तर रामेले छाता ल्याएको थिएन ।

५ उसको टाउनो दुखेको थियो तर उसले औषधि खाएको थिएन ।

६ उनीहरू इलामबाट आएका थिए तर उनीहरूले चिया ल्याएका थिएनन् ।

46

१ मेरा भाइले आज पानी पर्दैन भनेर बुवालाई भन्यो ।

२ त्यो अग्लो मान्छेले तिमी अँग्रेज हौ कि भनेर मलाई सोध्यो ।

३ आमाले तिम्रो साथीलाई भोक लाग्यो कि भनेर मेरी दिदीसँग सोध्नुभयो ।

४ शिक्षकले किताबहरू बन्द गर भनेर बच्चाहरूलाई अह्राउनुभयो ।

५ बुवाले भोलि बाहिर नजाऊ भनेर हामीलाई सल्लाह दिनुभयो ।

47

१ (तपाईंले) धेरै पियो खाना खानुभएकोले तपाईंलाई दिसा लाग्यो ।

२ (वहाँको) पेट दुखेकोले वहाँ स्कूल जानुभएन ।

३ (बाहिर) गर्मी भएकोले हामी बाहिर जाँदैनौं ।

४ (ऊसँग) कलम नभएकोले उसले चिठी लेखेन ।

५ (उनको) श्रीमान बिरामी हुनुभएकोले उनलाई दुख लाग्यो ।

48

१ हिजो आएका पाहुनाहरू सबै अँग्रेज हुन् ।

२ बाहिर पानी परेको छ । तिमीले गएको हप्ता बजारमा किनेको छाता लिएर जाऊ ।

३ तिमी नेपाल पुगेको महिना बैसाख हो ।

४ म नेपाल आएको यो दसौं पटक हो ।

५ तपाईंहरू बस्नुभएको घर धेरै पुरानौ छ ।

६ अस्ति शुक्रवार मैले तपाईंले लेख्नुभएको चिठी पाएको थिइनँ ।

७ ऊ भारतबाट आएको मान्छे (त) होइन ।

८ यो तिमीले आमालाई दिएको उपहार होइन ।

49

१ हिजो उनले उसले ताश खेलेको देखिन् ।

२ गएको महिना मैले उनले त्यो गीत गाएको सुनें ।

३ तीन दिन अघि उसले वहाँलाई घर आएको देख्यो ।

४ अस्ति बुधवार मैले तिमीले चुरोट खाएको देखें ।

५ गएको हप्ता वहाँले उनले हिन्दी बोलेको सुन्नुभयो ।

६ अस्ति उनीहरूले तिमीलाई स्कूल गएको देखे ।

50

१ अँग्रेजीमा पुल भनेको *bridge* हो ।

२ अँग्रेजीमा ओरालो भनेको *downhill* हो ।

३ अँग्रेजीमा हैजा भनेको *cholera* हो ।

४ नेपालीमा *letter* भनेको चिठी अथवा अक्षर हो ।

५ नेपालीमा *face* भनेको मुख अथवा अनुहार हो ।

६ नेपालीमा *month* भनेको महिना हो ।

51

१ बिहिवार, १० जनवरी १६२१

२ २०१६ साल चैत्र १० गते, मङ्गलवार

३ आइतवार, २६ नोवेम्बर १६५६

४ २०४२ साल फाल्गुण १ गते, शुक्रवार

52

१ सुरेन्द्रको दाइ जापान गएको दुई वर्ष भयो ।

२ सुरेन्द्रको दाइले जापानबाट एउटा राम्रो रेडियो पठाउनुभयो ।

३ दाइले दिएका क्यामेरा र रेडियो दुवै जापानमा बनेका हुन् । त्यसै कारण बलिया र राम्रा छन् ।

४ सुरेन्द्रको काका दार्जीलिङ्गबाट आउनुभएको थियो ।

५ सुरेन्द्रलाई एउटा क्यामरा मात्रै चाहिन्छ ।

६ किनभने सुरेन्द्रले काकाले दिएको क्यामेरा एउटा साथीलाई बेचेको छ ।

53

१ यदि (तपाईंलाई) थकाइ लाग्यो भने आराम गर्नुहोस् ।

२ यदि (तपाईंलाई) तिर्खा लाग्यो भने यो पानी खानुहोस् ।

३ यदि हाम्रा पाहुनाहरूलाई भोक लाग्यो भने म बजार गएर फलफुल र तरकारी किन्छु ।

४ यदि तिमी भोलि आएनौ भने आमा घरै बसैर रुनुहुन्छ ।

५ यदि म पाँच बजेसम्म अफिसमा आइनँ भने मलाई मन्दिरमा भेट्नुहोस् ।

६ यदि यो हप्ता बुवाले मलाई चिठी पठाउनुभएन भने म वहाँलाई घरमा फोन गर्छु ।

54

१. हिजो आएका पर्यटकहरूलाई यति खानाले पुग्यो ।

२. हामीलाई मदत गरेको शेर्पालाई दस रुपियाँले पुगेन ।

३. खाना पकाएकी आइमाईलाई एक किलो घिउले पुगेन ।

55

१ भोलि आउने पर्यटकहरूलाई यति खानाले पुग्दैन होला ।

२ हामीलाई मदत गर्ने शेर्पालाई दस रुपियाँले पुग्छ होला ।

३ खाना पकाउने आइमाईलाई एक किलो घिउले पुग्छ होला ।

56

१ भोलि मौसम साह्रै राम्रो होला ।

२ भोलि दिल्लीबाट काठ्माडौं पुग्न दुई घण्टा जति लाग्ला ।

३ भोलि नानीहरू खेतमा फुटबल खेल्लान् । उनीहरूको लुगामा हिलो लाग्ला ।

४ भोलि सीताले घर राम्रोसँग सफा गर्लिन् ।

५ भोलि दिदीले भात नपकाउलिन् दाइले पकाउलान् ।

६ भोलि घरमा पाहुनाहरू भएको कारणले उनीहरू स्कूल नआउलान् ।

57

लण्डनबाट नेपाल जान पाँच सय पाउण्ड लाग्छ र काठ्माडौं पुग्न पन्ध्र घण्टा लाग्छ । म विमानस्थलमा सधैं एउटा चाखलाग्दो किताब किन्छु । पोहोर साल नेपाल गएको बेलामा मैले एउटा मोटो उपन्यास किनें अनि यो पढ्न मलाई करीब दस घण्टा लाग्यो । म आउने साल फेरि नेपाल जान्छु होला अनि यस पालि चाहिं दुइटा उपन्यास किन्छु होला । नेपालमा म भद्रपुर गएँ । काठ्माडौंबाट बसमा जानुभयो भने एकदम सस्तो हुन्छ तर त्यहाँ पुग्न पूरै एक दिन लाग्छ । भद्रपुर जाने बसमा धेरै मान्छेहरू थिए अनि भद्रपुर जाने बाटो साह्रै खराब थियो । मैले त्यो यात्राको लागि कुनै किताब किनिन किनभने म एक-दुईजना नेपाली साथीहरूसँग गएको थिएँ । तपाईं भद्रपुर हवाईजहाजबाट जानुभयो भने धेरै पैसा लाग्छ तर समय धेरै लाग्दैन । भद्रपुर जाने हवाईजहाज हरेक बिहान दस बजे राजधानीबाट उड्छ । म अर्को साल फेरि भद्रपुर गए भने हवाईजहाजबाटै जान्छु होला ।

58

१ हामीले ईश्वरलाई पूजा गर्नुपर्छ ।

२ मेरो भाइले हरेक दिन दाल भात खानुपर्छ ।

३ आज बिदा हो, हामीहरू अफिसमा जानुपर्दैन ।

४ उनीहरूले हामीलाई त्यो कथा सुनाउनुपर्दैन ।

५ सीताले घर सफा गर्नुपर्दैन । त्यो काम एउटा नोकरले गर्नुपर्छ ।

६ आज मैले भात पकाउनुपर्दैन । मेरो श्रीमानले पकाउनुपर्छ ।

59

१ अब बुवा पशुपतिनाथको मन्दिर जानुपर्‍यो ।

२ अब तिमीले अलिकति भात खानुपर्‍यो ।

३ अब मचाँडै सुत्नुपर्‍यो ।

४ हिजो मैले धेरै काम गर्नुपरेन ।

५ हिजो किसानहरू खेतमा जानुपरेन ।

६ हिजो आमाबजार जानुपरेन ।

60

१ आमाले मेरा साथीहरूलाई हाम्रो घरमा रक्सी खान दिनुहुन्न ।

२ उनीहरूले हामीलाई मन्दिरभित्र जान दिन्छन् ।

३ दाजुले बच्चाहरूलाई बिहान टी० भी० हेर्न दिनुहुन्छ ।

४ बुवाले हामीलाई बेलुका बाहिर जान दिनुहुन्न ।

५ तपाईं पर्यटकहरूलाई मन्दिरमा जुत्ता लाउन दिनुहुन्छ ?

61

(A) यो कुन देवताको मन्दिर हो ? भित्र जान हुन्छ ?

(B) यो गणेशको मन्दिर हो । भित्र जान हुन्छ तर जुत्ता खोल्नुपर्छ ।

(A) यो धेरै पुरानो मन्दिर हो ?

(B) हो, धेरै पुरानो हो । मान्छेहरू हरेक दिन बिहान आएर गणेशको पूजा गर्छन् ।

(A) उनीहरूलाई हरेक बिहान किन आउनुपर्छ ?

(B) आउनुपर्दैन तर हरेक दिन यहाँ आउनु राम्रो हो । तपाईंले हरेक दिन गणेशको पूजा गर्नुभयो भने तपाईंको दिन सफल हुन्छ । त्यो हाम्रो एउटा विश्वास हो ।

(A) अब मैले के गर्नुपर्छ त ?

(B) तपाईंले भगवानको दर्शन गर्नुभयो, राम्रो भयो । मन्दिरको लागि अलिकति पैसा दिनुहोस् ।

(A) मसँग त्यति पैसा छैन । तर दस रुपियाँ दिन हुन्छ होला ?

(B) हुन्छ, ठीक छ । ल, आउनुहोस्, ढिलो भयो । अब हामीलाई पशुपतिको मन्दिर जानुपर्छ । त्यति टाढा छैन । हामी हिँड्यौं भने आधा घण्टामा पुगिन्छ ।

(A) पशुपतिको मन्दिरमा कुन देवताको पूजा हुन्छ ?

(B) त्यहाँ शिवजीको पूजा हुन्छ ।

62

१ म नेपाली बोल्न सक्छु ।

२ म नेपाली खाना पकाउन सक्छु ।

३ म यो किताब बुझ्न सक्छु ।

४ उनी नेपाली बोल्न सक्छिन् ।

५ उनी नेपाली खाना पकाउन सक्छिन् ।

६ उनी यो किताब बुझ्न सक्छिन् ।

७ तपाईं नेपाली बोल्न सक्नुहुन्छ ।

८ तपाईं नेपाली खाना पकाउन सक्नुहुन्छ ।

९ तपाईं यो किताब बुझ्न सक्नुहुन्छ ।

63

१. उसले हिजो सगरमाथा चढ्न पायो ।

२. उसले हिजो फोन गर्न पायो ।

३. उसले हिजो गुन्द्रुक खान पायो ।

४. उनीहरूले हिजो सगरमाथा चढ्न पाए ।

५. उनीहरूले हिजो फोन गर्न पाए ।

६. उनीहरूले हिजो गुन्द्रुक खान पाए ।

७. तिमीले हिजो सगरमाथा चढ्न पायौ ।

८. तिमीले हिजो फोन गर्न पायौ ।

९. तिमीले हिजो गुन्द्रुक खान पायौ ।

64

दुई हप्ता अघि मेरी दिदीको बिहा भयो । अहिले वहाँ धुलिखेलमा बस्नुहुन्छ । धुलिखेल भक्तपुरबाट झण्डै दस माइल टाढा छ । अस्ति आइतवार हामीहरू भिनाज्यू र दिदीको नयाँ परिवारलाई भेट्न गएका थियौं । धुलिखेल जान (लाई) हामीहरूले रत्न पार्कसम्म ट्याक्सी लिनुपर्‍यो । रत्न पार्कमा पाँचखाल जाने बस चढ्नुपर्‍यो । धुलिखेल पाँचखाल जाने बाटोमा पर्छ । रत्न पार्क पुगेपछि बुवालाई एउटा पसलमा जानुपर्‍यो । वहाँले उपहार किन्न बिर्सनुभएको थियो । बुवालाई लुगा, मिठाई र चुरा किन्न तीनवटा पसलमा जानुपर्‍यो । अलि ढिलो हुन लागेकोले आमालाई अलि चिन्ता लाग्न थाल्यो । तर धुलिखेल पुग्न एक घण्टा मात्रै लाग्छ अनि बसहरू एक एक घण्टामा छुट्छन् । बुवाले उपहारहरू किन्नुभएपछि हामीहरूले धुलिखेल जाने बस खोज्न थाल्यौं । एउटा नयाँ नीलो बसको छेउमा उभिएको मान्छे पाँचखाल पाँचखाल भनेर कराउन थालेको थियो । बुवा हाम्रो टिकट किन्न अफिसमा जानुभयो । बुवा टिकट लिएर फर्किनुभन्दा पहिला नै यो बस धुलिखेल जाने हो कि भनेर मैले चालकलाई सोधें । जाने हो भनेर उसले भन्यो । धुलिखेल नजाने कुरै छैन किनभने त्यहाँ राम्रो होटेल छ भनेर उसले भन्यो । धुलिखेलबाट पाँचखालको लागि बस जानुभन्दा पहिला नै सबै यात्रुहरू बिहानको खाना त्यहीं खान्छन् भनेर भन्यो । अकस्मात् पानी पर्न थाल्यो अनि हामीले बसभित्र बस्ने ठाउँ पायौं । केही मिनेटपछि हाम्रो यात्रा शुरु भयो ।

65

१ नेपालीहरू तराई क्षेत्रलाई मदेस भन्छन् ।

२ नेपाली भाषाबाहेक तराई क्षेत्रमा मैथिली, भोजपुरी, अवधी, थारू र अन्य भाषाहरू बोलिन्छन् ।

३ पहाडी क्षेत्रको जमीन प्राय जसो उकालो र ओरालो हुन्छ ।

४ नेपाली भाषाबाहेक पहाडी क्षेत्रमा नेवारी, गुरुङ्ग, मगर, लिम्बू, तामाङ्ग र राई जस्ता भोट-बर्मेली भाषाहरू बोलिन्छन् ।

५ नेपालका नदीहरूमध्ये कर्णाली, गण्डकी र कोशी महत्त्वपूर्ण छन् ।

६ घर पुग्नलाई धेरैजसो नेपालीहरू हिँड्नैपर्छ ।

66

१ यस गाउँका किसानहरू धान रोप्दैनथे । उनीहरू मकै रोप्थे ।

२ भात खाएपछि हामीले हात-मुख धुनुपर्थ्यो ।

३ चियापसलमा चिया पनि पाइन्थ्यो, खाने कुरा पनि पाइन्थ्यो ।

४ तिमी भारत गएर के काम गर्थ्यौ ? म चौकिदारको काम गर्थें ।

५ दाइहरू जुम्लामा बस्नुहुन्नथ्यो, दैलेखमा बस्नुहुन्थ्यो ।

६ म हरेक हप्ता उसलाई एउटा लामो चिठी लेख्थें ।

67

म पनौती भन्ने एउटा सानो शहरमा मेरो बुवा-आमासँग बस्थें । पनौती काठ्माडौं उपत्यकाको दक्षिण-पूर्व कुनामा पर्छ । म त्यहाँको एउटा सानो स्कूलमा पढ्थें । म एघार वर्ष पुग्नेबित्तिकै मैले त्यो सानो स्कूल छाड्नुपर्‍यो । त्यो बेलादेखि मैले भक्तपुर भन्ने शहरको एउटा ठूलो स्कूलमा पढ्नुपर्‍यो । मैले हरेक बिहान सात बजे बस लिनुपर्थ्यो । मेरा धेरैजसो साथीहरू पनि त्यही बसबाट जान्थे । साँझमा फर्किंदाखेरि हामीहरू गीत गाउँथ्यौं अनि पनौती आइपुगेपछि धेरै खुशी हुन्थ्यौं । मेरो घरभन्दा तल एउटा ठूलो नदी थियो । गर्मी महिनामा घर पुग्नेबित्तिकै हामी त्यो नदीमा पौडी खेल्न जान्थ्यौं । कहिलेकाहीं मेरा स्कूलका लुगाहरू भिज्थे अनि आमा रिसाउनुहुन्थ्यो । म घर आउनेबित्तिकै वहाँले ती लुगा धुनुपर्थ्यो अनि सुकाउन गाह्रो हुन्थ्यो । तर शनिवार बिदा भएको कारणले आमा मलाई शुक्रवार पौडी खेल्न दिनुहुन्थ्यो । भक्तपुरको ठूलो स्कूलमा पढ्दाखेरि मैले ठूलो भएपछि शिक्षक बन्ने निधो गरें । शिक्षक बन्ने आशाले मैले राम्ररी पढें । स्कूल छाड्नेबित्तिकै म त्रिभुवन विश्वविद्यालयमा पढ्न गएँ अनि हिजोआज म काठ्माडौंमा बस्छु । केही दिनपछि मैले मेरो अन्तिम परिक्षा दिनुपर्छ । अझै पनि मेरो शिक्षक बन्ने आशा छ । परिक्षामा सफल भएँ भने एउटा जागिर खोज्नुपर्ला ।

68

१ तपाईंको छोरा चाँडै निको होओस् ।

२ भोलि हामीहरू फिलिम हेर्न पोखरा जाऔं ?

३ हामीहरू तपाईंकी आमालाई के भनौं ?

४ तपाईंको जिन्दगी सुखी होओस् ।

५ आजको बस ढिलो होओस् ।

६ म तपाईंकहाँ कति बजे आऊँ ?

69

१ मलाई भोक लागेको भए म खपाखप भात खान्थें ।

२ पानी नपरेको भए उनीहरू भात खान आउँथे ।

३ पहाडमा खोलाहरू नभएको भए हाम्रो घरमा बिजुली हुँदैनथ्यो ।

४ बेलामा औषधि खाएको भए त्यो मान्छे अकालै मर्दैनथ्यो ।

५ साथीले गीत गाएको भए बेलुका झन रमाइलो हुन्थ्यो ।

1 If I had been hungry I would have eaten voraciously.

2 If it had not rained they would have come for a meal.

3 If there were no streams in the hills there would not be electricity in our house.

4 If he had taken the medicine on time that man would not have died an untimely death.

5 If a friend had sung a song the evening would have been even more enjoyable.

70

आज केही चिनेका मान्छेहरू हाम्रो घरमा साँझ छ बजेतिर खाना खान आउँदै छन् । म चार बजे विश्वविद्यालयबाट घर फर्किन्छु त घर रित्तै रहेछ ! अनि झोलामा साँचो छ कि भनेर हेर्छु त झोला पनि रित्तै रहेछ । साँचो कहाँ गयो होला त ? म सबै ठाउँमा खोज्छु तर पाउँदिन । भान्से साढे तीन बजे आउनुपर्थ्यो तर

अहिलेसम्म आएको छैन । सायद घरमा त आइसकेको होला तर पसलतिर गयो होला । घरमा चार बजेसम्म बसेको भए त यो समस्या आउने थिएन । झ्याल फोडेर भित्र जाऊँ कि ? विश्वविद्यालयमा फर्केर अफिसमा गएर साँचो खोजूँ कि ? खै, के गरूँ ? ल भान्से पनि आइपुगेछ । साँचो उसको हातमा रहेछ । मैले झ्याल फोडेको भए मेरो श्रीमानले मलाई गाली गर्नुहुन्थ्यो । सवा चार बजिसकेछ । ऊ मेरो लागि ढोका खोलिदिन्छ । श्रीमानलाई फोन गरेर अलिक छिटो घर आउनुहोस् भनूँ कि ? खै, के गरूँ ? पर्दैन होला । भान्सेले सबै खाना किनिसकेको छ । अब हामीलाई खाना पकाइदिन्छ ।

71

१ उनीहरू जाँड-रक्सी धेरै पिइरहेका थिए ।

२ गोपाल राम्रा राम्रा गीत गाइरहेको थियो ।

३ मेरो भाइ टाढाको एउटा स्कूलमा गइरहेको छ ।

४ खैरेनीबाट काठ्माडौंमा धेरै तरकारी आइरहेको छ ।

५ म यहाँबाट कीर्तिपुरसम्म हिंडेर गइरहेको थिएँ ।

72

१ भोक नलागे म खाजा नखाउँला ।

२ थकाइ लागे म आराम गरुँला ।

३ काठ्माडौं छाडेर जान मन नलागे काठ्माडौंमै बसुँला ।

४ नेपाली सिक्न गाह्रो लागे र हिन्दी सिक्न पनि गाह्रो लागे जापानी सिकुँला ।

५ गुन्द्रुक मीठो नलागे र आलु-तामा पनि मीठो नलागे कालो दाल खाउँला ।

73

म हिजो दाइसँग विमानस्थल गएँ । दिल्लीबाट हामीकहाँ बस्न केही पाहुनाहरू आइरहेका थिए । बिहानै हामीहरूले नेपाल एयरलाइन्स अफिसमा फोन गरेका थियौं अनि एउटी आइमाईले दिल्लीबाट विमान दिउँसो तीन बजे आइपुग्छ भनेर भनेकी थिइन् । त्यसो भए हामीले ठीक साढे दुई बजे घर छोड्नुपर्छ भनेर दाइले भन्नुभयो । विमानस्थलमा पुग्नेबित्तिकै दाइले विमानको बारेमा त्यहाँको कर्मचारीसँग सोध्नुभयो । मौसम खराब भएकोले विमान भरखरै मात्रै दिल्लीबाट उडेको छ भनेर कर्मचारीले दाइलाई भन्यो । त्यसो भए हामीहरूले कति बेरसम्म पर्खनुपर्ला भनेर दाइले सोध्नुभयो । अब नेपालतिर उडिरहेको छ एक घण्टाभित्र आइपुग्छ भनेर कर्मचारीले भने । हवाईजहाज ढिलो भयो र हामीले यहाँ पर्खनैपर्ला भनेर दाइले भन्नुभयो । तर बुवा-आमा घरमा पर्खिरहनुभएको छ भनेर मैले भनें, हजाई जहाज ढिलो भएको कुरा वहाँहरूलाई थाहा छैन नि । तिमी गएर वहाँहरूलाई फोन गर भनेर दाइले भन्नुभयो । हामीहरू हवाईजहाज आइपुगेपछि घर सीधै आउँछौं भनेर भनिदेऊ ।

Nepali–English glossary

Words marked* are transitive verbs.

अ	
अँ	yes
अँग्रेज	English
अँग्रेजी	English language
अँध्यारो	dark, darkness
अकालै	untimely
अक्षर	letter of alphabet
अखबार	newspaper
अग्लो	tall, high
अघि	ago, before
अचार	pickle
अङ्खोरा	jug, steel cup
अझ पनि	yet, still
अञ्चल	administrative zone
अटाउनु	to fit into a space
अढाई	two and a half
अथवा	or
अदुवा	ginger
अधिकृत	official
अनि	and, then
अनिकाल	famine
अनुचित	inappropriate
अनुभव	experience
अनुमति	permission
अनुसार	according to
अनुहार	face
अनौठो	strange, odd
अन्तिम	final, last
अपढ	illiterate
अपराध	crime, offence
अप्ठ्यारो	difficult, awkward
अफिस	office
अब	now, from now
अबेर	late, lateness
अभाव	lack, absence
अभ्यास गर्नु*	to practise
अमेरिकाली	American
अम्बा	guava
अम्रीकन	American
अरब	Arabia; the Middle East
अरू	other, more
अर्को	another, next
अर्थ	meaning
अलपत्र	untidy
अलि	quite, rather
अलिक	slightly
अलिकति	a small amount of
अलिपछि	after a little while
अवधी	Awadhi (language)
अवश्य	certainly
असफल	unsuccessful
असल	of good character
असाध्दै	extremely, very
असार (आषाढ)	third month of the Nepali year
असुविधा	inconvenience

असोज (आश्विन)	sixth month of the Nepali year
अस्ति	the day before yesterday; last week
अस्पताल	hospital
अहँ	no
अहिले	now
अहिलेसम्म	yet
अह्राउनु*	to order, command

आ

आँखा	eye
आँगन	courtyard
आँप	mango
आँसु	tear, tears
आइतवार	Sunday
आइपुग्नु	to arrive
आइमाई	woman
आउनु	to come
आकाँक्षा	ambition
आकाश	sky
आखिर	in the end, after all
आगो	fire
आज	today
आजकाल	nowadays
आठ	eight
आठौं	eighth
आत्मा	soul
आदर गर्नु*	to respect
आधा	half
आफू	oneself
आफै	oneself (emphasized)
आफ्नो	one's own
आमा	mother
आराम, आरामै	in good health
आराम गर्नु*	to rest
आलु	potato
आलु-तामा	potatoes and bamboo shoots
आवश्यक	necessary
आशा	hope

इ

इच्छा	wish, desire
इतिहास	history
इनार	well
इमान	honesty
इस्लामी	Islamic

ई

ईश्वर	the Lord; God

उ

उकालो	uphill; steep
उकुस-मुकुस	feeling of suffocation
उखान	proverb
उचाइ	height
उच्चारण	pronunciation
उठ्नु	to get up
उड्नु	to fly
उता	there, over there
उत्तर	north
उदाहरण	example
उनी	s/he (Middle)
उनीहरू	they (Middle)
उपत्यका	valley
उपन्यास	novel
उपयोगी	useful
उपहार	gift

उपाय	means
उभिनु	to be standing up
उमाल्नु*	to boil
उमेर	age
उम्लनु	to come to the boil
उसरी	in that manner
उसो	in that manner
उहाँ	see वहाँ

ऊ

ऊ	s/he (Low)

ए

ए	hey, oh, I see
एउटा	one, a
एक	one
एकदम	absolutely
एकनाले	single-barrelled
एकमात्र	one and only
एक्लै	alone

ओ

ओढ्ने	quilt
ओत	shelter from rain
ओरालो	downhill; steep

औ

औंला	finger, toe
औलो	malaria
औषधि	medicine

क

कक्षा	class
कण्डक्टर	conductor
कता	where? to where?
कता-न-कता	somewhere or other
कति	how many? how much?
कतिजना	how many people?
कतिवटा	how many things?
कतै	anywhere
कत्रो	how big?
कथा	story
कप	cup
कपडा	cloth
कपाल	hair (of the head)
कफी	coffee
कम	rarely, less, few
कमलपित्त	jaundice
कमिज	shirt
कम्तिमा	at least
कम्मर	waist
कराउनु	to shout, make a loud noise
करीब	approximately
करोड	ten million
कलकल	sound of running water
कलम	pen
कलिलो	young, tender
कलेज	college
कल्पना गर्नु*	to imagine
कविता	poem, poetry
कसको	whose?
कसरी	in what manner? how?
कसो?	in what manner? how?
कस्तो	like what? how?
कहाँ?	where?
-कहाँ	at the home of
कहिले?	when?
कहिलेकाहीं	sometimes

कहिल्यै	ever
कहीं	somewhere
काँक्रो	cucumber
काँटा	fork
काँध	shoulder
काउली	cauliflower
काका	younger paternal uncle
कागज	paper
कागती	lime
काट्नु*	to cut, to kill
कात्तिक (कार्त्तिक)	seventh month of the Nepali year
कान	ear
कान्छी	youngest girl
कान्छो	youngest boy
काम	work
काम गर्नु*	to work
कारण	reason
कार्यक्रम	programme
कालो	black
काहिंलो	fourth eldest
कि	or
किताब	book
किन	why?
किनभने	because
किनमेल	shopping
किन्नु*	to buy
किलो	kilogramme
किलोमिटर	kilometre
किसान	farmer
किसिम	type, kind
कीरा	insect, worm
कुखुरा	chicken
कुन	which?
कुनचाहिं	which one?
कुन्नि	I don't know
कुर्सी	chair
कुरा	thing, matter, talk
कुरा गर्नु*	to talk, converse
कुरुवा	a measure of weight equal to two **mānās**
कुर्कुच्चा	heel
कुर्नु	to wait for
कुवा	well
कुहिनो	elbow
कृपा	kindness, favour
के	what?
केन्द्र	centre
केटा	boy
केटी	girl
केरा	banana
केही	some, something
केही-न-केही	something or other
को	who?
कोट	coat
कोठा	room
-को दाँजोमा	compared with
कोदो	millet
-को लागि	for
कोसिस गर्नु*	to try
कोस	approximately two miles
कोसेली	gift
क्यामेरा	camera
क्यारे	I guess, I suppose
क्षमा	forgiveness

क्षमा गर्नु*	to forgive
क्षेत्र	area, region

ख

खतम गर्नु*	to stop
खतम हुनु	to end
खतरा	danger
खपाखप खानु*	to gobble up
खबर	news
खबर गर्नु*	to inform
खबरदार	beware!
खराब	bad
खल्ती	pocket
खसाल्नु*	to drop, post (a letter)
खसी	gelded goat
खस्नु	to fall; die
खाइनु	to be eaten
खाक	ash
खाजा	snack, light meal
खाना	food
खानु*	to eat, drink, consume
खाने कुरा	food
खाली	empty, only
खास	special, particular
खिच्नु*	to pull, take a photograph
खिल्ली	stick
खुकुरी	kukri knife
खुट्टा	leg, foot
खुर्सानी	chilli pepper
खुल्नु	to open
खुवाउनु*	to feed
खुशी	happy, happiness
खूब	very, thoroughly
खेत	irrigable field
खेती	farming, agriculture
खेतीपाती	farming, agriculture
खेल	game
खेल्नु*	to play
खै	well! what about?
खैरो	brown
खोइ	well! what about?
खोकी	cough
खोजी	search
खोज्नु*	to seek; try to
खोला	river, stream
खोला-नाला	rivers and streams
खोल्नु*	to open

ग

गजब	wonder, amazement
गट्टा खेल्नु*	to play a game with pebbles
गणित	mathematics
गते	day of a month in the Bikram calendar
गफ गर्नु*	to chat, converse
गरीब	poor
गर्नु*	to do
गर्मी	heat
गलत	wrong, incorrect
गहना	jewellery
गह्रुँगो	heavy
गाइड	guide
गाइने	minstrel
गाउँ	village
गाउनु*	to sing
गाग्री	water pitcher

गाडी	car, wheeled vehicle
गाली गर्नु*	to tell off
गाह्रो	difficult, hard
गीत	song
गुनासो	complaint
गुन्द्रुक	a traditional dish made from dried vegetables
गुरु	guru, teacher
गुरुङ्ग	Gurung (an ethnic group)
गोजी	pocket
गोलभेंडा	tomato
गौचर	cow pasture

घ

घटना	incident, event
घडी	watch, clock
घण्टा	hour, bell
घर	house, home
घरपति	landlord
घाँटी	throat, neck
घाट	steps beside river
घाँस	grass
घाम	sunshine
घिउ	ghee (clarified butter)
घुँडा	knee
घुमाउरो	indirect
घुम्नु	to turn, travel

च

चक्कु	knife
चढ्नु	to climb, mount
चना	chickpea
चन्द्रमा	moon
चम्चा	spoon
चराउनु*	to take to graze
चर्को	hot, loud
चर्पी	lavatory
चलाउनु*	to cause to move, drive
चल्नु	to move, go, function
चाँडै	quickly, immediately, early
चाँदी	silver
चानचुन	small change
चामल	uncooked rice
चार	four
चारौं	fourth
चाहनु*	to want to
चाहिनु	to be wanted, needed
चिउँडो	chin
चिउरा	parched/beaten rice
चिज	thing, item
चिठी	letter
चिनापर्ची	acquaintance
चिनियाँ	Chinese
चिनी	sugar
चिन्ता गर्नु*	to worry
चिन्नु*	to recognize, be acquainted with
चिप्लो	slippery
चिया	tea
चियापसल	teashop
चिया-सिया	tea and snacks
चिसो	cold, damp
चीन	China
चुरोट	cigarette
चूल्हो	stove, hearth
चैत (चैत्र)	twelfth month of the Nepali year
चोखो	pure, unsullied

चोटि	turn, time
चौकिदार	watchman, guard
चौथाई	one quarter
च्याउ	mushroom

छ

छक्क पर्नु	to be surprised
छर्लङ्ग	clearly
छाड्नु*	to leave, quit
छाता	umbrella
छाती	breast, chest
छाम्नु*	to feel with the hand
छायाँ	shade from the sun
छाला	skin
छिमेक	neighbourhood
छिमेकी	neighbour
छिटै	quickly
छिटो	quick, fast
छिन	moment
छुट्टिनु	to split, bifurcate
छुट्टी	time off work
छेउ	side
छैटौं	sixth
छोटो	short, brief
छोरा	son
छोराछोरी	sons and daughters
छोरी	daughter

ज

जंगल	jungle; uninhabited land
जटिल	complicated, difficult
जताततै	everywhere
जति	approximately, as much as
जनसंख्या	population
जन्म	birth
जन्मनु	to be born
जन्मस्थल	birthplace
जमीन	land
जम्मा	all together, in total
जम्मा हुनु	to gather, assemble
जर्मन	German
जलाउनु*	to burn
जवाफ	reply, answer
जसरी	in a similar manner to
जसो	in a similar manner to
जस्तो	similar to
जाँच	examination
जाँच्नु*	to examine
जाँड-रक्सी	alcoholic drink
जागिर	salaried job
जाडो	cold, coldness
जात	species, type, caste
जानिनु	to be known
जानु	to go
जान्नु*	to know
जिन्दगी	life
जिब्रो	tongue
जिल्ला	district
-जी	honorific suffix added to names
जीवन	life
जीवन-जल	diarrhoea remedy
जुत्ता	shoe, shoes
जूठो	impure, sullied, polluted
जे	that which
जेठ (ज्येष्ठ)	second month of the Nepali year

जेठो	eldest, elder
जोई	wife
जोर	pair
ज्यादा	more
-ज्यू	honorific suffix added to names

झ

झण्डै	almost
झन्	even more
झर्नु	to descend
झिक्नु*	to take out, extract
झिसमिसे	very early morning
झोला	bag
झ्याल	window

ट

टाउको	head
टाढा	distant, far
टिकट	ticket, postage stamp
टिप्नु*	to pick up
टी० भी०	TV
टुङ्गिनु	to come to an end
टुङ्ग्याउनु*	to bring to an end
टुप्लुक्क	suddenly, out of nowhere
टूरिष्ट	tourist
टेक्नु*	to stand, set down, rest on
टेबुल	table
टोक्नु*	to bite
टोपी	hat
टोल	town quarter
ट्याक्सी	taxi
ट्रक	truck

ठ

ठट्टा गर्नु*	to joke
ठाउँ	place
ठीक	fine, OK
ठूलो	big
ठेगाना	address

ड

डढ्नु	to scorch, burn
डर	fear
डलर	dollar
डाँडा	hill ridge
डाँफे	monal pheasant
डाक्टर	doctor
डाक्नु*	to summon, call for
डेढ	one and a half
डेरा	rented accommodation

ढ

ढिलो	slow, late, slack
ढोका	door, gate
ढोल	drum

त

तँ	you (Low)
त	but, though, however
तपाईं	you (High)
तयार	ready
तयार गर्नु*	to prepare
तर	but
तरकारी	vegetables
तराई	the Tarai region
तरुनी	young woman
तर्नु	to cross

तल	below, downwards
तलतल	craving
तथा	and
ताक्नु*	to take aim
तातो	hot
तामाङ्ग	Tamang (an ethnic group)
तारीख	day of a month in the western calendar
ताल्चा	door lock
ताश	cards
तिनी	s/he (Middle)
तिमी	you (Middle)
तिम्रो	your
-तिर	towards, near, at about
तिर्खा	thirst
तिर्नु*	to pay
ती	they, those
तीन	three
तीर्थस्थल	place of pilgrimage
तुरुन्त, तुरुन्तै	immediately
तेरो	your
तेल	oil, fuel
तेस्रो	third
त्यति	that much
त्यसरी	in that manner
त्यसो	in that manner
त्यस्तो	like that
त्यहाँ	there
त्यही	that very
त्यो	that

थ

थकाइ	tiredness
थप्नु*	to add, refill
थर	family name
थाक्नु	to become tired
थारु	Tharu (an ethnic group)
थाल्नु*	to begin, start to
थाहा	knowledge, information
थाहा पाउनु*	to find out
थियो	was
थुप्रै	lots of, heaps of
थोक	thing, matter

द

दक्षिण	south
दरबार	palace
दराज	drawer
दर्जा	class
दर्शन	sight, vision
दशक	decade
दस	ten
दसैं	Dasain festival
दसौं	tenth
दही	yoghurt
दाँत	tooth
दाइ	elder brother
दाउरा	firewood
दाजु	elder brother
दाज्यु	elder brother
दाह्री	beard
दाम	price
दाल	lentils
दालभात	lentils and rice
दाह-सँस्कार	funeral ceremony
दाहिने	right
दिउँसो	afternoon, daytime

दिदी	elder sister
दिन	day
दिनभरि	all day
दिनु*	to give
दिसा लाग्नु	to have diarrhoea
दुइटा	two (with non-human nouns)
दुई	two
दुईनाले	double-barrelled
दुख	sadness, pain, trouble
दुखी	sad, suffering
दुख्नु	to hurt
दुब्लो	thin
दुलहा	bridegroom
दुलही	bride
दुवै	both
दूध	milk
दूरदर्शन	Indian television service
दृश्य	view
देखाउनु*	to show
-देखि	from, since
देखिनु	to be seen, be visible
देख्नु*	to see
देब्रे	left
देवर	husband's younger brother
देवता	god, deity
देवी	goddess
देश	country
दोबाटो	crossroads
दोस्रो	second
दौडनु	to run
-द्वारा	by

ध

धनी	rich
धन्दा मान्नु*	to worry
धन्यवाद	thank you
धर्म	religion, righteousness
धर्मावलम्बी	religious adherent
दाग लाग्नु	to make a mark, stain
धान	growing rice
धारा	spring, watersource
धुनु*	to wash
धुम्रपान	smoking
धुवाँ	smoke
धूमधाम	pomp, splendour
धेरै	very, many
धेरैजसो	usually, mostly
धोबी	washerman
ध्यान दिनु*	to pay attention
ध्वनी	sound

न

न	negative particle
नक्सा	map
नगर पालिका	municipality, town council
नङ	fingernail
नजिक	close, nearby
नत्र	otherwise
नदी	river
नमस्कार	word of greeting
नमस्ते	word of greeting
नयाँ	new
नरमाइलो	unpleasant
नराम्रो	bad
नवौं	ninth

नाक	nose
नागरिक	citizen
नाति	grandson
नातिनी	granddaughter
नातेदार	relative
नानी	small child
नाफा गर्नु*	to make a profit
नाम	name
नि	you know; what about?
निकाल्नु*	to take out, extract
निको	well, healthy
निकै	very, extremely
निचोर्नु*	to press, squeeze
निदाउनु	to fall asleep
निद्रा	sleep, sleepiness
निधो गर्नु*	to decide
निबुवा	lemon
निम्तो	invitation
निम्त्याउनु*	to invite
नियम	rule
निराश	without hope
निर्वाण	Nirvana
निश्चय गर्नु*	to decide
निस्कनु	to emerge, come out
नीलो	blue
नुन	salt
नुहाउनु	to bathe
नुहाउने कोठा	bathroom
नेपाल भाषा	Newari (language)
नेपाली	Nepali
नेपालीभाषी	Nepali-speaker
-नेर	near to
नेवार	Newar (an ethnic group)
नोकर	servant
नोट	note
नौ	nine
नौनी	butter
न्यानो	warm

प

पकाउनु*	to cook
पक्का	ripe, firm, proper
पछि	after, later
-पछि	after
पटक	turn, time
पटक्कै	not even a little
पठाउनु*	to send
पढाउनु*	to teach
पढे-लेखेको	educated
पढ्नु*	to read, study
पण्डित	Pandit; a traditional scholar
पता लगाउनु*	to find out
पत्याउनु*	to believe
पत्रिका	magazine
पनि	also, even
पप सँगीत	pop music
पर	beyond, on the other side of
परम्परा	tradition
परिवार	family
पर्खनु	to wait
पर्नु	to fall
पर्यटक	tourist
पर्व	festival
पर्सि	the day after tomorrow
पल्लो	next, further

पल्ट	turn, time
पल्टनु	to lie down
पशु	animal
पश्चिम	west
पसल	shop
पस्नु	to enter
पहाड	hill
पहाडी	of the hill region
पहिरो	landslide
पहिला	previously, before, ago
पहिलो	first
पहेंलो	yellow
पाँच	five
पाँचौं	fifth
पाइनु	to be acquired, be available
पाइलट	pilot
पाइला	footstep, footprint
पाइला टेक्नु*	to take a step
पाउण्ड	pound
पाउनु*	to get, acquire, be able to, manage to
पाकिस्तानी	Pakistani
पाक्नु	to ripen, be cooked
पाखा	hillside
पाखुरा	upper arm
पाठ	lesson
पाठ गर्नु*	to recite
पाठ्य पुस्तक	textbook
पाथी	measure of quantity or volume equal to eight **mānās**
पानी	water, rain
पार गर्नु*	to cross
-पारि	on the far side of
पालन गर्नु*	to maintain, foster
पाला	heyday, turn, time
पाल्नु*	to rear, keep (livestock)
पासपोर्ट	passport
पाहुना	guest
पिउनु*	to drink
पिकनिक	picnic
पिठ्यूँ	back
पिन्सेन	pension
पिरो	spicy
पीपल	pipal tree
पीर गर्नु*	to worry, be troubled
पुग-न-पुग	almost
पुगिनु	to be reached
पुग्नु*	to be enough, suffice
पुग्नु	to arrive (there)
पुजारी	priest
पुण्य	religious merit
पुरानो	old
पुर्खा	ancestor
पुल	bridge
पुस्तक	book
पुस्तकालय	library
पुस्ता	generation
पूजा गर्नु*	to worship
पूरा	whole
पूर्णिमा	full-moon day
पूर्व	east
पूस (पौष)	ninth month of the Nepali year
पेट	stomach

पैसा	money; one hundredth of one rupee
पोई	husband
पोल्नु*	to burn
पोहोर	last year
पौडी खेल्नु*	to swim
पौने	less one quarter
प्याक गर्नु*	to pack
प्याज	onion
प्याजी	purple
प्रगति	progress
प्रजातन्त्र	democracy
प्रदेश	state
प्रधानमन्त्री	prime minister
प्रवचन	lecture, speech
प्रशस्त	plentiful
प्रश्न	question
प्रहरी	police, police officer
प्रहरी थाना	police station
प्राचीन	ancient
प्रान्त	province
प्रायजसो	mostly, usually
प्रारम्भ हुनु	to commence
प्रिय	dear
प्रियजन	dear people
प्रीति	love
प्रेम	love
प्रेमिका	girlfriend

फ

फरक	difference/different
फर्कनु	to return
फर्काउनु*	to cause to return
फर्किनु	to return
फर्सी	pumpkin
फलफुल	fruit
फल्नु	to fruit
फाँड्नु*	to smash, break open
फाइदा	benefit
फागुन (फाल्गुण)	eleventh month of the Nepali year
फिरिरि	rippling
फिर्ता दिनु*	to give back
फिर्ता लिनु*	to take back
फिलिम	film
फुकाल्नु*	to untie, take off
फुटबल	football
फुर्सद	spare time
फुल	egg
फुल पार्नु*	to lay an egg
फुल्नु	to flower, bloom
फूल	flower
फूलकोपी	cauliflower
फेला पर्नु	to be found
फोक्सो	lung
फोटो	photograph
फोन गर्नु*	to make a phone call
फोहोर	dirty

ब

बगर	riverbank
बगैंचा	garden
बग्नु	to flow
बच्चा	child
बजाउनु*	to play a musical instrument
बजार	bazaar, marketplace

बजे	at … o'clock
बज्यै	grandmother
बट्टा	packet
बढी	more
बढ्नु	to increase, advance
बत्ती	lamp, light, electricity
बनाउनु*	to make, mend
बन्द	shut
बन्द गर्नु*	to shut
बन्द हुनु	to be closed
बन्दा कोपी	cabbage
बन्दोबस्त	arrangements
बन्दूक	gun
बन्नु	to become
बयान	account, description
बर्मा	Burma
बलियो	strong
बर्सात	monsoon rain
बल्ल	eventually, at last
बल्ल बल्ल	eventually, at last
बस	bus
बस चढ्नु	to board a bus
बसाइँ सर्नु	to move home
बस्ती	settlement, village
बस्नु	to reside, sit down, stay
बहिनी	younger sister
बाँकि	left over, remaining
बाँदर	monkey
बा	father
बाखा	goat
बाघ	tiger
बाजि	turn, time
बाजे	grandfather
-बाट	from, by
बाटो	road, path, way
बाठो	clever, smart
बादल	cloud
बाबु	little boy
बारम्बार	repeatedly
बारी	dry field
बालुवा	sand
बाल्यकाल	childhood
बास	lodging
बास बस्नु	to lodge for a night
बासी	stale
बाहिर	outside
बाहुन	Brahmin
बाहेक	except for, apart from
बिगार्नु*	to spoil
बिग्रनु	to be spoiled, go to the bad
बिचरा	unfortunate
बिजी	busy
बिजुली	electricity
बिताउनु*	to spend (time)
बिदा	holiday, time off work, leave
बियर	beer
बिरलै	rarely, seldom
बिरामी	sick, ill
बिरालो	cat
बिसन्चो	unwell
बिर्सनु*	to forget
बिर्सिनु	to be forgotten
बिस्कुट	biscuit
बिस्तारै	slowly, carefully

बिहा	wedding, marriage
बिहा गर्नु*	to marry
बिहान	morning
बिहिवार	Thursday
बीच	between
बीचबाटोमा	on the way, en route
बुझिनु	to be understood
बुझ्नु*	to understand
बुधवार	Wednesday
बुवा	father
बूढा	old man, husband
बूढी	old woman, wife
बूढी औंला	thumb
बूढो	old, aged
बेंसी	valley floor
बेच्नु*	to sell
बेर	time
बेला	time, occasion
बेलायत	Britain, England
बेलुका	evening
बेस	better, good
बैंक	bank
बैसाख (वैसाख)	first month of the Nepali year
बोकाउनु*	to cause to carry
बोक्नु*	to carry
बोट	tree
बोतल	bottle
बोलाउनु*	to call, invite
बोलिनु	to be spoken
बोल्नु*	to speak
बौद्ध	Buddhist
ब्याटरी	battery

भ

भगवान	God
भटमास	soybean
भट्टी पसल	inn
भदौ (भाद्र)	fifth month of the Nepali year
भनाइ	statement, utterance
भनिनु	to be said, be called
भन्ज्याङ्ग	pass, col
-भन्दा	than
-भन्दा अगाडि	before, in front of
-भन्दा अघि	before
-भन्दा तल	below
-भन्दा पर	beyond
-भन्दा पहिले	before
-भन्दा माथि	above
भन्नु*	to say, tell
भन्सार	customs
भरखर, भरखरै	recently, just now
भरसक	as far as possible
-भरि	throughout, filling
भरिया	porter
भरे बेलुका	this evening
भर्ति	recruitment, enrolment
भर्नु*	to fill
भाँडा	pot, vessel
भाइ	younger brother
भाइ टीका	a special day on which women and girls anoint their brothers
भाउज्यू	elder brother's wife
भाग	share, portion
भाग्नु	to run away, escape

भात	cooked rice; a meal
भान्सा-कोठा	kitchen
भान्से	cook
भारत	India
भारतीय	Indian
भारी	load
भाषा	language
भाषण	speech, lecture
भिज्नु	to become wet
भित्ता	interior wall
भित्ते-घडी	wall clock
भित्र	within, inside
भिर्नु*	to strap on
भिसा	visa
भीड	crowd
भुइँ	ground
भूगोल	geography
भूटान	Bhutan
भूत	ghost
भूस्वर्ग	heaven on earth
भेक	area, district
भेट	meeting, encounter
भेट्नु	to meet
भेट्टाउनु*	to find, locate
भोक	hunger
भोको	hungry
भौगोलिक	geographical
भोजपुरी	Bhojpuri (language)
भोट	Tibet
भोट-बर्मेली	Tibeto-Burman
भोटिया	Tibetan
भोलि	tomorrow
भ्रमण	tour

म

म	I
मकै	maize, corn
मङ्गलवार	Tuesday
मङ्सीर (मार्गशीर्ष)	eighth month of the Nepali year
मट्टीतेल	kerosene
मतलब	meaning
मदत गर्नु*	to help
मदेस	Tarai (region)
मध्यरात	midnight
मध्य	mid-
-मध्यान्न	midday
-मध्ये	among
मन	heart, mind
मन पराउनु*	to like
मन पर्नु	to be liked
मन लाग्नु	to want to
मनाउनु*	to celebrate
मन्त्रालय	ministry
मन्त्री	minister
मन्दिर	temple
मर्नु	to die
मर्मस्पर्शी	touching, moving
महंगो	expensive
महत्त्वपूर्ण	important
महल	palace
महाविद्यालय	college
महिना	month
-मा	in
मा	mother
माइत	woman's natal home
माइल	mile

माग्नु*	to ask for
माघ	tenth month of the Nepali year
माछा	fish
माझ्नु*	to scrub, scour
मातृभाषा	mother tongue
मात्र, मात्रै	only
माथि	above, up
माना	a measure: 0.7 litres or 20 ounces
मानिस	person
मान्छे	person
मान्नु*	to agree, accept, believe
माफ गर्नु*	to forgive
माफी दिनु*	to forgive
माया	love, affection
माया गर्नु*	to love
माया मार्नु*	to forget a friend
मासु	meat
मास्टर	schoolmaster
माहिलो	second eldest
मिटर	metre
मिठाई	sweets
मित्र	friend
मिनेट	minute
मिरमिरे	very early in the morning
मिलाउनु*	to arrange, assemble, adjust, bring together, sort out
मिल्नु	to come together, match, fit, get along
मीठो	good-tasting
मुख	face, mouth
मुख्य	main, principal
मुटु	heart
मुठा	bunch
मुरी	measure of weight or quantity equal to 20 **pāthīs**
मुश्किल	difficult, difficulty
मूर्ख	fool
मूला	radish
मूसा	mouse
मृग	deer
मृत	dead, deceased person
मेच	chair
मेरो	my, mine
मैथिली	Maithili (language)
मैलो	dirty
मोक्ष	salvation, deliverance
मोटर	motorcar
मोटो	fat
मोल	value, price
मोहर, मोहोर	a half-rupee
मौसम	weather

य

यता	here, in this direction
यति	this much
यती	Yeti
यसपालि	this time
यसरी	in this manner
यसो	in this manner
यस्तो	like this
यहाँ	here
यहीं	right here
यातायात	transport

यात्री	traveller, pilgrim
याद	memory
यिनी	s/he (Middle)
यी	they, these
युवती	young woman
युवा	young man
यूरोप	Europe
यो	this
योजना	plan

र

र	and
रक्सी	liquor
रगत	blood
रङ	colour
रमाइलो	pleasant, enjoyable
रमाइलो गर्नु*	to enjoy oneself
रहर	strong desire
राई	Rai (ethnic group)
राख्नु*	to put, keep
राँगो	a male buffalo
राजधानी	capital
राजनैतिक	political
राजमार्ग	national highway
राजा	king
राज्य	country, state
राणा	Rana
राति	at night
रातो	red
रानी	queen
रामतोरियाँ	okra
राम्रो	good, nice
रायो	mustard
राष्ट्र	nation
राष्ट्रपति	president
राहदानी	passport
रिक्सा	rickshaw
रिजर्वेशन	reservation
रिन	debt
रिसाउनु	to be angry
रुक्नु	to stop
रुघा	head cold
रुघा-खोकी	cold and cough
रुचि	appetite
रुनु	to cry
रुपियाँ	rupee
रूख	tree
रूमाल	handkerchief
रे	particle indicating that the information imparted by the speaker comes from another source
रेडियो	radio
रेल	train
रेष्टुराँ	restaurant
रेसम	silk
रोक्नु*	to stop
रोटी	bread
रोपाइँ	the planting of a crop
रोप्नु*	to plant

ल

ल	there!
लखतरान	exhausted
लगाउनु*	to put on
लज	lodge

लसून	garlic
लाइन	line, queue
-लाई	to, for, at
लाउनु*	to wear
लाख	one hundred thousand
लाखौं	hundreds of thousands
लाग्नु	to be felt, affect, seem, apply, begin, cost, take time, be imposed, head for, set in
लाज	embarrassment, shame
लाटो	stupid
लानु*	to take away
लामो	long
लिनु*	to take
लिम्बू	Limbu (ethnic group)
लुगा	clothing, clothes
लुगा-फाटा	clothes
-ले	by, because of, due to
लेख्नु*	to write
लोग्ने	husband
लोग्नेमान्छे	man
लोटा	metal water pot
लौ	there! you see!
ल्याउनु*	to bring

व

वन	forest
वर्ष	year
वहाँ	s/he (High)
वहीं	right there
वाक्य	sentence
वातावरण	atmosphere, environment
वार	day of the week
वालेट	wallet
वास्तवमा	really, actually
विचार	opinion
विचार गर्नु*	to consider, think about
विज्ञान	science
विदेश	abroad, a foreign country
विदेशिनु	to go abroad
विदेशी	foreign, foreigner
विद्यार्थी	student
विद्यालय	school
विभाग	department
विमान	flight
विमानस्थल	airport
विरह	loneliness
विशेष	special, particular
विश्व-युद्ध	world war
विश्वविद्यालय	university
विश्वास गर्नु*	to believe, trust
व्यवसाय	occupation
व्यवहार	behaviour
व्याकरण	grammar
व्यापार	trade
व्यापारी	trader

श

शताब्दी	century
शनिवार	Saturday
शब्द	word
शरीर	body
शहर	city, town
शाकाहारी	vegetarian
शान्त	peaceful

शान्ति	peace
शासन	rule, regime
शिक्षक	teacher
शिक्षा	education
शिखर	mountain peak
शिवरात्री	Shivarati festival
शिवालय	Shiva temple
शील्ड	shield
शुक्रवार	Friday
शुभकामना	good wishes
शुभनाम	given name
शुरु गर्नु*	to start
शुरु हुनु	to begin
शून्य	empty, zero
शेर्पा	Sherpa (ethnic group)
श्रीमती	wife
श्रीमान	husband

स

-सँग	with
सँग-सँगै	together
सँगीत	music
संरक्षण	conservation
संवत	calendrical era
सँसार	world
सकिनु	to finish
सक्नु	to be able to
सगरमाथा	Mount Everest
सघाउनु*	to help, to assist
सजिलो	easy
सडक	street, road
सधैं	always
सन्चो	in good health
सन्तान	offspring
सपना	dream
सफल	successful
सफा	clean
सफा गर्नु*	to clean
सब	all
समतल	level, flat
समस्या	problem
समाचार	news
समाचार पत्र	newspaper
समाप्त	finished
सम्झना	memory
सम्झनु*	to remember
सम्झाउनु*	to remind, counsel
सम्पादक	editor
-सम्भावना	possibility
-सम्म	up to, as far as, until
सम्मान	honour, respect
सय	hundred
सरकार	government
सरकारी	governmental
सरस्वती	Saraswati (goddess)
सर्वनाश	disaster
सल्काउनु*	to set light to
सल्लाह	advice
सवा	plus one quarter
ससुराली	wife's parents' home
सस्तो	cheap
सस्तोमा	cheaply
सहयोग गर्नु*	to help
साँचो	true
साँचो	key
साँझ	dusk
साँस्कृतिक	cultural

साइकल	bicycle	सिमाना	border
साउन (श्रावण)	fourth month of the Nepali year	सिमी	bean
साग	greens	सिलसिला	series, sequence
साट्नु*	to exchange (money)	सीट	seat
साढे	plus one half	सीधै	directly, straight
सात	seven	सुँगुर	pig
सातौं	seventh	सुँघ्नु*	to sniff, smell
साथी	friend, companion	सुइँ-सुइँ	the sound of the wind
सानो	small	सुका	a quarter rupee
साबुन	soap	सुखी	happy
सामान	luggage	सुझाव	suggestion
सायद	perhaps	सुत्नु	to sleep; lie down
सारङ्गी	Nepali violin	सुत्ने कोठा	bedroom
सारी	sari; a woman's dress	सुदूर	remote, very distant
साल	year	सुनाउनु*	to relate, tell
साली	wife's younger sister	सुन्दर	beautiful
साहिंलो	third eldest	सुन्दरी	beautiful (woman)
साहित्य	literature	सुनिनु	to be heard, be audible
साहू	merchant; business proprietor	सुन्तला	orange
साहेब	term used to address a professional	सुन्नु*	to hear, listen
साह्रै	extremely	सुरक्षित	secure, protected
सिकाउनु*	to teach	सुविधा	convenience
सिकिस्त	gravely	सेतो	white
सिक्किम	Sikkim	सेलाउनु	to cool down
सिक्नु*	to learn	सोच्नु*	to think
-सित	with	सोध्नु*	to ask
सिद्धिनु	to end	सोफा	sofa
सिद्ध्याउनु*	to finish	सोमवार	Monday
सिनेमा-घर	cinema	स्कूल	school
सिपाही	soldier	स्थापना	establishment
सिमसिमे पानी	light rain	स्थिति	situation, circumstances
		स्नान गर्नु*	to bathe
		स्याउ	apple

स्वर	voice
स्वर्ग	heaven
स्वस्थ	healthy
स्वाद	taste, flavour
स्वादिलो	tasty
स्वास्थ्य	health
स्वास्नी	wife
स्वास्नीमानिस	woman

ह

हगि	right?, isn't that so?
हजार	thousand
हजारौं	thousands of
हजुर	sir, yes
हजुर?	pardon?
हजुरआमा	grandmother
हजुरबा	grandfather
हडताल	strike
हतपत	hurry
हतार	hurry
हप्ता	week
हराउनु	to be lost
हरियो	green
हरेक	every
हवाईजहाज	aeroplane
हाँक्नु*	to drive (a vehicle)
हाँस्नु	to smile, laugh
हाकिम	boss
हाड	bone
हात	hand, arm
हातमुख	hands and face
हानीकारक	harmful
हामी, हामीहरू	we
हाम्रो	our, ours
हालखबर	news
हावा	wind, air
हिँडेर जानु	to go on foot
हिउँ	snow
हिजो	yesterday
हिँड्नु	to walk, set out
हितैषी	well-wisher
हिन्दी	Hindi
हिन्दीभाषी	Hindi speaker
हिन्दुस्तानी	Indian
हिन्दू	Hindu
हिमाल	the Himalayas
हिमाली	Himalayan
हिलो	mud
हिसाब गर्नु*	to add up
हीरा	diamond
हुलाक घर	post office
हुनु	to be
हेर्नु*	to look
होचो	short-statured
होटेल	hotel
होस् गर्नु*	to be careful
है	do you hear?, OK?
हैजा	cholera

English–Nepali glossary

about (time)	-तिर	**-tira**
about (quantity)	करीब	**karīb**
abroad	विदेश	**videś**
acquire	पाउनु	**pāunu**
advice	सल्लाह	**sallāh**
advise	सल्लाह दिनु	**sallāh dinu**
after	-पछि	**-pachi**
afternoon	दिउँसो	**diũso**
age	उमेर	**umer**
ago	अघि, पहिले	**aghi, pahile**
airport	विमानस्थल	**vimānsthal**
alcohol	रक्सी	**raksī**
all	सब, सबै	**sab, sabai**
allow	दिनु	**dinu**
always	सधैं	**sadhaĩ**
angry, to be	रिसाउनु	**risāunu**
anyone	कोही	**kohī**
apple	स्याउ	**syāu**
arrive	पुग्नु, आइपुग्नु	**pugnu, āipugnu**
ask	सोध्नु	**sodhnu**
at home	घरै, घरमा	**gharai, gharmā**
bad	खराब, नराम्रो	**kharāb, narāmro**
bag	झोला	**jholā**
bangle	चूरा	**cūrā**
bank	बैंक	**baĩk**
become	बन्नु	**bannu**
before	-भन्दा अघि	**-bhandā aghi**
begin	शुरु गर्नु,	**śuru garnu,**
	शुरु हुनु	**śuru hunu**
	लाग्नु, थाल्नु	**lāgnu, thālnu**

belief	विश्वास	**viśvās**
below	तल	**tala**
big	ठूलो	**ṭhūlo**
black	कालो	**kālo**
blue	नीलो	**nīlo**
board (vb)	चढ्नु	**caḍhnu**
boil (vb)	उम्लनु	**umlanu**
book	किताब	**kitāb**
born, to be	जन्मनु	**janmanu**
boy	केटा	**keṭā**
Brahmin	बाहुन	**bāhun**
break	फोड्नु	**phoḍnu**
bridge	पुल	**pul**
bring	ल्याउनु	**lyāunu**
brother, elder	दाइ	**dāi**
brother, younger	भाइ	**bhāi**
buffalo	भैंसी	**bhaĩsī**
bus	बस	**bas**
bus station	बस बिसौनी	**bas bisaunī**
buy	किन्नु	**kinnu**
capital	राजधानी	**rājdhānī**
cards	ताश	**tāś**
central	मध्य	**madhya**
chair	मेच	**mec**
cheap	सस्तो	**sasto**
children	बच्चाहरू	**baccāharū**
Chinese	चिनियाँ	**ciniyā̃**
cholera	हैजा	**haijā**
cigarette	चुरोट	**curoṭ**
city	शहर	**śahar**
class	कक्षा	**kakṣā**
clean	सफा	**saphā**
clever	चलाक	**calāk**
climb (vb)	चढ्नु	**caḍhnu**

close	बन्द गर्नु	**banda garnu**
cloth	कपडा	**kapaḍā**
clothes	लुगा	**lugā**
cold	चिसो	**ciso**
coldness	जाडो	**jāḍo**
colour	रँग	**rãg**
come	आउनु	**āunu**
cook (n)	भान्से	**bhānse**
cook (vb)	पकाउनु	**pakāunu**
corner	कुना	**kunā**
cough	खोकी	**khokī**
country	देश	**deś**
cow	गाई	**gāī**
cry	रुनु	**runu**
cup	कप	**kap**
daughter	छोरी	**chorī**
day	दिन	**din**
day before yesterday	अस्ति	**asti**
decide	निधो गर्नु	**nidho garnu**
deity	देवता	**devatā**
Delhi	दिल्ली	**dillī**
diarrhoea	दिसा	**disā**
difficult	गाह्रो, अप्ठ्यारो	**gāhro, apṭhyāro**
dirty	मैलो	**mailo**
distant	टाढा	**ṭāḍhā**
door	ढोका	**ḍhokā**
downhill	ओरालो	**orālo**
drink	खानु, पिउनु	**khānu, piunu**
driver	ड्राइभर	**ḍrāibhar**
dry (vb)	सुकाउनु	**sukāunu**
each	हरेक	**harek**
easily	सजिलोसँग	**sajilosãga**
east	पूर्व	**pūrva**

easy	सजिलो	**sajilo**
eat	खानु	**khānu**
embarrassment	लाज	**lāj**
empty	रित्तो	**ritto**
English	अँग्रेज	**ãgrej**
evening	बेलुका	**belukā**
Everest	सगरमाथा	**sagarmāthā**
exam	जाँच	**jā̃c**
expensive	महंगो	**mahãgo**
eye	आँखा	**ā̃khā**
face	मुख, अनुहार	**mukh, anuhār**
family	परिवार	**parivār**
family name	थर	**thar**
farmer	किसान	**kisān**
fat	मोटो	**moṭo**
father	बुवा, बा	**buvā, bā**
fear	डर	**ḍar**
field	खेत, बारी	**khet, bārī**
find	पाउनु	**pāunu**
finish	सिद्ध्याउनु	**siddhyāunu**
first	पहिलो	**pahilo**
flight	विमान	**vimān**
food	खाना, भात	**khānā, bhāt**
foreigner	विदेशी	**videśī**
forget	बिर्सनु	**birsanu**
Friday	शुक्रवार	**śukravār**
friend	साथी	**sāthī**
from	-देखि, -बाट	**-dekhi, -bāṭa**
fruit	फलफूल	**phalphūl**
Ganesh	गणेश	**gaṇeś**
German	जर्मन	**jarman**
get	पाउनु	**pāunu**
ghee	घिउ	**ghiu**
gift	उपहार, कोसेली	**upahār, koselī**

girl	केटी	**keṭī**
give	दिनु	**dinu**
go	जानु	**jānu**
god	देवता	**devatā**
good	राम्रो	**rāmro**
granddaughter	नातिनी	**nātinī**
grandfather	हजुरबा	**hajurbā**
grandmother	हजुरआमा	**hajurāmā**
grandson	नाति	**nāti**
green	हरियो	**hariyo**
guest	पाहुना	**pāhunā**
half	आधा	**ādhā**
happiness	खुशी	**khuśī**
he (High)	वहाँ	**vahā̃**
he (Low)	ऊ	**ū**
he (Middle)	उनी	**unī**
head	टाउको	**ṭāuko**
head cold	रुघा	**rughā**
heard, to be	सुनिनु	**suninu**
heat	गर्मी	**garmī**
help	मदत गर्नु	**madat garnu**
here	यहाँ	**yahā̃**
Himalaya	हिमालय	**himālaya**
holiday	बिदा, छुट्टी	**bidā, chuṭṭī**
home	घर	**ghar**
hope	आशा	**āśā**
hot	गरम, तातो	**garam, tāto**
hotel	होटेल	**hoṭel**
hour	घण्टा	**ghaṇṭā**
house	घर	**ghar**
how much?	कति?	**kati?**
how, like what?	कस्तो?	**kasto**
how, in what manner?	कसरी?	**kasarī**
hunger	भोक	**bhok**

hurt	दुख्नु	**dukhnu**
husband	श्रीमान, लोग्ने	**śrīmān, logne**
I	म	**ma**
in	-मा	**-mā**
India	भारत	**bhārat**
Indian	भारतीय	**bhāratīya**
inside	-भित्र	**-bhitra**
interesting	चाखलाग्दो	**cākhlāgdo**
Japanese	जापानी	**jāpānī**
job	जागिर	**jāgir**
journey	यात्रा	**yātrā**
Kathmandu	काठ्माडौं	**kāṭhmāḍaũ**
key	साँचो	**sā̃co**
kilogramme	किलो	**kilo**
knowledge	थाहा	**thāhā**
language	भाषा	**bhāṣā**
last (previous week)	अस्ति	**asti**
last (year)	पोहोर	**pohor**
last (final)	अन्तिम	**antim**
late	ढिलो	**ḍhilo**
lateness	अबेर	**aber**
letter	चिठी	**ciṭhī**
liquor	रक्सी	**raksī**
live	बस्नु	**basnu**
lodge	लज	**laj**
London	लण्डन	**laṇḍan**
lose	हराउनु	**harāunu**
man	लोग्नेमान्छे	**logne-mānche**
many	धेरै	**dherai**
market	बजार	**bajār**
marry	बिहा गर्नु	**bihā garnu**
meat	मासु	**māsu**

meet	भेट्नु	**bheṭnu**
mile	माइल	**māil**
Monday	सोमवार	**somvār**
money	पैसा	**paisā**
month	महिना	**mahinā**
morning	बिहान	**bihāna**
mother	आमा, मा	**āmā, mā**
motorcar	मोटर	**moṭar**
my	मेरो	**mero**
name	नाम	**nām**
nearby	नजिक	**najik**
never	कहिल्यै पनि	**kahilyai pani**
new	नयाँ	**nayā̃**
newspaper	अखबार	**akhbār**
next day	भोलिपल्ट	**bholipalṭa**
nice	राम्रो	**rāmro**
night	राति	**rāti**
north	उत्तर	**uttar**
novel	उपन्यास	**upanyās**
now	अहिले, अब	**ahile, aba**
nowadays	हिजोआज	**hijoāja**
o' clock	बजे	**baje**
office	अफिस	**aphis**
official	अधिकारी	**adhikārī**
old	पुरानो	**purāno**
open (adj)	खुला	**khulā**
open (vb)	खोल्नु	**kholnu**
opinion	विचार	**vicār**
orange	सुन्तला	**suntalā**
order	अह्राउनु	**ahrāunu**
our	हाम्रो	**hāmro**
outside	बाहिर	**bāhira**
own	आफ्नो	**āphno**

packet	बट्टा	**baṭṭā**
passport	पासपोर्ट	**pāsport**
pen	कलम	**kalam**
people	मान्छेहरू	**māncheharū**
person	मान्छे	**mānche**
phone	फोन	**phon**
pick up	उठाउनु	**uṭhāunu**
place	ठाउँ	**ṭhāũ**
plane	हवाई जहाज	**havāī jahāj**
play	खेल्नु	**khelnu**
Pokhara	पोखरा	**pokharā**
police	प्रहरी	**praharī**
police station	प्रहरी थाना	**praharī thānā**
poor	गरीब	**garīb**
post office	हुलाक घर	**hulāk ghar**
potato	आलु	**ālu**
pound	पाउण्ड	**pāuṇḍ**
present	उपहार, कोसेली	**upahār, koselī**
problem	समस्या	**samasyā**
purple	प्याजी	**pyājī**
question	प्रश्न	**praśna**
quit	छाड्नु	**chāḍnu**
quite	अलि	**ali**
rain	पानी	**pānī**
reached, to be	पुगिनु	**puginu**
read	पढ्नु	**paḍhnu**
receive	पाउनु	**pāunu**
recently	भरखर	**bharkhar**
rest	आराम गर्नु	**ārām garnu**
restaurant	रेष्टुराँ	**resṭurā̃**
return	फर्किनु	**pharkinu**
rice (cooked)	भात	**bhāt**
rice (uncooked)	चामल	**cāmal**
rich	धनी	**dhanī**

river	खोला, नदी	**kholā, nadī**
road	बाटो	**bāṭo**
room	कोठा	**koṭhā**
rupee	रुपियाँ	**rupiyā̃**
sadness	दुःख	**duḥkha**
said, to be	भनिनु	**bhaninu**
Saturday	शनिवार	**śanivār**
say	भन्नु	**bhannu**
school	स्कूल	**skūl**
search	खोज्नु	**khojnu**
see	देख्नु	**dekhnu**
seen, to be	देखिनु	**dekhinu**
send	पठाउनु	**paṭhāunu**
she (High)	वहाँ	**vahā̃**
she (Low)	ऊ	**ū**
she (Middle)	उनी	**unī**
Shiva	शिव	**śiva**
shoes	जुत्ता	**juttā**
shop	पसल	**pasal**
since	-देखि	**-dekhi**
sing	गाउनु	**gāunu**
sister, elder	दिदी	**didī**
sister, younger	बहिनी	**bahinī**
sister-in-law	भाउजु, बुहारी	**bhāuju, buhārī**
sleep	निद्रा	**nidrā**
sleep	सुत्नु	**sutnu**
slowly	बिस्तारै	**bistārai**
smoke	चुरोट खानु	**curoṭ khānu**
soaked, to be	भिज्नु	**bhijnu**
some (people)	कोही	**kohī**
some (thing)	केही	**kehī**
somebody	कोही	**kohī**
sometimes	कहिलेकाहीं	**kahilekāhī̃**
son	छोरा	**chorā**

song	गीत	**gīt**
south	दक्षिण	**dakṣiṇ**
speak	बोल्नु	**bolnu**
spoken, to be	बोलिनु	**bolinu**
stay	बस्नु	**basnu**
straight	सीधा	**sīdhā**
strange	अनौठो	**anauṭho**
street	सडक	**saḍak**
student	विद्यार्थी	**vidyārthī**
student hostel	छात्रावास	**chātrāvās**
study	पढ्नु	**paḍhnu**
successful	सफल	**saphal**
suddenly	अकस्मात	**akasmāt**
summer	गर्मी	**garmī**
Sunday	आइतवार	**āitavār**
sweet sounding	मीठो	**mīṭho**
sweets	मिठाई	**miṭhāī**
swim	पौडी खेल्नु	**pauḍī khelnu**
table	टेबुल	**ṭebul**
take	लिनु	**linu**
take off	फुकाल्नु	**phukālnu**
tall	अग्लो	**aglo**
tasty	मीठो	**mīṭho**
taxi	ट्याक्सी	**ṭyāksī**
tea	चिया	**ciyā**
teacher	शिक्षक	**śikṣak**
tell	भन्नु	**bhannu**
tell off	गाली गर्नु	**gālī garnu**
temple	मन्दिर	**mandir**
tenth	दसौं	**dasaũ**
that	त्यो	**tyo**
there	त्यहाँ	**tyahā̃**
they	उनीहरू	**unīharū**
thirst	तिर्खा	**tirkhā**

this	यो	**yo**
thousands	हजारौं	**hajārau͂**
Thursday	बिहिवार	**bihivār**
Tibet	भोट	**bhoṭ**
ticket	टिकट	**ṭikaṭ**
time	बेला, समय	**belā, samay**
tiredness	थकाइ	**thakāi**
today	आज	**āja**
tomorrow	भोलि	**bholi**
tourist	पर्यटक	**paryaṭak**
towards	-तिर	**-tira**
Tuesday	मङ्गलवार	**maṅgalvār**
TV	टी० भी०	**ṭī. bhī.**
twice	दुई पटक	**duī paṭak**
umbrella	छाता	**chātā**
understand	बुझ्नु	**bujhnu**
understood, to be	बुझिनु	**bujhinu**
university	विश्वविद्यालय	**viśvavidyālaya**
until	-सम्म	**-samma**
up to	-सम्म	**-samma**
uphill	उकालो	**ukālo**
usually	धेरैजसो	**dheraijaso**
valley	उपत्यका	**upatyakā**
vegetables	तरकारी	**tarkārī**
very	धेरै	**dherai**
village	गाउँ	**gāũ**
violin	सारङ्गी	**sāraṅgī**
visit	जानु	**jānu**
voice	स्वर	**svar**
wait	पर्खनु	**parkhanu**
wash	धुनु	**dhunu**
washerman	धोबी	**dhobī**
watch	घडी	**ghaḍī**

water	पानी	**pānī**
we	हामी	**hāmī**
wear	लाउनु	**lāunu**
weather	मौसम	**mausam**
Wednesday	बुधवार	**budhavār**
week	हप्ता	**haptā**
well	राम्ररी	**rāmrarī**
west	पश्चिम	**paścim**
wet	भिजेको	**bhijeko**
what?	के ?	**ke?**
when?	कहिले ?	**kahile?**
where?	कहाँ ?	**kahā̃?**
white	सेतो	**seto**
whole	पूरा, पूरै	**pūrā, pūrai**
whose?	कसको	**kasko?**
wife	श्रीमती, स्वास्नी	**śrīmatī, svāsnī**
window	झ्याल	**jhyāl**
witch	बोक्सी	**boksī**
woman	आइमाई	**āimāī**
work	काम	**kām**
work	काम गर्नु	**kām garnu**
worry	चिन्ता गर्नु	**cintā garnu**
worship	पूजा	**pūjā**
write	लेख्नु	**lekhnu**
year	साल, वर्ष	**sāl, varṣa**
yellow	पहेंलो	**pahẽlo**
yesterday	हिजो	**hijo**
yet	अहिलेसम्म	**ahilesamma**
you (High)	तपाईं	**tapāī̃**
you (Low)	तँ	**tã**
you (Middle)	तिमी	**timī**